GOD'S SONG IN MY HEART

By
RUTH YOUNGDAHL NELSON

Daily Devotions

AUGUSTANA PRESS
ROCK ISLAND, ILLINOIS

GOD'S SONG IN MY HEART

Library of Congress Catalog Card Number 56-11912

Fourth Printing

PRINTED IN U·S·A·

AUGUSTANA BOOK CONCERN
Printers and Binders
ROCK ISLAND, ILLINOIS
1961

A Personal Word to the Friends Who Will Share This Book

WILL you please try to put these meditations to their greatest use? Each day, sing or read the hymn for the week. Then it will be yours to keep after seven times! So subtly does the law of memory work. These hymns are such rich devotional material in themselves, that they alone will bless your lives. The Christian witness of the authors will stay with you through each day of the week. Let the hymn live with you through the day. Sing or hum it while you work.

Have your Bible handy so that you can read the suggested passage before you read the meditation. In some instances space permitted the printing only of excerpts.

If you have friends who are using the book, it would be fun to get together once in awhile to review the hymns that you have learned. You will be well repaid by these experiences.

These pages have been written in a variety of settings. In the mountains of Livingstone, Montana; by the sands of Daytona Beach, Florida; in the rich, Pennsylvania Dutch country; in a motel in Birmingham, Alabama; on the coast of southern California—and then in the parsonage in Washington, D. C., and at Nelson's Käja at Moose Lake, Minnesota—these are some of the places where the writing has been done. In the midst of a speaking schedule, in the whirl of the demands of keeping house, and in between trying to serve as a pastor's wife, have these meditations been born. Only by the grace of God has the drawing apart been possible, and only because of His wonderful answer to prayer has the work been finished.

As far as possible the hymns were chosen because of their appropriateness to the church season—Lent, Trinity, Advent, as well as Christmas, Easter, Pentecost, Transfiguration, and All Saints' Day, all a part of the cycle.

The writer has one consuming desire: that on every page the reader might find the footprints of the eternal, life-giving Christ, and that each one might come to know Him as a personal Savior! Then from each life there will go the contagion of a song in the heart!

To my family:
my husband, Clarence;
our children, Lorraine,
Jonathan, David,
Elizabeth, and Mary,
I dedicate this book.

How many times our
sharing the Christ together
has put a song in the
heart!

Contents

Week *Hymn* *Page*

GOD'S SONG IN MY HEART

I Look Not Back

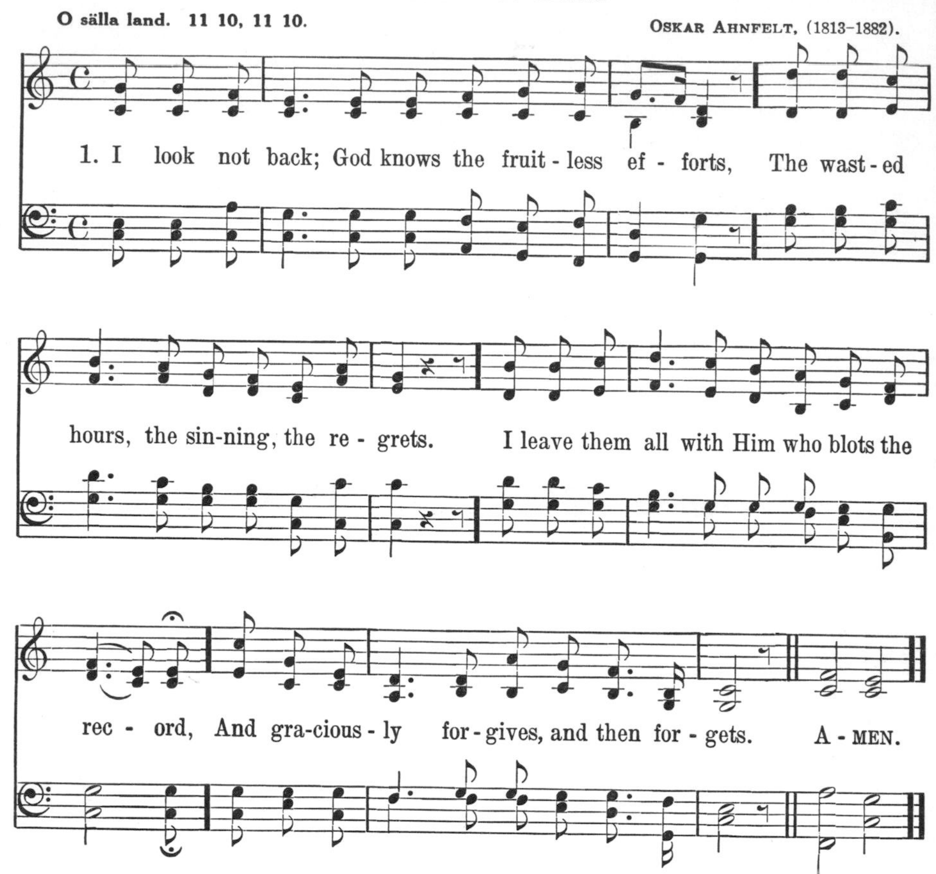

2 I look not forward; God sees all the future,
The road that, short or long, will lead me home,
And He will face with me its every trial,
And bear for me the burdens that may come.

3 I look not round me; then would fears assail me,
So wild the tumult of earth's restless seas,
So dark the world, so filled with woe and evil,
So vain the hope of comfort and of ease.

4 I look not inward; that would make me wretched;
For I have naught on which to stay my trust.
Nothing I see save failures and shortcomings,
And weak endeavors, crumbling into dust.

5 But I look up—into the face of Jesus,
For there my heart can rest, my fears are stilled;
And there is joy, and love, and light for darkness,
And perfect peace, and every hope fulfilled.

Annie Johnson Flint.

SUNDAY

I Look Not Back

Psalm 32

2 Corinthians 5:17

For if a man is in Christ he becomes a new person altogether—the past is finished and gone, everything has become fresh and new. (Phillips)

SO MANY people wallow in the mud of their past lives. They ooze dejection because the sins and regrets of their yesterdays haunt them. And instead of their regrets being a spur to a new beginning, they are the devil's way of planting the seed of despair.

William Cowper, the English poet, could speak with first-hand experience when he wrote:

Remorse, the fatal egg by pleasure laid,
In every bosom where her nest is made,
Hatched by the beams of truth, denies him rest,
And proves a raging scorpion in his breast.

Yes, remorse can be a hangover that will incapacitate us for today.

God has another word for us. This is a new year, a fresh calendar, a new day. If you have confessed your failings to Him, and accepted His forgiveness in Christ, then you too, can say, "The past is finished and gone, everything has become fresh and new."

What a reason for coming before His Presence with singing! Here is our chance to begin again. The words God speaks to us in His new covenant contain the note of victory over the past, and a fresh start. The writer of the Letter to the Hebrews, in quoting from the Book of Jeremiah, writes, "For I will be merciful toward their iniquities, and I will remember their sins no more."

Rejoice, then, that your sin is forgiven. Sing about the goodness of God in giving us a new day, yes, a new year.

One of our daughters, when as a first grader she had just learned to write on the blackboard at school, prayed the following prayer at our family devotions one morning:

Dear God, Please give me a clean blackboard today, and help me to do the writing. Amen.

"I look not back; God knows the fruitless efforts,
The wasted hours, the sinning, the regrets.
I leave them all with Him who blots the record,
And graciously forgives, and then forgets."

PRAYER: *Thank You, God, for this New Year and this chance to begin again. Thank You that in Christ my mistakes and omissions of last year are forgiven and forgotten. Help me to live the joy of Your salvation. In Jesus' Name. Amen.*

I Look Not Back

Psalm 103

Bless the Lord, O my soul;
and all that is within me,
  bless his holy name!
Bless the Lord, O my soul,
  and forget not all his benefits.
Psalm 103:1, 2

ALTHOUGH THE Lord does not want us to look back with vain regret, there is a backward look that He would have us take. That is the look that makes us count our blessings. The psalmist says, "and forget not all his benefits."

At the beginning of this New Year, it is good for us to look back in gratitude for all that the Lord has done. We step with new confidence into this day, as we take inventory of His sustaining help in the past. In Psalm 103 the writer speaks several times of the "steadfast love of the Lord."

What did God do for you this past year? Did He not provide the necessities of life? Was not His strength always sufficient, no matter how hard the task? Did He not keep open the line of prayer to His powerhouse of strength? Did He ever fail?

Those dark days that you had, were they not because you failed to look to Him, and relied upon your own resources? And those times that appeared so difficult when you experienced them, as you now look back, is there not something even in them for which you should praise Him?

As Christians we need more of the cheerful philosophy of the soldier who lost his leg in action. His remark to a sympathizing friend was, "Well, at least I am rid of that rheumatism in the knee that has bothered me for years."

The poet, George Herbert, has expressed what should be our desire in his prayer:

Thou hast given so much to me,
Give one more—a grateful heart;
Not thankful when it pleaseth me,
As if Thy blessings had spare days;
But such a heart, whose pulse may be
Thy praise.

"And forget not all his benefits." Today will be a better day if you remember them, and remembering also acknowledge that always there was His steadfast love. It is yours for this day, this year, too.

"But the steadfast love of the Lord
  is from everlasting to everlasting
    upon those who fear him."

PRAYER: *Lord God, your mercies are past my accounting. Thank You for Your steadfast love. Thank You that You have been sufficient, no matter how difficult the situation. Let my life praise You. Amen.*

TUESDAY

I Look Not Forward

Matthew 6:25-34

"Therefore I tell you, do not be anxious about your life . . . . Therefore do not be anxious about tomorrow, for tomorrow will be anxious for itself. Let the day's own trouble be sufficient for the day . . ." " But seek first his kingdom and his righteousness, and all these things shall be yours as well."
Matthew 6:25, 34, 33

HOW WE need to sing this song, "I look not forward"! Which one of us has not borrowed trouble from tomorrow? In so borrowing, we have depleted our resources for meeting the situations of the next day. The Bible tells us that worrying is a lack of faith, and that is sinful. Jesus has put it into such plain words: "Do not be anxious about tomorrow." This word of advice followed the object lesson that He had just taught. "Look at the birds of the air. . . . Consider the lilies of the field. . . . And yet your heavenly Father feeds them . . . clothes the grass of the field." "Are you not of more value than they?"

There are countless thousands who feverishly seek out fortune tellers and tea-leaf readers in their faithless attitude of wanting to probe the future. The Lord knew what He was doing when He planned for us to live one day at a time. When human beings try to substitute their wisdom for His, they get into trouble.

Our sainted mother often quoted verse 34 of this sixth chapter of Matthew. But she added another verse, as if it were a Siamese twin, "as your days, so shall your strength be." With the problems that inevitably come from raising ten children, she had found God's grace to be abundantly sufficient for each day, one day at a time.

A young girl tacking up a wall calendar at the beginning of the year said with a prophetic ring of her voice: "It's going to be a beautiful year." A friend standing by asked her, "How do you know it is going to be a beautiful year? A year is a long time." "Well," she said, "a day isn't a long time, and I know that it is going to be beautiful, because I am going to take a day at a time to make it so. Years are only days, when you come right down to it, and I am going to see that every single one of these three hundred and sixty-five days gets at least one beautiful thing into it."

Jesus tells us how to do this: "Seek ye first his kingdom and his righteousness." Put God in His rightful place, first, and walk by faith in His love, and you will be content to leave the future in His hands.

"I look not forward; God sees all the future,
The road that, short or long, will lead me home,
And He will face with me its every trial,
And bear for me the burdens that may come."

PRAYER: *We confess, O Lord, that too often we have borrowed trouble from tomorrow. Our future is in good hands when it is in Your pierced ones. Give us a faith that trusts You one day at a time. And daily remind us that You have promised strength sufficient for each day. In the name of the eternal Christ. Amen.*

I Look Not Forward

Hebrews 11

For he looked forward to the city which has foundations, whose builder and maker is God. . . . But as it is, they desire a better country, that is, a heavenly one. Therefore God is not ashamed to be called their God, for he has prepared for them a city. Hebrews 11:10, 16, 17

HERE IS a forward look that we are enjoined to have; the long look to our homegoing. Who does not love to anticipate going home, especially when home is synonymous with love?

So much of our thinking about death is pagan, as is our thinking about life. We forget that we are travelers and sojourners here, and that we are on the way that, short or long, will lead us home. Is it because we are not sure of the One who leads the way home, that we walk in fear? It was said of an old Puritan that "Heaven was in him before he was in heaven." Heaven is to be with Christ eternally. If He lives in you now, then, something of heaven is your experience, and the forward look is one of joyous anticipation. It is why Paul was able to say: "For to me to live is Christ, and to die is gain. . . . My desire is to depart and be with Christ, for that is far better."

Does this mean that we despise this life? Not at all. It does mean that the long look determines our sense of values. It means that our stewardship of life will be measured by the yardstick of eternity. But more than that, it means that there is no terminus. Heaven is an ongoing fulfillment of the joy we have known in Christ's presence here.

We were praying as a family for one of the elderly mothers of our parish. For some time she had been suffering with cancer. Then one night, one of our little girls prayed: "And please God, bless Grandma Anderson. I kind of think You ought to take her home with You, Lord, she has suffered so long. But, You know what's best, and anyway she's with You now and she will be with You then, so it really won't make any difference." The little child had caught the real significance of the forward look.

Lord, it belongs not to my care,
Whether I die or live;
To love and serve Thee is my share,
And this Thy grace must give.

Richard Baxter

PRAYER: *What wonderful provision You have made for us, Lord! Thank You for the blessed hope of being at home with You. Dwell with us even now in our earthly dwelling so that, living or dying, we are with You. In the name of our crucified Savior. Amen.*

THURSDAY

I Look Not Round Me

Luke 21:10, 11

Then he said to them, "Nation will rise against nation, and kingdom against kingdom; there will be great earthquakes, and in various places famines and pestilences; and there will be terrors and great signs from heaven."

IF EVER the roundabout look was a distressing one, it is so in our age. We are witnessing the knowledge of the miracle of the atom, including its use to destroy men; we live in a world of suspicion and distrust, of conniving and manipulation. We live in a world of surplus abundance, on the one hand, and primitive want on the other. It does not make sense. Nor is the answer to close our eyes and not see things as they are. That is not the pattern Christ set. He faced reality in its starkest form, and then proceeded to remedy or improve the situation.

For Christians who are alert there is a special significance to the signs of the times. In Luke 21:31 we read: "So, also, when you see these things taking place, you know that the kingdom of God is near." Victor Hugo has beautifully written:

Be like the bird
That, pausing in her flight
Awhile on boughs too slight,
Feels them give way
Beneath her, and yet sings
Knowing that she hath wings.

Here one is faced with the strange paradox that comes to every Christian. The knowledge of the wings gives one a sense of inner peace in a disturbed world, but the Presence that gives the peace gives also a holy compulsion to share the "how" of it with every living soul. There should be an urgency about our witness for Christ in times like these. Every soul we meet is a potential for the kingdom.

Bishop Thoburn said, "During my early years in India, I spent several months in a village and gained only thirteen converts. I returned there two years later and found eight hundred converts. No missionary had been there since I left. Every Christian had been a witness for Christ." This was the method of first century Christians in terrible times. Because of their witness, you and I have the gospel. Are you permitting the Lord to use you in times like these?

PRAYER: *Help us to remember, Lord, that even though there is tribulation in the world, You have overcome it; and give us the holy compulsion to redeem the days, for they are evil. Put a song upon our lips, and give wings to our feet, as we do Your bidding. In Jesus' Name. Amen.*

I Look Not Inward

Job 14:1-6

"Who can bring a clean thing out of an unclean?
There is not one."

Psalm 130:3

If Thou, O Lord, shouldst mark iniquities,
Lord, who could stand?

TO LOOK inward honestly is to recognize with Paul that "nothing good dwells within me." Examine, for instance, your motives for doing good. Is there not some tint of self, expressed in wanting credit for what you do, or at least wanting that it should be noticed and acknowledged? Is it not easier for you to believe the evil about your neighbor than it is to believe the good? And what about envy and jealousy? To keep looking inward is to despair. Failures, shortcomings, weak endeavors—these are what we see.

God, however, cannot work the miracle of His grace, unless we are willing to make an inward inventory, and bring our findings to the cross. A physician can best bring healing to a disease when he has diagnosed its character. It is why our daily prayer should be: "Search me, O God, and know my heart!" Dwight L. Moody once said: "You can always tell when a man is a great way from God—he is always talking about himself, how good he is. But the moment he sees God by the eye of faith, he is down on his knees, and like Job, he cries, 'Behold, how vile!' "

There is another inward look that is a stumbling block to Christ's indwelling. It can also be a cause for poor health. A nervous, sickly girl consulted a physician who told her she had "ingrowing feelings." "You think too much about yourself," he told her frankly. "What you need is to get away from yourself, and think of others and what you can do to help them." The girl went home and thought over what the physician had told her. By God's grace she applied his remedy, and soon became the picture of health.

The remedy begins with the simple prayer of the tax collector: "God, be merciful to me a sinner!" It finds its accomplishment in the daily fulfillment of the promise: "If we confess our sins, he is faithful and just, and will forgive our sins and cleanse us from all unrighteousness."

PRAYER: *Lord, let the inward look make us to acknowledge our sin, and our dependence on You. Put a song of gratitude upon our lips that our salvation does not depend upon our merit. Thank You that in love You have made it a free gift for anyone that will receive. In the name of our Redeemer, we pray. Amen.*

SATURDAY

But I Look Up

Hebrews 12

Therefore . . . let us also lay aside every weight, and sin which clings so closely, and let us run with perseverance the race that is set before us, looking to Jesus the pioneer and perfecter of our faith, who for the joy that was set before him endured the cross, despising the shame, and is seated at the right hand of the throne of God. . . . Therefore lift your drooping hands and strengthen your weak knees, and make straight paths for your feet, so that what is lame may not be put out of joint but rather be healed.

Hebrews 12:1, 2, 12

YOU SHOULD read this whole twelfth chapter of Hebrews, and sense the power of the conclusion to those who follow the directive of *looking to Jesus,* as it is found in the last two verses: "Therefore let us be grateful for receiving a kingdom that cannot be shaken, and thus let us offer to God acceptable worship, with reverence and awe; for our God is a consuming fire."

As you have gone from one verse to the next of our hymn for this week, have you not daily longed for the hope and undergirding of this final stanza? What we really should have done was to repeat this verse after the one assigned for each day, for to all the negatives, it is the positive answer.

I look not back—but I look up;
I look not forward—but I look up;
I look not round me—but I look up;
I look not inward—but I look up.

The great crying need of the world today is the upward look—to Jesus. It is the answer to your need. There is nothing in your past, nor in your future; there is nothing around you, nor within you, that can daunt you when you look to Him. Today God is saying to you, "Lay aside every weight—and look to him." Tell Him your burden. When you share it with Him, it becomes light.

A father was holding his little blind daughter on his knee. Just then a friend came in, and picking her up walked off with her down the garden. The little one expressed neither surprise nor fear, so her father said, "Aren't you afraid, darling?" "No," she replied. "But you don't know whose hand you hold." "No," was the prompt reply, "but you do, Father."

Someone looking to you, sees you *looking to Jesus.*

I lift my gaze beyond the night, and see,
Above the banners of man's hate unfurled
The holy figure that on Calvary
Stretched arms out wide enough for all the world.

WHEELOCK

PRAYER: *Lord, the Lifter up of our heads, help us daily to have the upward look. You are the answer to our need; You are the perfecter of our faith. We thank You. Amen.*

He Leadeth Me! O Blessed Thought!

Aughton. L. M. With Refrain. WILLIAM BATCHELDER BRADBURY, 1860.

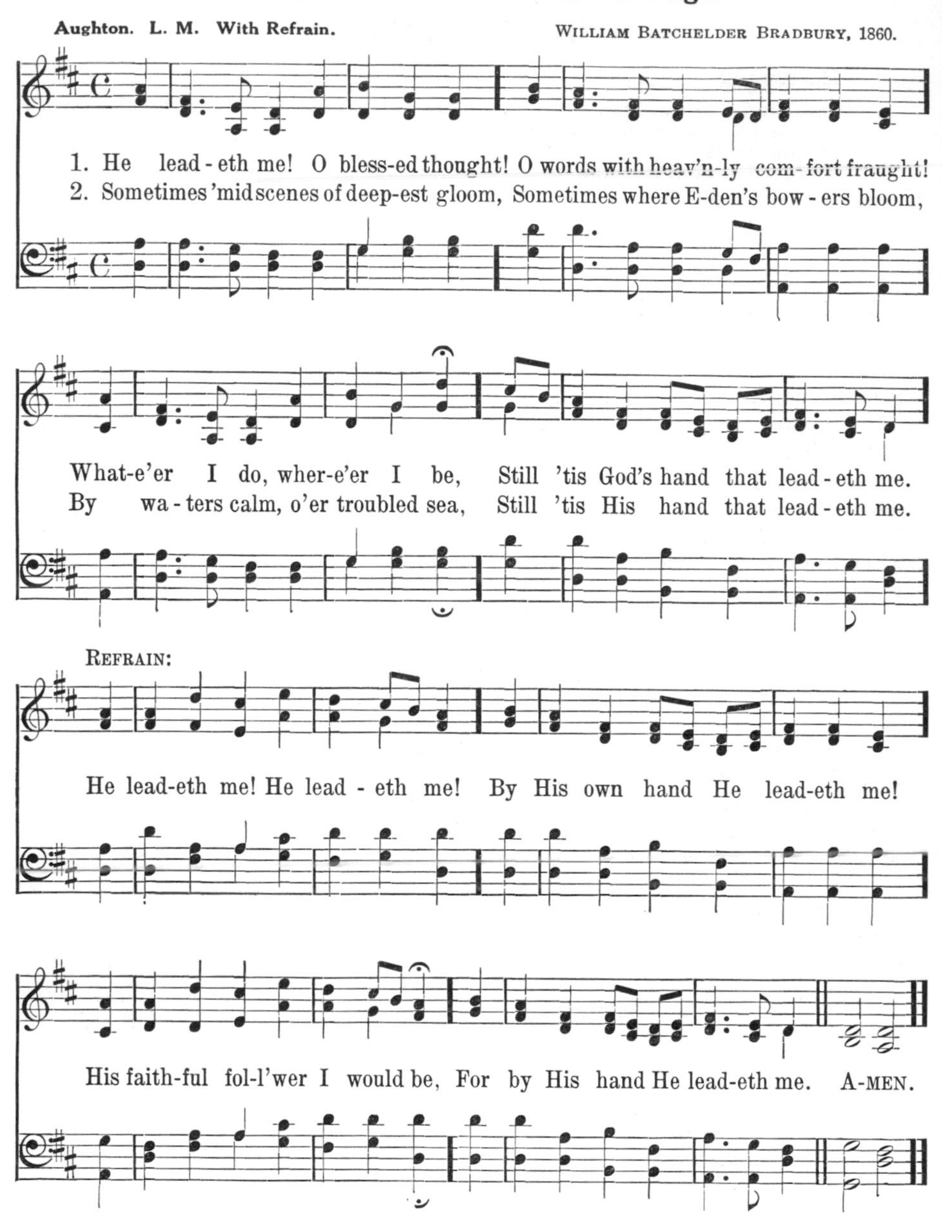

3 Lord, I would clasp Thy hand in mine,
Nor ever murmur nor repine;
Content, whatever lot I see,
Since 'tis my God that leadeth me.

4 And when my task on earth is done,
When by Thy grace the vict'ry's won,
E'en death's cold wave I will not flee,
Since God through Jordan leadeth me.

Joseph Henry Gilmore, 1859.

SUNDAY

He Leadeth Me

Deuteronomy 32:7-12

"... Like an eagle that stirs up its nest,
that flutters over its young,
spreading out its wing, catching them,
bearing them on its pinions,
the Lord alone did lead him,
and there was no foreign god with him."
Deuteronomy 32:11, 12

OUR BIBLE passage is a recounting of God's leading the people of Israel from a land of bondage to the land of promise. This is the kind of journey every soul must make, from the land of birth to the "place He has gone to prepare." He has never promised that it would be an easy journey. To the contrary, He made it very plain that following Him was to take up a cross, was to go against the stream, was to be often misjudged and maligned. How often we, who claim to be His followers, forget this.

Not only did He promise to go before, but He promised also His constant presence to those who will follow Him. The picture in our scripture today is a beautiful one. Have you ever studied the way of an eagle with its young? First there is the stirring up of its nest, born of the instinctive desire to see eaglets try their own wings; then the fluttering above them, eagerly watching their progress; then, as they awkwardly push out of the nest, the eagle dips underneath them, spreading its wings to catch them, should fear paralyze them, and bearing them on its pinions. So the Lord leads us.

Our song writer wants us to be aware that the Lord's leading is constant.

He leadeth me! O blessed thought!
O words with heav'nly comfort fraught!
Whate'er I do, where'er I be,
Still 'tis God's hand that leadeth me.

"Whate'er I do, where'er I be." In the monotony of the repetitious tasks of housekeeping; in the daily discipline of an office; in the extra volunteer tasks of love in your church and community—He leads you. I have arisen from my devotional time, and had Him lead me to the telephone to perform some errand for His kingdom, or to speak a word of encouragement to some soul. There is no magic about this leadership. The chorus of our song stipulates what our part must be if we are to know the joy of His going before. Did you take note—"His faithful follower I would be"?

If the eagles refuse to lift their wings to get out of the nest, the eagle's hovering and spreading of its wings are to no avail. So in your life, you will not know the blessing of His leadership, unless you want to be His faithful follower.

PRAYER: *We thank You, Lord, that You are our trailblazer. Today You would lead us in the way we should walk. Help us to be open to Your leading. Amen.*

He Leadeth Me

Sometimes 'mid scenes of deepest gloom

Romans 5:3-5

We rejoice in our sufferings, knowing that suffering produces endurance, and endurance produces character, and character produces hope, and hope does not disappoint us, because God's love has been poured into our hearts through the Holy Spirit which has been given to us.

THERE ARE those who feel that when you are a Christian, no trouble will befall you; that you will be spared the vicissitudes of life. This is a sugar-coated idea of what it means to follow the leading of Christ. Scripture again and again reiterates what it means to walk in His steps. Nowhere does it suggest that such walking will be on a bed of roses; that material success and physical comfort will be the lot of those who come after Him. Such a philosophy, placed next to Calvary, shrivels. When Paul said "in everything God works for good with those who love him," he did not have reference to the superficial trivia of our physical lives. He was speaking of our eternal souls.

This does not mean that there cannot be outward and physical blessings. These may well be the portion of many who follow Christ. Beware, though, if your soul is at ease. For following the Christ is a warfare from beginning to end. The devil never gives up, and can use material comforts to lull a soul to sleep. The Christian's joy is found in knowing that, though he must go through scenes of deepest gloom, he is not alone; there is One who has led the way. Yes, he knows that nothing can separate him from that One, if he will keep his eyes fixed on Him; and the sorrow to be endured will only make the goal more beautiful.

Have you desired an easy life for yourself and your children? Did you grumble and doubt the wisdom of God when trouble came your way? Can you not trust His leading, knowing that even though it is by the way of the cross, it will lead *home*? And let us not forget that Paul teaches us that suffering produces character.

Do not cheat thy heart and tell her,
 "Grief will pass away,
Hope for fairer times in future,
 And forget today."
Tell her, if you will, that sorrow
 Need not come in vain;
Tell her that the lesson taught her
 Far outweighs the pain.

ADELAIDE PROCTER

PRAYER: *Lord, help us to know that You are with us through scenes of deepest gloom. Make us willing to follow Your leading in the difficult places, too. In the name of the One who has gone before. Amen.*

He Leadeth Me

Sometimes where Eden's bowers bloom

Psalm 1

He is like a tree
  planted by streams of water,
that yields its fruit in its season,
  and its leaf does not wither.
In all that he does, he prospers.
Psalm 1:3

IS IT NOT wonderful to know that God's leading is for every situation? He is not just a helper for difficult times; He shares our joys, too. And their pleasure is double because He is with us. Is it not true that too often we take for granted the happy times, the countless blessings, the love of our families, the enrichment of friends? But how quick we are to speak of troubles, when they come!

What makes Eden for you? A clergyman overheard two women talking in a New York subway. With a whiny twang in her voice, one of them said to the other: "Oh, I don't know what I want now. Twenty years ago my ambition was to have a nice home in the suburb, with all the modern conveniences, a car, a trip to Europe, two children, and a fur coat. I have all these now, and I am still not satisfied. I don't know what I want." How does your criterion of Eden measure up to what she thought hers was?

What are some of the real things that make Eden for a woman? In my book, one of the first would be to be loved, and to love. And the latter produces the former. If you do not think you are loved enough, be sure that either the quantity or quality of your love is insufficient. Hand in hand with being loved is the joy of being needed. Yet many of us turn our backs on this door that is opened to us, and refuse to go in and claim the Eden that could be ours.

Perhaps today the Lord would have us know that, if we do not walk in the counsel of the ungodly, in everything in life there can be something of Eden. He says, "In all that he does, he prospers."

OUT OF THE VAST

There's a part of the sun in an apple,
  There's a part of the moon in a rose;
There's a part of the flaming Pleiades
  In every leaf that grows.

Out of the vast comes nearness;
  For the God whose love we sing
Lends a little of His heaven
  To every living thing.

AUGUSTUS BAMBERGER

PRAYER: *Lord, help us to be aware of the "Eden" places in our lives May the joy be doubled because You have led the way. Amen.*

He Leadeth Me

By waters calm

Psalm 121

The sun shall not smite you by day,
nor the moon by night.
Psalm 121:6

Psalm 119:165

Great peace have those who love thy law;
nothing can make them stumble.

IN BOTH of these Psalms the song writer suggests the key to calm waters in a Christian's life. In Psalm 121 the opening verse is:

I lift up my eyes to the hills.
From whence does my help come?
My help comes from the Lord
who made heaven and earth.

And in Psalm 119 we are told very plainly that those who love God's law have great peace. We are told where to look, and what to do, if we would increase the calm water places in our lives.

It is true that the hymn writer undoubtedly had in mind those days in our lives that seem less perturbed, without unexpected situations and difficulties. Yet most often is not this sense of calm waters something that can come from within? Have you found that things that disturb you mightily on some days, do not even cause a ripple on others? If you are very honest with yourself, will you not admit that, when you fail to look to the Source of your help, and fail to obey His laws, you can very quickly stir up a tempest?

When I think of Christ, something of the calmness of eternity that He generates for every one who embraces Him pervades my soul. In the midst of a howling mob that threw lying accusations at Him, He never said a word. This gift of His presence He will give to anyone who will wait upon Him.

Maybe this part of our song should make us stop and ask ourselves if we have the places of calm in our lives that we should have? Maybe we should take a look at ourselves and see how we react under difficult situations. If you find that the look is not a happy one, then know that He stands ready to help, He who is the source of eternal peace.

In some old castles are found deep wells meant to supply the garrison in time of siege. An aqueduct bringing water from without would be at the enemy's mercy; but over the well within the enemy has no power.

The peace that Christ gives is that of the spring within. He wants to lead you by waters calm.

PRAYER: *Thank You, Lord, for the peace that comes from knowing that You will lead us by waters calm. Thank You that You are the only source of lasting peace. Amen.*

THURSDAY

He Leadeth Me

O'er troubled sea

Psalm 27

When evildoers assail me,
 uttering slanders against me,
my adversaries and foes,
 they shall stumble and fall.

For he will hide me in his shelter
 in the day of trouble;
he will conceal me under the cover of his tent,
 he will set me high upon a rock.
Psalm 27:2, 5

WHAT A glorious, undergirding Psalm is the twenty-seventh! After recounting all the difficulties that were facing him, the psalmist boldly says, "of whom shall I be afraid?" and then reaffirms his faith in the words, "yet I will be confident." It is not how troubled the sea is that determines the course of your life; it is who the Pilot is. And again, it is not what happens to you; it is how you take it. Have there been times when you have felt the troubled seas were more than your frail craft could take? Did you remember His leading is sufficient for the most turbulent storm? The One who stilled the tempestuous waters of the Sea of Galilee has the power to guide your boat safely through any gale. And how you weather the storm is your witness to the world.

In the Pitti Palace at Florence there are two pictures which hang side by side. One represents a stormy sea with its wild waves, and black clouds and fierce lightnings of agony and despair. The other picture also represents a wild sea, tossed by as fierce as a storm; but out of the midst of the waves a rock rises, against which the waters dash in vain. In the cleft of the rock there are tufts of grass and flowers, and amid these, a dove is seen sitting on her nest, quiet and undisturbed by the wild fury of the storm.

It is this confidence in the midst of the world's fury that the psalmist writes about. "He will set me high upon a rock. And now my head shall be lifted up above my enemies round about me; . . . I will sing and make melody to the Lord."

I shall never forget the experience of having a young pastor, completely crippled with arthritis, sharing this psalm with me. For four years he had been bed-ridden, his body twisted and distorted with the disease that necessitated his giving up the active ministry. Yet what a ministry went from that bedside! In the middle of a sea of pain, with the howling of the skeptics around him, he witnessed to the leading of the Lord in a way that was unforgettable. As he planned his memorial service, he asked that this Psalm be read as though it were from him. The Lord will lead you, too, over any troubled sea you have to cross.

PRAYER: *Give me grace, O God, to give a steady witness even when the winds of the world make the going rough. Let me hear You say: "Be strong, and let your heart take courage." Amen.*

He Leadeth Me

So that I am

Content, whatever lot, I see

Philippians 4:4-13

Rejoice in the Lord always; again I will say, Rejoice . . .
Have no anxiety about anything . . .
for I have learned, in whatever state I am in, to be content. . . .
I can do all things in him who strengthens me.
Philippians 4: 4, 6, 11, 13

THIS SECTION of the fourth chapter of Philippians parallels what the hymn writer says in our stanza for today. Why could Paul say "I have learned, in whatever state I am, to be content"? Because he could do all things through the One who strengthened him. There are people who spend their lives looking longingly at other people, wishing they could be in their place. The other field is always greener; what happens to the other fellow is always better than what happens to you. Rest assured that this pattern of thinking is the recipe for a frustrated life. It is also a very common cause of ulcers. It comes from trying to walk alone.

Were you to go with any pastor on his round of sick calls, you would meet two kinds of people. There would be those who would complain about the situation they were in. Then there would be those who had found Paul's jewel. In prison? Ill? Forgotten? Far away from home? Yet content. Yes, we have sat by bedsides where, from the human viewpoint, there was nothing but cause for complaint.

One aged friend comes to mind. Relatives had absconded with the pension money; the doctor had said the patient would never walk again; yet such a sense of peace was in this room in that convalescent home, that one knew there was another Presence there. God can give us grace not to mull over our misfortunes, but to meet them head on victoriously!

The world is wide
In time and tide,
And God is guide;
Then do not hurry.

The man is blest
Who does his best
And leaves the rest;
Then do not worry.

CHARLES F. DEEMS

PRAYER: *There is so much of discontent in the world today, Lord. Help me to witness to the peace that comes from following You, knowing that no matter what the outer circumstances may be, Your presence can transform them. In Jesus' Name. Amen.*

SATURDAY

He Leadeth Me

When my task on earth is done . . . through Jordan

Psalm 23

Even though I walk through the
valley of the shadow of death,
I fear no evil . . .
And I shall dwell in the house of the Lord
for ever. Psalm 23:4, 6

WHAT MOTHER when she has been overborne by the multitudinous tasks expected of her, has not longed for the day when her task would be done? And could anything be sweeter than to relax an aching body on a comfortable bed? How many times I have thanked God that one of the things we are told about the life to come, is that there we shall find rest. And what a goal is ours—to dwell in the house of the Lord for ever.

Is your pattern of thinking and planning and working evidence of your following the Great Shepherd who leads the way? Is there a note of victory in your life, and of purpose? Are you constantly aware that you do not walk alone?

A church school class had been told the story of David and Goliath. Then the teacher asked, "Aren't you surprised that little David could defeat the Giant Goliath?" To which one little lad replied, "Why, no. It was two to one. God was fighting for David."

I remember hearing a great Chinese educator speak to a college assembly. He told how he was in a city in North China during the second World War, when the signal came foretelling an air raid. Being a stranger there, he made inquiry about an air shelter. He was informed there was none, because there was water so near the surface. The only recourse was to take one's rug and find a place in the field near by.

The scholar shared the pattern of his thinking as he waited for the final signal. He thought of all the degrees he had earned, and how he was considered a learned man. Then he looked at the illiterate lying next to him. How much better off was he than this poor man, now? He recalled what a comfortable balance he had in his bank back home, and how he had thought that it was a source of security. Then he glanced at the pauper on the other side, and realized that his money did nothing for him now. He began to get into a state of panic, when lines he had learned in the mission school in which he had been educated came to him: "The Lord is my shepherd . . . though I walk through the valley, I will fear no evil." Remembering who the Lord was, and what power was His, such peace came into his soul that he promised God that, should he live, he would go around the world telling people what it meant, when you faced walking through the valley, to have the Lord with you. He leads!

PRAYER: *Help me to be Your faithful follower. Lead me in the way everlasting. Amen.*

Thy Word Is Like a Garden, Lord

Edwin Hodder, 1868

Old English Melody

Thy Word

Is like a garden, Lord

Psalm 126:6; Mark 4:14-20; Isaiah 40:6-8

The grass withers, the flower fades;
but the word of our God will stand forever.

THE INSTABILITY of the spiritual life of many people is due to the fact that they depend upon their feelings, rather than the unchanging Word of God. Our hymn for this week should help us to evaluate in our own lives whether we have given God's Word its rightful place. Perhaps too many of us have done only nibbling, the kind that takes away one's appetite for a real meal. Too often our Bible reading has lacked joy. In Jeremiah 15:16 we read,

Thy words were found, and I ate them,
and thy words became to me a joy
and the delight of my heart;
for I am called by thy name,
O Lord, God of hosts.

"Thy word is like a garden, Lord, with flowers bright and fair." How closely is Scripture linked with creation! And rightly so, for the creation is the handiwork of the Creator. I remember being in the audience in a great church when the late Dr. George Washington Carver spoke. There was a huge basket of beautiful roses in front of him. He plucked one, and holding it in his hand and looking at it, he quoted Tennyson's immortal words:

Flower in the crannied wall,
I pluck you out of the crannies,
. . . but if I could understand
What you are root and all, and all in all,
I should know what God and man is.

Yet even more true is this of the Word. In the Gospel of John we are told that the Word was God. So, if we are searching for God, it is to the Word we must go, for there He is to be found.

Is it not interesting that the Bible uses the temporary quality of flowers that are picked to contrast the everlastingness of God's Word?

The flower fades;
but the word of our God will stand forever.

Here is where the sowing comes in. The inference is that a seed sown takes root and produces sheaves. That is what should happen in every life in which God's Word is real.

PRAYER: *Lord, forgive me that too often I have just glanced at the garden of Your Word, and have not made its beauty my own. Give me grace to take time to cultivate eternal truths in my life. Amen.*

Thy Word

Is like a deep, deep mine

Proverbs 20:15

There is gold, and abundance of costly stones;
but the lips of knowledge are a precious jewel.

"THE LIPS of knowledge are a precious jewel." It is interesting that Scripture should so evaluate itself. In another place we read, "The fear of the Lord is the beginning of wisdom." Since Scripture is the source of our knowledge of Him, it is the mine in which we should search.

Let us take a look at our reading! How much of it has to deal with eternal truth? And we want it easy to take, in sugar-coated capsule form. When did you sit down and really work through a section of Scripture yourself, probe its meaning, and contemplate its application in your life? Most of us have not done much more than surface mining, and those resources quickly run out. With a shrug of our shoulders we say somewhat flippantly, "Well, there is so much I cannot understand," and with that we dismiss God's injunction to "search the scriptures." We too often treat it as a magic formula which, having been dutifully mumbled, will now produce the desired good for our lives. We need to study the Bible and not about the Bible.

The late Dr. John R. Mott wrote:

To do God's work we must have God's power.
To have God's power we must know God's will.
To know God's will we must study God's Word.

To those who know the joy of "mining" God's Word there is a thrill that no words can describe. To be studying a daily portion, and to have some word for you come leaping out of the pages, must parallel the feeling a miner has when he locates a find. Dr. Kierkegaard, the Danish theologian, says that the Bible is a personal letter from God to you, with your name on it.

Yes, there will be many passages that you do not understand, and there will be many others that will take on a new meaning for you each time that you read them, like a facet of a jewel catching a sunbeam. Always, and this is God's promise, for the one who earnestly seeks there will be treasures in abundance, and the-not-understood passages, one leaves with God until the day of His revealing.

"Seek, and you will find."

PRAYER: *Make me a miner, Lord. Give me grace daily to set aside time to search the Scriptures. Let mine be the joy of hearing You speak personally to me through its pages. In Jesus' Name. Amen.*

Thy Word

Is like a starry host

Psalm 8

When I look at thy heavens, the work of thy fingers,
  the moon and the stars which thou hast established;
what is man that thou art mindful of him,
  and the son of man that thou dost care for him?
Psalm 8:3, 4

HOW ANYONE can study astronomy, and not bow in adoration before the Creator of the starry host, is more than I can understand. It is to cry out with the psalmist: "Praise him, all you shining stars!" There are the miracles of their pattern their placement, their numbers. Consider the Milky Way. Here are more stars than man has been able to number. Brilliant Greek minds, during what was supposed to be one of the most erudite periods of history, tried to count them. They thought that they were being extravagant when they suggested that there might be three thousand, or possibly, four thousand of them. Yet when God spoke to Abraham, hundreds of years before, He intimated that the number of stars was beyond man's counting. God's Word is like a starry host. The light to be found for our daily living is incalculable. An American professor has written these lines:

When I am overmatched by petty cares
  And things of earth loom large and seem to be of moment,
How it soothes and comforts me
  To step into the night and feel the airs of heaven fan my cheek
And gaze into those all uncharted seas
  Where swim the stately planets. Such as these
Make mortal fret seem light and temporal.

RICHARD BURTON

The experience of the poet with the stars of the physical world is like the one that a seeker in the spiritual world has when he gazes into the firmament of God's Word. Values come clear; things take their right perspective. Try it.

Some years ago a lady went to consult a famous New York physician about her health. She was a distraught, nervous woman. After listening to her complaints, the doctor gave her this brief prescription: "Go home and read your Bible an hour a day, then come back to me a month from today." She thought it sounded silly, but it was inexpensive medicine, so she decided that she would try it. In a month she went back to the doctor's office and asked him how he knew what she needed. For answer, the physician turned to his desk. There, worn and marked, lay an open Bible. "Madam," he said, "if I were to omit my daily reading of this Book, I would lose my greatest source of strength and skill."

PRAYER: *Help me, O Lord, to look into Your Word, and explore the wonders of its firmament. Give me grace daily to seek its light. Amen.*

Thy Word

Is like an armory

2 Samuel 22:2-20

> The Lord is my rock, and my fortress, and my deliverer;
> The God of my rock; in him will I trust: he is my shield,
> and the horn of my salvation, my high tower, and my
> refuge, my saviour. 2 Samuel 22:2, 3 (KJV)

IN OUR generation the word "war" has been a common one in everybody's vocabulary. When it has not been a hot war, it has been a cold one; and the matter of defense has occupied not only much of our national concern, but also of our country's budget. In the matter of building a physical defense, we have all too often neglected the armory of the soul, and so have faced our days unprepared.

In the Bible one finds equipment to fight the battle against temptation, against worry, against fear. There is a weapon for every foe. But all the weapons in the world do no good, if one does not know where they are and how to use them. Men may die of thirst next to a spring, if they will not put forth the effort to take a drink. It is an astounding thing to discover how men flounder around, trying every kind of defense in the battle of life, and ignore the inner fortress that can be theirs, if they earnestly turn to the Bible.

On board a boat crossing the ocean, I was in conversation with a woman from another part of our country. As we shared one with the other, she told me her story. She had spent a great deal of time and much money for months seeking psychiatric help. Then someone opened for her a page of Scripture and in a short time, as she pursued this source of help, she was well again, and able to be about normal living. As she finished her story she said, "And all this was there all the time, free for me to take!"

Surely every one of us should be grateful for the skills that psychiatry has been able to bring to mental illness. But real psychiatrists will tell you that the fundamental principles of their science are to be found in the words of Jesus. And they are in God's armory for the use of anyone who wants them.

Whittier has said it succinctly in these lines:

> We search the world for truth. We cull
> The good, the true, the beautiful,
> From graven stone and written scroll,
> And all old flower-fields of the soul;
> And, weary seekers of the best,
> We come back laden from our quest,
> To find that all the sages said
> Is in the Book our mothers read.

PRAYER: *What a resource You have given us, Lord, for life's every battle. Help us to use the weapons that are at our command. Amen.*

Thy Word

Has been preserved

Psalm 119:89

For ever, O Lord, thy word
is firmly fixed in the heavens.

Matthew 24:1-14

"And this gospel of the kingdom will be preached throughout the whole world, as a testimony to all nations." Matthew 24:14

"Heaven and earth will pass away, but my words will not pass away." Matthew 24:35

THE STORY of the preservation of the Bible through the ages is a fascinating one. Any script other than one of divine origin would long have perished, if men had made the same effort to destroy them as they have made to destroy the Scriptures. But even as God's Word is powerful and "sharper than any two-edged sword," so according to His promise it is also imperishable. Even in a physical way this has been true.

In Bohemia, traveling through a district where the Bible was not permitted to be read, a colporteur was surprised to find a locksmith who knew the Bible well. He learned that seventeen years before, all the copies of the Bible had been gathered together, and a bonfire made of them. A gust of wind carried away two burning pieces, which the locksmith had picked up and read. The first words that caught his eye were, "Heaven and earth will pass away, but my words will not pass away." So impressed was he, that he and his father saved a whole Bible out of the burning, and became Bible readers and Bible students.

Or there is that telling incident from the life of Adoniram Judson. He had just completed his translation of the Bible into Burmese, when the war broke out between Burma and England. Judson was thrown into prison under suspicion of being an English spy. For nineteen months he was bound in fetters and kept in a loathsome cell.

Mrs. Judson, knowing that the manuscript would be found and seized in her home, at first buried it. Then, fearing that it would decay if left longer in the ground, she wrapped it about with cotton and of it made a pillow for her husband in the cell. Once the pillow was stolen by soldiers, but Mrs. Judson redeemed it by giving them a better one. One night Dr. Judson was hurried off to another prison, and his pillow was thrown into the prison yard. There one of his faithful converts took it home, because it had belonged to his beloved teacher. Dr. Judson mourned for his Bible, but long afterwards to his great joy, found it uninjured in the house of his convert.

Whether or not you use it, God's Word will endure. But how will you endure, if you do not use it? Using it, you will be empowered to endure anything!

PRAYER: *In a transitory world, we give You thanks, Lord, for the things that endure. Thank You that Your Word is everlasting. Amen.*

FRIDAY

Thy Word

Is to be hidden in the heart

Psalm 119

O that my ways may be steadfast
  in keeping thy statutes!
I have laid up thy word in my heart,
  that I might not sin against thee.
Psalm 119:5, 11

JUST READING God's Word is not the final answer, although that is a wonderful beginning. Surface exposure is not enough. Sometimes those who get a great deal of this application immunize themselves against the real shot. It is the Bible in one's heart and in one's life that is potent.

How much of the Bible do you know from memory? When did you last memorize a section? With our mentally lazy ways, there is a real danger of our ignoring a source of power that is life changing. And when the Bible is laid up in your heart, there is not any place where you cannot call it forth, and have God talk to you.

I shall never forget when my mother was lying ill in the hospital. Our little boys were only one and two years of age at the time, and there had to be planning and bustle at home, in order that daily I might be at her side. One day I was particularly weary, and the news had not been favorable. As I was driving along alone, I wondered how I could step into my mother's room with calm. The thought of losing her was overwhelming. Then, as surely as though God had been physically in the car with me, He spoke to me, through words my mother had taught me: "I know whom I have believed and I am sure that he is able to guard until that Day what has been entrusted to me." With calm, yes, even with joy, I was able to greet my mother and visit with her.

An observer noticed a strange phenomenon down in a railroad yard. One of many boxcars that were temporarily halted there was filled with railroad ties that had been thoroughly soaked in creosote solution. It was a warm day, and all the other cars were buzzing with insect life around them, but this one car was completely free of pestiferous bugs. The clean, antiseptic creosote created an atmosphere that was so uncongenial to the pests that they avoided it. So it is with God's Word laid up in your heart. It is inimical to the presence of temptations and worries, and is a source of abundant living.

PRAYER: *I have been mentally lazy, Lord, about learning Your Word. Forgive me, and stir up my powers that I may hide its treasure in my heart. Amen.*

SATURDAY

Thy Word

Reveals my Savior

John 1:1-14

And the Word became flesh and dwelt among us, full of grace and truth.

John 20: 31

But these are written that you may believe that Jesus is the Christ, the Son of God, and that believing you may have life in his name.

WHAT MORE can be said about the Savior than the Bible already reveals? From the detailed prophecies of the Old Testament to the spectacular fulfillment of them in the New Testament, one has a complete picture of what the Son of God is like. One need but to study.

Take Isaiah, for example. In that great book, listen to the descriptive titles used for Christ: Immanuel, Mighty God, Everlasting Father, Prince of Peace, Righteous King, Divine Servant, Arm of the Lord, Anointed Preacher, Mighty Traveler. Or listen to the characteristics this same prophet lists as pertaining to the promised Messiah: Wisdom, spiritual discernment, justice, righteousness, silence, gentleness, perseverance, radiance, meekness, vicarious suffering, sinlessness, greatness, saving power. Need one say any more about the Divine Redeemer?

Those who would seek a Savior should search the Scriptures.

In the city of Washington there is a unique and remarkable copy of the Constitution of the United States. If one examines it closely, it seems to be a jumble of strange lettering and distorted lines. However, if you will step back a bit and get the total perspective, you will find to your amazement the likeness of George Washington.

And so it is with God's Word. There are those who, emphasizing out of proportions certain sections, come out with a mumbo-jumbo religion. To get a total picture of Scripture, to seek to find the crimson thread of Christ's redemptive blood in the story of creation, in the books of history, through the pages of the prophets, and the poetry of the psalms; to walk with Him along the shores of Galilee and on up to Jerusalem; to live through the dramatic days of the early church, and to see countless times the transforming power of the presence of Christ in lives, is to let Him walk right into your life, and take His pre-eminent place there. Yes, to those who seek, God's Word reveals the Christ.

PRAYER: *Speak, Lord, through Your Word. Help me to see Your picture therein. Amen.*

Beautiful Saviour! King of Creation

Schönster Herr Jesu. 5 5 7, 5 5 7.

Silesian Folksong.
HOFFMANN VON FALLERSLEBEN'S Volkslieder, 1842.

3 Fair is the sunshine,
Fair is the moonlight,
Bright the sparkling stars on high;
Jesus shines brighter,
Jesus shines purer
Than all the angels in the sky.

4 Beautiful Saviour!
Lord of the nations!
Son of God and Son of Man!
Glory and honor,
Praise, adoration,
Now and for evermore be Thine!

Münster Gesangbuch, 1677.

Beautiful Savior

King of Creation

Job 38

"Where were you when I laid the foundation of the earth?" Job 38:4

John 1:3

All things were made through him, and without him was not anything made that was made.

SOMEONE HAS said, "Nature is the glove on the hand of God." You need but go in search of two leaves alike, yes, even two blades of grass alike, to bow in adoration and wonder before the Creator of such infinite variability. Surely, if the "glove" is a series of miracles beyond our understanding, how much more wonderful is the Hand that created the glove?

In the thirty-eighth chapter of Job are posed some classic questions. "Where were you when I laid the foundation of the earth? Tell me if you have understanding. . . . Who determined its measurements—surely you should know!" This question is not insignificant when you consider that, were the measurements of the earth, or its distance from the sun, one fraction greater or less, life would be impossible, because of frigidity on the one hand, or fire on the other.

Or if you deal in gardens, are you not often filled with wonderment that from one brown bulb comes a red tulip, and from another a golden yellow one? It is not surprising that a poet of the seventeenth century, John Dryden, was compelled to write:

> This is a piece too fair
> To be the child of Chance, and not of Care,
> No Atoms casually together hurl'd
> Could e'er produce so beautiful a world.

A minister asked an old man his reasons for believing in the existence of God. The reply was: "Sir, I have been here going hard on seventy years. Every day since I have been in this world I see the sun rise in the east and set in the west. The North Star stands where it did the first time I saw it. The seven stars and Job's Coffin keep on the same path in the sky and never turn out. It ain't so with man's works. He makes clocks and watches. They may run well for a while; but they get out of fix and stand stock-still. But the sun, and the moon, and the stars keep the same way all the while."

The One who is your Beautiful Savior is the King of Creation. Could you trust your life into more capable hands?

PRAYER: *Savior, forgive us that so often we make You so small. We are grateful that creation is in such all-wise and all loving hands. Make us more aware of Your Presence in the things about us. Amen.*

Beautiful Savior

Son of God

Matthew 16:13-20

Simon Peter replied, "You are the Christ, the Son of the living God."
Matthew 16:16

Matthew 3:17

And lo, a voice from heaven, saying, "This is my beloved Son, with whom I am well pleased."

Matthew 17:5

A voice from the cloud said, "This is my beloved Son, with whom I am well pleased; listen to him."

John 3:16

"For God so loved the world that he gave his only Son."

THAT CHRIST is the Son of God has been the stumbling block for many people through the ages. They are willing to admit that He was a wonderful man, or a great teacher, or an outstanding reformer. But that He is the only Son of God,—there they hedge. Yet this is the basic claim that He makes for himself again and again in Scripture. It is the major premise that makes valid for us His mediation with the Father. As far as I am concerned, this claim of His must be true, or He is a liar. And if so, then how can He be a great teacher, or great anything else?

Throughout the Old Testament, like a crimson thread, there runs the promise of His coming. The Gospels record the fulfillment, in miraculous detail, of all that was foretold. The Book of Acts and the epistles relate the epic of the kingdom He established on earth, and reiterate and reaffirm His basic claim that He is the Son of God.

A Jewish soldier had been attending services where he had heard much of the character and teaching of Christ. He went to his Rabbi and said, "Rabbi, the Christians say that Christ has already come, while we claim that he is yet to come." "Yes," assented the Rabbi. "Well," asked the young soldier, "when our Christ comes, what will he have on Jesus Christ?"

If the fact that Christ is the Son of God has been a stumbling block to some is true, it is also true that to countless millions this fact has been their only hope of salvation. "There is no other name under heaven given among men by which we must be saved."

Who do you say that He is? From the need of your innermost heart today, are you willing to acknowledge Him as your Beautiful Savior, Son of God? Such a confession invites Him into your heart, and gives you courage to face whatever may come of life or death, because you will never have to face it alone.

PRAYER: *Beautiful Savior, I would acknowledge You to be the only Son of God, and my Redeemer. Such matchless love I cannot understand, but I can gratefully accept it. Thank You for coming to earth. Amen.*

Beautiful Savior

Son of Man

Philippians 2:5-8

Christ Jesus emptied himself, taking the form of a servant, being born in the likeness of men. And being found in human form he humbled himself and became obedient unto death, even death on a cross.

HOW GRATEFUL I am that God in His divine wisdom chose to reveal himself in the form of a man. Here is a picture that I can understand, for He was like us in all things, except that He was without sin. He knew hunger, weariness, disappointment, rejection, and therefore He understands anything that befalls me.

As a woman I am grateful that, though the Lord of Glory walked this earth in a time when women were held in small repute, ye He counted every one worthy of His attention; so that He redeemed a Mary Magdalene, He loved the hospitality and understanding of Mary and Martha, He paused to share with the Samaritan woman. As a mother, I have adored Him for taking little children in His arms and blessing them.

God's plan was remarkable in another respect, too. Dr. C. F. Andrews, the great Christian from India, has succinctly put it: "For the supreme miracle of Christ's character lies in this: that He combines within Himself, as no other figure in human history has ever done, the qualities of every race. His very birthplace and home in childhood were near the concourse of the two great streams of human life in the ancient world, that flowed East and West. Time and place conspired, but the divine spark came down from above to mold for all time the human character of the Christ, the Son of Man."

NO DISTANT LORD

No distant Lord have I, loving afar to be.
Made flesh for me He cannot rest until He rests in me.

I need not journey far this dearest friend to see.
Companionship is always mine; He makes His home with me.

I envy not the twelve. Nearer to me is He.
The life He once lived here on earth He lives again in me.

Ascended now to God my witness there to be,
His witness here am I because His Spirit dwells in me.

O glorious Son of God, Incarnate Deity,
I shall forever be with Thee because Thou art with me.

MALTBIE BABCOCK

PRAYER: *Thank You, Lord, that You were willing to humble Yourself and become flesh like us. Thank You that You want eternally to dwell in us. Amen.*

Beautiful Savior

Light of my soul

Isaiah 9:1-8

The people who walked in darkness have seen a great light; those who dwelt in a land of deep darkness, on them has light shined. Isaiah 9:2

John 8:12

And again Jesus spoke to them saying, "I am the light of the world; he who follows me will not walk in darkness, but will have the light of life."

THOSE OF us who lived in the era of street gas lamps, have an unforgettable memory. Night would be descending, when way down the street could be seen a pinpoint of light. It crisscrossed from side to side. The nightly wonder of the darkness before, and the lighted path behind, is something I shall never forget. And the lamplighter was always someone very special because he was a part of this transformation.

When the Light of the World enters a human life, darkness goes. He goes into every corner of the heart and ferrets out what might be lurking there. Perhaps this is why so many people refuse to let Him be the Light of their souls. There are things in their lives they would rather not have revealed.

But if you have walked in darkness, you know what a stumbling way it is. You bruise yourself on obstacles and trip on unsuspected objects unseen in your path. How different is all this when Christ, the Light, shines upon your way. Where there is gloom, He comes with His sunshine; where there is sin, He comes with His cleansing; where there is fear, He comes with His love.

NEVER NIGHT AGAIN

The soft light from a stable door
Lies on the midnight lands.
The Wise Men's star burns evermore
Over all desert sands.

Unto all peoples of the earth
A little Child brought light,
And never in the darkest place
Can it be utter night.

No flickering torch, no wavering fire,
But Light—the Life of men.
Whatever clouds may veil the sky,
Never is night again!

LILIAN COX

Jesus said, "He who follows me will not walk in darkness."

PRAYER: *In this world of darkness, Lord, be my light. Expose any areas of my heart that have been kept from You. Today let me walk in Your light. Amen.*

Beautiful Savior

My Joy

Psalm 34

I will bless the Lord at all times;
his praise shall continually be in my mouth . . .
Look to him and be radiant;
so your faces shall never be ashamed.
Psalm 34:1, 5

TOO OFTEN as Christians we give the impression that following the Lord is the most joyless pursuit in the world. No wonder that those whose lives we touch are not drawn to Him! When we speak of the joy that Christ is to His followers, we do not mean a giddy, superficial kind of mantle that one dons. Of the One we follow it was said, "who for the joy that was set before him endured the cross." For us, too, a part of the joy will be that there is a work for us to do; there is love for us to share. Is it not true that the joyless people you know are the ones who are thinking about what people are not doing for them, or those who feel they are no longer needed?

Or to get a little nearer home, is it not true that the joyless times in your life have not necessarily been when there has been sorrow, but rather when you have indulged in self-pity? The joy Christ gives is one that is an undergirding even through sorrow, an undertone of sustaining strength that has in it something of the music of eternity. Often it may be that your happiest times might even be your hardest times.

The psalmist tells what the key is. "Look to him, and be radiant!" In his letter to the Galatians, Paul speaks of one of the fruits of the Spirit as being joy.

We have a dear friend whom we visit who is in a home called "The Home for the Incurables." That surely is rather a joyless name! But not so the guest whom we know there. Ninety-three years young, bedridden and crippled from a stroke, there is, nevertheless, an atmosphere in her room that is akin to the joy of heaven. With her alert mind and lively sense of humor, she makes one's visit to her an experience that sends one forth with a new incentive. Why? She looks to her Savior. He has never failed her. He has promised to prepare a home for her. Her joy is in acknowledging what He has done. When people have been with you, do they leave with a sense of joy?

One of Hadyn's friends asked how it was that his church music was almost always cheerful and even festive. The great composer replied: "I cannot make it otherwise. I write according to the thoughts I feel. When I think upon God my heart is so full of joy that notes dance and leap as it were from my pen, and since God has given me a cheerful heart, it will easily be forgiven me that I serve Him with a cheerful spirit."

Look to Him—and be radiant!

PRAYER: *Forgive, Lord, my long-faced moments when I have belied Your presence in my heart. Help me to impart the joy of salvation! Amen.*

Beautiful Savior

My Crown

Isaiah 28:5, 6

In that day the Lord of hosts will be a crown of glory, and a diadem of beauty, to the remnant of his people; and a spirit of justice to him who sits in judgment, and strength to those who turn back the battle at the gate.

THE CROWN is the symbol of one who reigns. It denotes power, and suggests that there are subjects who do the bidding of the one who wears it. So it is with the Christian. The kingdom over which the One who is our Crown reigns, is the Kingdom of Love. Its subject is our will. It takes the stubborn pride that so often is a part of us, and bends it into being willing to ask for forgiveness. It gives orders to energies that in their natural course would be bent on making things comfortable for us, and directs them into doing things for others. When Jesus is the Crown of your life, He patterns your thinking, He motivates your energies, He directs your footsteps.

And what a King this Savior is! He asks nothing of His subjects that He himself has not been willing to do first. And more than that, He promises to be close to His followers when they are on His errands, and to be their enabling. He has assured us that to be a part of His kingdom is to be on the victorious side. "In the world you have tribulation; but be of good cheer, I have overcome the world."

And what, you ask, is the cost of this crown? Perhaps this is the most amazing part of it all. You see, it does not cost a thing, and then again, it costs everything. It does not cost a thing because the King in love came to earth and walked with men, and finally died on a cross, sinless though He was, in order that justice might have its due. The justice that had to be met was the judgment of your sins. The King paid the ransom for you. He is asking you to accept eternal life from Him as a free gift of His love; only that you believe what He did for you.

Then again, it costs you everything for, once having accepted the gift, all that you are and have become His. Your life wears His crown.

Two young soldiers were talking about the service of Christ. One of them said, "I can't tell you all that the Lord is to me. I do wish that you would enlist in His army."

"I am thinking about it," answered his comrade, "but it means giving up several things; in fact, I am counting the cost."

An officer passing at that moment heard the remark, and laying his hand on the shoulder of the speaker, said, "Young friend, you talk of counting the cost of following Christ, but have you ever counted the cost of not following Him?"

PRAYER: *Lord, whose presence crowns our lives with all that is good, reign in each day of our living. Thank You for the knowledge that when we accept Your crown, victory is ours. Amen.*

SATURDAY

Beautiful Savior

Lord of the Nations

Psalm 86:8-10

There is none like thee among the gods, O Lord,
nor are there any works like thine.
All the nations thou hast made shall come
and bow down before thee, O Lord,
and shall glorify thy name.
For thou art great and doest wondrous things,
thou alone art God.

Jeremiah 10:7

Who would not fear thee, O King of the nations?
For this is thy due;
for among all the wise ones of the nations
and in all their kingdoms
there is none like thee.

SOMETIMES WE forget that nations as well as individuals are mortal. And so we become beset by fear because of some rising tyranny, or some power-drunk monarch. I am not proposing that we just sit and twiddle our thumbs as these things happen. God wants us to be so busy in the promulgation of His kingdom that these fears will find their rightful place in the promises of God. We need to bend every effort and enlist every energy that our nation will acknowledge and serve God; and if we do this, we shall not have much time to be concerned with the fear of kingdoms rising around us. Back in 1787, Benjamin Franklin said, "I have lived, sir, a long time—and the longer I live, the more convincing proofs I see that God governs in the affairs of men." Napoleon looking back on St. Helena said, "There are two world powers: the sword and the spirit. The spirit has always vanquished the sword."

No nation is any stronger than its individual citizens. Even as our nation will endure only if it acknowledges Christ to be Lord, and follows His teachings also in relation to its fellow men in the world around, so also we must as individual citizens take inventory as to who is first in our lives and put into practice what He has taught us in regard to our neighbor.

There are those who feel that government is something entirely apart from God, and that He should have nothing to do with it. There is the story about the farmer who was looking at his young, springing crop of oats which held high promise. Someone stepped up to him and said, "This is a fine crop." The farmer replied, "Yes, if God Almighty will only let it alone, it will be a fine crop." Then, according to the story, the crop stopped where it was. God Almighty had let it alone. Do we need to stop and remember that He is Lord of the nations to know how much we need His guidance and counsel?

PRAYER: *As we view disturbing situations around the world, Lord, make us mindful that You are the Ruler of nations. Help us to bend every effort to sharing You with all the world. Amen.*

Our Times Are in Thy Hand

Glezen S. M. E. K. GLEZEN.

2 Our times are in Thy hand,
Whatever they may be,
Pleasing or painful, dark or bright,
As best may seem to Thee.

3 Our times are in Thy hand;
Why should we doubt or fear?
A Father's hand will never cause
His child a needless tear.

4 Our times are in Thy hand,
Jesus, the Crucified;
The hand our many sins have pierced
Is now our guard and guide.

5 Our times are in Thy hand:
We'll always trust in Thee,
Till we have left the weary land
And all Thy glory see.

William Freeman Lloyd, 1841, a.

Our Times Are in Thy Hand

Our Times

Psalm 31:14-16

But I trust in thee, O Lord,
  I say, "Thou art my God."
My times are in thy hand;
  deliver me from the hand of my enemies and persecutors!
Let thy face shine on thy servant;
  save me in thy steadfast love!

Romans 13:11-14

Besides this you know what hour it is, how it is full time now for you to wake from sleep. For salvation is nearer to us now than when we first believed. Romans 13:11

IF YOU were to ask folks what they think about the times in which we live, you would be apt to get two diametrically different answers. There would be those who would say: "We are living in terrible times! Communism, immorality, fighting, godlessness of all kinds are at hand. These are terrible times!" And none could but say that they were right.

But there would be another group. Their response might be something like this: "These are remarkable times in which we live! Think of the speed by which we may travel! Think of the miracle of radio and television! Of modern aids to housekeeping! Think of the boon that new drugs afford to those who are sick! Think of the possibilities of the atom! It's a wonderful time in which to be alive!" And they, too, would be right.

There is one thing to which both of these parties would have to agree, however. St. Paul says it in his letter to the Romans: "It is full time now for you to awake from sleep. For salvation is nearer to us now than when we first believed." Yes, whatever our attitude may be, we know we are nearer the end of our time on this earth today than we were yesterday.

Again the Apostle Paul has a word for us. He tells us to redeem the time because the days are evil. Shakespeare has put it into classic verse when he says:

Make use of time, let not advantage slip;
Beauty within itself should not be wasted:
Fair flowers, that are not gathered in their prime
Rot and consume themselves in little time.

The story is told of a naturalist in the Scotch Highlands who desired to secure a rare flower growing down on the side of the cliff. He offered to pay a boy liberally, if he would consent to be lowered, so that he could recover the flower. At first the lad hesitated but finally said: "I'll go down if Father holds the rope."

PRAYER: *In times like these, Lord, we want the more to walk with You. Thank You that we may know that You will deliver us from the hand of our enemies, and save us in Your steadfast love. Amen.*

Our Times Are in Thy Hand

A Strong Hand

Psalm 89:8-13

O Lord God of hosts,
  who is mighty as thou art, O Lord,
with thy faithfulness round about thee?
Thou dost rule the raging of the sea;
When its waves rise, thou stillest them.
Thou hast a mighty arm;
    strong is thy hand, high thy right hand.

THE WAY many Christians whimper and wail when there are hard tasks to be done, or difficult burdens to be borne, could lead folks to think that theirs was a namby-pamby kind of God who must be quite powerless to help them. How entirely different that is from reality! For the Lord never fails. It could be that our connection with Him is weak; that we are not "plugged in" to His strength.

The word strength comes from a word signifying to be twisted together. When we say with the psalmist, "The Lord is the strength of my life," then we acknowledge that our lives are twisted together with God. God and my soul are as two strands intertwined. Mine may have no strength at all; but while it is twisted together with God, it is invincible. So we might well say with the psalmist: The Lord is "my strong deliverer." Are we holding His strong hand?

When I have faith to hold Thee by the hand,
I walk securely, and methinks I stand
More firm than Atlas; but when I forsake
The safe protection of Thine arm, I quake
Like wind-shaked reeds, and have no strength at all,
But, like a vine, the prop cut down, I fall.

FRANCIS QUARLES

Perhaps our trouble is that we do not stop often enough to consider God's power. As I write this, there is being sounded all over the nation's capital the warning of Hurricane Ione. We are being told to expect winds that may reach the velocity of ninety miles an hour. Men know all about many things, but as yet they are powerless to stay the storm or to control the wind. There is One who walked on the Sea of Galilee, stilled its tempestuous waves, and reached out a saving hand to Peter whose small faith caused him to sink. He is walking across the sea of life today, extending His strong hand to you.

A Korean was once asked, "Can you do it?" with reference to some church work. His reply was, "We ask questions such as, 'Can you do it?' about men's work, but not about God's work."

PRAYER: *Thank You, Lord, for Your strong hand that is ours for the taking. Give us the faith that permits Your strength to pour into our lives. Amen.*

Our Times Are in Thy Hand

Pierced Hand

Luke 24:36-40

And he said to them, "Why are you troubled, and why do questionings arise in your hearts? See my hands and my feet, that it is I myself."

John 20:27

"Put your finger here, and see my hands; and put out your hand, and place it in my side; and do not be faithless, but believing."

WHAT CAN you tell about a person from looking at his hands? The practice of palmistry goes back to three thousand years before Christ. Even though today we know that most of it is based on the imagination, there is this much of truth in it: you can tell pretty well what a man does in the line of work by looking at his hands. The father of the so-called "art" in its modern form was Lavater, an eccentric priest. The work that had been assigned to him as a candidate for the holy orders was to stand at the doorway of the chapel, holding a velvet bag for offerings. He kept his eyes down as a symbol of his humility; thus he became a close observer of hands. It was a matter of no great skill to read the character of the giver in this way. A hand of velvet, plump and unctious, told of worldly ease; a hard, horny hand indicated honest toil; a thin hand, armed with talons suggested a shylock casting in his alms.

We need neither magic nor artifice in our observation of the hands of our Lord. They are pierced hands, and the story they tell is the most beautiful one ever told. It is the story of divine Love suffering through hell in order that sinners like you and me might know eternal joy. It was by His hands that our Lord hung on the cross, and by doing that He opened heaven's gate to let us in.

A little girl caused quite a consternation in her home one day, when she returned from school and reported that she had been punished by her teacher for the first time in her life. Pressed to give the reason, she confessed to a particularly grave fault. "But you never did a thing like that!" her mother protested. "No, of course I didn't," came the answer, "but no one would own up to it, and something had to be done about it, so I held up my hand." That is what happened on Calvary. The pierced hand that was held up releases all who will look to it.

On one occasion, following unspeakable suffering in a filthy prison, the great missionary Adoniram Judson appeared before the King of Burma, and asked permission to go to a certain city to preach. "I am willing for a dozen preachers to go, but not you," was the answer, "not with those hands! My people are not such fools as to take notice of your preaching, but they will take notice of those scarred hands." Oh that the world would listen to the One who says, "See my hands . . ."

PRAYER: *Today, Lord, I would take Your pierced hand anew. Thank You for offering it so freely. Thank You for Your matchless love. Amen.*

Our Times Are in Thy Hand

A Guarding Hand

Psalm 18

Thou hast given me the shield of thy salvation,
and thy right hand supported me,
and thy help made me great. Psalm 18:35

THE ENTIRE Eighteenth Psalm is a glorious recording of God's guarding hand. The psalmist echoes the theme in the heart of each one of us that has experienced this, when he concludes: "For this I will extol thee, O Lord." For those of us living in New Testament times there should be an additional paean of praise, for we have the benefit of what the song writer says:

"The hand our many sins have pierced,
Is now our guard."

It is the tested hand of eternal love that is waiting to guard us from all evil; that wants to hold us in the hollow of His hand. Why, then, should anyone ever be afraid?

Even being in places of peril need hold no fear for you, if your being there is a part of your following God's will. There is safety in the perils that God chooses for us. There is danger in the "safe" places of the world. "Is it safe to work among the lepers?" was asked of a great missionary to India. The man's selfless life had been a blessing to countless afflicted men. To the question, his answer was, "Yes, it is safer to work among the lepers, if it's my job, than to work anywhere else."

Not always do we accept the guarding that God's hand would give us. If we cannot see where it will lead us, we rebel, and try to plan our own way out. We are like the bird about whom the poet Wordsworth has written. The winged creature was swept from Norway by a storm. With desperate effort it battled its way against the storm, eager to wing its way back to Norway. But all was in vain, and so at last it yielded, expecting the gale to carry it to its death. Instead, the gale carried it to sunny England, where it found forest glades and green meadows.

If your life is hidden in the hollow of God's hand, you are in the safest place in all the world.

Though hosts encamp around me,
Firm to the fight I stand;
What terror can confound me,
With God at my right hand?

JAMES MONTGOMERY

PRAYER: *For Your outstretched hand which can guard against all evil, we thank You, Lord. Empower us to walk in the peace that comes from holding Your hand. Amen.*

Our Times Are in Thy Hand

Guiding Hand

Isaiah 58:11

"And the Lord will guide you continually,
and satisfy your desire with good things,
and make your bones strong;
and you shall be like a watered garden,
like a spring of water, whose waters fail not."

John 16:13

"When the Spirit of truth comes, he will guide
you into all the truth."

PERHAPS a pertinent question for us to stop and ask ourselves today would be, Where are we going? You see, your destination will determine very much who your guide will be. Is it because so many people have no goal, but just aimlessly live from day to day, that there is such a sense of muddled confusion abroad in the world?

How can we know God's guidance? There are special ways in which God speaks. First, through the Scriptures. Is it not on the days when you have not stopped to listen to Him that you have known confusion and uncertainty? If you would have Him for your guide, you must take time to listen to His instructions. Then there is the voice of our own higher judgment. If you are very honest, you will recognize that voice. It will not ask, "What will this do for me?" but rather, "How will I best serve God?" The Lord guides in another way, too: through providential circumstances. One door closes; another door opens. At the time circumstances seem completely frustrating, but as we look back we are able to see in our frustrations the wonderful guiding hand of God.

This was the experience of a missionary who had to return from a foreign field because of ill health. One Sunday, lying in the hospital, she looked out of her window and saw streams of people going to church. Thinking of the few Christian workers there were in China, she said to the doctor when he came in, "Oh doctor, I'm not needed here. I'm needed in China." Looking straight into her eyes, he responded wisely: "You are needed wherever you are!" And the patient realized anew that it is for the commander of his forces alone to choose the spot where each soldier shall be on duty. The Lord used her in that hospital in a remarkable way, and through her inspiration several young people dedicated their lives to the field that she had to leave.

Have you ever gone through the Mammoth Cave in Kentucky? One visitor tells what happened when he and his party were guided through the one known as The Cathedral. The guide mounted a rock called "The Pulpit," and said that he would preach a sermon. It was a very short one. He simply said: "Keep close to your guide." It was a very practical one, for the party soon found out that, if they did not keep close to their guide, they would certainly be lost in the midst of so many precipices and pitfalls.

PRAYER: *So much of the time we just wander aimlessly, Lord. Give us a sense of Your direction. Keep us close to You. Amen.*

Our Times Are in Thy Hand

Inclusive Hand

Psalm 96:3

Declare his glory among the nations,
his marvelous works among all the peoples!

Isaiah 45:22

"Turn to me and be saved,
all the ends of the earth!
For I am God, and there is no other."

THE HANDS of God would include the entire world! Scripture tells us that God wants everyone to be saved, that He would have no one perish. The Bible is replete with "whosoever" and "everyone" and "all" and "each." How thankful we should be for this reiteration, for it is our assurance that we are also included.

Has that been our witness as a Christian Church, or as individual Christians? One of the most shameful facts of our generation has been that eleven o'clock on the Sabbath morning has been the least inclusive hour of the week in our national life. If God is one, He cannot be a tribal, or national, or racial deity. G. A. Studdert-Kennedy has stated it well when he says: "You can't buck the universe. It was meant to be a family. If you treat it as a battleground everybody loses. There are enough Christian laymen to transform society from its present predicament of conflict and insecurity into a scene of harmony, peace, and effective living—if these Christian laymen understood the Gospel and took it seriously."

That is a big IF. It begins with you. Are you inclusive, like the heart of God, in your outreach? To the ends of the earth? Yes, behind iron curtains, and bamboo curtains, and every other kind of man-made blocks? But more than that! Are you inclusive in witnessing to God's big heart in your own community, in your own neighborhood? Have you ever heard church people say, "Well, they are just not our kind"?

The story is told of Sophie Brugman who had been praying to become a foreign missionary. One day the Lord put it into her heart to ask these questions: "Where were you born, Sophie Brugman?" "In Germany," was the answer. "Where are you now?" "In America." "Well are you not a foreign missionary? Now who lives on the floor above?" "A family of Swedes." "And who above them?" "Why some Swiss." "And who in the rear?" "Italians." "A block away?" "Some Chinese." Then Sophie's comment was, "And I have never said a word to these people about Jesus Christ. It is no wonder that I am not sent thousands of miles away when I do not care enough about those at home to speak to those at my very door."

It is not home or away. It is everywhere—all. Christ's hand is inclusive.

PRAYER: *Take off our blinders, Lord, and give us Your concept of the world. Help us to yearn that all might be saved, and to be aware that the person next door to us is our brother. Amen.*

Our Times Are in Thy Hand

An everlasting hand

Deuteronomy 33:27

"The eternal God is your dwelling place, and underneath are the everlasting arms."

Isaiah 46:4

"Even to your old age I am He, and to gray hairs I will carry you. I have made, and I will bear; I will carry and will save."

WHAT A word for our day! There is the fear of the new found power of science for destruction; there is the fear of other ideologies and what they can mean to our safety; there is the fear of disease: of cancer and heart failure and other ravagers of the body; there is the fear of loss of position or prestige or wealth; or the fear of lack of it. In such a world we are given these words: "The eternal God is your dwelling place, and underneath are the everlasting arms of God." In a world that seems insecure and uncertain there stands One who is changeless and sure. He offers you His hand. And as you take it, eternity is in you.

An old Puritan said that heaven was in him before he was in heaven. That is exactly the experience that we should have as Christians. Paul enjoins us to "lay hold on eternal life." It is a thing of the future, and it is a thing of the present. Do you know this ongoing sense of eternity within you? If you have it, you should be easy to live with, for its fruits are the kind that make living good: calmness, patience, hope, joy, peace, and the inclusive kind of love about which we spoke yesterday. Petulance, pride, envy, worry, covetousness—these must go out of the window, if the eternal presence of our loving God is to dwell within us. And this will make such a difference in your sense of values. Things take on a different perspective in the light of eternity.

Above the triple doorways of the Cathedral of Milan there are three inscriptions. Over one is carved a beautiful wreath of roses and underneath is the legend, "All that which pleases is for the moment." Over the other is sculptured a cross, with the words, "All that which troubles is for the moment." But over the great central entrance of the main aisle is the inscription, "That only is important which is eternal." Witnessing of some of the same spirit, a great cathedral in one of our American cities has inscribed in stone outside of its portals: "And of His kingdom there shall be no end."

Are you investing your life in the things which are eternal?

As this week draws to a close, let us take a look at the proffered hand of God. For times like these He offers us a strong hand, a pierced hand, a guarding hand, a guiding hand, an inclusive hand, and an everlasting hand. Have you grasped it?

PRAYER: *Dwell in us Lord God, here, and give us the awareness that Your indwelling is eternal. Amen.*

I Will Not Be Afraid

G. E. M. Govan

So we go singing onward;
So we go singing onward;
We're looking upward,
And traveling homeward
To Him, unafraid.

I Will Not Be Afraid

He goes before me

Isaiah 45:2

"I will go before you and level the mountains, I will break in pieces the doors of bronze and cut asunder the bars of iron."

IS THERE any fear that is so devastating to one's inner peace as the fear of the unknown? Our imaginations work overtime in creating horrible monsters in the shadow world of those experiences which may lie ahead of us. Take, for instance, the case of someone who is about to have an operation. In anticipation, he conceives of every possible complication and usually envisions the most dire results. Often we do not even share these fears with anybody, but behind our brave smile they lurk and gnaw.

Or there are those fears that mothers so often carry for their children. What will happen to them in their future life, and how will they meet temptation when they are away from home? When they are little, we worry about the diseases that they may get, the accidents they may have, the bad influences to which they may be subjected. Most of us have permitted fears for things that will never happen to dominate many hours of our lives, and to make us miserable.

Then have you had the experience of having someone say: 'Why I had that same operation a couple of years ago, and I never felt better in my life than I do now." Or a grandmother will witness: "How well I remember many fretful, concerned times as the children grew up. The things that never happened were often the things that I had feared the most; and anything that we did have to face we were always given strength for."

Friend, your future holds nothing that your Lord does not know about. He goes ahead and blazes the trail so that the pathway will never be too hard.

If you have ever lived in snow country, do you remember the experience of fresh snow piled high, and of your having to cross the white expanse? Then someone with heavy boots says, "Let me go first. I'll blaze a trail." You find yourself putting your feet in his tracks, and the way is made easy because a friend went before. Your Lord and Savior has done that for all of life for you. He has blazed the trail and made the path for you to follow. Then why do you fear?

This day let the refrain make glad your heart, as you accept the challenge of it from His hand:

I will not be afraid!
He goes before me.

PRAYER: *Forgive me, Lord, that I have feared the future, when all the while You are willing to lead the way. Help me this day to remember that Your promise is that You will go before and level the mountains. And so, no matter how difficult the future may seem, let the witness to my family and my friends be one of calm strength—Your gift to those who follow You. In Jesus' Name. Amen.*

MONDAY

I Will Not Be Afraid

He is beside me

Isaiah 43:1, 2

"Fear not, for I have redeemed you; I have called you by name, you are mine. When you pass through the waters I will be with you; and through the rivers, they shall not overwhelm you; when you walk through fire you shall not be burned, and the flame shall not consume you."

EACH NEW day is a journey we travel. It may be that we will not even leave the house in the course of the day, yet our soul, the real person, daily is on the great journey of life.

Our song for the week was born on a journey; a journey of hungry, weary bodies, leaving their homes to seek refuge in the road ahead. From out of the hearts of the Christian Chinese this song came as they were leaving their land to head westward, fleeing from the enemy whose bombings could well mean their lives. Upon their backs they carried whatever earthly possessions they could retrieve.

Madame Chiang Kai-Shek in her beautiful book, *The Sure Victory,* vividly describes this trek and the ensuing years of living in dank, air-raid shelters to the "music" of almost incessant bombing. Out of such an experience, this song was born.

It must have been that in some of those hearts, the words that had been planted by missionaries were being remembered. "When you pass through the waters, I will be with you; and through the rivers, they shall not overwhelm you." It must have been that they remembered who it was that made this promise. Those who had tried Him had found that He never failed.

You are journeying today. Have you asked Him to walk beside you? What happens then is that in His company one becomes oblivious of the rocks, or the pull up the hill, or the inclement weather. The atmosphere His presence creates is an asbestos of love that is our sure protection.

When I was traveling with the Florida Chain of Missionary Assemblies, my kind hostess in one town was waiting to drive me to my next appointment. As we drove along, we shared the things of the soul, and became oblivious of the passing miles. In this instance, we were so engrossed, we even overshot our destination.

In a more wonderful way, the oblivion of the road becomes ours when He is beside us. Only—He never loses the way.

Sing it today as you work, through whatever tasks you may face,

"I will not be afraid;
He is beside me."

PRAYER: *Come into my heart with Your transforming presence now, Lord. I claim Your promise to be with me. Whatever this day may bring, it will not be too hard for You. Give me joy as I meet its opportunities, and let everything I do be done as in Your presence. In Jesus' Name. Amen.*

TUESDAY

I Will Not Be Afraid

His arms are underneath me

2 Samuel 22:32-34

"For who is God, but the Lord?
And who is a rock, except our God?
This God is my strong refuge,
and has made my way safe.
He made my feet like hinds' feet,
and has set me secure on the heights."

Deuteronomy 33:27

"The eternal God is your dwelling place, and underneath are the everlasting arms."

TO HAVE an uncertain footing is to live in fear. It is true both when you are walking and when you are driving. To be going along on ice, not knowing when your equilibrium may be lost, is not a happy experience. Nor is driving pleasant when the road is a glaze, and you feel that the rear end of your car may slide out from under you at any time.

Our souls often find themselves in such positions. We have something of the stomach-disturbing kind of a feeling of being uncertainly suspended in space—and without wings.

What an undergirding then is God's Word! "Who is our rock, except our God?" Then the writer goes on to tell us that God has made our feet like hinds' feet. In other words, they were made for climbing. To feel secure, does not mean that we carefully stay put. In fact, God's directives are just the opposite. We are made to climb, to seek loftier heights for our soul. He provides the climbing apparatus, and always "underneath are the everlasting arms." What an adventure life becomes with this knowledge! Even while we dare to do hard things, our hearts can be at rest in God's promised undergirding, if we are daring for Him.

How many times in the parsonage this has been our source of strength! God gives a vision of work to be done that stirs you out of your comfort. (It would be so easy just to let things remain as they are.) You turn to folks on whom you thought you could depend, and they hesitate. The forces of your congregation are divided—yet the vision of what God wanted done seemed so clear to you. He had spoken through His Word, and further directed you in prayer. Then He had followed by opening up the opportunity. Yet those on whom you thought you could depend were not so sure. How good, then, to know that the Rock has not failed.

A man came to a friend and said, "I have failed in business. The bottom has dropped out." The bottom never drops out for those who will accept the protection of the everlasting arms. The partial drop then only becomes the means of a higher flight.

PRAYER: *Thank You Lord, that I need never depend upon any foundation of my own making. Thank You for the daily challenge of climbing, and the strength that comes from knowing that I need never be afraid, because underneath are the everlasting arms. In Jesus' Name. Amen.*

I Will Not Be Afraid

His love enfolds me

2 Thessalonians 2:16, 17

Now may our Lord Jesus Christ himself, and God our Father, who loved us and gave us eternal comfort and good hope through grace, comfort your hearts and establish them in every good work and word.

Jeremiah 31:3

"I have loved you with an everlasting love; therefore I have continued my faithfulness to you."

IN THE thirty-first chapter of Jeremiah the writer tells some of the fruits of this wonderful love of God for us. He speaks of singing aloud with gladness, of shouting, and giving praise. In the twelfth verse he says, "And they shall be radiant over the goodness of the Lord." And again in the thirteenth verse, "I will turn their mourning into joy, I will comfort them, and give them gladness for sorrow." Later in the same chapter the Lord says: "For I will satisfy the weary soul, and every languishing soul I will replenish." No wonder that in chapter 32:17 Jeremiah says, "Nothing is too hard for thee, who showest steadfast love to thousands." Paul, in his letter to the Thessalonians picks up from here when he tells us, because of this love and the eternal hope that it brings, "Comfort your hearts and establish them in every good work and word."

His love enfolds us. What serenity of spirit that should bring to every soul! As I ponder on this thought, and let it seep into my very being, I am a little girl again with a thousand fears struggling to possess me. What other people thought of me (did they not laugh when I was awkward?), what the consequence of some childish sin would be (here I suffered the torments of a very vivid hell), or what were those strange figures that must be lurking in the dark corners of my bedroom at night, and what evil they might portend. Then comes the remembrance of timidly sharing these with my beloved mother, one by one, and knowing the sense of her enfolding love, as she would take me in her strong arms and dispel each of the bogies in turn. There was something of God in that experience—in her arms, in her strong faith, and it has never left me.

A man once asked his friend to take him to the sea, about which he had heard but which he had never seen. On reaching the shore, and gazing out into the water, the man said, "Is this all? Is this the mighty sea of which I have heard?" "Yes," his friend replied, "this is all. But get upon it. Trust your bark to it, and you will find that it will take you around the world."

So with the eternal love of God. It will take you through the world and land you on the blissful shore of eternity. His love enfolds you—you need not be afraid.

PRAYER: *Thank You, God for Your Love revealed in Christ, Your Son and my Savior. Thank You that it is sufficient for each day's need and for eternity. Help me this day to walk in it. In Jesus' Name. Amen.*

THURSDAY

I Will Not Be Afraid

I'm looking upward

Psalm 34

Look to him, and be radiant;
so your faces shall never be ashamed.
This poor man cried, and the Lord heard him,
and saved him out of all his troubles."
Psalm 34:5, 6

READ THIS whole psalm. It is brimming over with the sufficiency of the upward look. It challenges to the scientific approach: "O taste and see that the Lord is good!" Then it follows with a lesson in how to live in the fear of the Lord.

The world promises you all kinds of things in a few streamlined lessons. How many of us have known the folly of heeding advertisements that read: "How to Get Slim Without Dieting—But Quick!" Or, "How To Be Glamorous in Three Short Lessons." In the thirty-fourth Psalm, there is put forth for you a way to walk that has on it the signature of the bank of heaven. Are you drawing on it? Sometimes I think it is because the procedure is so simple that people ignore it. They agonizingly try to work out their own way—and find themselves bankrupt.

The story is told of a man who was sick and asked his friend to take his bank book in and have it balanced. The friend asked if the sick man did not want to write out a check to be cashed at the same time, for he knew that he needed money. "I don't dare do that," he replied, "for I am afraid that there is very little, if anything to my credit." The friend performed the errand, and lo, when the book was balanced there was a credit of one hundred and fifty dollars. Upon examining the book, the sick man said, "How foolish I was to worry about my need for money, when I had it in the bank all the time. All I needed to do was to have my book balanced."

Is not that our trouble often spiritually? We fail to know or acknowledge our resources, and so we go around "broke"!

I will not be afraid—I am looking upward. Look to Him; you will be radiant. Your resources are unlimited. They bear the signature of the One who said, "All authority in heaven and on earth has been given to me." Each promise has the seal of the cross.

A terrific storm was raging, and in one home two of the larger children were frightened, both giving way to sobs. A five-year-old lad, not at all afraid, soon wearied of their weeping and blurted out: "Stop your bawlin! Don't you suppose God knows His business?"

PRAYER: *God, You are the Lifter up of my head. Forgive me that there have been times when I have spurned the radiance that You had to offer through faith. Let me walk this day looking up—unafraid. In Jesus' Name. Amen.*

I Will Not Be Afraid

Traveling Homeward

2 Corinthians 5:1

For we know that if the earthly tent we live in is destroyed, we have a building from God, a house not made with hands, eternal in the heavens.

John 14:1-4

"Let not your hearts be troubled; believe in God, believe also in me. In my Father's house are many rooms; if it were not so, would I have told you that I go to prepare a place for you? And when I go and prepare a place for you, I will come again and will take you to myself, that where I am you may be also. And you know the way where I am going."

A LITTLE girl was running along, and she was asked if she was not afraid to go through the cemetery at night. "Oh no," she said, "I'm not afraid, for my home is just beyond." This is the story Bishop Quayle told at the funeral of his colleague, Bishop Smith. Is anyone ever afraid to go home?

As I pondered this, I realized that there are times when children are very apprehensive about their homegoing. Basically, there are two reasons for such fear: the child has done some wrong for which he fears he may be held accountable; or home to the individual does not evoke the kind of memories God meant it to do.

In regard to the first fear, is it not wonderful to know about the forgiveness of God because of what His Son, Jesus Christ, did for us? If we go home with Him, we are assured of a welcome, and a blotting out of all our ugly past. We need not be afraid! As Christians we can know that there will be a welcome for us, if we have repented of our sins, and accepted forgiveness through Christ Jesus. We can know it with the certainty of God's Word. And there will be the open arms of the One who has so repeatedly given the invitation to us.

In regard to the second fear, knowing God in Christ will eliminate that. And the few things that Scripture tells us about our heavenly home are more than sufficient. No tears, no sorrow, no parting, no sin—and Christ will be there! In fact, He has promised to come and take us to this wonderful home.

Coming down to the lobby of a hotel in a foreign country, we found a woman we had met on the train, very disturbed. "How come," she said, "you got a room when you arrived at the same time I did?" "Why, we made reservations here some time ago," was our reply.

I will not be afraid to go home, if my reservation through the grace of God in Christ has been made. Such blessed assurance brings a foretaste of heaven to our earthly home. Is it with unexcelled joy you can sing, "I'm traveling homeward"?

PRAYER: *Thank You, Lord, that Your preparation for us is for all eternity. Thank You for the joyous expectancy of going home. Keep our feet this day on that path. In Jesus' Name. Amen.*

SATURDAY

I Will Not Be Afraid

I'll go singing onward

Isaiah 51:11

And the ransomed of the Lord shall return,
and come with singing to Zion;
everlasting joy shall be upon their heads;
they shall obtain joy and gladness,
and sorrow and sighing shall flee away.

IN A description of Zion in the early part of this fifty-first chapter of Isaiah we are told:

"Joy and gladness will be found in her,
thanksgiving and the voice of song."

This, then, should be the atmosphere attending one whose trust is in God, and in whose heart dwells the eternal Christ. It is essential that women in their homes become aware of their responsibility in this respect. It is one thing to have a song when things are going nicely and folks are responding to you properly. It is another to give a feeling of sustained music when the going is rough. The witness of a mother whose attitude in the midst of frustration and pressures is one of calm and confidence will be an undeniable one in the lives of her children, yes, to the entire neighborhood.

A friend was telling about an experience she had when coming home late one night. It was in the city of Minneapolis, and she had to walk through the Washington Avenue section. She had been helping a person in distress and had been oblivious of the lateness of the hour. Knowing that she had been on an errand for the Lord, she set out with confidence toward her home and a much needed rest.

She had been walking about a block, when her heart skipped a beat as she heard heavy, rhythmic steps behind her. At first she did not even dare to look, not knowing what she might see. However, the uncertainty was causing her heart such a feeling of panic that she finally glanced quickly behind her. Her worst fears were justified. Seemingly following her on this dark street was a great big bruiser of a man. Then the Lord put a song on her lips, and though her heart was catapulting, from her throat there came the old familiar hymn:

Rock of ages, cleft for me,
Let me hide myself in Thee.

Imagine her surprise, and relief, and gratitude, when she found that a bass voice belonging to the man she had feared picked up the melody with her, and joined her in the singing of the hymn.

PRAYER: *Give me such a song in my daily living, Lord, that the message of faith, and hope, and love will be radioed from my home. In Jesus' Name. Amen.*

O Master, Let Me Walk with Thee

Washington Gladden, 1879

H. Percy Smith, 1874

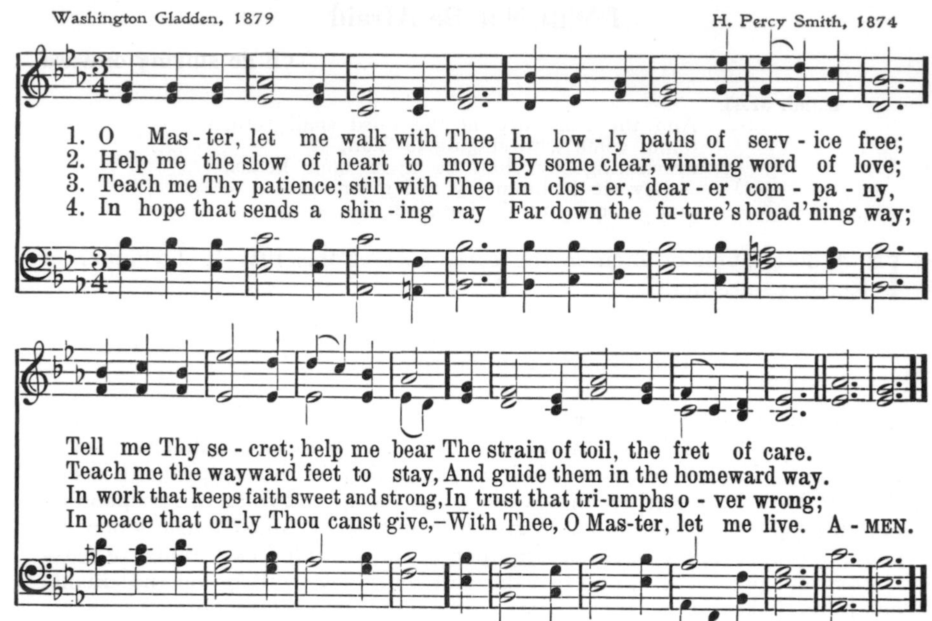

SUNDAY

O Master, Let Me Walk with Thee

In lowly paths of service free

Deuteronomy 5:33

"You shall walk in all the way which the Lord your God has commanded you, that you may live, and that it may go well with you, and that you may live long in the land which you shall possess."

Micah 6:8

He has showed you, O man, what is good; and what does the Lord require of you but to do justice, and to love kindness, and to walk humbly with your God?

WHEN WE pray for a walk with the Master, we need to be aware of where that walk will lead us. Too often our feet lag on the pathway where He leads, because we did not take a long enough look to count the cost before we started out. It is why He warns us of the dangers of the second mile. Have you not experienced in your life starting out enthusiastically in some work for Him, and then finding yourself bogging down, and losing interest when the glamor of the first enthusiasm was gone? Today, let us take inventory as to our attitude toward the kingdom work to which He has called us.

The song writer speaks of "lowly paths of service free." Micah writes of lovingkindness and walking humbly before our God. I am wondering if here is not the key to some of our lethargy for the tasks that God would have us do. The lowly paths are not to our liking. How often in church work someone is offended because he was not given proper credit for what he did! Many a preacher's life has been made miserable because of this kind of attitude. O what a blessing to kingdom work are those folks who are willing to walk in lowly paths of service, and find sufficient reward in that they are following the One they love.

As women, we need to look to our attitudes toward homemaking. Housework can very easily become drudgery. The ceaseless monotony of dishes, diet, and dirt can overwhelm a person. It is only by the grace of the constant presence of Christ that even the everyday tasks can have a glow.

Something of this spirit, it seems to me, was the greatness of Abraham Lincoln. He wrote: "If, in your judgment, you cannot be an honest lawyer, resolve to be honest without being a lawyer." In his own life, the humblest person, the most insignificant burden, were his concern.

"There are strange ways of serving God,
You sweep a room, or turn a sod;
And suddenly to your surprise,
You hear the whir of seraphim,
And know you're under God's own eyes,
And building palaces for Him."

PRAYER: *Remove from my heart, Lord, the spirit of pride and ego. Make me Your willing servant, and give me such a song in my heart, that I may do the humblest tasks with joy. In Jesus' Name. Amen.*

MONDAY

O Master, Let Me Walk with Thee

Tell me Thy secret

Psalm 91:1

He who dwells in the shelter of the Most High,
who abides in the shadow of the Almighty,
will say to the Lord, "My refuge and my fortress:
my God, in whom I trust."

TO FIND the secret of the peace and power of our Lord's life is to walk through the Gospels with Him, seeking it. Having found it there, the challenge is to try it for your own life. It is not hard to find. Whenever Christ needed renewal, whenever the throngs that crowded in upon Him had depleted His strength, He went up to the mountains, or out into the desert, or somewhere alone, to pray. It was a matter of recharging the battery of His soul with the everlasting power of His heavenly Father.

What my quiet time with the Lord means to me I can never adequately put into words. It is then that He takes the burdens; it is then that He forgives the sin, and so removes the obstacles; it is then that He gives the directives for the day. My prayer is that these devotionals may be a part of such a time for you. It is why they are always grounded on Scripture. For that is how He talks to me, and the remembrance of what He has said, I carry with me in my heart through the day. What a glorious walk each day becomes with such a beginning!

This is not to say that there will not be difficulties. In Christ's life it was to be strengthened for the difficulties that He drew apart. It is to say that, no matter what happens, such resources will be yours that you will be able to meet anything that comes.

The secret of Christ's strength is yours for the asking and taking. If you are to walk with Him, it is essential.

Mid all the traffic of the ways,
Turmoils without, within,
Make in my heart a quiet place,
And come and dwell therein:

A little shrine of quietness,
All sacred to Thyself,
Where Thou shalt all my soul possess,
And I may find myself.

. . . .

A little place of mystic grace,
Of self and sin swept bare,
Where I may look upon Thy face,
And talk with Thee in prayer.

JOHN OXENHAM

PRAYER: *Teach me Thy secret, Lord, of calm in the midst of storm. Give me the strength to discipline myself to a daily quiet time with You. Amen.*

TUESDAY

O Master, Let Me Walk with Thee

Help me bear the strain of toil

Psalm 55:17, 22

Evening and morning and at noon I utter my complaint
and moan, and he will hear my voice.
Cast your burden on the Lord,
and he will sustain you;
he will never permit the righteous to be moved.

A READING of this entire psalm would be helpful. In verse six, we read "O that I had wings like a dove! I would fly away and be at rest." Every woman who has known the monotony of housekeeping (unless she does it with a glory!) will have breathed this cry for release sometime or other. You have had days when everything seemed to pile up, and the pressure of things needing to be done so overwhelmed you that you could not get started on anything. You suffered very much under the strain of toil. What to do?

The psalmist gives the first step: cast your burden on the Lord. Somehow in just the telling there is a balm. Many a day I have groaned out, "God, there is so much that I ought to do today that it just looks impossible. Besides that, I'm tired already!" And my Lord has said to me, "Daughter, I never ask anyone to do everything at once. Take one thing at a time, and trust me for the rest." And every time I have trusted, He has not failed!

Often our weariness comes because everything seems in such confusion. What a gift it is to be able to organize! It is a gift that every one can develop. Take the confusion of the kitchen, when the table has been cleared of the dirty dishes hurriedly in order to get the dessert served. You have worked hard to get the meal; it has been quickly consumed; the disordered remnants now are before you. You can do one of two things: you can say, "I can't stand it," and tear your hair; or you can say, "I can't stand it," and set about organizing it into a dishwashing victory. It is mostly that you need to begin somewhere.

The Lord can make out of humdrum tasks an opportunity to witness to His sufficiency. I love the lines from Elizabeth Barrett Browning's sonnet that reads: "I love you to the level of every day's most quiet need." To the Christian there is this challenge of the level of everyday's repeated toil; and we would repeat what has been said before: it is to take one task at a time.

A certain lady had a serious accident which necessitated many months of confinement. When the physician had finished his work and was about to leave, she asked, "Doctor, how long shall I have to lie here helpless?" "Oh, only one day at a time," was the cheery response.

As we walk with the Master, He becomes our burden bearer, and we learn the lesson of facing one task at a time.

PRAYER: *For work to do, Lord, I thank You. Make me constantly aware that You do not expect of me more than You give me strength to do. But help me not to seek refuge in my own confusion. In Jesus' Name. Amen.*

O Master, Let Me Walk with Thee

Help me bear . . . the fret of care

1 Peter 5:7, 10

Cast all your anxieties on him, for he cares about you. And after you have suffered a little while, the God of all grace who has called you to his eternal glory in Christ, will himself restore, establish and strengthen you.

A WINDOW of a downtown shop in Washington had this caption on it: "Brood over your troubles and you'll hatch a batch of them." Is not that exactly what many of us do? The brooding process is reproductive and, instead of only a couple of cares we find we have a battalion. However, when the Lord really walks with you, this does not happen. You cannot brood over troubles and at the same time give heed to Him speaking to you, when His Word says: "Have no anxiety about anything, but in everything by prayer and supplication with thanksgiving let your requests be made known to God." Philippians 4:6. I have found that the phrase "with thanksgiving" is the key that unlocks the verse, for no matter what the fret is, when I begin to think of the things for which I have to be thankful, any anxieties fade into insignificance.

As you grow in Christian grace, there should be less and less of anxiety. As you study the life of Christ, you will find that under every pressure He was serene. He was tired, and hungry, and thirsty, and in pain, yes. But never fretful. His mind was stayed on God His Father.

In this respect, I cannot follow the thinking of the hymn writer. There should be no bearing the fret of care. There will be care—yes—all through life. But the fret of it comes only when we refuse to release ourselves in the great promises of God. And the fretting action is a disintegrating and incapacitating thing that cripples not only the soul but the body as well.

Beecher has put it well: "It isn't work that kills men; it is worry. Work is healthy; you can hardly put more upon a man than he can bear. Worry is rust upon the blade. It is not the revolution that destroys the machinery but the friction. Fear secretes acids; but love and trust are sweet juices."

The continuation of Paul's word in the fourth chapter of Philippians is: "And the peace of God, which passes all understanding, will keep your hearts and your minds in Christ Jesus."

PRAYER: *Forgive us Lord, for fretting and being anxious. May we be true yoke fellows with You in our walk, so that we will, indeed, find that our "yoke is easy and our burden is light." In Jesus' Name. Amen.*

O Master, Let Me Walk with Thee

Help me the slow of heart to move

Acts 20:35

In all things I have shown you that by so toiling one must help the weak, remembering the words of the Lord Jesus, how he said, "It is more blessed to give than to receive."

Romans 15:1, 2

We who are strong ought to bear with the failings of the weak, and not to please ourselves; let each of us please his neighbor for his good, to edify him.

TODAY'S SONG section is the follow-up antidote for fret. First, we cast our burdens on the Lord; then, we share our brother's burden. As surely as we follow this procedure, so surely will we be having a glorious walk with our Lord. It is the basic recipe for a life that is abundant.

What a description of the Master is contained in the words which tell us that "Christ is able to sympathize with us in our weaknesses"! Would you walk with Him? Then share in His concern for those who do not know Him; share in that concern enough to do something about it. Would you walk with Him? Then be His beckoning hands and seeking feet in your neighborhood, in your community, to the ends of the world. Nothing draws people more closely together than working together in one spirit. The more you share in His great concern for others, the less you will know of fret, and the more of joy and blessedness.

There is a story told about Louis Agassiz when he was a boy in Switzerland. One day he and his little brother thought they would cross a frozen lake and join their father. The mother anxiously watched them from the window, till at length they came to a crack in the ice more than a foot wide. Her heart failed her. She knew the older boy could make it across that break in the ice, but she feared the little boy would also try it, and she was sure his legs were not long enough. She was too far away for her to call and be heard. She sat frozen with fear. Then she saw Louis get down on the ice, his feet on one side of the crack and his hands on the other, like a bridge, and his little brother crept over him to the other side.

Would you walk close to the Master? Then you be the bridge by which the slow in heart can find Him. Today, seek out someone, and share with that one what God has done for you. Prepare the way by prayer—and yours will be a glorious walk.

PRAYER: *Put upon my heart, Lord, those for whom I should be concerned. Make me earnest in prayer on their behalf, and then use me as a channel for Your love to flow into their lives. In Jesus' Name. Amen.*

O Master, Let Me Walk with Thee

Teach me the wayward feet to stay

Hosea 6:1

"Come, let us return to the Lord; for he has torn, that he may heal us; he has stricken, and he will bind us up."

2 Corinthians 5:20

So we are ambassadors for Christ, God making his appeal through us. We beseech you on behalf of Christ, be reconciled to God.

NO ONE is ever going to be nagged into the kingdom. Sometimes wives, without realizing it, try to use this method on their errant husbands. Nor is the threatening method effective. Children have gone in reverse many times when this means has been used. Nor is the "holier than thou, looking down your nose" attitude one that produces. There is a real temptation for those who know the Lord to sit in judgment. Often that judgment is legalistic, and has in it the flavor of the Pharisee. Maybe we do not do some of the things our neighbors do, but what about our thoughts? Spiritual pride is a stench in the nostrils of God. Nor will it ever stay the wayward feet.

How, then, can we be used of the Lord to be helpful to others? First, we must confess that we are sinners in God's sight, and that only by the miracle of His redeeming grace, can we walk with Him. This identifying ourselves with the sinner is the first step. When I go out to the prison for our weekly Bible Class, it is only when I share with the women there that I am a sinner and need daily forgiveness that they will listen to what God has done for me. And every time I am with those girls, I well know that there I would be but for the grace of God. All my life I have been taught what is right and wrong, and have been surrounded by love. Many of them have never known any direction. God will judge differently from our standards.

"Teach me the wayward feet to stay"—what is the lesson the Lord has for me? Yesterday's song verse had it: "By some clear winning word of love." Is there not someone today for whom you could be God's channel for this winning word, this kind deed?

Do you remember in an early reader the story of the contest between the sun and the wind, as to which was the more powerful? They decided to settle their dispute by experimenting on a man, to see which could get him to remove his coat. The wind was first, and blew and blew with all its ferocity. But the more it blew, the more tightly the man drew his coat about him. Then the sun came out, and poured its warmth down. First the man unbuttoned his coat, and before long he had taken it off, and was carrying it over his arm. We can learn from the sun.

PRAYER: *I would be Your ambassador, Lord. Give me the winning word of love that will stay the wayward feet. I bungle so often. Help me! Amen.*

SATURDAY

O Master, Let Me Walk with Thee

Teach me Thy patience

James 5:7, 8

Be patient, therefore, brethren, until the coming of the Lord. Behold, the farmer waits for the precious fruit of the earth, being patient over it until it receives the early and the late rain. You also be patient. Establish your hearts, for the coming of the Lord is at hand.

IT IS interesting to note in the new translation, the synonyms that have been used for patience. For instance in Luke 21:19, endurance is used instead of patience. The same substitution has been made in Hebrews 10:36. Whether the word be patience or endurance, of this one thing we are sure: it is a quality that most of us are very short of, and it is a quality that is synonymous with the mercy of God.

Imagine a farmer fussing and fuming because he does not see the green sprouts the day after he has planted the seed! Not only would he make everybody around him miserable, but he would be a pretty wretched man himself, and a sure case for ulcers. On the other hand, if after he has planted the seed he goes about doing the other things at hand, all the while that he is tending the seed, he will in due time be rewarded with a harvest.

As mothers, we need in such a great measure this patience of our Lord. This beautiful virtue can be a grace whereby in us our loved ones can see something of the love of God. The amount we have of it will depend upon how close our walk with Him is.

What an arithmetic lesson Christ gave to impetuous Peter! We are enjoined to forgive to the point of seventy times seven. And who would keep account that long? What we need to do is to reflect on the Lord's infinite patience toward us. Eternity is long, and love is endless.

Surely many times Susanna Wesley's patience must have been tried with her extraordinarily large family to take care of. Her husband was observing her once when she was dealing with the children. Finally he turned to her and said, "How could you have the patience to tell that blockhead the same thing twenty times over?" "Why," she replied, "if I had told him but nineteen times, I should have lost all my labor."

If we could push ajar the gates of life,
  And stand within, and all God's workings see,
We could interpret all this doubt and strife,
  And for each mystery could find a key.
But not today, Then be content, poor heart!
  God's plans, like lilies pure and white, unfold:
We must not tear the close-shut leaves apart—
  Time will reveal the calyxes of gold.

MARY RILEY SMITH

PRAYER: *Teach me Your patience, Lord, and help me to walk with such trust that I may reflect something of the calm of Your presence. Amen.*

Jesus, Keep Me Near the Cross

Near the Cross. 7 6, 7 6. Trochaic. With Refrain. WILLIAM HOWARD DOANE, (1831–1915).

1. Je - sus, keep me near the cross, There a pre - cious foun - tain,
2. Near the cross, a trem - bling soul, Love and mer - cy found me;

Free to all, a heal - ing stream, Flows from Cal - v'ry's moun - tain.
There the Bright and Morn - ing Star Sheds its beams a - round me.

REFRAIN:

In the cross, in the cross Be my glo - ry ev - er,

Till my rap - tured soul shall find Rest be - yond the riv - er. A - MEN.

3 Near the cross! O Lamb of God,
Bring its scenes before me;
Help me walk from day to day
With its shadows o'er me.

4 Near the cross I'll watch and wait,
Hoping, trusting ever,
Till I reach the golden strand
Just beyond the river.

Frances Jane (Crosby) Van Alstyne, 1869.

SUNDAY

Jesus, Keep Me Near the Cross

There a precious fountain

Psalm 36:9

For with thee is the fountain of life;
in thy light do we see light.

Revelation 21:6

. . . "To the thirsty I will give water without price from the fountain of the water of life."

IN DEUTERONOMY 8:7 we read of the promise of the Lord to bring the children of Israel into a land not only of water brooks but of fountains and springs flowing among the valleys and hills. Not until I walked those barren, tawny hills of Palestine in the dry season, did I begin to realize what a fountain would mean to a thirsty soul. As we were driving across the desert, we saw a young Arab lad come running across the sand with his hand going up and down to his lips to indicate his thirst. The driver stopped the car, and took out the bottle of water he had on hand, offering it to the boy. The boy hesitated, and we were amazed, for he obviously was parched. We learned from our driver that the hesitation was due to the fact that the water was in the kind of bottle that might have held alcoholic beverages. In Arabic the driver explained to him that it was just water, and again offered him the bottle. But the thirsty lad shook his head and went away rather than take a chance. As far as he could tell, there might have been fire water in the bottle.

The average village in Bible lands depends upon a fountain or well for its water supply. In the little town of Nazareth we watched folks gather their water from the well that could have been the one the Lord's mother came to. Outside of Jericho there is Elisha's fountain, and it was a modern anomaly to see folks carrying water on their heads, some in gourds and beautiful pottery pieces, and others in Standard Oil cans!

The fountain in Palestine is its very lifeline. Where there is no water, the people perish.

So it is with the fountain that the song writer speaks of. The psalmist gives you an idea of the kind of spiritual water that flows from the fountain that springs from the cross. In verse ten, he prays, "O continue Thy steadfast love to those who know you." In Revelation we are told that the water is without price (that is, to us). It is ours for the taking.

Recall Jesus' conversation with the Samaritan woman at the well. His promise holds today: "Whoever drinks of the water that I shall give him will never thirst." It is at the cross you will find the fountain. As you come, acknowledge your sin and your need of a Savior, and claim His free gift. You will find that your thirst is quenched.

PRAYER: *Help me, Lord, to accept the free gift of living water that You have provided for all who will believe in the cross. Let me daily drink of this life-giving stream. Amen.*

Jesus, Keep Me Near the Cross

Free to all

Isaiah 55:1

"Ho, every one who thirsts, come to the waters; and he who has no money, come, buy and eat!"

Romans 3:22, 23

For there is no distinction; since all have sinned and fall short of the glory of God, they are justified by his grace as a gift, through the redemption which is in Christ Jesus.

IN THE three little words "free to all" there are two very basic thoughts for our Christian faith. The first is that salvation is something that needs no money, nor prestige. It is, "Ho, everyone who thirsts," and again, "They are justified by his grace as a gift." Is that why so many spurn it?

There is the strange psychology that possesses us and that makes us think that if the price tag (from the world's point of view) on something is low, then the thing cannot be of much value. Yet the most beautiful things in life are free: sunsets, the moon on a silvery lake, a little child's face looking up, a rose. We could go on and on. Make your own list. Yet in this eternal gift from God of His Son there is the paradox that, although it is free to us, it cost Him everything. Maybe that is our point of forgetting. He who is the King of glory, humbled himself and made himself in the form of man, and became obedient to death, even the death on the cross. His is the cost; to us it is free. Through all eternity I shall never cease to wonder at this. And, had I a thousand lives, I could never thank God enough for this matchless gift and its transforming power in my life.

Not only is the gift free, but it is for everyone. That is the most inclusive word there is. It comes right out from the page and speaks to you. God is offering you a free gift. Whether you receive or reject it will determine the abundance of your life here on earth as well as for eternity. The message of the Christmas angel was that the good tidings should be to all people. Some of our human exclusions look pretty small in the light of this.

Dwight L. Moody calls our attention to the fact that in Noah's ark, a little fly was just as safe as an elephant. It was not the elephant's size and strength that made him safe; it was the ark that saved both the elephant and fly. Rich or poor, learned and unlearned, we can only be saved by the blood of Christ.

Ho, every one who thirsts, come!

PRAYER: *Thank You, God, for the free gift of everlasting life. Thank You that it is not something just for the future, but that the joy of it is mine, now. Thank You that it is for everyone. In Jesus' Name. Amen.*

TUESDAY

Jesus, Keep Me Near the Cross

A healing stream
Flows from Calvary's mountain

Isaiah 53:5

But he was wounded for our transgressions, he was bruised for our iniquities; upon him was the chastisement that made us whole, and with his stripes we are healed.

Psalm 103:3

Who forgives all your iniquity,
who heals all your diseases.

IN VARIOUS parts of our country, as well as around the world, there are certain springs whose water people claim have healing powers. There are those who will travel thousands of miles to seek such healing. I do not presume to argue about the healing power of either water or herbs. I constantly marvel at God's creation and its undiscovered potential. This I know, however: For any person, for every disease, there is healing right at hand that we do not begin to utilize. The process of that healing begins with the cleansing that comes from confessed sin; it continues in the experience of forgiveness; wounds are healed as irritations and grudges against others are overcome by the grace of God; and the peace of His presence and the awareness of His strength as your resource, are the best immunization for any disease that can be found.

This is not to say that a Christian will never be sick. There have been saints who have spent years on beds of pain, and for that we cannot always understand the reason. Some of the most beautiful pulpits I have known have been bedsides like these. As the soul finds its healing in the great Physician, what happens to the body becomes less and less significant. The Lord himself said, "Do not fear those who will kill the body, but rather fear him who can destroy both body and soul in hell." I love to walk through the pages of the New Testament with my Lord. What a glorious refrain there is: "He healed every one that came to Him."

For a Christian there is a daily healing that is necessary. The infections of the world so quickly can cause irritations that produce fevered tempers and hot tongues. The Great Physician's touch is the prescription that is sure.

Long, long ago the hands of Christ
Were nailed upon a tree,
But still their holy touch redeems
The hearts of you and me.

LESLIE SAVAGE CLARK

PRAYER: *Great Physician, come even now with healing for my heart. Forgive my sin. And, Lord, You are the only real healing for the nations. Use me to share this remedy. In Jesus' Name. Amen.*

Jesus, Keep Me Near the Cross

Bring its scenes before me

Matthew 26:75

And Peter remembered the saying of Jesus, "Before the cock crows, you will deny me three times."

John 2:22

When therefore he was raised from the dead, his disciples remembered that he had said this; and they believed the scripture and the word which Jesus had spoken.

SOMEONE HAS said: "The spiritual life is much like a watch—very liable to run down." Undoubtedly this is why God has given us memories: to keep us wound, so that we may be in running order.

Sometimes when a friend is going away, he will give us a gift, and say: "Every time you look at this, you will think of me." The Lord instituted His Holy Supper for this purpose: "This do in remembrance of me." Lent, too, is that kind of reminder—a bringing before us the scenes of the cross, and what it cost the Father to offer this free gift. Peter remembered—and repented; the disciples remembered—and believed; the early church remembered—and received power. Will the days of Lent produce such results in your life? The haunting question that cries for an answer in all ages is: "Is it nothing to you, all you who pass by?"

The day we walked the via Dolorosa is an unforgettable one. The gospel incidents became so real. We had previously gone to the Garden of Gethsemane and seen the old olive tree whose roots might have been those of the tree that was kind to our Lord. We had knelt by the rock that might have been the one where He agonized; and with overwhelming remembrances crowding in, we were barely able to whisper: "Lord, in my life, Your will be done." Then the walk up the narrow cobblestone street. Here was the place where the women wept for Him; here was where He stumbled with the cross, and Simon took up the burden; and then, finally, the hill to Golgotha, and the cross.

As a mother, I tried to envision what that meant to His mother—the agony, the seeming hopelessness, the awful injustice. And the poor, defeated, and frightened disciples! What a way to usher in a new kingdom!

All of it——His agony, all the hatred that was poured out upon Him, all the vile abuse He took—it was for me. Again He looks down from the cross and His eyes find mine. I can hear Him say:

"This I have done for thee;
What hast thou done for me?"

PRAYER: *Remembering the scenes of the cross, Lord, I am aware in a small measure of how great Your love for me is. Let my gratitude, and the dedication of my life, be a witness of my awareness. In Jesus' Name. Amen.*

THURSDAY

Jesus, Keep Me Near the Cross

Help me walk from day to day
With its shadow o'er me

Psalm 17:8

Keep me as the apple of the eye;
hide me in the shadow of thy wings.

Psalm 91:1, 2

He who dwells in the shelter of the Most High,
who abides in the shadow of the Almighty,
will say to the Lord, "My refuge and my fortress
my God, in whom I trust.

THERE ARE other beautiful references in Scripture to the power of the shadow. The tabernacle is spoken of as a shadow for the day; Isaiah mentions a shade from the heat—the shade of a great rock in a weary land; and "in the shadow of His hand He hid me." And in Lamentations we read: "Under his shadow we shall live among the nations."

It is well to background our thinking by calling to mind the terrific heat of the Palestinian desert. Even a bird flying overhead, casting a shadow, is a source of relief. It is good to think, then, that when one walks from day to day with the Lord, one knows the constant cooling of the shadow of His wings. The shadow of the cross extends the outstretched arms of God to all the world. Within those arms there is relief from fret, there is a dissolving of fear, there is a cleansing from guilt—in fact, there is the healing for whatever ails you.

Sometimes our own shadow negates the shadow of the cross. We balk at the Gethsemane prayer, and want our own way. The big "I" overshadows everything else, and our days are tense and fretful. Then we cast a shadow on His wonderful name, a ghastly shadow that portends evil. It is said of the great sculptor, Michaelangelo, that when at work, he wore over his forehead, fastened on his artist's cap, a lighted candle, in order that no shadow of himself might fall on his work. To each Christian there comes the challenge of so walking day by day that our passing by will have in it something of the healing of the Almighty. That must have been true of Peter, for we are told in the Book of Acts that cripples and sick folk were brought to him that "his shadow might fall on some of them." You remember that after a miracle, the people wanted to proclaim Paul a God. How quick he was to set them right as to the source of his power!

When people say nice things about you, do you witness to the Source of all goodness? In the heat of today's living, do folks find in you the healing of the shadow of the cross?

PRAYER: *I would confess, Lord, that often I cast a shadow over everything. It is my comfort, my wishes that are uppermost. Forgive! Give me grace to walk, day by day, in the shadow of the cross. In Christ's Name. Amen.*

Jesus, Keep Me Near the Cross

Near the cross I'll watch and wait

Matthew 26:40, 41

And he came to the disciples and found them sleeping; and he said to Peter, "So, you could not watch with me one hour? Watch and pray that you may not enter into temptation; the spirit indeed is willing, but the flesh is weak."

Mark 13:35, 36, 37

"Watch therefore—for you do not know when the master of the house will come, in the evening, or at midnight, or at cockcrow, or in the morning—lest he come suddenly and find you asleep. And what I say to you I say to all: Watch."

IS THERE anything worse than to fight sleep? I shudder at the memory of the agony of sitting at an evening service, surrounded by people, with a splendid sermon being preached, yet fighting sleep with all the will power I had. It might be good to recall some of the preliminaries and circumstances. The church is warm and comfortable, so you get yourself into the most relaxed position possible. Maybe the lights are a little low, and the music is soft and soothing. You find you have to push yourself to rise to sing the hymn, but between a yawn or two you half-heartedly join in. Then you settle down for the sermon. You find your head is pretty heavy, so you prop your elbow on the hymnbook on your lap, and rest your head in your palm. Not bad! But before you know it the mellifluous voice of the preacher becomes fainter and fainter, and your head becomes too heavy for your hand which has decided also to relax. You jerk up quickly, furtively look around you to see if anybody has observed, and start all over again. What a struggle!

Not unlike this one is the daily one in our lives, to keep our souls awake and watching. Comforts, ease, yes, even the pleasant surroundings for which we all strive, are sometimes the drug that inures us to the necessity of watching. It is so easy to be at ease in Zion. Churches have fallen asleep with this kind of opiate. People have resented being made aware of the needs of their surrounding community as well as the world. On the portal of many churches could there well be hung the sign "Do not disturb." In how many church parlors has there not been sung the soothing lullaby, "We've always done it this way before."

Dr. Phillips uses a good catchword in his translation, "Keep a good look-out." Sleepy customs officers sometimes let contraband in because it seems of small bulk. Strong castles have been taken by armed men, hidden in innocent-looking carts. Souls have been lost to eternity because of the "little foxes that spoil the vineyards." To His disciples, to you from the cross the Lord is saying, "Keep a good look-out. I may return any day."

PRAYER: *Lord, make me an alert watchman. Give me the long look that sees opportunities to serve. Keep me watching—near the cross. In Jesus' Name. Amen.*

Jesus, Keep Me Near the Cross

'Til I Reach the Golden Strand

Hebrews 11:8-10

By faith Abraham obeyed when he was called to go out to a place which he was to receive as an inheritance; and he went out, not knowing where he was to go. By faith he sojourned in the land of promise, as in a foreign land, living in tents with Isaac and Jacob, heirs with him of the same promise. For he looked forward to the city which has foundations, whose builder and maker is God.

WHAT A difference it makes to have a destination! Even in the way you do your work it makes a difference. If there is a definite objective you wish to achieve, you set about doing the things to accomplish this. However, on those days when there seems to be no particular deadline, you accomplish very little. So it is with life. The long look to the golden strand, the forward look to the eternal city, give motivation and purpose to life that brings something of the atmosphere of the "other shore" right down to earth, right into your every-day living. The accuracy of your direction and your rate of sailing are directly dependent on how near you stay to the cross. The wind for filling the sail is to be found on Golgtha's Hill.

The story is told of a ship that was becalmed by a sea without a ripple. The ship was dependent upon the wind to fill its sails. Not a breeze stirred. But while the men were hanging idly about, one of them saw a little pennant on the top of the highest mast begin to rise and sink. The order was given to spread the sails and in a little while the vessel was moving slowly but steadily forward. No ripple was upon the water, not a breeze swept the deck, but under the influence of the higher currents the vessel was going forward on its course.

So it is with our lives. Looking to the cross for our motivation, our purpose, we find in our every day the current to move our craft along to the golden shore. It means we sail each day with confidence; it means we sail each day without fear. The cross is God's signature, written in His own blood, that assures us, if we accept it, of safe journey to the "city which has foundations, whose builder and maker is God."

A friend who was in the First World War told of an experience he had aboard a ship as a marine. The ship was sailing in perilous waters, infested by submarines. There was an air of tenseness in the crew, for each one knew that in a flash he might be facing eternity. This friend came upon the Captain with his binocular field glass, scanning the horizon. "Do you think, Captain, that we'll reach the other shore?" was his query. The Captain paused for a long moment, and then quietly but with confidence replied, "It depends upon which other shore you mean. I don't know what the next hours will bring to this ship, but as for the ship of my life, it will reach the golden shore whatever happens, for Christ is my Captain."

PRAYER: *Thank You Lord, for your great promises and Your wonderful provisions. Keep me near Your cross today, that my sails may have the set of eternity. In Jesus' Name. Amen.*

Master, No Offering

Love's Offering. 6 4, 6 4, 6 6 4 4. EDWIN POND PARKER, 1888.

3 Some word of hope for hearts
Burdened with fears,
Some balm of peace for eyes
Blinded with tears;
Some dews of mercy shed,
Some wayward footsteps led,
Dear Lord, to Thee.

4 Thus, in Thy service, Lord,
Till eventide
Closes the day of life,
May we abide.
And when earth's labors cease,
Bid us depart in peace,
Dear Lord, to Thee.

Edwin Pond Parker, 1888.

Master, No Offering

Costly and sweet,
May we like Magdalene
Lay at Thy feet

Matthew 26:6-11

But Jesus, aware of this, said to them, "Why do you trouble the woman? For she has done a beautiful thing to me." Matthew 26:10

TOO OFTEN our giving is measured by a comparison with what others have done. The Lord's measuring stick is another one. In His sight, the gift is large or small in proportion to what you have; it is acceptable according to the degree of cheerfulness with which it is given.

In the twenty-fifth chapter of Matthew we are told the story of the talents. Here the truth of proportionate giving is made very plain. The "Well done" of the Master was to each of the servants that had produced in proportion to what they had been given. One of the compelling thoughts of Lent is what the Lord has done for us. The concommitant thought in the heart of each one of us should be: "What have I done for Him?"

When one speaks of giving, erroneously enough, people begin to feel of their purses. What you do with your purse contents should be an effect rather than a cause. Too many of us are like the man who was being pressed to give for missions. He tried to excuse himself, but the deacon pressed him to give. He explained to the deacon that he had to pay his debts first, then he would give. Knowing that this was but an excuse, the deacon reminded him that he owed the Lord the most of all, and ought to pay Him. To which the man answered, "Faith, deacon, I know it; but then, He doesn't crowd me like my other creditors."

No, the Lord will never crowd you. The acceptable gift to Him is the one that comes from the heart. It was this about Mary Magdalene's gift that made it so acceptable.

It is the absence of this basic gift that we so often try to camouflage. This is what we mean by getting down to the cause of our giving. It is Dr. Jowett who points out that Paul's liberality can be traced to Calvary; all his giving had its roots in the cross.

Would you like to know what your spiritual health is? Then consider your attitude toward your giving to kingdom purposes. Do you give with the same joy that you give to your children? Is your giving the essence of gratitude for what God has done for you? Yes, as the poet has said,

Still, as of old,
  Man by himself is priced.
For thirty pieces Judas sold
  Himself, not Christ.

PRAYER: *Lord, You do not ask of me that which I do not have. Nor do You want that which is given grudgingly. May the compulsion of my giving be my overwhelming love for You. Amen.*

Master, No Offering

Yet may love's incense rise
Sweeter than sacrifice

Ephesians 5:1, 2

Therefore be imitators of God, as beloved children. And walk in love, as Christ loved us and gave himself up for us, a fragrant offering and sacrifice to God.

IS THERE anything that so transforms the face of a woman as to be in love? Something of the beauty of the heart-expression is caught in the features and glows out of the eyes. A young husband, in describing his wife who had just become a mother, said of her: "Why, she just glows. Stars just shoot out all over from her." Paul speaks of Christ's love, evidenced in His giving himself up for us as a fragrant offering.

What gift, then, is most acceptable to God? "A broken and contrite heart, O God, thou wilt not despise." That is why Mary Magdalene's gift was so acceptable. It was the fragrance of the gift of her heart. This is what the Lord asks for and loves. In Proverbs 23:26 is recorded His request: "My son, give me your heart."

Think through your gifts to the Lord, to His church, to the extension of His kingdom. What has been the motivation for the giving? If you have begrudged the gift, if you have complained about too much asking, if you have looked longingly at material things for which you might have spent the money, then you have known very little joy in the gift. Then the giving gives off a stench rather than a fragrance.

It is not your money the Lord wants, it is you. He wants your mind, so that the pattern of your thinking will follow His; He wants your time, so that every moment you will be aware of His presence; He wants your talent, so that the fragrance of His presence within you will permeate whatever atmosphere you are in. To say that you are giving Him your hands, and to withhold your heart, is to fool yourself.

A man came to a watchmaker and gave him the hands of a clock saying, "I want you to fix these hands. They just don't keep correct time any more." "But where is the clock?" asked the watchmaker. "Why, that is out at Indian Creek in our home," was the reply. "But," said the repair man, "I can't make things work unless I have the clock." In disgust the customer retorted, "You just want the clock so that you can charge me more. All I want fixed is the hands. You had better give them back to me."

The incense of a loving heart is a fragrance to God and the gifts that flow therefrom are acceptable in His sight. The most fabulous gift carries a stench when the heart is withheld.

PRAYER: *Scrutinize my gifts, Lord; look deep into my heart. May my love for You motivate all my living and my giving. In Jesus' Name. Amen.*

Master, No Offering

Daily our lives would show
Weakness made strong

2 Corinthians 12:9

His reply has been, "My grace is enough for you: for where there is weakness, My power is shown the more completely." Therefore, I have cheerfully made up my mind to be proud of my weaknesses, because they mean a deeper experience of the power of Christ. I can even enjoy weaknesses, suffering, privations, persecutions and difficulties for Christ's sake. For my very weakness makes me strong in Him (Phillips).

TO ONE who has not experienced it, this statement of Paul's would seem like a strange paradox. To be proud of one's weakness! That is not the song of the world! But neither does the world know the indescribable joy of finding the source of strength that is in Christ. If one is strong in one's own right, there is no need for another source of strength. To those of us who feel inadequate for any day on our own power, there is the glorious assurance that the resources of God are ours for the taking; that in our weakness, we become strong in a way that could otherwise never happen.

We have mentioned before how the word strength comes from a word signifying twisted together. "The Lord is the strength of my life," "God is the strength of my soul." My life is twisted together with God's. The one strand may have no strength at all, but when it becomes twisted with the Strong One, the strength of the latter is added as long as they are wound together.

If your life is hid with Christ in God, His strength is your daily portion. Is this your witness? So many of us become victims of our own complaining and whining. We whimper about all the work we have to do, and all the obstacles. Then we wonder when our children do the same.

A naturalist was studying a cocoon in which a butterfly was struggling to be free. He heard it beating against the sides of its prison, and in his sympathy for it, he took a knife and cut away the fragile walls and released the little captive. To his amazement, it was not the beautiful creature he had expected to see. It lay struggling on the table, unable to walk or fly. The Creator had so designed it that its struggle for freedom was a part of its preparation for life. And so "weakness made strong" in our lives can be an offering of faith and love to our Creator.

PRAYER: *Lord, I would thank You that for each day Your strength has been sufficient, and that in my weakness and inadequacy, I have known most fully the joy of Your strength and its daily provision. In my home let this be my witness. In Jesus' Name. Amen.*

Master, No Offering

Toilsome and gloomy ways
Brightened with song

Psalm 42

"By day the Lord commands his steadfast love;
and at night his song is with me,
a prayer to the God of my life." Psalm 42:8

THE FORTY-SECOND Psalm is the autobiography of a soul that scrapes the bottom of despair, and yet comes up with "Hope in God; for I shall again praise him, my help and my God." The taunt of the enemy, "Where is your God?" is answered in the same way. "Toilsome and gloomy ways, brightened with song." Have you tried giving this expression of faith as a gift to your Master? When things have seemed the darkest, when the monotony of the multitudinous daily tasks has weighed down your spirit, then have you tried singing praise to your God? What a difference a song can make! Even down to the very toes there goes something of the strength of it, so that nimbleness is given to the feet and lightness to the step.

A song is a beauty treatment for the face, too, for when one smiles, one sings best. How often I have heard our choir director tell the singers to smile. A song and a smile go together, and change a growl and a frown. Try it and see.

The tonic of a song is not limited to the singer. It has healing and an uplift for everyone who hears. It radiates faith and joy through a home.

Do you remember the story of Browning's "Pippa Passes"? The little girl had one free day in all the year from the slavery of her factory work. What would you do with such a day, were you she? There was a song in her heart for the gift of this day, and so she arose early to make the most of it. Out she went into God's beautiful world, singing as she went. Her songs were of love, its constancy, its forgiveness. Her songs were of faith and hope because of the goodness of God. At the end of her day, she mused about the way she had wasted it. Yet little did she realize the many-pronged effect of her singing. Lover's quarreling in a room by which she passed paused to listen, and made up; a mother and son who were maligning each other in anger heard her song, and found a meeting ground of understanding; a young man despairing of life, and planning his end, took new hope as he listened to her song.

Yes, toilsome and gloomy ways can be lightened by song, when that song is inspired by faith in a sufficient Savior. And the effect of the singing is two-fold: it changes the day for the singer, and it puts a new song of hope into the heart of the listener. Try it.

PRAYER: *Forgive, Lord, that too many times my soul has been downcast. Give me a song even in the night of gloom and toil. Bring to my remembrance that You approached Jerusalem with singing. Amen.*

Master, No Offering

Some deeds of kindness done

Ephesians 4:31, 32

Let all bitterness and wrath and clamor and slander be put away from you, with all malice, and be kind to one another, tenderhearted, forgiving one another, as God in Christ forgave you.

WHAT A lovely string of pearls the days of a year would be, if every day's bead had the luster of some deed of kindness! Many of us look longingly at the lives of others, thinking how abundant they seem, and bemoan our own lusterless days. Yet the opportunities for abundant living begin at home. They are to be found in the daily search for that which will make the lives of those around us more comfortable, more rich.

A young Southern girl said to a lady who, though she was eighty, still attracted all whom she met. "Tell me the secret of your charm. Teach me to fascinate people as you do." "My child," was the response, "remember just this: in the alphabet of charm, there is no such letter as 'I'; it is all 'you.'" Our Lord gave the directive in very specific words: "Whoever would be great among you must be your servant." Then again, He told us that if we would find our lives, we must be willing to lose them.

Notice that Paul speaks of the things that must be eliminated before the fruit of kindness will grow. His words, sadly enough, describe too many of the situations that we find ourselves in: bitterness, wrath, clamor, and slander. These by the grace of God must be put away. An effective procedure is to start being kind. Try saying some kindly thing to each member of your family today. Follow this practice with every one you meet. Follow up the words with deeds. What a day you will have! And this kind of day multiplied will make an abundant life!

In the Book of Proverbs, a perfect woman is described. One of the attributes about which the writer speaks is that "the law of kindness is on her tongue." Today, you can make this gift to your Lord: some deed of kindness done.

If I knew that a word of mine,
  A word, not kind or true,
  Might leave its trace
  On a loved one's face,
I'd never speak harshly, would you?

If I knew the light of a smile
  Might linger the whole day through
  And brighten some heart
  With a heavier part,
I wouldn't withhold it, would you?

ANONYMOUS

PRAYER: *Give me grace, O Lord, daily so to walk in Your love, that the fruits of my life will be kindness. Help me to begin today, and begin at home. Amen.*

Master, No Offering

Some souls by patience won

Luke 8:15

"And as for that in the good soil, they are those who, hearing the word, hold it fast in an honest and good heart, and bring forth fruit with patience."

IF THERE is a quality that the devil tries to discourage, it is patience. Possibly it is because he knows that in the final analysis, God will conquer. What a word with which to meet the impatient one: "In the world you have tribulation; but be of good cheer, I have overcome the world." In the great adventure of soul winning, patience is a must. God's timepiece is different from ours. Sometimes the patience of a whole lifetime is rewarded by the redeemed soul of a loved one. Something of this is in the parable of the sower of the seed which Luke relates, "and bring forth fruit with patience."

One can well understand why the Lord used the figure of planting in His sharing of the workings of the kingdom. To dig an insignificant little brown seed down into the soil, and expect anything to happen, is indeed an act of faith. To one who did not know the process, those days when nothing happens, when even a tiny green shoot does not appear, would seem hopeless. And even after the shoot comes, the long period of growth with first the leaves, and then the blossom, and then the ripening fruit, would seem almost endless.

By this same process of following God's instructions, then in patience and with faith and hope waiting, keeping the soil in condition by prayer, souls are won. Many a mother could testify to a lifetime of waiting and praying for her children; many a wife has lived through long years with a mate before she was given to see the fruit of her prayers; many a pastor has knocked on the door of people's hearts time after time, and has left a parish without seeing any visible response to his knocking. Then to his successor the door is opened. The Lord gives us to know that this is His way. Paul says, "So neither he who plants nor he who waters is anything, but only God who gives the growth."

Is there someone for whom you have been praying and about whom you are discouraged? Why do you not this day make your gift of patient waiting to the Master? Trust Him, in His good time, to bring it to pass. Accepting His promises, live as though you already have the answer. Let there be the note of victory in your daily walk, because you know that in His wonderful way the fruit will come with patience.

PRAYER: *Teach the lesson of all growing things, O Lord; give me the patience to know that in due season we will reap, if we faint not. Let Your patience in me be the means of some soul being won. In Jesus' Name. Amen.*

Master, No Offering

Some word of hope for hearts
Burdened with fear

Psalm 34:4

I sought the Lord, and he answered me,
and delivered me from all my fears.

Isaiah 41:10

Fear not, for I am with you,
be not dismayed for I am your God;
I will strengthen you, I will help you,
I will uphold you with my victorious right hand.

TODAY'S WORLD is filled with fear-ridden people. They are in every crowd of which you are a part. You meet them down any street. Over eighty percent of the people in our hospitals today are there because of mental illness. The cause of this illness is basically a fear of some kind or other. For some, it is a fear of something that they have done in the past; for some, it is the fear of their being all alone, of no one's caring for them; and for others, it is the fear of being defeated, of feeling incapable of coping with the situations of life.

It is wonderful to know that for each of these our Lord had a very special word. To the first group He says, "Be of good cheer, your sins are forgiven you." To the second group He says that He will never leave them nor forsake them. To the third group He has another word of cheer: "In the world you have tribulation; but be of good cheer, I have overcome the world." Paul gives an additional witness in "I can do all things in him who strengthens me." And how many times are we not reminded that with men things may be impossible, but with God all things are possible.

Here, then, are the words of hope for hearts burdened with fears. The question is with what conviction can you speak them. Ought we to say to ourselves: "Physician, heal thyself"? Are you living victoriously in the knowledge of the power of God to take care of you under any circumstances? Does your life have about it the sense of peace that comes from freedom from fear? Do you have the "fear nots" of God so hidden in your heart that you can readily share them? What words for this day:

"Fear not, for I am with you";
"Fear not, I have redeemed you";
"Fear not, you shall not be ashamed."

An aged Korean woman was asked what benefits she received from Jesus. She answered, "I will tell you one thing. Before I was a Christian I never slept through the night without awakening at some time and lying in a cold sweat for fear the evil spirits would bring some disaster on my family. Now when the sun sets I commit my family into the hands of God, and sleep clear through till morning."

PRAYER: *Forgive us the absence of faith, Lord, that makes it possible for fear to possess us. Give us such a sense of Your undergirding that daily we may share it with others. Amen.*

When I Survey the Wondrous Cross

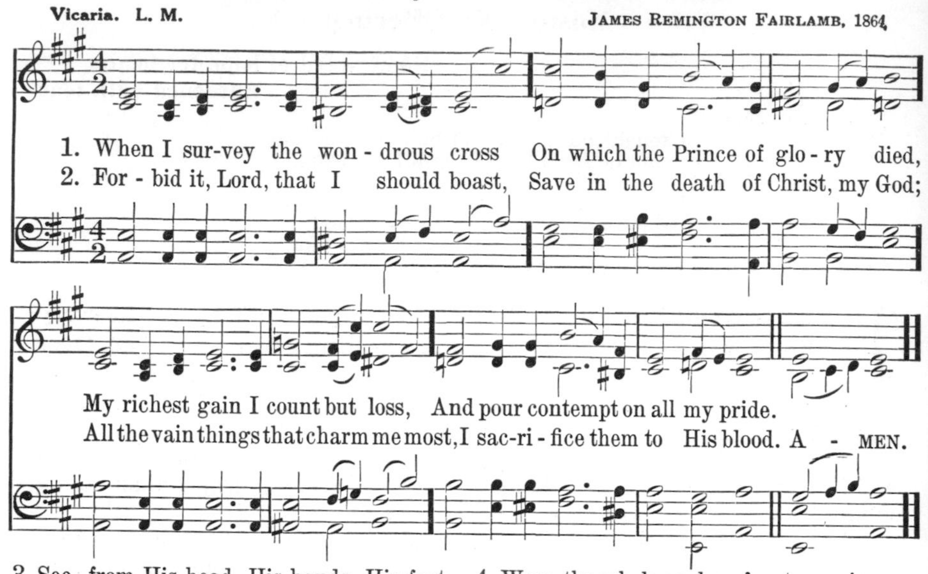

3 See, from His head, His hands, His feet,
Sorrow and love flow mingled down!
Did e'er such love and sorrow meet,
Or thorns compose so rich a crown?

4 Were the whole realm of nature mine,
That were a tribute far too small;
Love so amazing, so divine,
Demands my soul, my life, my all.

Isaac Watts, 1707, **a.**

SUNDAY

When I Survey the Wondrous Cross

On which the Prince of Glory died

John 19:17-22

So they took Jesus, and he went out bearing his own cross, to the place called the place of a skull, which is called in Hebrew Golgotha. There they crucified him, and with him two others, one on either side, and Jesus between them. Pilate also wrote a title and put it on the cross; it read, "Jesus of Nazareth, the King of the Jews." John 19:17-19

THE PURPOSE of Lent is to take a long look at the cross, and determine for our own life what its meaning is. It is to walk with our Lord, the via dolorosa, and ask ourselves what effect His being nailed to a cross has on us. If we have never had this great confrontation personally, some day in our lives it will have to be. For those of us who have chosen to follow the Christ, the Lenten look is a time of reconsecration; a time of holding up anew our values in life to the light of the cross.

Lent

To search our souls
To meditate,
Will not suffice for Lent.
To share the cross,
To sacrifice,
These are the things
God meant.

Jane McKay Lanning

Around the cross on that first Good Friday there were many people watching. Someone has said that they might be divided into three groups. First, there were the soldiers. They were there because they had to be and their reaction was largely one of apathy. Then there were the rulers. These were the ones responsible for Christ's being there. Theirs was an active attitude of antagonism and hatred. Finally there were the women and the disciples. What aching, heavy hearts they must have had to see the One they loved, the One who had done nothing but good to all who came to Him, come to such a perfidious end! I have often wondered what went on in the hearts of all the people in that vast crowd who had known the wondrous touch of Christ's healing hand. Before the cross, three groups: in the soldiers, apathy; in the rulers, antagonism, hatred; in the women and disciples, sympathy. Apathy, antipathy, sympathy in those who surveyed the cross.

Would the same classifications hold today? Only, in the last class there must be more than sympathy, for we have known the victory of the resurrection; we have been privileged to know the why of the cross. In the resurrection power, too, there is the grand "Amen" as to who Christ is!

PRAYER: *Call me aside these days, Lord, to look at the cross and its meaning for my life. Make me aware of who the Prince of glory is and what He did for me. In His name. Amen.*

When I Survey the Wondrous Cross

My richest gain I count but loss

Philippians 3:7, 8

But whatever gain I had, I counted as loss for the sake of Christ. Indeed I count everything as loss because of the surpassing worth of knowing Christ Jesus my Lord.

Matthew 16:26

"For what will it profit a man, if he gains the whole world and forfeits his life?"

SOMEONE HAS said, "What we truly and earnestly aspire to be, that in some sense, we are." And so it is that the things that we count as gain in our lives reveal what our goal is. For what are most people striving?

There is wealth. Oh, how people struggle for it, and how many sell their souls for it. Too often it possesses them, and there is no more cruel master than money. The danger of losing it becomes an obsessing fear, and the using of it becomes an agony. Yet if you speak to many young people today about their aim in life they will say, "I want to do something that will make me get rich quick!"

A man was riding on a train and struck up a conversation with the man next to him. They began to talk about their goals in life. "Oh," said the one, "I want first of all to make a lot of money." "Then what?" his friend asked. "Oh, then I want to travel all around and see the world," he responded. "Then what?" was the friend's persistent question. "Then what, phooey!" said the man, as he left his interrogator to go into the club car to drown the necessity for an answer.

Or there is position and name. Mothers will send their daughters to fashionable schools when the family budget can ill afford it, in order that their darlings may have the prestige that such a school is supposed to bring. Women frantically try to climb the social ladder.

Then there is pleasure. What an alluring enchantress is this enticing person. She has so captivated many that they would do anything to embrace her. The story of Samson and his shorn hair is a real in the lives of many today as it was in the life of the Old Testament strongman.

In the final analysis, what cannot be stolen, nor is variable, nor will be gone when you awaken in the morning?

It is the faith that you find when you survey the wondrous cross. In its light, the temporal things take on their right value, and living a life rich in the presence of the Crucified One becomes the directive for your every day.

As you look at the cross, evaluate your striving; as you look at the cross, check on the use of your time; as you look at the cross, measure the amount of your giving. Can you say, "I count everything as loss because of the surpassing worth of knowing Christ Jesus my Lord"?

PRAYER: *Help me, O Lord, to use the measuring stick of Your love against my life. Give me the evaluation that comes from surveying the wondrous cross. Amen.*

When I Survey the Wondrous Cross

And pour contempt on all my pride

Proverbs 8:13

The fear of the Lord is hatred of evil. Pride and arrogance and the way of evil and perverted speech I hate.

WHAT A multitude of varying forms, this tool of the devil takes! A Christian magazine lists them in this fashion:

Some are proud of their lace,
Some are proud of their race;
Some are proud of their face;
Others are proud of their grace.

Yes, there are even people who are proud of their humility! A husband, finding his wife adjusting some frills at her mirror, and taking a good deal of time to survey the effect, said to her, "How conceited you are, my dear. You are always looking at yourself in the glass." Quickly replied the wife, "I'm sure that I'm not conceited. I don't think that I am half as pretty as I really am."

Perhaps no pride is more insidious or uglier than spiritual pride. Under the guise of sanctity it often covers its identity. It goes to church and wears a sanctimonious air. It belongs to women's organizations in the kingdom work, and is a block to the channel for God's love. How can you recognize it? It is sensitive; quickly displays hurt feelings; it wants praise, wants to be recognized, wants special attention! It compares itself with those who more obviously have fallen into sin, and quickly sits in judgment; it finds alibis for itself at every turn of the road, and is never willing to face up to any mistake. It is the most dangerous and the most arrogant of all prides. But it cannot live at the foot of the cross.

It is revealing to see Paul's increasing sense of unworthiness as he grows in the grace of Christ. First, he acknowledges himself to be a sinner; then a couple of years later, he speaks of himself as being chief of sinners. The closer he came to the Lord, the less worthy he felt himself to be, and the more contempt he poured on all his pride. The way to cultivate humility is not by self-contemplation, but by the contemplation of Christ.

Someone passing down a Glasgow street, saw a crowd at a shop door, and had the curiosity to look in. There he saw an auctioneer holding up a grand picture, so that all could see it. When he got it in position, he remained behind it, and said to the crowd, "Now look at this part of the picture, and now this other part." The observer commented that the entire time that he was there, he never saw the person, only the picture. That is the way to work for Christ. You decrease, that He may increase.

PRAYER: *Scrutinize every corner of my heart, Lord, to ferret out any pride that might be lurking there. Help me to take such a sure look at the cross, that I will pour contempt on all my pride. In Jesus' Name. Amen.*

When I Survey the Wondrous Cross

Forbid it, Lord, that I should boast

Ephesians 2:8, 9

For by grace you have been saved through faith; and this is not your own doing, it is the gift of God—not because of works, lest any man should boast.

WE ARE living in an age that is constantly boasting of man's achievements. Magazines run articles on self-made men. Scientific discoveries and inventions are recounted as if man had made the universe. Too often biographies and autobiographies are a recounting of personal achievement. In the light of the cross, we need to stop and ask ourselves from whom all things come.

In the old days, when organs often had a hand pump behind them to supply the wind necessary to produce sound, it took two to perform. The story is told of a musician who used his young brother as his pumper. There came a time when the young lad felt that he was not getting any credit, as he was always behind the scenes. They were to play at an especially important occasion. Before he began the performance, the musician turned to his audience and said, "I will now play for you Beethoven's Sonata." He then sat down to his instrument, but found to his utter amazement that no sound came. Then he heard a voice from behind the organ: "Say, 'we,' say, 'we,' or there won't be any playing."

A real temptation to mothers is to boast about their children. Grandmothers are prey to this temptation, too. Is not your boast then about your own flesh and blood? You might just as well be saying commendable things about yourself.

There is one thing about which we should boast, though. Our song writer knew it, for he says:

Forbid it, Lord, that I should boast,
Save in the cross of Christ, my God.

Here then is something we should speak of. Psalm 44:8 reads: "In God we have boasted continually, and we will give thanks to thy name for ever." Again in Psalm 34:2 we read:

My soul makes its boast in the Lord;
Let the afflicted hear and be glad.

Salvation is a free gift of God! If you boast of your own achievements, people become weary, and often it degrades them for what they have not accomplished; if you boast in the Lord, the afflicted hear and are glad.

PRAYER: *For all the times I have wanted acknowledgment for something I have done, forgive me, Lord. Thank You for the grace that makes salvation a gift, and let all my boasting be to share Your wondrous love. In Jesus' name. Amen.*

THURSDAY

When I Survey the Wondrous Cross

See from His head, His hands, His feet,
Sorrow and love flow mingled down!

Luke 23:33, 34

And when they came to the place which is called The Skull, there they crucified him, and the criminals, one on the right and one on the left. And Jesus said, "Father, forgive them; for they know not what they do."

PERHAPS THE gift of everlasting life, bought for us by the blood of Christ, we take lightly, because we do not often enough stop to consider the cost. The ignominy of the cross, the humility to the King, the taunting and the shame, besides the physical torture, would seem to be enough to make us realize the price God paid for our salvation. But in addition to this, there was the identification in Him of all our sins; He who was sinless became loathsome to His Father, a God of justice as well as mercy, in order that from this time on He might plead our cause when we otherwise would be doomed. Yet in the midst of all this agony that embraced eternity, He prayed for His persecutors, "Father, forgive them; for they know not what they do."

Revealment

They planned for Christ a cruel death;
  Steel pierced His hands and feet and side;
They mocked His last expiring breath,
  And thought their hate was satisfied.

. . . .

They did not know that on the hill
  Eternal love was satisfied;
That Christ, who hung there, triumphed still.
  . . . . And only cruel death had died!

JOHN RICHARD MORELAND

In Ireland a teacher once asked a boy if there was anything God could not do, and the little fellow said: "Yes, He cannot see my sins through the blood of Jesus Christ."

See from His head, His hands, His feet,
  Sorrow and love flow mingled down!
Did e'er such love and sorrow meet,
  Or thorns compose so rich a crown?

PRAYER: *Thank You, Lord, for Your love and compassion. Thank You for Your cross which I can only dimly understand. As I look to Calvary during these days of Lent, reveal Your amazing love to me. In Your name. Amen.*

FRIDAY

When I Survey the Wondrous Cross

**Were the whole realm of nature mine,
That were a tribute far too small**

1 Peter 2:4-10

Come to him, to that living stone, rejected by men but in God's sight chosen and precious; and like living stones be yourselves built into a spiritual house, to be a holy priesthood, to offer spiritual sacrifices acceptable to God through Jesus Christ. . . . But you are a chosen race, a royal priesthood, a holy nation, God's own people, that you may declare the wonderful deeds of him who called you out of darkness into his marvelous light.

IT IS awfully easy to give away what we do not have. Someone who cannot sing has a glib tongue to say, "If I had a voice, I would dedicate it." By the same token, someone who has very little money can comfortably say, "If I had the wealth that she has, what I wouldn't do with it!" Would you? So it is easy for us to say with the song writer, "Were the whole realm of nature mine, That were a tribute far too small"; but not having those resources, we fold up and do nothing. This reasoning is what makes the Christian Church less effective than it should be today.

A woman went to a lawyer to make a will. She began to enumerate fabulous sums that she wanted to give away. After a while the lawyer stopped her and said, "Pardon me, but how much money do you have?" "Oh," was her response, "I haven't anything, but I'm just having the fun of giving all this away." When you survey the wondrous cross, the question is not what you would give if you had the whole realm of nature; the question is: what are you giving now? What about your life dedication?

In the Epistle of Peter, we are challenged to be living stones. What kind of tribute to the crucified Christ is your everyday living? What are you doing with what you have? You stand beneath His cross, and marvel at what He did for you. Then you glibly offer an excuse when His church asks for a part of your devotion, your time. Beneath the cross, take a long look at the things that keep you from giving a more total consecration to the church which is His body here on earth. Has the power of the cross permeated every area of your life?

Suppose you were to buy a house, and on the day that you were to move in the previous owner said, "Here are the keys to eight rooms. I have reserved two rooms. I want to keep four tigers in one, and two reptiles in another. All the rest of the house is yours." Ludicrous, you say? Yet such withholding is what too many of us practice even in the light of the cross.

PRAYER: *Lord, help me to witness with what I have to the redeeming love that I know through the power of Your crucifixion. This day, Lord, I dedicate to You. In Your name. Amen.*

SATURDAY

When I Survey the Wondrous Cross

Love so amazing, so divine,
Demands my soul, my life, my all

Matthew 16: 24, 25

Then Jesus told his disciples, "If any man would come after me, let him deny himself and take up his cross and follow me. For whoever would save his life will lose it, and whoever loses his life for my sake, will find it."

YES, TO FOLLOW Christ and really know the joy of it means an all-out commitment. Does that seem like a strange paradox, to know the joy of taking up a cross? One has but to try it to experience its fulfillment. The people who are really miserable are the halfway people. There is nothing so agonizing as indecision. You know how true that is about the smallest thing. Once you have made up your mind to it, even the most difficult task is not too formidable. It is the indecision of commitment to it that is agony.

How true this is of our lives. Many people in the church do not know the joy of Christ's presence because they cannot make up their minds between Him and the world. They think they can live with a part of them for each, and the result is they know little joy on either side.

Faraday, the great chemist, learned a vital lesson when he was but a boy. He earned his bread by selling newspapers out in the street. One day he was waiting for the morning issue outside the Edinburgh Press, and passed the time away by thrusting his head and arms through the railings of the iron gate. He was a born metaphysician and began to speculate on which side of the railings he was. "My head and my hands are on one side," he said to himself, "and my heart and my body are on the other." The gate was opened hastily before he could disengage himself, and the wrench he received taught him, as he said in after life, that all true work required head and heart and hands to be on the same side.

Through the ages some glorious chapters have been written when this choice has been made. They would include a Livingstone, a Judson, a Grenfell, a Schweitzer, a Kagawa, and countless others. The heroes of the total commitment are written in the Book of Life.

You have read the story about the Indian who was very poor, but whose heart was filled with the wonder of Jesus' love for him. When the collection plate was passed, he said, "Put it down a little lower." When it was lowered, he said, "Still lower," until it was put on the floor. Then he stepped into it. He wanted to give himself.

PRAYER: *I want to face up to this total consecration, Lord. As I survey the cross, I see that only all is enough. Help me to take up my cross, and follow. In Jesus' name. Amen.*

Dear Lord and Father of Mankind

Rest (Maker). 8 6, 8 8 6. FREDERICK CHARLES MAKER, 1887.

2 In simple trust like theirs who heard,
Beside the Syrian sea,
The gracious calling of the Lord,
Let us, like them, without a word
Rise up and follow Thee.

3 O Sabbath rest by Galilee!
O calm of hills above,
Where Jesus knelt to share with Thee
The silence of eternity
Interpreted by love!

4 Drop Thy still dews of quietness,
Till all our strivings cease;
Take from our souls the strain and stress,
And let our ordered lives confess
The beauty of Thy peace.

5 Breathe through the heat of our desire
Thy coolness and Thy balm;
Let sense be dumb, let flesh retire;
Speak thro' the earthquake, wind, and fire,
O still, small voice of calm.

John Greenleaf Whittier, 1872

Dear Lord and Father of Mankind

Forgive our feverish ways

Luke 10:40

But Martha was very worried about her elaborate preparations and she burst in, saying,

"Lord, don't you *mind* that my sister has left me to do everything all by myself? Tell her to get up and help me!"

But the Lord answered her,

"Martha, my dear, you are worried and bothered about a great many things. Only a few things are really needed, perhaps only one. Mary has chosen the most important thing and you must not tear her away from it!" (Phillips)

ONE WOULD think, with all the electric appliances to aid women in housework, that there would be more time for meditation and quietness; more time to sit at the feet of the Lord, and get directions for living; more time to run His errands. Just the converse is true. Again and again I have had women say to me, "But how do you find time to read the Bible and pray? The days are just too full!" Indeed the days are too full, if this be the case, or is it that our sense of values has gone awry? Someone has said: "Your date book is your creed. What you believe in, you find time for!"

Why do so many of us fill our lives with such feverish activity? Could it be that we are afraid to be quiet before God, and the "many things to do" is a coverage? I love the word of the Lord to Martha—"only a few things are really needed, perhaps only one." I think of the elaborate table we struggle to set, and then find ourselves so utterly exhausted that we cannot enjoy our guests when they come.

Slow Me Down, Lawd

Slow me down, Lawd. Ah's going too fast,
Ah can't see mah brother when he's walking past.
Ah miss a lot of good things day by day,
Ah don't know a blessing when it comes mah way.

Slow me down, Lawd. Ah wants to see
More o' the things that's good for me.
A little less o' me an' a little more o' You.
Ah wants the heavenly atmosphere to trickle through.

Let me help a brother when the goin's rough.
When folks work together it ain't so tough.
Slow me down, Lawd, so I can talk
With some of your angels. Slow me down to a walk.

ANON

PRAYER: *Forgive my feverish ways, Lord, and give me a right sense of values. Amen.*

Dear Lord and Father of Mankind

Reclothe us in our rightful mind

Matthew 9:4

But Jesus, knowing their thoughts, said, "Why do you think evil in your hearts?"

Romans 12:3

For by the grace given to me I bid every one among you not to think of himself more highly than he ought to think, but to think with sober judgment, each according to the measure of faith which God has assigned him.

BUT JESUS knowing their thoughts." Reading this word of Scripture, are you frightened or relieved? On the one hand it is frightening to think that the pure, all-seeing eye of God looks into every crevice of your mind. There is nothing hid from Him. On the other hand, it is a good, clean, free feeling to know that God knows you as you really are, and still loves you. Of course He does not love your wicked thoughts, or your selfish ones; but if you are willing to confess them, He will forgive, and remember them no more. There is no point in your trying to put up a front with Him.

I remember when Dave was just a little lad with a chubby face. He had done something naughty, so as I concluded my reprimand, I said to him, "I still love you, Dave, even when you are naughty, although your naughtiness makes me feel very bad. God still loves you, although it hurts Him, too, when you are naughty." He went into his room to chew on that one for a while, but before too long he came to see me and said piously, "Mother, I still love myself, too, even when I'm naughty." If as adults we were to be honest, we should have to make something of the same confession as Dave.

The hymn writer prays to be reclothed in a rightful mind. This is a very basic, significant prayer. Scripture says "As a man thinks, so he is." Every day we are becoming more like our thoughts. If they are mean and selfish, we cannot prevent ourselves from becoming so; if they are unclean and evil, our character and conduct will inevitably be shaped by them. What you are thinking is very important.

Our Scripture suggests one of the tempting thought patterns that produce no good: "to think of himself more highly than he ought to think." This is a chronic disease of the mind—selfishness. Its progeny are envy, suspicion, pride, touchiness.

But Scripture has a positive word for us, too, in regard to our thinking. It is well worth memorizing, and is like the balm of Gilead for a fretful spirit: "If you believe in goodness and if you value the approval of God, fix your minds on the things which are holy and right and pure and beautiful and good." (Phillips)

PRAYER: *Too often, Lord, my thinking has been fretful and peevish. Help me to think Your thoughts after You. In Jesus' Name. Amen.*

Dear Lord and Father of Mankind

In purer lives Thy service find

1 Corinthians 10:24, 33

Let no one seek his own good, but the good of his neighbor.
Just as I try to please all men in everything I do, not seeking my own advantage, but that of many, that they may be saved.

HERE WE are given the antidote for selfish, unhappy thinking. It is what the hymn writer means when he says, "In purer lives Thy service find." To be clothed in a rightful mind is not the whole answer. Thinking God's thoughts after Him sets in motion a whole chain of things. It means that you think of your neighbor's need, and how you can help him. It means that your chief desire is to serve. For this day, what are your plans? Will they include lovingkindness to some one who will not be expecting it? Have you thought of how you might make the return of the family to the home base more pleasant? Will they anticipate coming home, because in you they will find a haven of peace and a source of inspiration? This is an area in which today's woman has given too little thought. In the desire to equal men in all things, we have lost sight of the peculiar opportunity that is ours to set the atmosphere of our homes. Often in our shortsightedness, we have yielded a place of tremendous influcnce. Our selfishness has been the blind that has caused us to forfeit a wonderful opportunity.

An amusing, yet significant, story is told of a minister who came out of a hotel one day, whistling. A little boy, playing near by, heard him and said, "Is that the best that you can do?"

"No," said the minister; "can you beat it?"

The boy said that he could, and the minister said, "Well, let's hear you." The little fellow began to whistle, and then insisted that the minister should try again. He did so, and the boy acknowledged that it was good whistling. As he started away, the little fellow said: "Well, if you can whistle better, what were you whistling that way for?"

Wherever the Lord has put us, there is an opportunity to serve. Are you doing it as unto the Lord, to the best of your ability? In your feverish seeking for something somewhere else, maybe you are overlooking the fullness of life that can be found in serving the Lord right where you are.

What of your home, your neighborhood, your church? Are you seeking the good of the other person?

PRAYER: *Help me to lose myself, Lord, in serving others where I am. Help me not to seek my own good, but rather the good of those about me. In my losing, let me find You. In Jesus' name. Amen.*

Dear Lord and Father of Mankind

In deeper reverence, praise

Isaiah 52:9

Break forth together into singing,
you waste places of Jerusalem;
for the Lord has comforted his people,
he has redeemed Jerusalem.

IN THE poem, "Seedtime and Harvest," John Greenleaf Whittier the Quaker author of our hymn for this week, expresses something of the faith that brings depth to this phrase, "in deeper reverence, praise." His duty, as he saw it, was to sow the seed, knowing that God would take care of the harvest. With such a frame of mind, marveling at the miraculous way God works, in quiet wonder and adoration he lifted his heart in praise. As a little boy, his life was one of struggle in which hard work and drudgery were the daily fare. One day he sat before the kitchen fire and wrote:

And must I always swing the flail
And help to fill the milking pail?
I wish to go away to school;
I do not wish to be a fool.

Through hard work, he was able to attend Haverhill Academy for two seasons. So to some extent his ambition was realized.

If we are really to praise the Lord in deeper reverence, we should daily remember who He is: the Creator of all the universe, the King of kings who has all power in His hands, and also your Elder Brother and Savior, the One who was willing to die for you that you might live with Him for ever. No wonder another poet has written:

What language shall I borrow
To thank Thee, dearest Friend?

He loves to hear His praise spoken, but more than that, He loves the witness of daily living. He loves the gratitude of a heart that spills over into lovingkindness in the lives of others.

Sam had this spirit in a big way. He was always saying, "Praise the Lord." One day his boss gave him some extra money with which to buy a steak as a special treat. Down the street he went, swinging his purchase, his mouth drooling in anticipation of the feast that was ahead. A huge hound had smelled a good meal for himself, and before Sam could protect the package, he had grabbed it and run off with it. A friend, standing near by said, "Now Sam, surely you won't say, 'Praise the Lord.' " With a sparkle in his eye, he quickly replied, "Yes, sir. I say, 'Praise the Lord I still have my appetite.' "

PRAYER: *In quiet adoration, Lord, my heart would pay its tribute now. You do more for me than I can ever ask or think. Let my life praise You. In Jesus' name. Amen.*

THURSDAY

Dear Lord and Father of Mankind

In simple trust like theirs who heard, . . .
The gracious calling of the Lord

1 Corinthians 1:26, 27

For consider your call, brethren; not many of you were wise according to worldly standards, not many were powerful, not many were of noble birth; but God chose what is foolish in the world to shame the wise, God chose what is weak in the world to shame the strong.

WHO WERE the men that were called to follow the Christ beside the Syrian Sea? Mostly fishermen they were—men from the most ordinary walks of life. Apparently their capacity, too, was very average. Up to this time no great ambition had stirred them. They had been quite content to eke out a living, a bare subsistence for themselves and their families. Their intellectual background was "mine-run." They were not the so-called "men of wisdom" of their day. In his Letter to the Corinthians, Paul tells us that not many wise, not many powerful, not many of noble birth are called. Why? Do you think it is that the Lord does not want them? No, it is only because their wisdom becomes an obstacle; their position becomes a hindrance; their noble birth becomes their undergirding. They too often trust in these, rather than in simple faith to look to the Lord for their resources. Thank God, in every age there have been those so especially endowed, who have been willing to come to the place where we all must begin, a simple, childlike trust in the Lord.

Is it not wonderful that every one of us is called of the Lord? No matter what our gifts, no matter who we are, no matter where we are, the Lord is calling: Rise up and follow me!

Notice the next significant thing the hymn writer speaks about: those who heard the call. There is where the rub is. Do the alluring sounds of the world so fill our ears that we cannot hear God's call? Has it been so long ago that we listened that we have only a faint remembrance of that call?

Then we have this matter of simple trust. Isaiah sends out the call: "Who among you . . . who walks in darkness . . . yet trusts in the Lord?" Do we remember whom it is we trust?

For today, hear the calling of the Lord. In simple trust step out on faith and do His bidding. Yours will be a rewarding experience!

PRAYER: *Lord, give us open ears to hear Your call. Then, Lord, may Your spirit so work in us that we may have this simple trust, even when things are dark. In Jesus' name. Amen.*

FRIDAY

Dear Lord and Father of Mankind

Breathe through the heat of our desire
Thy coolness and Thy balm

Psalm 107:28

Then they cried to the Lord in their trouble,
and he delivered them from their distress.

Matthew 8:26

And he said to them, "Why are you afraid, O men of little faith?" Then he rose and rebuked the winds of the sea; and there was a great calm.

HAVE YOU been in a violent storm and known the sweet peace of the ensuing calm? What the Lord wants us to do is to carry that calm right through the storm. When He said to His disciples, "Why are you afraid, O men of little faith?" He was grieved that they did not remember that He had always taken care of them. He had evidenced His sufficiency on every occasion. Yet, here they were, acting as if that had never been their experience.

Often the "heat of our desire" stirs up a storm of tornado proportions. Is there a calm center, no matter how high the winds? Sometimes when we are endeavoring to further the Lord's cause, we find ourselves in such a storm. In such a time, are we aware that He is in our boat, and so we need not be afraid? Yes, even the winds and the waves of our tempestuous desires will obey Him, if we will but hear the "still, small voice."

Notice that our hymn line says:

Breathe through the heat of our desire
Thy coolness and Thy balm.

This inner peace is not something that you can buy in a package nor purchase in twenty easy lessons. It is something that you breathe; that grows and develops in you as "in him you live and move and have your being." It is to know Christ's presence in all that you do; it is to be aware of His values in your desires and aspirations. When you have the assurance that you walk in the will of God, then indeed you have peace.

Besides having this inner peace for ourselves, we have something to impart to others. I think of what it means to children to sense this in their parents. The witness of a deep, undergirding faith is the finest heritage parents can give their children.

God give me sympathy and sense,
And help me keep my courage high;
God give me calm and confidence,
And, please, a twinkle in my eye.

ANON

PRAYER: *Help us, Lord, to check our desires with Your will. Through the stormiest waters, give us the calm of Your presence. In Jesus' name. Amen.*

Dear Lord and Father of Mankind

Speak thro' the earthquake, wind, and fire

Psalm 46

God is our refuge and strength,
  a very present help in trouble.
Therefore we will not fear though the earth should change,
  though the mountains shake in the heart of the sea;
though its waters roar and foam,
  though the mountains tremble with its tumult. Psalm 46:1-3

WHAT TIMES we are living in! The report for the Red Cross in the year 1955 showed the greatest number of disasters in its history. Earthquakes, floods, hurricanes, besides plane and train accidents, were at a maximum. One becomes sober remembering that the Lord mentions these things as happening in great numbers when the end of the world shall be. Should this sobering be fear, or how would the Lord speak to us?

Again there should be an inventory of our values. If Christ should come today, would we be at the tasks that He would have us do? Is there some soul that would be fearful at His coming, because we had failed to speak to Him about what our faith means to us? What about the world? It is the burden of His heart; is it ours? Is the passion of our lives that every soul around the earth should know about His redeeming love?

Life is uncertain at best. You are here today; it is in God's hands whether or not you will be here tomorrow. Today's opportunity will never come back to you. This evening this day will be gone! Have you used it for Him?

No disaster is greater than His undergirding will help us bear. He is sufficient for anything that may come. Yes, even through the valley of the shadow, He will be with you, if you have accepted His grace.

A great woman lecturer found herself in a boat in a harbor of Japan when a volcano erupted. The disturbance of the sea that followed appeared to be the end for all on board the ship. Those unprepared to face eternity were in a frenzy, acting like mad people. At first, this woman found herself quaking for fear, then the words of the forty-sixth Psalm came to her: "Though its waters roar and foam." Immediately she sensed the adequacy of God, and that that word was hers for just a time like this. She was given such calm that she was able to be a wonderful help to all the others on board that ship. The word she passed along was: "God is our refuge and strength."

PRAYER: *Teach me Lord, in all the things that are happening about me, the lesson of Your undergirding love. Let these things accelerate the compulsion of my sharing. In Jesus' name. Amen.*

Rock of Ages, Cleft for Me

Toplady. 7 7, 7 7, 7 7. THOMAS HASTINGS, 1830.

3 Nothing in my hand I bring,
Simply to Thy cross I cling;
Naked. come to Thee for dress;
Helpless. look to Thee for grace;
Foul. I to the fountain fly:
Wash me, Saviour, or I die!

4 While I draw this fleeting breath,
When my eyelids close in death,
When I soar to worlds unknown,
See Thee on Thy judgment throne;
Rock of ages, cleft for me,
Let me hide myself in Thee.

Augustus Montague Toplady, 1776, a.

Rock of Ages

Cleft for me

1 Samuel 2:2

"There is none holy like the Lord; there is none besides thee; there is no rock like our God."

THROUGHOUT ALL the ages, philosophers have pondered the longing in the human heart for bolstering and immortality. George Herbert, an English poet, has explained it by saying that when God made man, from the glass of His creation He poured out all the attributes with their potential until there was but one left; that was rest. Then He stayed His hand to consider. "For," He said, "if I should give him this gift, too, he might worship the gift instead of the Giver." And so the gift of rest was withheld, in order that man with his eternal restlessness might find his home in God.

Something of succumbing to this temptation was the experience of Jeshurun who waxed fat, grew sleek, and scoffed at the God of his salvation. Isn't Jeshurun's temptation one that faces us each day? As we sing this hymn this week, let us look to the Rock from which we are hewn.

The hymn was born out of a deep need, filled by a simple childlike faith in God's wonderful plan of salvation. It is so simply put that a child can understand it, and yet it so serves to satisfy a human hunger that it is one of the most popular of all hymns. Augustus Toplady, the author, at the age of sixteen attended an evangelistic service in a barn in Dublin. The preacher was an unlettered man, but the sincerity of what he was saying gripped the young man in his audience, and he dedicated his heart and his life to God. His life span was short, for he died at the age of thirty-eight. The impact of his witness, however, has gone down through the centuries.

He witnessed to the complete adequacy of this Rock in life and death before he passed on. Just a few hours before he breathed his last, he exclaimed: "My heart beats every day stronger and stronger for glory. Sickness is no affliction, pain no curse, death itself no dissolution." When he was ill, some friends expressed the hope that he might be made well. But to this he said, "No mortal man can live after the glories which God has manifested to my soul." The Rock of Ages was already so vital a part of his life, that he spoke of already enjoying heaven in his soul.

That Rock was cleft for you, too.

PRAYER: *Thank You for the witness, Lord of those who have gone before. Thank You for the everlasting adequacy of the Rock of salvation. In Jesus' name. Amen.*

Rock of Ages

Let me hide myself in Thee

Galatians 2:20

I have been crucified with Christ; it is no longer I who live, but Christ who lives in me; and the life I now live in the flesh I live by faith in the Son of God, who loved me and gave himself for me.

A FRIEND of Augustine's days of dissipation came to him, after he had given himself to Christ, and tried to persuade him to join her again. "I haven't changed," she argued, as she used her wiles on him. "But I have," was his quick reply. And he could well have added, "it is no longer I who live, but Christ lives in me." Many of us do not find the joy in our Christian life that we should because we have not been willing to make this all-out commitment. Many of us are very vague even about what we believe. It is said that the devil once asked a dying man, "What do you believe? Fearful that he might be caught in some heresy the poor man responded, "What the church believes." "And what does the church believe?" the devil demanded. The merry-go-round answer was, "What I believe."

Would you be able to give a clear-cut witness about what you believe? Many of us have accepted the church of our fathers without ever making a personal spiritual search for ourselves. Salvation cannot be inherited. Your relationship to Jesus Christ is between you and Him. He has promised to every one who will seek that he will find. Is it that too many of us do not want to pay the price? For that is a total commitment, a complete hiding ourselves in Him; it is to be able to say that it is no longer you who live, but that Christ lives in you.

What a wonderful hiding-place! It is a protection from the ambitions of the world that can eat at the soul like a cancer; it is a coverage from any fear that could haunt; it is a place of peace and power.

This does not mean that you escape from the world, and withdraw. Rather, it means that you walk down the streets, and live abundantly. For when you are hid in Him, you run His errands, you do His work—always, however, with His empowering.

A missionary to India asked a Hindu to help him translate this hymn into one of the dialects. The opening words were:

> Grey old stone, split for my benefit,
> Let me get under one of your fragments.

Because too many of us want a fragmentary religion, are not willing to be all-out-hidden, we do not know the joy of possessing the Rock of Ages. Can you say,

> "It is no longer I who live,
> but Christ who lives in me."

This prayer by Dale Evans Rogers could well be ours today: *I shall not rest, O Father, until at last I rest in Thee; until I find peace in giving Thee my hunted, haunted soul. Amen.*

Rock of Ages

Not the labors of my hands
Can fulfill Thy Law's demands

Romans 4:13-15

The promise to Abraham and his descendants, that they should inherit the world, did not come through the law but through the righteousness of faith. If it is the adherents of the law who are to be heirs, faith is null and the promise is void. For the law brings wrath, but where there is no law, there is no transgression.

WHAT ARE the law's demands? That you should be perfect, as your heavenly Father is perfect. Is there any human being who on any day can fulfill this? Yet there are those who believe that they can stand on judgment day with their own poor works in their hands, and be received by a just and holy God. They will say, "I haven't broken any of the commandments. I've tried to do what is right."

Let us take a look at the commandments! Have you put God first in everything and loved Him more than anybody else? Have you loved your neighbor as yourself? (Do you criticize yourself as readily as you do him?) Have you remembered the Sabbath Day, to keep it holy, attending the house of the Lord, and visiting the sick and the lonely on the rest of the day? Have you had respect and honor for those in authority as well as for your own parents? And what about this matter of killing? Have you never hated anybody, or had any unkind feelings toward anyone? Of course, you are free from adultery! You have never had unclean thoughts, or been a party to suggestive movies and the like! What about bearing false witness? Have you always spoken well of your neighbor, and put the most charitable construction on all his actions? Then, there is this matter of covetousness. Can you say that you have never desired for your own, some possession of your neighbor? What could I ever do that would be adequate compensation before a holy, all-seeing God for my daily sinning?

We are guilty also for all the things we should have done but which we have neglected to do.

I have not cut my neighbor's throat
My neighbor's gold I have not stole;
I have not spoiled his house or land,
But God have mercy on my soul
For I am haunted night and day
By all the things I have not done.
O unattempted loveliness!
O costly valor, never won!

MARGUERITE WILKINSON

PRAYER: *Disturb us, Lord, so that we will get to the heart of things and acknowledge our sin as it really is. Show us our need of a Savior! In His name. Amen.*

Rock of Ages

Thou must save and Thou alone

Luke 19:9, 10

And Jesus said to him, "Today salvation has come to this house, since he also is a son of Abraham. For the Son of man came to seek and to save the lost."

Luke 20:17

"What then is this that is written: 'The very stone which the builders rejected has become the head of the corner' "?

IN THE fourth chapter of the Book of Acts, when Peter is called to answer the question put to him by the rulers, he answers:

"This is the stone which was rejected by you builders, but which has become the head of the corner. And there is salvation in no one else, for there is no other name under heaven given among men by which we must be saved."

In these days when there is so much of synthetic religion, it is essential that we should know on what rock we stand. Paul speaks of the stone that the builders rejected becoming a stone of stumbling to some. And Jesus tells us that whoever falls on that stone will be broken to pieces. He adds that when it falls on anyone, it will crush him. The claim of Christianity is that Christ is *the Way,* not *a* way. This unyielding claim is anchored in Christ's own words.

The witness that Canon Chandra Ray of Pakistan gave I shall never forget. He was brought up in a wealthy Hindu home. When he was twenty, his mother, sensing a restless spirit, took him on a pilgrimage to a Hindu shrine, thinking this would satisfy him. He related with what expectancy he went, hoping that the yearning within him would find some fulfillment. But the experience was like a dud. He was disillusioned and heartsick at the emptiness of what he found. Then he began searching. He sought the truth in all the religions with which he had had any contact: Buddhism, Confucianism, Islam, and the others. Always there was the same blind alley: by your good works you won for yourself your place in the future life. He had not contacted Christianity or the Bible, until one day he met a young man, whom the doctors had told that he was going blind. One night the young man said to Chandra Ray, "My eyes are very bad. The doctor is to take one last look tomorrow, but he has said that I am going blind. Will you read to me?" and he put into his hand a New Testament. Chandra Ray had never seen it before, and the impact of what he read that night was so great, that he took the Book home, and read it through the night. You know what followed: he found the Savior through the Book. He told us that the thing that captured him was this having access to the Father because of what Christ had done for us. "There is no other religion," he said, "where you can find such a way."

PRAYER: *Savior, thank You for being the Way. I claim the salvation You offer in Your love. Amen.*

Rock of Ages

Nothing in my hand I bring
Simply to Thy cross I cling

Romans 8:1, 2

There is therefore now no condemnation for those who are in Christ Jesus. For the law of the Spirit of life in Christ Jesus has set me free from the law of sin and death.

John 3:14, 15

"And as Moses lifted up the serpent in the wilderness, so must the Son of man be lifted up that whoever believes in him may have eternal life."

CALL TO mind that story from the Old Testament. Again and again, by their lack of faith, the children of Israel had sinned against God. Now their punishment was this onslaught of venomous snakes, whose very bite was the doom of death. But the God of justice is a God of mercy also, and in His infinite love He provided a way. Moses was given instructions to put a brazen serpent on a cross with the promise that whoever looked to this cross should be spared from the poison and be saved. And so it was.

The miracle of the Bible is its togetherness. That from the first story in the Book of Genesis, and then running all the way through, sometimes on the surface, and then again being caught in the intricacies of the weaving there should be, this crimson thread can hardly be explained away. It is all a part of God's wonderful plan. Yet through all the ages, even as in those days when Jesus walked on this earth, people have repudiated it because it has been so simple. Or could it be that the repudiation is due to the fact that the price of our pride must be paid in order to acquire faith?

The story is told of a young man coming to Dr. Dwight L. Moody and saying, "If you will answer this list of questions, then I will become a Christian." Mr. Moody replied, "If you will become a Christian and start tonight, and then come to me tomorrow morning, I will answer every question on your list." The man said, "Sir, I will come." He went home to seek the source of his coming. That night he accepted Christ as his Savior. The next morning he came back to Dr. Moody's house, his face shining, and said, "Mr. Moody, I will not have to put you to the trouble of answering the questions. They have all been answered." Christ is the only answer.

The last lines of poetry my mother quoted she used as a conclusion to the last devotional period she led for her women's group in her church. What a farewell word!

"The hands of Christ seem very frail
For they were broken by a nail;
But only they reach heaven at last,
Whom these frail, broken hands hold fast."

PRAYER: *Thank You for the cross, O Lord. Thank You that the way of salvation is so simple that even a child can understand. Help me to share the faith that is all of life to me. In Jesus' name. Amen.*

Rock of Ages

Naked come to Thee for dress

2 Corinthians 5:1-4

We know, for instance, that if our earthly dwelling were taken down, like a tent, we have a permanent house in Heaven, made not by man, but by God. In this present frame we sigh with deep longing for the heavenly house, for we do not want to face utter nakedness when death destroys our present dwellings—these bodies of ours. So long as we are clothed in this temporary dwelling we have a painful longing, not because we want just to get rid of these "clothes" but because we want to know the full cover of the permanent house that will be ours. (Phillips)

AS A child or adolescent, did you ever have the dream of being on the street in full view of everybody, and being only partially clothed, or entirely naked? Even now, I cringe when I think of the embarrassment I felt in my dream. As an adult, I have often thought that something like that will be our feeling when we stand before our Maker, unless we accept the wardrobe He is willing to supply. From Him, nothing can be hid, and every evil intent, every ungenerous thought, every ugly word will be exposed.

But there is another way. He has provided, in His infinite love, a gown for our presentation. Its design is from eternity; its first cutting was that Christmas when the angels sang; it began to take form those thirty-three years that the Great Designer walked on this earth; it was completed at Calvary. Ever since the occasion when His seamless robe was gambled for at the foot of the cross, it has been available to any one who would accept it. The dying thief did, and was accepted by the King. As Paul says, "We do not want to face utter nakedness when death destroys this dwelling." But God has made provisions.

In Edna St. Vincent Millay's "Ballad of the Harp Weaver" is depicted a mother who was so poor that she broke up the chairs for fuel, and who hardly had a crust for her hungry son. In spite of this lack, the son's remembrance is of his mother sitting on the one good chair, singing and weaving. In the morning when he arose, "there sat his mother in the one good chair," with her hands in the harp strings frozen dead.

"But piled up beside her
And toppling to the skies
Were the clothes of a king's son
Just my size."

Our Lord, in the gift of His life, provides eternity's wardrobe for everyone who will come for it. Before Him, in our own right, we stand naked. But in the robe of our Elder Brother, we are properly clothed for our presentation to the King.

PRAYER: *Clothe me, Lord, in Your righteousness. Amen.*

SATURDAY

Rock of Ages

When I soar to worlds unknown,
See Thee on Thy judgment throne

Romans 5:1, 2

Therefore, since we are justified by faith, we have peace with God through our Lord Jesus Christ. Through him we have obtained access to this grace in which we stand, and we rejoice in our hope of sharing the glory of God.

IN DR. BERNHARD ANDERSON'S book, *Rediscovery of the Bible,* there is presented in challenging form the thought of God's part in the destiny of history, the necessity of the long look, and a measuring stick of judgment that includes the good of all, and what is good from God's viewpoint. Our perception is earth-bound and material.

During the Lenten season we try to get a new sense of the eternal. We measure our lives anew in the light of the cross. One must have a single eye with a long look, to do this. When we stood in the refectory which houses DaVinci's "The Last Supper," and gazed at that matchless painting at the end of the room, our guide came to us and said, "Close one eye, and with your hand make a telescope with the other. Then focus that eye entirely on thc Lord. That is the only way to see the picture at its best." What a difference it made when we followed his instructions. Now it seemed as if the Christ were alive and talking.

For the eyes of the soul, these instructions hold, too. A singleness of eye, focused on the Lord is adequate preparation for launching out into the world's unknown.

We stood at Scala Sancta in Rome, and watched the succession of travelers kneel their way up those steps. At given intervals there are notations: "365 days of purgatory have been expiated," and so on. Our hearts were heavy as we watched people going through these motions, and thinking this was the way to eternal salvation. One man with crippled legs was going through agonies, pulling each one up. We recalled that it was at this spot where Luther's soul broke into open rebellion. From everything that he had read in Scripture, he knew that this could not be God's way. He recounted that salvation was not of works, lest any man should boast, and so he took his stand on the affirmation of Scripture that makes it possible for any one of us to stand before the judgment throne unafraid, because of Christ's gift to us. "Through him we have obtained access to this grace."

"Rock of ages, cleft for me,
Let me hide myself in Thee."

PRAYER: *For the Rock of our salvation, for Your free gift to us of everlasting life, we thank and bless You, Lord. To the ends of the earth, we would share this message of eternal hope. Amen.*

O Sacred Head, Now Wounded

Herzlich thut mich verlangen. 76, 76. D. HANS LEO HASSLER, 1601 and 1613.

2 How art Thou pale with anguish,
With sore abuse and scorn!
How does that visage languish,
Which once was bright as morn!
What Thou, my Lord, hast suffered,
Was all for sinners' gain;
Mine, mine was the transgression,
But Thine the deadly pain.

3 Lo, here I fall, my Saviour,
'Tis I deserve Thy place:
Look on me with Thy favor,
Vouchsafe to me Thy grace.
Receive me, my Redeemer;
My Shepherd, make me Thine,
Of every good the Fountain,
Thou art the Spring of mine!

4 What language shall I borrow
To thank Thee, dearest Friend,
For this Thy dying sorrow,
Thy pity without end!
O make me Thine forever,
And should I fainting be,
Lord, let me never, never,
Outlive my love to Thee.

5 Forbid that I should leave Thee;
O Jesus, leave not me;
In faith may I receive Thee,
When death shall set me free.
When strength and comfort languish,
And I must hence depart,
Release me then from anguish
By Thine own wounded heart.

Bernard of Clairvaux, (1091–1153).
Paul Gerhardt, 1653.

O Sacred Head, Now Wounded

With grief and shame weighed down

Isaiah 53:4, 5

Surely he has borne our griefs
and carried our sorrows;
yet we esteemed him stricken,
smitten by God, and afflicted.
But he was wounded for our transgressions,
he was bruised for our iniquities;
upon him was the chastisement that made us whole,
and with his stripes we are healed.

IN EVERYONE'S life there come times when you feel that no one can possibly understand the weight of your sorrow. You feel desperately, unutterably alone. Maybe it is an unconfessed sin, one that you hardly dare to acknowledge to yourself; maybe it is a hidden fear about a loved one, a suspicion of something about which you do not even want to think. These agonies of yours, as well as the weight that every soul carries—these were borne by the matchless sacred Head. Nevermore need you carry your burden alone. His head was bowed on Calvary's hill in order that He might forever be the "lifter up of your head." Prophetically the psalmist calls out:

Why are you cast down, O my soul,
and why are you disquieted within me?
Hope in God; for I shall again praise him,
my help and my God.

In the life of a Christian, then, there should never be moments of desperation. The moods of "throwing up your hands," and "tearing your hair," should become less and less frequent as your awareness of Christ's presence within you grows.

"And with his stripes we are healed!" From the challenging life of Adoniram Judson, the great missionary to Burma, there is the incident that has in it the human counterpart of what Christ did for us. Mr. Judson's servant was being tried in court for stealing. He was found guilty by the judge, who meted out fifteen whiplashings as punishment. Then Mr. Judson stepped forward and said: "Your honor, I am responsible for this man. Please let me take these lashings for him." So vividly did this illustrate for the servant the wonder of God's love in Jesus that Mr. Judson had for several years been trying to teach, that that servant became the first convert.

Lent is the time that in our hearts we take a new picture of that sacred Head, in order to keep in remembrance, that "with his stripes we are healed."

PRAYER: *We are overwhelmed, Lord, by the magnitude of Your love, and we are shamed by our small faith. Come into my life today with the priceless healing of Your presence. Amen.*

O Sacred Head, Now Wounded

Now scornfully surrounded

Isaiah 53:3

He was despised and rejected by men;
a man of sorrows, and acquainted with grief
and as one from whom men hide their faces
he was despised, and we esteemed him not.

ANYONE WHO has ever tried to give the Christian witness of faith knows a little about this being despised and rejected of men. This experience will be yours in greater measure, if you try to apply the teachings of the Lord to everyday life, to your community, to the world. Read about the great Christians of the ages, and you will read a succession of stories of rejected men and women, whose very sanity was questioned. Study the application of any Christian directive in any age, and you will find that the leaders with vision were often misunderstood and much-maligned people. It is in part the meaning of taking up a cross to follow Him; it is why nothing but a total commitment of devotion is sufficient.

This is not to say that you set out deliberately to antagonize people. On the contrary, the things that the Apostle Paul tells us we should "put on" as new creatures in Christ are the very virtues that should make for friends: kindness, mercy, forbearance, longsuffering, meekness, and so on. But it is also to be aware that following Christ is no bed of roses; that men will malign and misunderstand; that for every period of growth there will be pain.

How quick men are to say: "Where is your God?" Sometimes within our own family circle, if there are those who do not follow the Christ, we may have this invective flung at us. What comfort then it is to know that even through this kind of trial our Lord came, and so is sufficient to see us through.

Can you comprehend the things that they said about Him? They called His hand. "If thou art the son of God . . ." Scripture tells us they stuck out their lips, wagging their heads. How does anything you have ever had to take for His sake compare with that?

We need to beware of getting a martyr complex. In your own heart you know how easy this can be. It becomes an obnoxious stench, and can drive away those who may be seeking. Rather, the challenge of our daily walk should be one of gratitude for God's sufficiency, a constant awareness of our own sinfulness, an exuberant joy in the miracle of His using us as instruments of His love. This was the indomitable, unanswerable spirit of the disciples of the early church. Is it ours today?

PRAYER: *It was for me, Lord, that You were despised and rejected of men. Search out my heart, today, so that I do not become a part of the rejection. And so give me the grace of Your Holy Spirit, that I may with wisdom witness fearlessly and in love. In Your Name. Amen.*

TUESDAY

O Sacred Head, Now Wounded

With thorns Thine only crown

Matthew 27: 28, 29

And they stripped him and put a scarlet robe upon him, and plaiting a crown of thorns they put it on his head, and put a reed in his right hand. And kneeling before him they mocked him, saying, "Hail, King of the Jews!"

IN ONE of our Christmas hymns, we sing: "No more let thorns infest the ground." This really has a true Palestinian background, for there are few lands of equal size that have so many varieties of prickly plants. And it was to this land that the King of glory came! One section around Mt. Hermon has such an abundance of them that it has been given the name of "District of the Thorny Burnet." Certain varieties make impenetrable fences.

Thorns on the altars of Israel were evidences of sin. Micah spoke of wicked men as "worse than a horny hedge." Certain thorny herbs have needles which, when they get into a wayfarer's sandals, prove to be a real tribulation. To have nettles and thorns in a nomad's tent is a great source of woe, as Hosea 9: 6 declares. The torture crown of Christ may have been of the species *Calcotome illosa,* which is grown near Jerusalem. Crusaders identified it as Spina-Christ.

The little country of Palestine may well represent my heart, for here, too, is an area where the thorns of sin thrive. And every one of them was a part of that crown which pierced that noble brow. Remembering this with remorse and shame, I want to remember, too, that the thorns did form a crown. Even the ignominy of the material cannot obliterate the significance of this. In fact, the very material makes the crown more significant. A crown signifies a king, and power. In Christ, God's almighty power over my sins was forever revealed. It is my victory badge. The kingdom of my heart, where the thorns so quickly thrive and choke out the wheat, through the power given to me by this Monarch, can now be weeded out—daily. As you sing this strong beautiful hymn this week, even though it is written in a minor key, let there be in your singing the note of victory. The very crown of thorns is a part of it. There is no sin that He cannot conquer; there is no situation that you may have to face that is too difficult for Him. "And of his kingdom there shall be no end." Why, when you choose to follow Him, you are following the victor! Yes, the one who is victorious over any tribulation in this life as well as the life to come.

PRAYER: *Thank You, Lord, that You were willing to bear the crown of thorns. Reign now as King of my heart, and let there be such a victory in my living as to draw others into Your kingdom. In Your Name. Amen.*

O Sacred Head, Now Wounded

Once reigning in the highest
In light and majesty

Psalm 93: 1, 2

The Lord reigns; he is robed in majesty;
the Lord is robed, he is girded with strength.
Yea, the world is established; it shall never be moved;
thy throne is established from of old;
thou art from everlasting.

WHEN WE follow the story of the passion of our Lord, how often we forget that the One who was nailed to a cross is the same One who reigned and reigns over all the earth. The slivered cross seems a far cry from an omnipotent King who has the whole world in His hand. Yet in these facts is the wonder of Calvary; in this paradox is the greatest witness to God's love.

A Ballad of Wonder

My Lord came to me once a King
  A crown was on His hair.
I never knew that anything
  Could be so regal fair.
My Lord came to me once a King.
  I stopped my dream to stare.

My Lord came to me once a Child.
  His eyes were dark and wide.
He was so sweet and small and mild
  I dreamed I could have cried,
But when He looked at me, He smiled,
  And all my tears were dried.

My Lord came once—(Shall it be said
  I did but dream He came?)—
A crown of thorns was on His head,
  But in His heart a flame,
He came alone, unheralded,
  And signed me with His name.
I am no more the same.

Eleanor Slater

Yes, it is to wonder—a Babe in a manger, a man on a cross, a King of kings—such is the One who stands at the door of every human heart, seeking admission.

"I am no more the same."

PRAYER: *King of glory, so quickly do I forget who You are, and from whence You came! King though You are, You will dwell with me! Forgive me for ever keeping You outside the door! Forgive me for ever withholding any portion of my heart from You. Claim me as Your own, O King Eternal! Amen.*

O Sacred Head, Now Wounded

Dishonoured now Thou diest,
Yet here I worship Thee

Philippians 2:5-11

Have this mind among yourselves, which you have in Christ Jesus, who, though he was in the form of God, did not count equality with God a thing to be grasped, but emptied himself, taking the form of a servant, being born in the likeness of men. And being found in human form he humbled himself and became obedient unto death, even death on a cross. Therefore God has highly exalted him and bestowed on him the name which is above every name, that at the name of Jesus every knee should bow, in heaven and on earth and under the earth; and every tongue confess that Jesus Christ is Lord, to the glory of God the Father.

WHAT A pattern God has set for us to follow: "Have this mind among yourselves, which you have in Christ Jesus." In his line, "Dishonoured now Thou diest," the song writer takes us to the very root of this following for, if we are to live to Christ, we must die to self. Our own desires and ambitions we will be willing to crucify, in order to follow the Lord of love.

Christ's final step of victory was the cross. It just preceded the resurrection. As you think back over your life, what have been your greatest moments? Have they been moments of exaltation, when you have been lauded and men have spoken your praise? Have they been moments of physical pleasure, when your senses have been satisfied momentarily? Have they been moments when you have won an argument, or your ego is inflated? In my life, as I look back, often the "broken times" are the mountaintops spiritually. These are the times when, in my own inadequacy, my complete leaning has had to be on my Savior. In the life of our Lord the moment that seemed to be defeat was the moment of the greatest victory the world has ever known. Eternal Love suffered the ignominy of the cross, in order that from henceforth anyone who would look to the Crucified One might share in everlasting life.

But give heed to the next portion of the Apostle Paul's writing, "Therefore God has highly exalted him." Today, will you bring your adoration to Him? Even now as you are pausing in quietness, is there a sense of worship and wonder at His love for you? It will do something to your day, if this is the mood you will carry with you from these moments. For living gratitude puts a light in the eye, and a spring in the step, and tenderness to the hand, and lovingkindness on the lips.

PRAYER: *In the busyness of this day, O Lord, I would pause to pay my tribute to the "name which is above every name." So captivate my mind and heart that the fragrance of these moments of worship will permeate the whole day. In Jesus' Name. Amen.*

O Sacred Head, Now Wounded

What language shall I borrow
To thank Thee, dearest friend

2 Corinthians 9:11-15

You will be enriched in every way for great generosity, which through us will produce thanksgiving to God; for the rendering of this service not only supplies the wants of the saints but also overflows in many thanksgivings to God. Under the test of this service, you will glorify God by your obedience in acknowledging the gospel of Christ, and by the generosity of your contribution for them and for all others. . . . Thanks be to God for his inexpressible gift!"

SOMEONE HAS said, "Gratitude is the memory of the heart." There is no language like the language of our life to speak our thanks. In our day, more and more words have become ineffective because of our abuse of them. Hollywood has led us in the game of "super," "colossal," "gigantic," "surpassing all others" kind of vocabulary. Yet it is not alone in our age that there has been this feeling of the inadequacy of words. The Apostle Paul could not find superlatives enough in his vocabulary to express his gratitude for what Christ meant to him. Such phrases as, "exceeding abundantly," "more abundantly than all that we ask or think," "immeasurable greatness of his power," are an indication of his coming to the limit of his words. But his life was another thing! This springtime, this resurrection time, how much of the note of thanksgiving is there in your life?

Humans, like buckets, can be divided into two groups: The story is told of this bucket conversation on the way to the well. "How dismal you look," said one bucket to the other, as they were going to the well. "Ah," replied the other, "I was reflecting upon the uselessness of our being filled; for let us go away ever so filled, we always come back empty." "Dear me, how strange to look at it in that way!" said the other bucket. "Now, I enjoy the thought that, however empty we come, we always go away full."

Does the language of your living express the gratitude that you know for what Christ has done for you? What about your generosity in what you do for others, in the causes of the kingdom? What would this barometer indicate about the climate of your soul?

Martin Luther very succinctly has said: "So this is now the mark by which we all shall certainly know whether the birth of the Lord Jesus Christ is effective in us: If we take upon ourselves the need of our neighbors."

PRAYER: *Dear Lord, there are no words adequate enough to express my gratitude and love for what You have done for me. Let my living speak more loudly. In Jesus' name. Amen.*

O Sacred Head, Now Wounded

Lord, let me never, never
Outlive my love to Thee

Romans 8:35-37

Who shall separate us from the love of Christ? Shall tribulation, or distress, or persecution, or famine, or nakedness, or peril or sword? . . . No, in all these things we are more than conquerors through him who loved us. For I am sure that neither death, nor life, nor angels, nor principalities, nor things present, nor things to come, nor powers, nor height, nor depth, nor anything else in all creation, will be able to separate us from the love of God in Christ Jesus our Lord.

IT IS interesting to note that the hymn that is our choice for this week has shown in three different tongues with equal effect the wonder of God's great gift to us in the death of His Son, and our boundless indebtedness to Him. It was first written in Latin by the saintly Bernard of Clairvaux in the twelfth century; then, five centuries later, Paul Gerhardt, known as the greatest of all Lutheran hymnists, gave it a splendid translation into the German; and James Alexander of Princeton, gave us our classic English words. No theme has any right to be more universal than the one of Christ's love for us and our gratitude to Him. To have accompanying these words, music which Bach with his God-given genius took from a rather frivolous folksong and made into the medium of the "Passion Chorale," is to have a fitness of song that surely must have been born in heaven. For human hearts everywhere it is a vehicle for sharing the wonder of God's love.

In his book *The Story of Our Hymns,* Dr. E. E. Ryden relates the telling incident from the life of a missionary to India, Christian Schwartz. In 1798 he lay dying. His Indian friends gathered around his bed, and sang in their own Malabar tongue the last verses of the hymn. The dying missionary joined in the singing until his voice was silenced in death. "Lord, let me never, never, Outlive my love to Thee." Gloriously, triumphantly, his request was granted.

Paul lists some of the things that might well separate us from the love of Christ. Persecution, want, distress, evil powers—none of these, he says, nor anything else, can separate us from the love of God in Christ Jesus. Paul could speak from experience, as can countless people about the world today who are being compelled to endure many of these things rather than deny their Lord.

Sometimes I wonder if the subtle, respectable "other gods" are not more dangerous to a Christian than these more obvious difficulties. Prosperity, popularity, possessions, power, pleasures, pride—are some of these keeping you from giving an unqualified witness to the love of God in Christ Jesus?

PRAYER: *How long I live, Lord, is not important. How much I live for You, that is the question. Search my heart! In Jesus' name. Amen.*

I Know That My Redeemer Lives

Federal Street. L. M. HENRY KEMBLE OLIVER, 1832.

3 He lives, and grants me daily breath;
He lives, and I shall conquer death;
He lives my mansion to prepare;
He lives to bring me safely there.

4 He lives, all glory to His Name!
He lives, my Jesus, still the same;
O the sweet joy this sentence gives,
I know that my Redeemer lives!

Samuel Medley, 1775.

SUNDAY

I Know That My Redeemer Lives

What comfort this sweet sentence gives

Luke 24:38

And he said to them, "Why are you troubled, and why do questionings rise in your hearts? See my hands and my feet, that it is I myself; handle me, and see; for a spirit has not flesh and bones as you see that I have."

SUPPOSE EASTER had not been! Can your mind conceive the desolate prospect life would be without the Easter hope? Think of what winter would be without the promise of spring! Imagine experiencing night without the sure knowledge of a dawn to follow! Christ's resurrection from the dead was the great exclamation point of all history. The stone rolled away, the tomb empty, were the greatest news the world has ever heard. But, you ask, how can I know that Christ arose?

The disciples in their dullness and doubt asked the same question. And the Lord said to them, "Handle me, and see; for a spirit has not flesh and bones as you see that I have." He was sure that this doubt would eat away the joy of faith, and so He appeared to them several times and in different places. Thomas undoubtedly voiced the composite doubt of all ages when he said that, unless he could touch and feel, he would not believe. The Lord gave him this concrete opportunity, but also added, "Blessed are those who have not seen and yet believe."

From a historical viewpoint, we have contemporary historians like Josephus who attest to the fact of Christ's resurrection. And also from a historical viewpoint, a faith whose foundation was a basic lie could not revolutionize men's lives, nor would it spread to the ends of the earth. The tests of the things that are real are their permanence and their universality.

But there is a still more potent way of knowing the resurrection of the Lord. That is to live it in your own life. Test the truths that Christ taught; test them in the laboratory of life; test them for yourself, and then draw your own conclusion.

A dying Scotchman was asked "Have you a glimpse of glory now, my brother, that you are dying?" At such a question, he roused himself and said, "I'll have none of your glimpses now that I am dying. Why, I have had a full look at Him for forty years."

The power of Christ's resurrection is something for us to experience here and now. It is the power that conquers evil and brings hope to life again; it is the power that puts hate to rout, and causes love to grow. To have Christ living in you now is to know daily the joy of resurrection.

PRAYER: *We praise and adore You, Lord, for what Your resurrection means in our lives. We thank You that we may experience it firsthand, if we will but try You. Oh, give us grace and power to share the glory of this message around the world. In Your Name. Amen.*

MONDAY

I Know That My Redeemer Lives

He lives to bless me with His love

Luke 24:31, 32

And their eyes were opened and they recognized him. . . . They said to each other, "Did not our hearts burn within us while he talked to us on the road, while he opened to us the scriptures?"

John 15: 7, 9

"If you abide in me, and my words abide in you, ask whatever you will, and it shall be done for you."

"As the Father has loved me, so have I loved you; abide in my love."

TO WALK daily in the love of God is to live abundantly. Anyone who travels on the road with the Christ will have a burning heart. Why is it that so often our lives lack luster? Why is it that there are times in our lives when the tenor of them is a monotone, a daily repetition of tasks almost without meaning? Could it be that we have not exposed ourselves enough to the Redeemer?

Someone brought back from Germany a little phosphorescent matchsafe. One night in a company, he asked that all the lights be turned off that he might show his friends its magic. To his disappointment and chagrin, the matchsafe had no shine at all. He concluded that he had been swindled. The next day he examined the box more closely, and read the instructions: "If you wish me to shine, keep me in the sunlight." He followed the directions, put it out where the sun's rays could be absorbed, and then in a dark room, and found that it had a brilliant glow. In the Book of Jude we read, "Keep yourselves in the love of God." That is the recipe for burning hearts.

The redemptive love of Christ is often shown in the self-effacing love of His followers. It is only His resurrection power that can make us willing to forget our own comfort in order to ease another's pain.

A beautiful story comes to us from one of our mission fields. One of the missionaries was far from robust in health, and found it very exhausting to sit on the floor according to the natives' custom. She was used to the back support that we westerners have learned to lean upon. The love of one of her pupils was sensitive enough to be aware of the missionary's need. She glided behind her, and with her own body supported the body of her teacher, back to back. The pupil was afraid that the beloved teacher was not using the offered help enough, and so she whispered, "If you love me, lean hard!"

And the One who arose from the dead is saying to you, "If you love me, lean hard on my grace. It is sufficient."

PRAYER: *Words are so inadequate, Lord, to express our gratitude for the blessing of Your love. Always, as we have received it, we have had burning hearts. We would so expose ourselves to it that we might reflect in the lives of others something of the glow. In Jesus' name. Amen.*

TUESDAY

I Know That My Redeemer Lives

He lives to plead for me above

1 John 2:1, 2

My little children, I am writing this to you so that you may not sin; but if any one does sin, we have an advocate with the Father, Jesus Christ the righteous; and he is the expiation for our sins, and not for ours only but also for the sins of the whole world.

WHAT AN adequate Redeemer! Not only did He pay the price for our sins with His suffering and death, but He continues to follow through! He now pleads our cause before our Holy God.

Weekly, I teach a Bible Class at Occoquan, the District of Columbia's prison for women. As I have come to know the histories of some of the women there, I have found that there have been instances where they have been "framed" by crafty people; and because the lawyer appointed by the judge did not believe them, they have had to take sentences for crimes of which they were innocent. There was no adequate advocate standing by them to present their case.

Our resurrected Redeemer not only pleads our case with the Judge (and we are guilty), but He paid the fine and took the penalty on our behalf on that black Good Friday when He hung upon the cross. And now He lives to make intercession for us; that is, if we know Him.

John, the epistle writer, tells us how we may be sure that we know Him. He says: "If we keep his commandments. He who says 'I know him' but disobeys his commandments is a liar, and the truth is not in him; . . . he who says he abides in him ought to walk in the same way in which he walked."

In a large gathering of men, a preacher gave everybody a chance to give their objections to Christianity. The list was long and telling: "Church members are no better than others." "Their lives are inconsistent." "Yes," said the preacher, "that is true." "The ministers are no good," said another "Unhappily that is true, too," said the preacher. "There are hypocrites in the church," "The church is a rich man's club," and so on down the line went the accusations. When they were through, the pastor read off the whole list, then said, "Boys, you have objected to us pastors, to the church, to church members, and to other things, but you have not said one word against the Master!"

What kind of representative of Him are you?

PRAYER: *Forgive us, Lord, that too often our lives deny that we know You. Thank You that with infinite love and endless patience You plead our cause before God's throne, and make possible the forgiveness of our sins. In Jesus' name. Amen.*

I Know That My Redeemer Lives

He lives my hungry soul to feed

John 6:27, 33-35

"Do not labor for the food which perishes, but for the food which endures to eternal life, which the Son of man will give to you. . . . For the bread of God is that which comes down from heaven, and gives life to the world." They said to him, "Lord, give us this bread always." Jesus said to them, "I am the bread of life; he who comes to me shall not hunger, and he who believes in me shall never thirst."

IN EVERY country, throughout all ages, bread has been, and is, a mainstay of diet. In the Bible there are more than two hundred references to bread. The traditional Bible Land bread is the sort resembling stones in the Judean desert. It is flat and coarse, appetizing when fresh, and flabby when a day old. Taking the three measures of meal mentioned in Jesus' parable of the leaven, the housewife let it rise until its bulk was increased; then at the proper stage, she made it into flat loaves for her oven or sent it to the community baker. As we walked the streets of Jerusalem, we saw a young lad carrying a flat tray of raising bread dough on the top of his head. He must have been headed for the community baker. Unfortunately, the flies had discovered the rising dough, and for all the world it looked like raisin bread.

For the Passover and other feasts, unleavened bread was customary. Whichever kind it is, bread is a product in every land and with every people.

It is not to be wondered at, then, that the Lord used it as a symbol of what He is to humanity. The staff of life, the basic source of strength, that which supplies vigor—this is bread. And this is what He is to anybody who will receive Him.

As a woman, are you often overwhelmed by all the time you must spend in the preparation of food? The Lord warns us that there is a danger of laboring so for the bread that perishes that we will neglect the Bread which endures to eternal life. Is not this a real danger in the home? Mothers often spend themselves on the material well-being of their children to the place where they have little to offer in the way of spiritual nourishment. We need not neglect the one for the other; it is to keep the sense of eternal values straight.

How many times our children have come in and exclaimed at the fragrance of the home-baked bread that pervaded the house! So it is with those whose daily fare is the resurrected Bread of Life. In homes where He is shared, there is a fragrance!

PRAYER: *Bread of Life, thank You for the source of sustenance and strength You are to my soul. Thank You, that there is no hunger of the spirit for which You are not sufficient. Help me to labor for that which is eternal. In Your name. Amen.*

THURSDAY

I Know That My Redeemer Lives

He lives to help in time of need

Psalm 91:3-6

For he will deliver you from the snare of the fowler
  and from the deadly pestilence;
he will cover you with his pinions,
  and under his wings you will find refuge;
his faithfulness is a shield and buckler.
You will not fear the terror of the night,
  nor the arrow that flies by day,
nor the pestilence that stalks in darkness,
  nor the destruction that wastes at noonday.

THE ENTIRE Ninety-first Psalm is a glorious affirmation of what it means to have God as one's resource in time of need. It pleases the Lord that we should turn to Him, and believe that He will help us. An earthly father has a sense of joy when his children have enough confidence in him to ask his help. It is an evidence of a bond of love that exists between parent and child. So our heavenly Father rejoices that we have confidence in Him.

How many times do we fret and try to worry our own way out of some difficult situation! Our very fretting incapacitates us from getting a true perspective of the problem at hand, and from finding a solution. All the while, the crucified Savior is eager to help; is waiting for us to call upon Him. Those of us who have experienced His help again and again can testify to His skill in unraveling a snarled situation, or in lifting a fog when the sailing seemed hopeless. He lives to be our help in time of need! This is a part of the great gift of Easter.

In this same psalm we read, "For he will give his angels charge of you to guard you in all your ways." Have you known the ministering of these angels?

My husband had a beautiful experience in his visiting an old friend who had had a very critical operation. He paused at her bedside the day after to have a brief devotion. She was in pain, and told him how she had not been able to sleep or get any sense of rest. He paused at her bedside only long enough to speak this verse about the angels, and to pray a prayer that this might be her experience in the coming night. Because she was critically ill, he was at her bedside the next morning. Her greeting was unforgettable. "Pastor," she said, "you left the angels here last night. I had such a sense of their ministering that I knew relief from my distress, and sank into a wonderful sleep. Oh, I cannot be grateful enough!"

He lives to help you. Has yours been the rich experience of calling upon Him?

PRAYER: *Always when we have called upon You, Lord, You have answered and helped. Thank You that You stand waiting in whatever situation we find ourselves. Thank You that nothing is too hard for You. Teach us to lean upon You more each day. In Jesus' name. Amen.*

I Know That My Redeemer Lives

He lives and grants me daily breath

Ezekiel 37:5

"Thus says the Lord God to these bones: 'Behold, I will cause breath to enter you, and you shall live.'"

Acts 17:24, 25

"The God who made the world and everything in it, being Lord of heaven and earth, does not live in shrines made by man, nor is he served by human hands, as though he needed anything, since he himself gives to all men life and breath and everything."

HAVE YOU paused today to thank God for the gift of breathing? I dare say that it is one of the many things that you and I take for granted. Yet, if you have ever had to struggle for your breath, and have known anything of the agony of feeling that it just is not there, you will also be aware of the gratitude that we should show to God for daily breath. That in the beginning He should have breathed into us His own breath is a thought that should fill us with an overwhelming sense of His love. That the daily miracle of lungs which contract and expand and are a part of the entire complicated mechanism of our bodies is evidence of His constant care, should make us want to fall down and worship Him. It might be well for us at this moment to pause and thank Him for the gift of breathing. That the Lord has provided a filter through the nose to keep out things which cause infection; that the lung area, if stretched out, would measure two thousand square feet, yet the Creator has been able to compact it in a sponge-like organ so that it can be contained in a small portion of our bodies—all of this should fill us with wonder and gratitude for the daily gift of breathing.

But just to breathe is not really living, unless you comprehend the total mechanism of breathing. It has two parts: inspiration and expiration. Inspiration is a complicated process. An order is sent to the brain from the diaphragm, and it becomes flattened. This acts like a suction pump. The amount of room in the chest is increased, and the air from the outside is sucked in. The brain, which governs the whole process, sends an order down to the voice box, so that a wide opening is made there between the vocal chords for the air to pass through. Expiration, or breathing out, is quite different. When there are no obstructions, it is done with ease.

How little of all this intricate mechanism my lay mind can understand! Yet the overwhelming miracle of it we so quickly take for granted. The resurrected Lord daily gives me breath. He would also breathe into my soul each day the breath of eternity, the sweet fragrance of His presence. Then from my life He has a right to expect the concomitant expiration of His love into the lives of others.

PRAYER: *For the miracle of life, Lord, for the daily breath which enables us to share in the work of this world, we thank You. Keep the lungs of our souls filled with the breath of heaven. In Jesus' name. Amen.*

I Know That My Redeemer Lives

He lives my mansion to prepare

John 14:1-3

"Let not your hearts be troubled; believe in God, believe also in me. In my Father's house are many rooms; if it were not so, would I have told you that I go to prepare a place for you? And when I go and prepare a place for you, I will come again and will take you to myself, that where I am you may be also."

2 Corinthians 5:1

For we know that if the earthly tent we live in is destroyed, we have a building from God, a house not made with hands, eternal in the heavens.

IN THE King James' translation of these first verses of John 14 the word mansions is used instead of rooms. Dr. Phillips' translation makes it sound as if the Lord were right in the room talking to us. "It is true that I am going away to get a place ready for you, but it is just as true that I am coming again to welcome you into My own home, so that you may be where I am. You know where I am going and You know the road I am going to take."

Jesus is preparing a home for us. What a home that will be! All the interior decorators in the world will stand in awe before His handiwork. He who made the galaxy of stars, who takes the backdrop of a sunset to glorify a day, who can cause weeds and shrubs and rushes to come alive with His touch; He who conceived a pansy face, and a branch of dogwood, orchids, and roses, dandelions, and daisies—what a home He will prepare!

How much is there of this anticipation in your attitude to the life hereafter? Does the tone of your daily living evidence that this is the home to which you are going? Is there such a note of faith as to your prospect that others will want to seek it, too? Are you able to witness to them that your security is not in anything that you have done, but only in Christ's completed work of salvation on the cross—so that your homegoing is not a "maybe" or "I hope so," but is sure through faith in Him?

What a foretaste of heaven is a home where Christ lives! What memories are made as He shares!

An old Scotch minister was disturbed because he feared death and so was powerless to comfort others. Toward the end of his life he moved. Yet when the furniture had all gone, the old preacher lingered in the home where his children had been born and where his sermons had been prepared. At last his servant came to him and said, "Sir, everything's gone; and the new house is better than this one. Come away." This preached to him a lesson he never forgot. God has prepared for his children a home "much better than this one."

PRAYER: *We lift our hearts in adoration, Lord, for Your wonderful plans for us. In our daily living, let there be the joy of that anticipation. In the name of our Redeemer, because of whom this anticipation is possible. Amen.*

More Love to Thee, O Christ

2 Once earthly joy I craved,
Sought peace and rest;
Now Thee alone I seek,
Give what is best;
This all my prayer shall be,
More love. O Christ, to Thee,
More love to Thee.

3 Then shall my latest breath
Whisper Thy praise;
This be the parting cry
My heart shall raise;
This still its prayer shall be,
More love, O Christ, to Thee,
More love to Thee.

Elizabeth Prentis.

SUNDAY

More Love to Thee, O Christ

Hear Thou the prayer I make

Deuteronomy 10:12-16

"And now, Israel, what does the Lord your God require of you, but to fear the Lord your God, to walk in all his ways, to love him, to serve the Lord your God with all your heart and with all your soul, and to keep the commandments and statutes of the Lord, which I command you this day for your good? Behold, to the Lord your God belong heaven and the heaven of heavens, the earth with all that is in it; yet the Lord set his heart in love upon your fathers and chose their descendants after them, you above all peoples, as at this day. Circumcise therefore the foreskin of your heart, and be no longer stubborn."

IF EACH morning of these next seven days we pray as a prayer the words of this hymn, this will be a rich week, and the Holy Spirit will find new access to our hearts. Are you willing to go on such an adventure? It will mean that the Lord's requirements of us will daily become more clear; it will mean that this love which He asks of us will grow and bear fruit. Is that what you earnestly want in your heart?

The condition of the asking is made pointed in the first verse of our hymn, "on bended knee."

The bended knee is not so much a physical posture, (although that can be very helpful in keeping the focus of our attention on the One to whom we are praying) as it is a condition of the heart. As to the physical posture of prayer, the Bible speaks of several different ones. Besides the numerous references to kneeling, we are told of bowing, of being on the face before God, and of standing. It is the matter of the heart's attitude that is the key. Our Scripture points this up in a rather shocking figure to a modest mind. Yet it strongly illustrates this "bended knee" attitude that is essential to effective prayer. "Circumcise therefore the foreskin of your heart, and be no longer stubborn."

The devil works overtime to get us to resist God. And he does it in some of the most subtle ways. Refusal to acknowledge sin, harboring resentment and envy, being subject to touchy feelings, wallowing in hurt pride, thinking in terms of selfishness and our own wills—these are some of the devices he uses. The devil has no time for bended knees when they are an evidence of a broken and a contrite heart. "And be no longer stubborn" is a word that I need every day.

Man-like is it to fall into sin,
Fiend-like is it to dwell therein,
Christ-like is it for sin to grieve,
God-like is it all sin to leave.

FRIEDRICH VON LOGAN

PRAYER: *Bend the stiffness of my heart, O Lord, so that I will be open to Your love. Reveal the areas of resistance in my life. I want more love to Thee. In Jesus' name. Amen.*

More Love to Thee, O Christ

Once earthly joy I craved

1 Samuel 12:21

"And do not turn aside after vain things which cannot profit or save, for they are vain."

Isaiah 55:2

"Why do you spend your money for that which is not bread, and your labor for that which does not satisfy?"

UNDOUBTEDLY THE honest confession of the heart of any one of us would be that "once earthly joy we craved." Perhaps even at this point in our lives there may lurk some of this craving. Today let us take a look at those things that the world holds dear; those will-o'-the-wisps for which countless millions are striving.

Which one of us would not like to have a million dollars at his disposal? And, of course, we talk glibly about all the good we would do. But would we? The Lord knew the temptation of riches when He spoke about the needle's eye. Yet Scripture gives us to know that riches can be used to the glory of God, and all of us know people who have so dedicated their means. After all, there is no virtue in just being poor; it is the importance that wealth plays in our life that is the criterion.

Which one of us does not want to be liked and admired? And what price some people are willing to pay for this fleeting sensation! In the Book of Acts we read that it is better to be a God pleaser than a man pleaser. Yet how many of us mothers have not sacrificed everything that our children might be popular. Surely this is behind the distorted sense of values in many homes where dancing lessons are much more important than anything connected with the church, Christ's body here on earth. Often young people, and older ones, too, will compromise their moral standards to be what they believe is popular.

Or there is outward appearance. Is there any woman who has not had the secret longing in her heart at some time or another to be the winner at a beauty pageant? And what agonies women will go to, to try to erase wrinkles, or make their bodies conform to the fashion line!

Have you known the battle of this earthly craving in some line or other? Has the satisfying of such a craving ever brought you any lasting joy?

PRAYER: *Forgive, O God, my blindness in counting as of value many things which are only for the moment. Thieves break through and moth and rust corrupt so many of the things for which I have spent myself. The praise of men is fickle, and the wealth of the world is as shifting sand. Help me today to give to You these earthly things that I have craved. In Jesus' name. Amen.*

More Love to Thee, O Christ

Sought peace and rest

Jeremiah 8:10, 11

"From the least to the greatest every one is greedy for unjust gain; from prophet to priest every one deals falsely. They have healed the wound of my people lightly, saying, 'Peace, peace,' when there is no peace."

Isaiah 59:8

The way of peace they know not, and there is no justice in their paths; they have made their roads crooked, no one who goes in them knows peace.

PERHAPS THERE is no word that haunts the minds and hearts of men more today than the elusive "peace." As nations and as individuals, we have this longing for peace. The increasing number of suicides attest to the blind alley down which so many travel. The abundance of literature on peace of mind is a witness to a need and a longing. The tragedy is that people will not accept the only path to peace. They will try every other method and become disillusioned, and often while so doing will pass right by the Prince of Peace with His outstretched hands.

It seems to me that this same futile search for peace in the manufacturing of devastating military weapons is the wrong track on which our world is running today. Peace is something that is manufactured in the heart of God, and only as we become a part of that Great Heart, whose product is forgiving love, can we know peace.

The great Indian Christian, Sadhu Sundar Singh, who found his peace of soul as he renounced the world to follow his Christ, tells the following story: As he was crossing the mountains, he met a girl of good family. She was on a pilgrimage, and her bare feet were bleeding. In answer to his question she said, "I am looking for rest and peace, and I hope to get them before I get to the end of this pilgrimage. If I do not, I shall drown myself." How strange it is that people who are born Christians, and have these gifts without taking all this trouble, should care so little for them, while this wealthy girl had given up her home and all that she cared most for to seek salvation. She did not find peace on that pilgrimage, but she met a missionary who told her about Christ. When Sadhu Sundar Singh saw her again, she told him that she had found all and more than she sought. "Men may kill me," she said, "if they like. I have found the better part that shall never be taken away from me."

Has your heart been longing for peace and rest? The labyrinthian ways of the world are not the answer; drowning yourself in forgetfulness will not bring it; earthly joys are not the answer—but there is One! More of Him, tomorrow.

PRAYER: *You know this longing in my heart for peace, Lord. Direct it until I find my peace in Your forgiving love. In Jesus' name. Amen.*

More Love to Thee, O Christ

Now Thee alone I seek

John 6:68, 69

Simon Peter answered him; "Lord, to whom shall we go? You have the words of eternal life; and we have believed, and have come to know, that you are the Holy One of God."

IT IS that simple—Christ is our peace. When we give up all the struggling and all the trying to work our own way out, and are weary unto death, there He is, the fulfillment of all that we were seeking, and more. As we turn our eyes to Jesus, and permit His presence to flood our hearts, He supplies the peace and rest for which we had been seeking. An unknown poet has expressed it simply:

I cannot think but God must know
About the thing I long for so;
I know He is so good and kind,
I cannot think but He will find
Some way to help, some way to show
Me to the thing I long for so.

One of my unforgettable childhood memories is of the time that I told my mother a lie. She had made a fresh chocolate cake with "gooey" frosting, and had told me not to touch it while she went to the store. But a little voice inside of me continued to tempt me, and I started to run my finger along the edge of the plate to scoop up some of that frosting. In climbing to get myself in better position for this operation, I knocked down a favorite blue cream pitcher. Quickly I forgot all about the frosting, and gathered up the broken pieces of the pitcher to dispose of them, so there would be no tell-tale evidence. When my mother came home, she was going to make some coffee for a friend, and looked for her cream pitcher. Not finding it, she asked me if I had seen it. Glibly I lied; then I tried to drown my disturbed conscience by doing any number of "covering" things. I jumped rope faster and harder than ever before; I sang to myself; I hop scotched; but all to no avail. But the voice of conscience inside of me grew louder and louder, until I wanted to scream. Then I flung myself into the house and into my mother's arms and sobbed out my guilt, and asked for forgiveness. Never shall I forget the feeling of her strong arms around me, and her forgiving love enfolding me. That experience as a child, was a foretaste of what my soul would know as it found its forgiveness in Christ, and knew the peace of resting in His everlasting arms.

PRAYER: *Call us home to Your heart, O Christ, from our devious paths. Daily teach us that our rest is to be found in Your forgiving love. Give us such oneness of purpose that others will see the joy of following You. Amen.*

More Love to Thee, O Christ

Give what is best

Matthew 7:7-11

"Ask, and it will be given you; seek and you will find; knock and it will be opened to you. For every one who asks receives, and he who seeks finds, and to him who knocks it will be opened. Or what man of you, if his son asks him for a loaf, will give him a stone? Or if he asks for a fish, will give him a serpent? If you then, who are evil, know how to give good gifts to your children, how much more will your Father who is in heaven give good things to those who ask him?"

THE LORD'S use of illustrations right from out our everyday lives has always been a source of comfort to me. In this portion He is talking to fathers who are fishermen. He calls to their minds the times their children have been hungry, and have asked for bread. Would anyone of them give their children stones, He asks, when they needed bread? Or again, when they pulled in their nets full of fish, and their little ones came running to ask for the fish that were too small for them to sell, which one of them would give his child the serpent that had been caught in the net instead of the fish? Then our Lord really drives the nail home. If human fathers know how to give what is good for their children, how much more will not our heavenly Father give good gifts to those who ask for them?

When the song writer makes his petition, "Give what is best," it is preceded by the prayer, "More love to Thee, O Christ." Trust is born of love; the more we love God, the more we will trust Him, the more we will be sure that His will is best. The wonderful part of this trust, too, is that it is the very source of peace, and God's bank has never gone bankrupt. It is not so with us humans. In the state of Pennsylvania there was a man, eighty years of age, who went to a city in which many years before he had invested some three thousand dollars in a bank. Now he wished to withdraw fifty dollars. Imagine his consternation on learning that the bank had failed eleven years ago, and all his life savings had been swept away. It is never so with God. It can be truly said of Him that His resources never fail.

Not only are God's resources endless, but His wisdom is perfect. How often we forget this, and want to superimpose our human wants. If our child asked for a razor, we certainly would not give it to him, knowing that it might be the means of his hurting himself. Often our children ask for more candy than is good for them. As wise parents, we deny their request, knowing that by so doing we will be saving their teeth. In the same way, often our Heavenly Father must deny us things that we think we would like, because He knows they would work to our harm.

PRAYER: *Dear Lord, help me so to grow in my love for You, that daily I will trust You to give what is best. You have so wonderfully blessed my life, and I thank You. In Jesus' name. Amen.*

More Love to Thee, O Christ

**Then shall my latest breath
Whisper Thy praise**

1 Peter 2:9

But you are a chosen race, a royal priesthood, a holy nation, God's own people, that you may declare the wonderful deeds of him who called you out of darkness into his marvelous light.

Psalm 35:28

Then my tongue shall tell of thy righteousness and of thy praise all the day long.

ONE SENSES, as one makes this hymn one's own, that it must have been born out of a great need. Such is the case. Elizabeth Payson Prentiss, the author, was blessed with an unusually fine home. Her father, a clergyman, was a man of deep faith. Her own home, too, which was established later, was a very happy one. However, all through her life, she bore the affliction of a body that was not well. Nevertheless, through her physical pain, her spirits rose, and daily became more radiant and beautiful. She became famous for a story she wrote entitled: "Stepping Heavenward." She said the purpose of the book was for the strengthening and comforting of other souls. Something of the outflowering of the mood of the hymn is to be found in her words: "To love Christ more is the deepest need, the constant cry of my soul. . . . Out in the woods and on my bed, and out driving, when I am busy and happy, when I am sad and idle, the whisper keeps going up for more love, more love, more love!"

In our experience we have often found that it is not so often those who have so many obvious blessings that are quickest in their praise of their Lord. Rather, it is those on beds of illness, or others that are going through trials, that most readily witness to His sustaining love. As I write this there comes to my mind the little ninety-three-year-old lady in the Washington Home for the Incurables. She had a stroke two years ago, and has had a completely paralyzed left side since then. Yet such is the radiance that glows from that room, that our young people vie with one another for the privilege of visiting her. Why is this? Because Hulda uses every opportunity to whisper His praise. And often her voice is not much more than a whisper. At ninety-three she has taken to writing poetry whose entire theme is gratitude and praise to God. From her little face there is the radiance of one who has trusted her Master to give what is best, who can only speak of the marvels of His love as she knows it in her Savior, and withal the joyous anticipation of her journey home, when she will be with Him forever. Is this same spirit of adoration and gratitude your first thought in the morning and your last thought at night?

PRAYER: *I would praise You, Lord, for Your bounteous love to me. Forgive me for the whining times. Let there be such a note of victorious exaltation in my living that each day will show forth Your praise. In Jesus' name. Amen.*

SATURDAY

More Love to Thee, O Christ

This still its prayer shall be
More love, O Christ, to Thee

John 21:15-17

When they had finished breakfast, Jesus said to Simon Peter, "Simon, son of John, do you love me more than these?" He said to him, "Yes, Lord; you know that I love you." He said to him, "Feed my lambs." A second time he said to him, "Simon, son of John, do you love me?" He said to him, "Yes, Lord; you know that I love you." He said to him, "Tend my sheep." He said to him the third time, "Simon, son of John, do you love me?" . . . And he said to him, "Lord, you know everything; you know that I love you." Jesus said to him, "Feed my sheep."

WHICH ONE of us does not like to be told again and again that we are loved? A husband and wife relationship is kept warm and vibrant with sincere repetition of the declaration of love. A parent and child experience is enriched and grows with the expression of love one for the other. When did you last tell the folks in your family circle that you love them? There is another Father who desires to hear His children speak of their love for Him. So many of our prayers are filled with our petitions, our wants, and our needs. It must be like sweet music in the ears of God to have a child simply declare his love without asking for something.

I can remember the system we used when at college. A letter would be full of gratitude for the kind of parents we had and all that they did for us. Then after the signature, there would be the significant postscript: "P.S. I'm broke." Our prayer song this week calls for something over and beyond such an expression of love.

Adolphe Monod, a famous French evangelist of the middle of the nineteenth century, made this significant statement shortly before he died in 1856: "I have strength for nothing more than to think of the love of God; He has loved us—that is the whole of dogmatics; let us love Him—that is the sum total of the ethics of the Gospel."

Three times the Lord asked Peter to reiterate his love. Were these to erase the threefold denial? Daily we deny Him in some fashion or another. Do we daily declare our love? So we must do, if we would get firsthand our marching orders.

The following verse was found by the writer of our hymn on the flyleaf of one of her favorite books:

One hour with Jesus! How its peace outweighs
The lavishment of earthly peace and praise;
How dearer far, emptied of self to lie
Low at His feet, and catch, perchance, His eye,
Alike content when He may give or take,
The sweet, the bitter, welcome for His sake.

PRAYER: *Take the love of my heart, this day, Lord. Each day I pray that it might increase. You know that I love You. For Jesus' sake. Amen.*

This Is My Father's World

Maltbie D. Babcock, 1901

Traditional English melody
Arr. by Franklin L. Sheppard, 1915

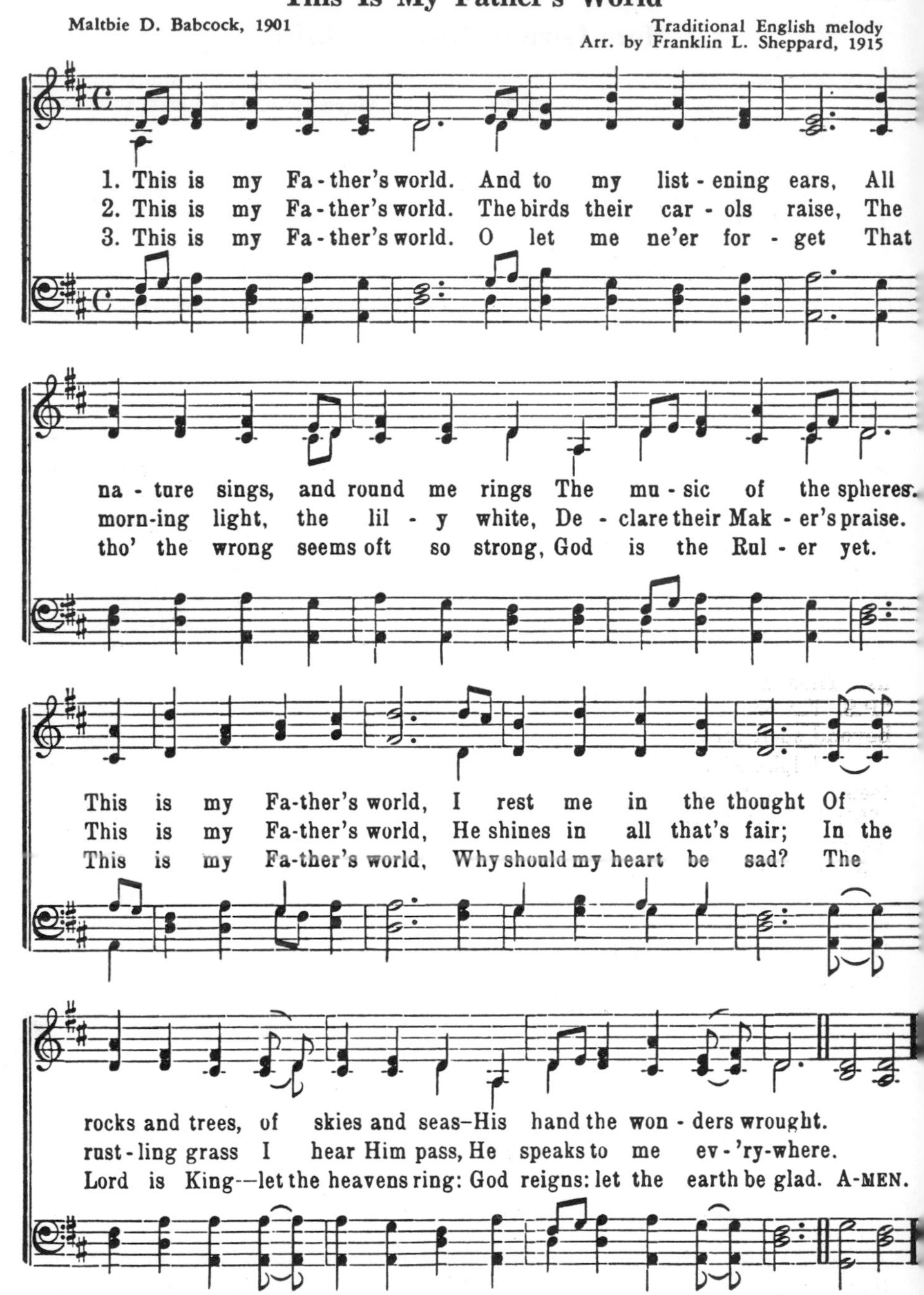

This Is My Father's World

Nehemiah 9:6

"Thou art the Lord, thou alone; thou hast made heaven, the heaven of heavens, with all their host, the earth and all that is on it, the seas and all that is in them; and thou preservest all of them; and the host of heaven worships thee."

HOW VERY much we take for granted in the world about us! When you think of the discoveries and inventions that we have witnessed in our lifetime, and then are aware that this power in nature was there all the time, you realize how little we know and appreciate the wonderful world that the Lord has made. Surely there is no better time than the spring of the year in which to be aware of the glory of creation, and the loving hand that formed the delicate beauty of a cherry blossom, as well as the majesty of a snow-capped mountain.

There is healing for our souls in this contemplation. It gives us a sense of certainty in a world of loose moorings and fear. The things of God are changeless: the stars in their course; day and night; birth and death; seed time and harvest—these are all a part of His eternal plan. Your soul will be strengthened, if daily you remember this. God has made the world and us and as Nehemiah says, He preserves all of them.

But there is something more personal that the hymn writer suggests than just the wonder and strengthening that comes from the knowledge of God's creation. Notice the personal pronoun, "my." And then pause at the intimate term, "father." "This is my Father's world." And because I am His child and His heir, I have a part in its possession. The sunrise and the sunset are mine; the fragrance of lilac and lily of the valley is something I need not purchase in a perfumery; the beauty all about me—is *mine.*

This day, then, in gratitude to God, let us give thanks for the immeasurable wealth that is ours in God's beautiful world. Let us pray for sensitive eyes and discerning hearts and minds, so that we may be more aware of the beauty all about us. Let us pause before a bud, or stop to enjoy the exquisite tracery that young green leaves make against a spring sky. You go on your own treasure hunt today, and then share your discovery with your family and with your friends. And tonight, before you close your eyes in sleep, call forth in panoramic array the pictures, one by one, of God's beautiful world—and yours.

PRAYER: *Thank You, Father, for the indescribable beauty of Your world. Thank You that it is mine to enjoy. Thank You that You are such a loving Father. In Jesus' name. Amen.*

This Is My Father's World

And to each listening ear,
All nature sings

Psalm 65:12, 13

The pastures of the wilderness drip,
the hills gird themselves with joy,
the meadows clothe themselves with flocks,
the valleys deck themselves with grain,
they shout and sing together for joy.

POETS THROUGH the ages have told of the music that is to be found in nature. It is Wordsworth who gives us this descriptive picture of the music of the ocean:

Listen, the mighty being is awake,
And doth with his eternal motion
Make a sound like thunder everlasting.

Have you not stood on a seashore and heard this rhythmic diapason of God's great water organ?

Or maybe the musical quality you like the best is the soughing of the winds in the pine trees; or the gentle dripping of rain on leaves. In all of nature the listening ear finds "the joy-of-being-created" sounds that are as natural to creation as breathing. It is the symphony of praise rendered to the Creator.

However, the song writer rightly stipulates that it is to the listening ear that all nature sings. Many people do not really hear music because they have not trained their ear; and many souls do not know the joy of the inner song because their ears cannot hear the music of God.

The story is told of a great naturalist who was walking down a busy New York street with a friend. All at once the scientist paused and said, "Listen!" The friend stopped, but all that he could hear was the usual rumble of traffic, and screeching of brakes, and scuffling of feet on pavement. The student of nature, however, amidst all this uproar, had heard the chirping of a little cricket, and by following his ear, had been able to locate the little insect, in a crevice between two buildings.

What do you hear? To what sounds is your ear sensitive? Is it quick to pick up the rejoicing, and slow to record the moaning? You are a blank record in the Creator's hand; you determine what shall be passed on of what you hear. Listen today for the singing of God's creation; eliminate the static of pressured living, and pass on to another soul the message of the serenity of God.

PRAYER: *So often, Lord, my ears have been clogged with the sound of wheels, and the jangle of coins. Give me listening ears to the beauty all about, and help me to pass this recording along to others. In Jesus' name. Amen.*

This Is My Father's World

I rest me in the thought
Of rocks and trees, of skies and seas;
His hand the wonders wrought

Psalm 96:11-13

Let the heavens be glad, and let the earth rejoice;
let the sea roar, and all that fills it;
let the field exult, and everything in it!
Then shall all the trees of the wood sing for joy
before the Lord, for he comes,
for he comes to judge the earth.
He will judge the world with righteousness,
and the peoples with his truth.

THE BIBLE is constantly using the figures of nature to express spiritual qualities. How often is not the Lord spoken of as a rock, and how many times is our thinking directed to the heavens! However, perhaps it is the tree that has played the most important part, for it was on a tree that the Lord of heaven gave the signature of His love to the world. It is significant then that in Job 14:7 we read "For there is hope for a tree, if it be cut down, that it will sprout again, and that its shoots will not cease." Then we are told that, though the root grows old in the earth and its stump dies, yet it may put forth branches like a young plant. Eternity is in a tree.

This was very vividly brought home to us when we walked through the garden that might have been Gethsemane. The gnarled old olive tree had roots that could well have belonged to the trees that were kind to our Lord. It was the fruit of a tree in the heart of the Garden of Eden that Satan used as a bait to tempt man, and it is the "fruit" of the tree on the hill of Golgotha that gives life everlasting.

Do the things of nature speak to you about eternity? All about us there are evidences of the wonders of God's handiwork. Do you see them? Every rock should remind us of the strength and certainty of our Lord. And every tree is a reminder not only of what the Lord has done for us, but also of what He expects of us. The Bible tells us that a man who does not walk in the council of the ungodly shall be like a tree planted by the rivers of waters. It further teaches us that you can tell what kind a tree is by its fruit.

Someone has said that every tree has a voice of its own. The oak roars, the beech shrieks, the elm has a deep groan, the ash moans, the pine whistles, the birch sighs, the mulberry sings, and the willow weeps. What kind of music does your life add to the great choir of nature?

PRAYER: *From the beauty about me, Lord, from the wonder of Your handiwork let me learn the lessons of eternity. Help me to see in all creation the glory of the Creator. In Jesus' name. Amen.*

This Is My Father's World

The birds their carols raise

Song of Solomon 2:11,12

"For lo, the winter is past,
the rain is over and gone.
The flowers appear on the earth,
the time of singing has come,
and the voice of the turtledove
is heard in our land."

WHAT HAUNTINGLY desolate places are forests where there are no birds! And who has not wondered at the beauty of sound that can be produced by a little feathered friend sitting on a branch. Even as I write this, from out the big oak tree in our back yard, there goes forth the call to a mate, and from another tree, there comes the answer. I am the eavesdropper! Yes, it is the time of the singing of the birds! You and I must acknowledge that this is our Father's world when we observe His wonderful providence even for every sparrow. It was to highlight faith in God's awareness and care that Jesus called attention to the sparrow. Is it to be wondered at that the little creatures pour out their adoration in song to such a God?

The arctic tern is a case in point as to the wonder of God's way with a bird. Flying thousands of miles over water, the feathered flier, newly hatched from its nest, unerringly makes its way to its destination, and without a visible compass.

From the stories of the Egyptians we learn that they believed that in the flight of a bird there well might be the passage of some mortal soul to its eternal home. The hoopoe they venerated because they felt that it eavesdropped on their secrets and would reveal them. From this has come our phrase, "A little bird told me!"

In the spring of this year, there is something that the birds would tell you. It is a message of faith and serenity even through the storms; it is the challenge to sing of the beauty of the earth and the wonder of God's love. It is to remind you that a song sung from the heart finds a sounding board in the heart of another. This day, as you give ear to the song of the birds, will you in turn sing a song of faith? A Christian philosopher of India has put beautifully into figure language the lesson of faith that there is in nature about us:

As a little bird flies into the leafy vastness of a tree,
As a little rivulet flows into the swelling vastness of a sea,
As a little seed sinks into the spreading vastness of the earth,
Lord, let me come to Thee.

PRAYER: *Lord give me ears to hear the music that is all about in Your beautiful world, and give me lips that will pass it on. In Jesus' name. Amen.*

This Is My Father's World

The morning light, the lily white
Declare their maker's praise

Matthew 6:28, 29

"And why are you anxious about clothing? Consider the lilies of the field, how they grow; they neither toil nor spin; yet I tell you, even Solomon in all his glory was not arrayed like one of these."

WHAT WOULD it be like to have the morning hours come and have no accompanying light? The dawn of each new day is a witness to the faithfulness and love of our Creator. Do you remember each day, as you awaken to a new morning, to thank Him for this gift? Too many of us have "alarm-clock" nerves and "early morning" dispositions! The cure for such afflictions is to greet each new day with a sense of gratitude for the gift of it, and the concomitant remembrance that God has promised that, no matter how difficult the tasks of the day, His grace will be sufficient for them.

"So up and away, for this is your day!"

Not only does the morning light witness to the constancy of God's love, but every flower that you see speaks of His providence. The lily white—from a brown bulb; the yellow, white, and purple crocuses pushing through the ground; a cherry tree in bloom—what a style show! Where is there beauty comparable to this? The Lord really takes us to task for our mundane worrying about clothes and the like, when He calls attention to the beauty of the flowers, and suggests that if God so clothes the lily of the field, should He not the more take care of us? Would He justifiably be able to say to you: "O you of little faith"?

The song writer uses the words: "In the rustling grass, I hear Him pass . . ." This calls to mind the unconscious witness that you and I ought to be to His presence within us.

A poet has said:

Who has seen the wind?
Neither you nor I;
But when the trees bow down their heads
The wind is passing by.

Is the spirit of your everyday living: the way you greet each new day; the way you trust the Lord for provisions; the way you acknowledge His sufficiency for whatever you may have to meet; in all of these is it a witness to others that this is your Father's world, and that He dwells in you?

PRAYER: *Give me grace each morning new, Lord, to take the day out of Your good hand. Help me to be reminded by every blossom, that You care and provide; and please, Lord, let others see in me the witness of Your presence. In Jesus' name. Amen.*

This Is My Father's World

O let me ne'er forget
That though the wrong seems oft so strong
God is the ruler yet

2 Corinthians 2:14

But thanks be to God, who in Christ always leads us in triumph, and through us spreads the fragrance of the knowledge of him everywhere.

2 Corinthians 4:16, 17

"So we do not lose heart . . . . For this slight momentary affliction is preparing for us an eternal weight of glory beyond all comparison.

IN A Christian's life, there are often times of discouragement when it seems that it is the wicked who prosper and the causes of righteousness that are defeated. But our perspective is very short, and our sense of timing is impatient. The Apostle Paul offers thanks to God who *always* leads us in triumph through Christ, and uses us in turn to spread this fragrance of victory wherever we go. Again in Corinthians he speaks of slight, momentary afflictions as compared with the glory of eternity. It is this perspective that we need more of in our Christian living. In a world of tribulation, we should be the ones sounding the note of victory and hope to the rest of the earth, because we follow the One who was able to say, "Be of good cheer, I have overcome the world."

Is the spirit of your every day one of optimism, built on the solid rock of faith in God's ultimate victory, and rooted in His promises which you have tried? Do your associates, your family, enjoy having you around because you breathe hope and assurance? Such can be the gift you share, if you build on the promises of God. A shifting, doubting, uncertain world today needs such a witness desperately.

The story is told of an old man who was visited by the minister. He was so crippled with rheumatism, that he was unable to move out of his chair except as someone would help him. He had his Bible open in front of him. The pastor noticed that the word "proved" was written often in the margin. Fingering through, he found such passages as "God is our refuge and strength, a very present help in trouble," and there in the margin was "proved." Again there was the passage, "This poor man cried, and the Lord heard him and delivered him out of all his troubles," and there again in the margin was "proved." And so on through the whole Book. The man's spiritual biography was contained in those marginal notes.

PRAYER: *Let there be a note of victory in my living, Lord, that will speak of Your power and love; that will witness to Your conquering of even the final enemy, death. Help me daily to speak a word of hope to others. In Jesus' name. Amen.*

This Is My Father's World

Why should my heart be sad?
God reigns: let the earth be glad

Philippians 4:4, 5

Rejoice in the Lord always; again I will say, Rejoice. Let all men know your forbearance. The Lord is at hand.

IT WOULD be a wonderful tonic for all of us daily to read the entire book of Philippians. It is short, and actually would not take more than ten minutes. Here is a letter written from prison by a man who was imprisoned because he witnessed to God's love in Christ. Yet the letter bounces with gladness, and uses superlatives to emphasize the joy of salvation. We who bear the name of Christian have done our Lord's cause an injury by our droopy mouths and furrowed brows and long faces. Of our Lord himself, we are told that He went singing to Jerusalem and even endured the cross, because of the joy that was set before Him.

Let us take a look at the preliminary thought of the rejoicing one in this fourth chapter of the letter to the Philippians. In the first verse, Paul enjoins those to whom he is writing to stand fast. Here is a prerequisite for gladness. Many people today are obsessed by unhappiness because they are uncertain about life's basic values. Their lives are successions of indecision and "yes, but." For the rejoicing song to flow from a heart, there must be a sense of a rock, of a fortress, of the protection of One who never slumbers nor sleeps, and whose resources are adequate for any situation that may come. Here is the stuff out of which songs are made! Here is the key to unlock the door to the House of Gladness.

There is a following thought to the rejoicing text that is significant, too. "Have no anxiety about anything, but in everything by prayer . . ." How many of us really practice this act of faith and for how long? The sixty-four dollar question is, do you really believe that "in everything God works for good with those who love him"? Believing this, you should be able to rejoice through everything.

Listen to the witness of two precious saints who were able to say, "I am glad!" Mary H. Mossman's witness is:

"I am glad the dear Lord has permitted me to be entirely deaf. I am shut in as in a closet with my Lord."

Fanny Crosby spoke these words:

"Oh, I am so glad the dear Lord permitted me to be blind since I was six weeks old. Why, He could not have done a better thing than to suffer blindness to come to me—He has shut me in with himself."

PRAYER: *Give us such a sense of rejoicing in our living, Lord, that no matter what may befall us, we will be glad because of Your victorious presence. In Jesus' name. Amen.*

God Moves in a Mysterious Way

London New. C. M.

PLAYFORD'S Psalter, 1671.
Altered from the Scotch Psalter, 1635.

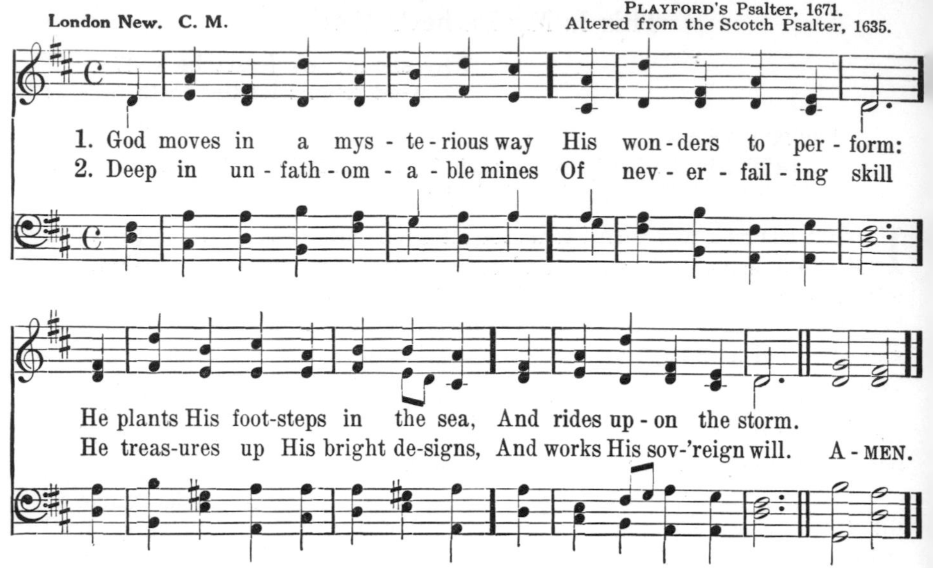

3 Ye fearful saints, fresh courage take:
The clouds ye so much dread
Are big with mercy, and shall break
In blessings on your head.

4 Judge not the Lord by feeble sense,
But trust Him for His grace;
Behind a frowning Providence
He hides a smiling face.

5 His purposes will ripen fast,
Unfolding every hour;
The bud may have a bitter taste,
But sweet will be the flower.

6 Blind unbelief is sure to err,
And scan His works in vain;
God is His own interpreter,
And He will make it plain.

William Cowper, 1774.

SUNDAY

God Moves in a Mysterious Way

His wonders to perform

Romans 11:33-35

O the depth of the riches and wisdom and knowledge of God!
How unsearchable are his judgments and how inscrutable his ways!
"For who has known the mind of the Lord,
or who has been his counselor?"
"Or who has given a gift to him that he might be repaid?"

WHEN I was teaching a course in English literature in high school, one of the refreshing delights amidst the humdrum routine of grammar that the course also required, was to come to the life of a man like the author of this hymn, William Cowper. No one would read his story and not be moved. As you learn this hymn this week, let the witness of the turbulent life out of which it was born, speak to you.

At the age of six, William Cowper lost his mother. A highly sensitive child, early showing signs of mental illness, he felt this load even more than a normal child. One is made aware of this in his poem, written many years later: "On the Receipt of My Mother's Portrait." The story is told that when he was passing through one mental crisis, he was obsessed by the idea that it was the divine will that he should drown himself in the Ouse River. When he was driven to the spot to which he felt he had been directed, a man was there, and so Cowper returned home. Then he tried to throw himself on a knife, but the blade broke. Next he tried to hang himself, but the rope parted. It was when he recovered from this horrible experience that he wrote this hymn. His personal realization of God's overruling providence swept in upon his soul. Through the years the Lord has used it mightily to bring this witness to the lives of others.

O the depths of the riches and knowledge of God. Yet how often we finite beings seek to plumb it. Unable to understand the mysteries of the Almighty's ways, we beat our fists against the wall, or petulantly cry out, "How can there be a God?"

Those of us who are mothers can know a little bit of how God must feel, when our children, having been denied something, pester us with the question, "But why, Mother? Why can't I? Just give me one good reason!" It is not always easy to put into words reasons which they can understand, because the perspective of time, and the importance of things from their viewpoint varies so much from ours.

You know what the answer is: a love so great that, even though it cannot see, it trusts. As you make this hymn yours, may your faith grow strong in the knowledge that "He does all things well."

PRAYER: *Lord, there are many things that I do not understand. But Your love for me on Calvary, and Your daily presence in my heart—these are enough. Continue to strengthen my faith. In Jesus' name. Amen.*

MONDAY

God Moves in a Mysterious Way

He plants His footsteps in the sea

Job 26:10, 12

"He has described a circle upon the face of the waters at the boundary between light and darkness."

Job 38:8-11

"Or who shut in the sea with doors, when it burst forth from the womb; when I made clouds its garment, and thick darkness its swaddling band, and prescribed bounds for it, and set bars and doors, and said, 'Thus far shall you come, and no farther, and here your proud waves be stayed'?"

THE WRITER of this hymn makes us pause to take inventory of the evidences of God's providence and power in the world about us. If you want to treat yourself to a real injection of this, read again the Book of Job. Here the self-sufficient man is confronted with the magnitude of the power of the Creator as the miracles of the world about us are pointed out.

Have you not often wondered about the boundaries of the sea? Have you not stood in awe at the power of a storm? I have remembrances as a little girl of peeking through the window of our lake cottage while a terrific storm was raging, and seeing huge oak trees uprooted as if they were the frailest plants. I remember also the comforting feeling of knowing that God could control the wind that had such power.

It must have been quite an experience for the disciples when their frail craft was being buffeted so frighteningly on the turbulent waters of Galilee. Did they forget that Jesus was on board, even though at the moment He was not in sight? Did they forget all that they had so recently seen Him do? However, to their credit, let it be said that in their distress, they turned to Him. "And he said to them, 'Why are you afraid, O men of little faith?' Then he rose and rebuked the winds and the sea; and there was a great calm. And the men marveled saying, 'What sort of man is this, that even the winds and sea obey him?' "

The One who plants His footsteps on the sea would also like to direct your life. The storms of life, tempestuous emotions, the lightning and thunder caused by the friction of personalities—these all can be brought within the orbit of His control, if you will do the bringing. In Psalm 65 we hear the psalmist address praise to God,

"who dost still the roaring of the seas,
the roaring of their waves,
the tumult of the peoples."

How He yearns to still the tumult of the peoples of the world today! His power of love is available. You and I must be the conductors. Today, wherever you go, will you bring a sense of His calm?

PRAYER: *Quiet the churnings of our hearts, O Lord. The waves of the world so quickly engulf us. Help us to bring to every situation in which we find ourselves this day the calm and peace of Your presence. Amen.*

God Moves in a Mysterious Way

The clouds ye so much dread
Are big with mercy

Psalm 103:15-18

As for man, his days are like grass; he flourishes like a flower of the field; for the wind passes over it, and it is gone, and its place knows it no more. But the steadfast love of the Lord is from everlasting to everlasting upon those who fear him, and his righteousness to children's children, to those who keep his covenant and remember to do his commandments.

THE R.S.V. translation uses the term "steadfast love" as a synonym for mercy. In my way of thinking it is more meaningful because in addition to a sense of forgiveness for past sins, it has an ongoing commitment of God's sustaining love. In a world where so very few things can be depended on, the word "steadfast" is like a rock to which submerged wayfarers may cling.

When you are facing a difficult situation, where do you look? To the magnitude of the thing that confronts you? Why not try looking to the resources that are yours as Christians? There is no cloud so big but that the One who is your Savior can ride it. Scripture tells us, "He rides upon the storm." The amazing thing is that these ominous clouds that we permit to darken our lives so quickly are big with mercy. Whatever our problem or situation may be, we need to hold it up alongside the "steadfast love" of God, for then fear is dissipated and gloom dispelled. For me, always, the sunshine of His presence has worked this miracle.

Sometimes I wonder if we like to grovel in our own inadequacies. Some people seem to pride themselves on what they are not able to do. They are obstacle people, who feel it is their mission in life to point up all the difficulties. Such was not the spirit of the early church. Because of Christ's enabling, nothing was too hard nor was there any trouble that could not be borne or surmounted. With Him, everything is possible. This was the dynamic that sent an ordinary band of men and women into a pagan world and revolutionized the old pattern of thinking.

It will do the same for you. Faith in Christ changes night to day. It makes out of difficulties, opportunities. It makes heroes out of cowards, and conquerors out of slaves. His steadfast love, His wonderful mercy are your enabling. Let Him dispel the clouds that keep you living in the shadows.

PRAYER: *Thank You, Lord, for Your steadfast love. Thank You that no situation we face is too difficult, if You are with us. Enable us to live victoriously. In Jesus' name. Amen.*

God Moves in a Mysterious Way

Judge not the Lord by feeble sense,
But trust Him for His grace

Isaiah 55:8, 9

"For my thoughts are not your thoughts, neither are your ways my ways, says the Lord. For as the heavens are higher than the earth, so are my ways higher than your ways and my thoughts than your thoughts."

THERE IS a fable called "The Devil's Wedge." It tells of how Satan announced that he was going to retire from business, and that all his tools would be for sale. The chief ones were malice, envy, hatred, jealousy, sensuality, vanity, deceit. There was one, however, in a separate compartment, that was priced higher than all the rest. It was discouragement. When the devil was asked about the exorbitant price of this one, he said: "That is the most useful weapon of all my tools. It is worth more than all the rest put together. I can pry open and get into a man's conscience with discouragement when nothing else avails me."

The Wild White Rose

It was peeping through the brambles, this little wild white rose,
Where the hawthorne hedge is planted, my garden to enclose;
All beyond was fern and heather on the breezy, open moor;
All within was sun and shelter and the wealth of beauty stored;
But I did not see the fragrance of floweret or tree,
For my eyes were on that rosebud,
And it grew just too high for me.

In vain I strove to reach it through the tangled mass of green;
It only smiled and nodded behind its thorny screen.
Yet all that summer morning, I lingered near the spot.
O why do things seem sweeter when we possess them not?
My garden buds were blooming, but all that I could see,
Was that mocking little, wild, white rose
Growing just too high for me.

So in life's wider garden, there are buds of promise too,
Beyond our reach to gather, but not beyond our view;
And like the little charmer that tempted me astray,
They steal out half the brightness of many a summer day.
O hearts that ache with longing for some forbidden tree
Look up and learn a lesson from my white rose and me.
'Tis wiser far to number the blessings at your feet,
Than ever to be longing for just one bud more sweet.
My sunbeams and my shadows, fall from a pierced hand;
I can surely trust His wisdom since His heart I understand.
And maybe in the morning, when His blessed face I see,
He will tell me why my white rose grew just too high for me.

PRAYER: *When things look difficult and dark, Lord, we still trust You. You know what is best! Amen.*

God Moves in a Mysterious Way

**His purposes will ripen fast,
Unfolding every hour**

1 Corinthians 13:9-12

For our knowledge is imperfect and our prophecy is imperfect; but when the perfect comes, the imperfect will pass away. When I was a child, I spoke like a child, I thought like a child, I reasoned like a child; when I became a man, I gave up childish ways. For now we see in a mirror dimly, but then face to face. Now I know in part; then I shall understand fully, even as I have been fully understood.

WHAT A distorted idea one can get from only a partial picture! And how different things look from a distance! Nature teaches this same truth in a thousand different ways. Imagine judging what a gladiola was going to be like from the color and size of the bulb! Or who could conceive of an oak from an acorn? A little babe in a mother's arms hardly looks like the President of the United States, and yet we know that each president has been such a babe. The unfolding plan of God's marvelous creation in nature is something we all take for granted. Yet in the spiritual realm, we often want to see the end from the beginning, and chafe and distrust at any ripening process.

Our Scripture teaches us that the mark of a spiritually mature person is the kind of faith that patiently awaits an unfolding of God's wonderful ways. "Now we see in a mirror dimly, but then face to face." All the unanswered questions of this life, will have their fulfillment in eternity. As Christians we need to develop the Christlike quality of patience. Through difficult situations, in adverse times, to believe in the purposes of God is to have the kind of faith that is a mighty witness. Children in whose home such a faith has been lived, have a priceless heritage. Is that your gift to your children?

Sometimes adverse situations create new ideas. Ingenuity is born when quick adjustments have to be made. One rather windy afternoon a small boy at a lakeside resort launched a little boat that he had made. The breeze filled the sails immediately, but instead of carrying the small craft on its course, capsized it and sent it straight to the bottom. The little owner of the boat looked sober for a moment, and then with a philosophical composure remarked, "That's a good wind for kites," and set about flying a kite. We could learn from this lad. When a door is closed for us, it could well mean that another is to be opened, if we wait upon the Lord and trust Him. Friend, this day give over to the Lord every frustration, every defeat. Wait upon His unfolding love—and you will be living abundantly!

PRAYER: *Like petulant children, Lord, who want to know the "why" now, so often we have come to You. Forgive us. Forgive our lack of faith and patience. Help us to grow in patience and in love. In Jesus' Name. Amen.*

God Moves in a Mysterious Way

**The bud may have a bitter taste,
But sweet will be the flower**

2 Corinthians 4:16-18

So we do not lose heart. Though our outer nature is wasting away, our inner nature is being renewed every day. For this slight momentary affliction is preparing for us an eternal weight of glory beyond all comparison, because we look not to the things that are seen but to the things that are unseen; for the things that are seen are transient, but the things that are unseen are eternal.

Romans 8:18

I consider that the sufferings of this present time are not worth comparing with the glory that is to be revealed to us.

WHAT A word from the Apostle Paul for us! If any man had tasted bitterness from the world's viewpoint, Paul had. Suspicioned by his own countrymen, flogged for witnessing to the love of Christ, and thrown into jail on the same count; suffering an affliction of the flesh that some Bible students have believed to be a form of epilepsy, persecuted and pursued, maligned and mistreated, yet withal singing in prison, rejoicing in affliction, praying for his enemies—this is the Paul who speaks and says, "Do not lose heart." Do you think things have been rough for you, friend? Sit down and make a list of your afflictions. Write them on paper. Then look at them in the light of what Paul endured. What was his secret?

Today's Scripture gives us the key: "For this slight momentary affliction is preparing for us an eternal weight of glory." In the poet's words, "The bud may have a bitter taste, but sweet will be the flower." What happens to us is not important. How we take it, is. In the alchemy of time, this will be the criterion for our lives.

It is Henry Ward Beecher who has said that men think that God is destroying them because He is tuning them. He describes the violinist who tightens up the string until the tense chord sounds the concert pitch. The tightening process is not to break it, but to use it tunefully.

I like the story of the little boy who had been given new skates. He fell so frequently that a tenderhearted spectator said to him, "I wouldn't stay on the ice and keep falling down so; I'd just come off and watch the others." The tears of the last fall were still rolling over the rosy cheeks, but the child looked down to his shiny new skates and up to the face of the stranger, and said, "I didn't get some new skates to give up with; I got 'em to learn how with!" Persistence, and faith that has a long look, make a couple that will never know defeat. Have you made their acquaintance?

PRAYER: *Help us to trust You for the end result, Lord, as we walk Your way, and give us a song in the heart that has in it the note of victory that You made possible on Calvary. Amen.*

SATURDAY

God Moves in a Mysterious Way

God is His own interpreter
And He will make it plain

1 Corinthians 4:5

Therefore do not pronounce judgment before the time, before the Lord comes, who will bring to light the things now hidden in darkness and will disclose the purposes of the heart. Then every man will receive his commendation from God.

IN THE previous chapter in this letter to the Corinthians, Paul says, "For the wisdom of this world is folly with God." Again in this same line he quotes from Job: "He catches the wise in their craftiness." Has it not been characteristic of our age that we have worshiped at the throne of the mind? How very much has been written and spoken, of man's achievements! It is amazing, too, that so much credence is still placed on man's wisdom, when so many of our fixed ideas have had to give way in the scientific field. How we need to learn all over again that the fear of the Lord is the beginning of wisdom.

That is not to say that the Lord does not want us to develop our God-given brains. It is to say that He does not want us to worship them. He is asking that we acknowledge Him in all our ways.

The recent witness of a great scientist here in Washington is one that we will not soon forget. This man had a very important position in the Oak Ridge plant. He was overwhelmed by the fact of man's knowledge being put to destructive use. He was haunted by the fact that he ought to do something about this awful trend. He turned his back on the world of science and went to the seminary, and has become an ordained minister. His idea is that he wants to bring every influence to bear on the human heart that will determine the use of these destructive weapons. Man's wisdom can be a destructive robot.

The closing chapter of William Cowper's life has in it something of what the last lines of his hymn say. Bishop Moule relates the story. "About half an hour before his death, his face, which had been wearing a sad and hopeless expression, suddenly lighted up with a look of wonder and inexpressible delight. It was as if He saw the Savior, and as if he realized the blessed fact, 'I am not shut out of Heaven after all!' This look of holy surprise and of joyful adoration remained until he had passed away, and even as he lay in his coffin the expression was still there. One who saw him after death wrote that 'with the composure and calmness of the face, there mingled also a holy surprise.'" The Lord had made it plain.

PRAYER: *We acknowledge, Lord, that Your ways are right. Help us to see things out of Your eyes, and in patience to await the explanation of those things that we do not understand. We know Your heart; we trust Your wisdom. In Jesus' Name. Amen.*

O Happy Home, Where Thou Art Loved the Dearest

Aline. 11 10, 11 10. JOHN VICTOR BERGQUIST, 1924.

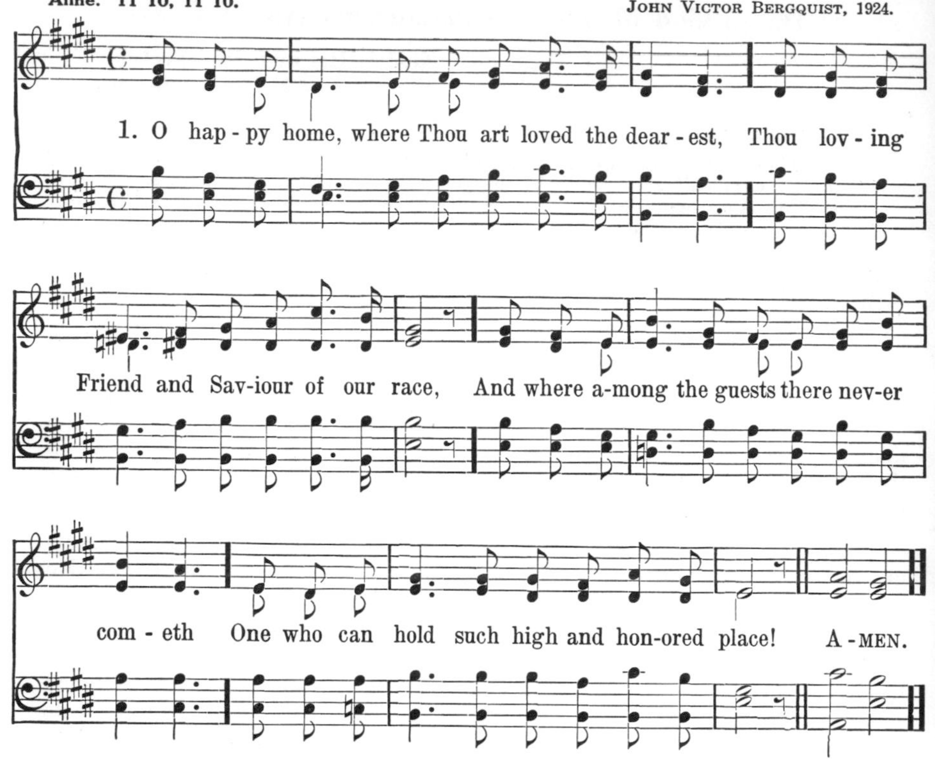

2 O happy home, where two, in heart united,
In holy faith and blessèd hope are one,
Whom death a little while alone divideth,
And cannot end the union here begun!

3 O happy home, whose little ones are given
Early to Thee in humble faith and prayer,
To Thee, their Friend, who from the heights of heaven
Guides them, and guards with more than mother's care!

4 O happy home, where each one serves Thee lowly,
Whatever his appointed work may be,
Till every common task seems great and holy,
When it is done, O Lord, as unto Thee!

5 O happy home, where Thou art not forgotten
When joy is overflowing, full and free,
O happy home, where every wounded spirit
Is brought, Physician, Comforter, to Thee.

6 And when at last all earthly toil is ended,
All meet Thee in the blessèd home above,
From whence Thou camest, where Thou hast ascended,—
Thine everlasting home of peace and love.

Carl Johann Philipp Spitta, 1833.

SUNDAY

O Happy Home, Where Thou Art Loved the Dearest

Thou loving Friend and Savior of our race

Joshua 24:14, 15

"Now therefore fear the Lord, and serve him in sincerity and faithfulness; put away the gods which your fathers served beyond the River, and in Egypt, and serve the Lord. And if you be unwilling to serve the Lord, choose this day whom you will serve, whether the gods your fathers served in the region beyond the River, or the gods of the Amorites in whose land you dwell; but as for me and my house, we will serve the Lord."

PERHAPS THERE is no subject so commonly discussed, nor whose condition is so frequently deplored, as today's home. Transportation has provided such convenient ways of getting away from home—and quickly! Mechanical amusements in public places with the crowd have been an easy out for entertainment. The complexities of modern living, with their concomitant tensions, competitions, and frustrations have developed an atmosphere of neurosis that is too often a far cry from the sentiment, "Be it ever so humble, there is no place like home." Yet historians and statesmen and plain ordinary people are agreed that "as goes the home, so goes the nation." To each one of us, then, there comes the challenge, "What can we do about our homes?"

First of all, perhaps, we ought to define home. You may be a single person, and so quickly you will say, "Well, this doesn't have anything to do with me. I'm not a mother." It is true, that in its most common usage, the word "home" suggests a family unit. Webster's first definition, however, is "one's dwelling place." Another one the Dictionary uses is the "abiding place of one's affections." More simply some one has said that home is where the heart is. So whether we are one or many, we have a home. It may be a room, an apartment, or a house; the size is not the determining factor. The important thing for each one of us to face is, "Who is first in our home?" To know whose spirit dominates, whose voice is the master, is to know the atmosphere and spirit of your home. We are not concerned whether or not yours is a matriarchal setup, or a patriarchal one. But who is "boss" in a larger sense is the very lifeline of the home.

"As for me and my house, we will serve the Lord." Is that the caption written in spirit over your doorway? Is Jesus Christ the final authority in your home? As we learn this recipe for a happy home in our hymn for this week, may God give us grace to take inventory, and true up the walls that have been leaning. May we establish anew the true Cornerstone.

PRAYER: *I want my home, Lord, to be a place where You dwell. I want Your will to be the guide for all decisions. Bless all homes, everywhere. In Jesus' Name. Amen.*

MONDAY

O Happy Home, Where Thou Art Loved the Dearest

And where among the guests there never cometh
One who can hold such high and honored place

Luke 10:38-42

Now as they went on their way, he entered a village; and a woman named Martha received him into her house. And she had a sister called Mary, who sat at the Lord's feet and listened to his teaching. But Martha was distracted with much serving; and she went to him and said, "Lord, do you not care that my sister has left me to serve alone? Tell her then to help me." But the Lord answered her, "Martha, Martha, you are anxious and troubled about many things; one thing is needful. Mary has chosen the good portion, which shall not be taken away from her."

IN OUR Scripture portion for today is borne out the definition of home which we tried to establish in yesterday's devotion. Apparently, none of these folks who made up this Bethany home were married. Let us remind ourselves again then, that home is the atmosphere you create where you live.

So often Martha's distorted sense of values is pointed out that we forget to consider the commendable things about her. When Jesus entered Bethany, it was Martha who received Him into her house. In John 11:5 we read: "Now Jesus loved Martha and her sister and Lazarus." And later in this same wonderful story of Jesus' raising Lazarus from the dead, we are told that it was Martha who, when she heard that Jesus was coming, went out to meet Him. In their conversation that followed about her dead brother and the resurrection, it was Martha that gave the good witness: "Yes, Lord; I believe that you are the Christ, the Son of God, he who is coming into the world." Martha knew and loved the Lord as well as did Mary, and welcomed Him into their home. On what score was it that the Lord gently reprimanded Martha, this woman who was always so eager to receive Him and welcome Him to her home?

There are two or three little key words that we might look to. Notice that we read "Martha was distracted . . ." It certainly was not her preparation for caring for the Lord's physical needs that was wrong. It was that this was bothering her. It is pointed up again in the Lord's response to her. Jesus said, "You are anxious and troubled about many things." Martha's anxiety and distraction about what she was doing spoiled the gift of her hospitality.

Has that been true of you? Has sharing your home with others become a burden rather than a joy? Then there is no blessing with the hospitality. Could it be that our pride enters in here? Do we fuss so about what we are going to have to eat, and how our homes look, that we are too worn out to enjoy our guests when they come?

To share in love is to know the joy of Christian hospitality.

PRAYER: *Forgive the times I have been anxious and troubled about unimportant things. Give me joy in sharing my home. In Jesus' Name. Amen.*

TUESDAY

O Happy Home, Where Two in Heart United

In holy faith and blessed hope are one

2 Corinthians 6:14-16

Do not be mismated with unbelievers. For what partnership have righteousness and iniquity? Or what fellowship has light with darkness? What accord has Christ with Belial? Or what has a believer in common with an unbeliever? What agreement has the temple of God with idols?

IN ALL THE talk today about compatibilities for folk who are to be married, how much emphasis is placed on the thing that can resolve any difference that may ever arise, and that can weld two people together into a union that is a foretaste of heaven? Where husband and wife have as their first love the Christ, there is a happy home. There is a home that will weather any vicissitude; there is the prospect of growing old lovely, because each passing year is a growing nearer to Him, together. Why is it that in the matter of marriage so many mothers have such a false sense of values?

I speak of the distorted values that mothers often have, because I have known mothers who thought they were good Christians, who would pride themselves on the "catch" their daughters had made. What were the criteria of the success of the catch? Would they be something like this: fine appearance, good family, lucrative position, lovely home, snappy car, brilliant mind. In the divorce courts of our nation you will find cases where there have been all of these—and yet broken homes.

Where two are in heart united and in holy faith and blessed hope are one, it is not to say that there will never be any difference of opinions or times of tension. The devil does not give up that easily. It is to say that for such times there is a resource that never fails. If two people are willing to go to God, and ask for direction about a thing on which they disagree, there at His throne they will meet, and their difference will be dissolved.

The Lord has a word for those who are unequally yoked. He does not recommend that you leave your mate. He suggests that, through prayer and your living the Christian life in your home, you may be the means of so witnessing to the Christ that your mate will be won to Him. Sometimes it is His presence in our silence, when we are tempted to nag, that gives the best witness.

To many, marriage is a god. Whenever a soul places anything before his love of God, life gets out of focus. But when two souls are knit together in a first love of Christ, there you will have a happy home.

PRAYER: *We would pray, O Lord for our young people that You would guide them in their choice of their mates. Give them grace always to put You first, Lord. In Jesus' name. Amen.*

O Happy Home Whose Little Ones Are Given

Early to Thee in humble faith and prayer

Deuteronomy 6:4-7

"Hear, O Israel: The Lord our God is one Lord; and you shall love the Lord your God with all your heart, and with all your soul, and with all your might. And these words which I command you this day shall be upon your heart; and you shall teach them diligently to your children, and shall talk of them when you sit in your house, and when you walk by the way, and when you lie down, and when you rise."

Matthew 19:14

But Jesus said, "Let the children come to me, and do not hinder them; for to such belongs the kingdom of heaven."

FORTUNATE CHILDREN are those whose parents dedicate them to the Lord from the very beginning. The atmosphere in which a child is reared will unconsciously affect his whole life.

One thing is sure: the atmosphere must be genuine. No one can detect hypocrisy and deceit more quickly than a child. If on the Sabbath you profess to love the Lord with all your heart and your neighbor as yourself, and the rest of the week ignore God, and complain about the church; if you sing lustily on Sunday about a holy walk with God, and on Monday practice bigotry, something will happen to the spiritual witness that you make in the lives of children who know you. It may be nieces and nephews; it may be grandchildren; it may be children in the neighborhood. A pastor was commending religion to a young boy. He expressed the hope that the boy would give his life to the Lord in his youth. "Look at your sister Sarah," he said. "How much that dear girl enjoys her religion." "Sarah may enjoy her religion," said the boy, "but nobody else in the house does."

Our Scripture speaks of talking about the things of God in our home and around the table. It would be interesting to have a tape recording of some table conversations when the participants did not know the recordings were being made. Actually, recordings are being made every time there are children listening. When you are together as a family, do you share how the Lord answers prayer? Do you acknowledge Him in all your ways? As you talk about your neighbor, do you put the most charitable construction on all his actions? Little children have sensitive ears and observing eyes and ready hearts.

A mother was telling her little girl about Samuel and his mother. She said to the child, "Samuel was dedicated to the Lord before he was born." Quickly, the little girl said, "You dedicated me before I was born, too, didn't you, mother?" Truthfully the mother said that she had not. Then the girl replied: "Then I'll kneel by you now, and you'll dedicate me, won't you?"

PRAYER: *For all little children everywhere, Lord, we pray. Help us not to be stumbling blocks in their way. Give us grace to point the way to You. Amen.*

O Happy Home Where Each One Serves Thee Lowly

Whatever his appointed work may be

John 13:12-15

When he had washed their feet, and taken his garments, and resumed his place, he said to them, "Do you know what I have done to you? You call me Teacher and Lord; and you are right, for so I am. If I, then, your Lord and Teacher, have washed your feet, you also ought to wash one another's feet. For I have given you an example, that you also should do as I have done to you."

Philippians 2:3

Do nothing from selfishness or conceit, but in humility count others better than yourselves.

1 Corinthians 10:31

So, whether you eat or drink, or whatever you do, do all to the glory of God.

THE TROUBLEMAKER in all of human relations is *self*. It is so in the home. Envy, jealousy, pride, hurt feelings—all are the fruits of the demon that is love of self. Look back into your life, to some time when there was dissension with some one. Be very honest with yourself, as before God. In your attitude at that time was there not something of a defense of yourself, of your thinking that you were not getting your due, or proper acknowledgment was not being made of your efforts?

The Lord sets us the example in what He himself did. He who is the King of glory, the Creator of all the universe, stooped to the most lowly task a man in those days could do. He washed His disciples' feet.

Paul in his letter to the Philippians tells us that in humility we should count others better than ourselves. What a difference this would make in our attitude to the things that need to be done for others! Instead of a defensive attitude, a feeling that we had to protect ourselves, we would have an attitude of seeking ways where we could be more helpful.

Then in Corinthians we are given a third suggestion. Do everything to the glory of God. The spirit of a home, the atmosphere of an office, the air of a schoolroom, can be transformed if there is but one person who day after day will live this kind of dedication. It "takes"!

When our children were home we all shared in the cleaning. Each had his appointed task. Sometimes I would have to ask one of them to do an extra job. We chuckle now when we remember the conversation. "Son, would you like to empty the wastepaper basket?" "Mother, don't ask me 'would you like to.' Just say 'Empty the waste basket.'" To which I would reply, "No, if you wouldn't like to be that helpful, I don't want you to do it."

Our attitude in what we do for others is an unconscious expression of our relationship to God.

PRAYER: *Give us joy in serving others, Lord. Help us to sense Your presence in every thing we do. Through Your Holy Spirit, give us such an attitude in our homes. In Jesus' Name. Amen.*

O Happy Home Where Thou Art Not Forgotten

When joy is overflowing, full and free

Psalm 92:1-4

It is good to give thanks to the Lord, to sing praises to thy name, O Most High; to declare thy steadfast love in the morning, and thy faithfulness by night, to the music of the lute and the harp, to the melody of the lyre.

For thou, O Lord, hast made me glad by thy work;
at the works of thy hands I sing for joy.

SURELY IT is true that many people think of the Lord as some one to call upon only when they are in trouble. We turn to Him as to a plumber's helper, to open up the works when they get clogged. Many children have never seen the witness of Christ sharing in the happy times—in fact, multiplying them. Often they get the impression that Christianity is something gloomy and heavy, an imposing of restrictions, when in actuality it is exactly the opposite. It is joy unspeakable; it is freedom from life's worst enslavements; it is happy anticipation. It is all of these, and more, because it is the person of Jesus Christ living in you daily.

That is why Christianity is a singing religion; it is why memories of a Christian home will bless a person during his whole life. "My!" said a neighbor to a Christian mother, "The young people that go in and out of your house seem always to be having such a happy time!" Yes, it is good to give thanks, to sing praises to the Most High. I have felt His presence again and again, as the laughter has rippled around our table. In our parental home the twinkle in my mother's eye, her sense of humor, God-given as a lift through many very difficult days, were as real a part of her Christian witness as her unforgettable prayers. Every family should know the joy of Christ's presence in their fun.

"I saw in my dreams," says a poet, "two fountains flowing side by side. One was a fountain of joy and the other of tears. And a voice said to me, 'These two fountains flow together all through life.' God makes them flow together that from one his children may learn gratitude, and from the other trust."

Do the work that's nearest,
Though it's dull at whiles,
Helping, when you meet them,
Lame dogs over stiles;
So in every hedgerow
Marks of angels' feet,
Epics in each pebble
Underneath our feet.

CHARLES KINGSLEY

PRAYER: *In all of our living, Lord, through every part of every day, be near. Thank You for the joy Your presence brings. Thank You that the laughter that is shared with You has in it the sound of the joy bells of heaven. Give us rejoicing grace. In Jesus' name. Amen.*

SATURDAY

O Happy Home Where Every Wounded Spirit

Is brought, Physician, Comforter, to Thee

Malachi 4:2, 3, 6

"But for you who fear my name the sun of righteousness shall rise, with healing in its wings. You shall go forth leaping like calves from the stall. And you shall tread down the wicked, for they will be ashes under the soles of your feet, on the day when I act, says the Lord of hosts. . . . And he will turn the hearts of fathers to their children and the hearts of children to their fathers, lest I come and smite the land with a curse."

TO SAY that there ever is a home where at some time or another there are not wounded spirits is to belie the truth of our human nature. As long as we live we must fight with the powers of darkness. But a Christian home knows the resources of a Great Physician whose very presence is healing for a wounded spirit. If folks would only invite Him in, what a difference there would be in our divorce courts! Some of the most beautiful remembrances we have as a family are those when by the power of the Holy Spirit we have come and asked forgiveness one of the other, and known this cleansing and healing that the Living Lord brings.

Honestly now, can you carry a feeling of resentment and ill will toward anyone after you have earnestly been on your knees in prayer? And when God gives you grace to go to the person against whom you have had an infested spirit, do you not find that He has already been there to prepare the way?

We glibly talk about our desire for world peace, and criticize the leaders of the world because the spirit of war seems so dominant. Peace can only come through each individual. The place really to work for world peace is in our homes and through our personal relationships. As you read this will you not ask the Great Physician to search out your heart? For every wound the balm of His love is the only cure that will last. If brought to Him, fretful spirits find peace, angry hearts are calmed.

Maybe you cannot always get the co-operation of the other patient. Remember, first we are told, "Physician, heal thyself." Then through prayer you can bring a cure when the other person is not even aware of it. An American visited one of our mission stations. Times had been hard, and they had had so few supplies. The nurse who was guiding them opened a very nice looking medicine cabinet. It was empty. Distressed, the tourist said, "Why, this is awful. Your cabinet is empty!" Smilingly, the nurse replied, "It's full of faith."

For wounded spirits in a home, in any group in the world, there is the Great Physician who has healing in His hands. Are we not foolish, if we know these resources and do not use them?

PRAYER: *Forigve\ us, Lord, that often we have gone around carrying infected areas in our hearts. Yes, we have been carriers of fretful fever and malignant malice. Come with the Sword of Your spirit, and cut out the diseased sections. And come with the healing of Your love. In Jesus' name. Amen.*

Faith of Our Fathers, Living Still

St. Catherine. 8 8, 8 8, 8 8.

HENRI FREDRICK HEMY, 1865.
Alt. by JAMES GEORGE WALTON, 1871.

2 Our fathers, chained in prisons dark,
Were still in heart and conscience free;
How sweet would be their children's fate,
If they, like them, could die for thee!
Faith of our fathers, holy faith!
We will be true to thee till death.

3 Faith of our fathers! we will love
Both friend and foe in all our strife:
And preach thee, too, as love knows how,
By kindly words and virtuous life:
Faith of our fathers, holy faith!
We will be true to thee till death.

Frederick William Faber, 1840.

SUNDAY

Faith of Our Fathers, Living Still

Living still

2 Timothy 1:5-7

I am reminded of your sincere faith, a faith that dwelt first in your grandmother Lois and your mother Eunice and now, I am sure, dwells in you. Hence I remind you to rekindle the gift of God that is within you through the laying on of my hands; for God did not give us a spirit of timidity but a spirit of power and love and self-control.

THROUGH THE years there has waged the old battle as to which has the more powerful influence, heredity or environment. In the matter of the spirit, there is something to be said for both sides. Scripture speaks of the blessings and the curses that are felt to the "third and fourth generation." On the other hand, regardless of what your forefathers were, the Lord requires a personal faith of you. To rely on your inheritance from them is a mistake. In fact, because of that very inheritance, more will be required of you.

The miracle of the life of the Christian faith is well worth studying. That a little band of ordinary men and women, in that first century after Christ, should have made the impact on the pagan world of their time that they did, is miracle enough to give us pause; but that this faith has lived on through all the succeeding centuries, so that it is spreading to the ends of the earth, is such an explosive fact, one wonders how agnostics can answer it. There is but one answer. This faith is not of men, it is of God, who came to earth to reveal His heart of love. So it is not only timeless; it is universal. And even as the early Christians were accused of turning the world upside down, so today, whenever Jesus Christ enters a life, there is a revolution and, "the former things have passed away, . . . I make all things new."

When the Apostle Paul writes to Timothy, he points up the twofold realization of our faith. He reminds him of the faith of both his grandmother and his mother, and then enjoins him to rekindle the gift of God within him. To pass along the faith that is our inheritance, this is what we must do. It will never stay alive if we depend only on the coals that have been given to us. We must add both coals and breeze, so that there will be live fire to pass on to the next generation.

The story is told of the man who was always boasting about his ancestors. Somebody said to him, "You remind me of the potato." "Why?" asked the boaster. And his friend replied, "Because everything good about you is underground."

A heritage of a Christian faith is a wonderful gift from God. To be kept, it must personally be used by the one so endowed. Is your faith antique or contemporary?

PRAYER: *Thank You, God, for the rich heritage that is ours who have Christian parents. Rekindle in us the flame, that we may pass the torch to those who follow. In Jesus' name. Amen.*

Faith of Our Fathers

In spite of dungeon, fire, and sword

Acts 5:41, 42

Then they left the presence of the council, rejoicing that they were counted worthy to suffer dishonor for the name. And every day in the temple and at home they did not cease teaching and preaching Jesus as the Christ.

Matthew 5:11

"Blessed are you when men revile you and persecute you and utter all kinds of evil against you falsely on my account."

TOO MANY people think that Christianity promises a bed of roses. Nowhere in Scripture can one find any basis for such a belief. The history of the heroes of our faith is a history of persecution, of being maligned and lied about. It is a glorious history of courageous men and women, imprisoned, burned at the stake, slain, given to wild beasts, but with superhuman power facing the future unafraid. If you are in search of ten easy lessons to a secure life, do not look to the Bible; do not follow the Christ. But if you want to know the way to rich, abundant, vibrant living, then take up your cross and follow Him.

Moses had to give up the palace and all the privileges of the son of a princess, to take his stand at the side of the people of God. Even then, they often turned upon him, blamed him and maligned him. But his marching orders were from another voice, and thus, in spite of all opposition, he went on.

Paul was cast into prison again and again, often after being beaten. Yet there he was, singing at midnight in the jail, thanking God that he was counted worthy to suffer. He headed for Jerusalem with the full knowledge that this trip might mean his death. Fearlessly he proclaimed his Damascus Road experience. He was able to say: "For to me to live is Christ, and to die is gain."

Have we taught our young people that this is the kind of life to which they are called? Have we passed along to them the armor that will equip them for this kind of battle? The battleground of the soul is no place for namby-pambies, nor first milers. But engaging in the battle for souls is the most exhilarating life there is. You are never in the battle alone; your major weapon is love; and at your command are resources that can never be used up.

The pages of history throb with the valor of people who have dared to live the Way.

PRAYER: *How soft we have become, Lord, and how easy we want things to be! Forgive us, and stir us. Make us aware that there is a battle going on, and that we have to take sides. If we are not for You, we are against You. Give us courage! Amen.*

Faith of Our Fathers

O how our hearts beat high with joy
Whene'er we hear that glorious word

Matthew 7:24

"Every one then who hears these words of mine and does them will be like a wise man who built his house upon the rock."

Matthew 15:6-9

"So, for the sake of your tradition, you have made void the word of God. You hypocrites! Well did Isaiah prophesy of you, when he said: 'This people honors me with their lips, but their heart is far from me; in vain do they worship me, teaching as doctrines the precepts of men.'"

IN THE fifteenth chapter of the Gospel of Matthew we have examples of two kinds of inheritance. In the first instance, the Lord excoriates the Pharisees for the way they twisted the word of God. They maneuvered it to fit their way of living. Then in the second instance there is a warm word of approval of the Canaanitish woman. Her faith was the avenue for her daughter's healing. It may thrill us to read about the faith of our fathers; we may brush away a sentimental tear when we review the hardships they endured for their faith; but unless the Word that was the bread of life for them becomes bone and marrow of our spiritual bodies, God will say of us, "This people honors me with their lips, but their heart is far from me." The woman of Canaan heard the Lord and believed, and her daughter was made whole. Jesus gives it to us in a nutshell: "Every one then who hears these words of mine and does them will be like a wise man who built his house upon the rock."

Can your family share Scripture one with another? Is there a growing understanding and learning of this Word in your life, so that you sense the power of it, and are able to share its message with others? God's Word is not a book on a table. Some people treat the printed Word as if it were some kind of hocus-pocus magic! It is that Word in your heart, ordering your day, setting a pattern for your thinking, sending you on God's errands, that is the real Word. It must come out of the printed page, and become muscle and peace of mind and heartbeat.

There has never been a revival of any power, unless its empowering was the Word of God. Nor will we have one in this generation, unless we get our families to turn to the Bible, and there find the One who is the way, the truth and the life. There are intellectuals today who boast about the fact that they know very little about this Book. Yet, with a sweep of the hand, they consign it to children and old people. How academic is that procedure, and how consistent with an open mind?

Every time anyone has honestly come to God's Word, seeking whatever truth there may be therein, he has found the Christ.

PRAYER: *Make us aware, Lord, of the power that there is in Your Word. Give us grace to share it in our homes. Keep us growing spiritually. In Jesus' name. Amen.*

Faith of Our Fathers

Our fathers, chained in prisons dark,
Were still in heart and conscience free

Isaiah 61:1

The Spirit of the Lord God is upon me, because the Lord has anointed me to bring good tidings to the afflicted; he has sent me to bind up the brokenhearted, to proclaim liberty to the captives, and the opening of the prison to those who are bound.

Romans 8:21

Because the creation itself will be set free from its bondage to decay and obtain the glorious liberty of the children of God.

2 Corinthians 3:17

Now the Lord is the Spirit, and where the Spirit of the Lord is, there is freedom.

AS THE hymn writer suggests, it is not the outward bars that make the real prison. Although freedom of one's body is certainly something to thank God for, yet imprisonment of the flesh is as nothing as compared with an enslaved soul. The real tragedy of our prisons is that there is a duality of imprisonment in most of the cases. On the other hand, I dare say that not a day goes by but that we meet enslaved people. Or maybe closer yet at home, not a day goes by but what we have to fight some enslavement.

There are the more obvious slaveowners: alcoholism, dope, sex perversion. To be sure these are now called diseases. By whatever name, there is but one Physician who can really bring freedom. There are the more subtle sins that often sit in the pew: pride, envy, jealousy, hurt feelings, laziness, bigotry. Many a soul has been grounded, because the spiritual wings were bound by one of these.

Some of our women were cleaning our altar in our church. One very attractive young woman was down on her knees with a scrub pail and brush at the foot of it. A friend came up to her and said, "Why Virginia, you'd never do this at home. You're just like a slave." To which the young woman replied, "Slave of God! I cannot think of anything that would be more wonderful than that."

Are you in heart and conscience free? Do you know the glorious liberty of the forgiveness of sins in Christ Jesus? Do you know freedom from hatred toward anybody? Have you let Christ give you release from ill will? Have you permitted Him to break the bonds of self that have enslaved you?

"Where the spirit of the Lord is, there is freedom."

PRAYER: *For the freedom there is in Christ Jesus, we thank You, God. We thank You that it is for everyone, everywhere. We are grateful that there is no enslavement that You cannot break. Such freedom needs to be shared. Use us! Amen.*

Faith of Our Fathers

**How sweet would be their children's faith,
If they, like them, could die for thee**

Matthew 26:33

Peter declared to him, "Though they all fall away because of you, I will never fall away." Jesus said to him, "Truly, I say to you, this very night, before the cock crows, you will deny me three times." Peter said to him, "Even if I must die with you, I will not deny you." And so said all the disciples.

SOMETHING IN the words of this part of our hymn disturbs me. First of all, it has in it the suggestion of Peter's glib promise, broken before the crowing of the cock. Then I wonder what our fortitude would be like in the face of danger on Christ's behalf, when I observe how we cower in the face of public opinion, and when I see how we compromise for public approval. Who can say that he would be strong in front of a firing squad, when at a cocktail party he feels constrained to conform, for fear of being thought queer; when in a crowd he remains silent when he should speak up for the right? Are physical and moral courage unrelated?

Amazingly enough, around the world today, thousands of Christians are having to make even this other choice. In Kenya, a woman was strung up five times until she was insensate, and then lowered to regain consciousness. Each time she was asked if she would deny Christ and take the Mau-Mau vow. Each time she spoke of her love for Him, and prayed for her persecutors. Gloriously she went home to be with her God. In that same parish a young couple, leaving a little child, were both killed because they would not conform to the pagan demands, but only kept praying. When the memorial service for them was announced, the invitation went out, "Come to the wedding. Mary and John have gone to be with Christ. Come to the wedding!" The British government acknowledges that the most potent force withstanding the criminal onslaughts of the Mau-Mau in Kenya today is this handful of Christians, whose armor is love, and whose weapon is prayer. Of one thousand Anglicans, six hundred have been martyred. They died for their faith.

In East Germany, the young people are called up before their school assemblies, and asked if they will denounce their Christian youth group. If they denounce, they may stay in school; if they refuse, they are taken out of school and sent in to the salt mines which, should they survive, means a life of slavery. Many of them are choosing Christ!

Some of these things were being shared by a missionary in a college class. At the conclusion, he said to the young Americans, "Of course, any one of you, faced with such a choice, would make it for Christ!" And the young man who related this said he was haunted by the question: "Would we? Would *we?*"

PRAYER: *My words are glib, Lord. Yet even these falter when I fear what the crowd will say. Give me courage to live for You. Amen.*

Faith of Our Fathers

We will love both friend and foe
In all our strife

Matthew 5:43, 46

"You have heard that it was said, 'You shall love your neighbor and hate your enemy.' But I say to you, Love your enemies and pray for those who persecute you. . . . For if you love those who love you, what reward have you?"

IN ANOTHER section of Scripture we are told that if your enemy compels you to go one mile, go two. The late Senator Barkley gave a definition of freedom in connection with this verse that I have not been able to forget. He said that when you are going the first mile you are a slave, you are under compulsion. But when you start out on the second mile, you are a free man, for that you are doing on your own. Again, the Bible speaks of feeding our enemies when they are hungry, and returning good for evil. Yesterday when we spoke of dying for Christ, we spoke of the courage that it takes to live for Christ. In today's lesson there is a classic example of this very thing. Have you the love and daring to bless your enemies, and do good to them? What an adventure for a nation to try! It has never been tried in the history of the world. It is the weapon before which the devil has no defense. Try it in your personal relations.

A remarkable story comes to us from a chaplain who was with a company in North Africa in the last war. The chaplain had seen a tremendous change take place in the life of a rough sergeant. He went to him and asked him what had happened. This is his story. He said, "You know that young stripling of a lad in our company, Chaplain, who looks as if he hardly needs to shave. Well, every night before the lights were out, he would take his Bible, and read it. It irritated me, and I made life as miserable for him as I could with the help of the other boys. He just kept it up as if he hadn't even heard our jibing. One night the rain was worse than usual. And this clay isn't the thing that I enjoy most. We finished sentry at near midnight and I came into the barracks soaked to the skin, with my boots heavy with clay. I was mad. Couldn't figure out why I had to be in this awful place. I felt in my bones that if that kid came in and read his Bible that night, I'd explode. And he did, and sure enough, I exploded. I took one of my dirty boots and hit him on one side of his head, and took the other dirty boot and hit him on the other side of his head. But there was not a whimper. He finished reading the Book and turned out the lights. The next morning when I awoke, there were my boots, under my bed, all cleaned and polished. Chaplain, I couldn't take that sitting down. What a fellow had, that would make it possible for him to do that, I wanted, too. Now we read our Bibles together, and I'm beginning to understand a little the difference that it makes when Christ Jesus lives in your heart."

PRAYER: *You prayed for Your enemies, Lord. You want us to be second milers! Give us daring to try Your way. Amen.*

Faith of Our Fathers

And preach thee, too, as love knows how,
By kindly deeds and virtuous life

Matthew 5:14-16

"You are the light of the world. A city set on a hill cannot be hid. Nor do men light a lamp and put it under a bushel, but on a stand, and it gives light to all in the house. Let your light so shine before men, that they may see your good works and give glory to your Father who is in heaven."

SOMEHOW AS I copied these words from the Gospel of Matthew my mother came before me. She has been gone from us in the body for twenty years now. But what she was in our home, to all ten of us children, is described in this verse; a light on a stand that gives light to the whole house. Her faith was like that. It was the kind of faith that made her fun to have around; the kind of faith that was always thinking of happy surprises for people; the kind of faith that was never too tired to listen to your troubles; the kind of faith that taught her children the joy of Christian living, and the inner peace that comes from the forgiveness of sins. When she came into a room, you loved it, and when she was not there, something very vital was gone.

Her sympathy for the underdog, her heart of compassion for those in want, her sense of the importance of every individual in God's great democracy—all stemmed from her very close association with One, Jesus of Nazareth, whom she knew as Redeemer and Friend. They say we grow like those with whom we associate. His light shone through her. Daily she met Him in private conference, and before the day was over, she would share Him with us, too. When she talked to Him in prayer, I knew that He was right in the room. And you could tell that He was her best friend. There had been some very rough times in her life. But He always steadied the boat for her. For her children, she wanted most of all that they should know this Friend, too.

Warren Partridge says that Christlike mothers are wonderful soul winners. They are the most successful evangelists in the world. He tells the story of a young infidel who contemplated the character of his mother. "I see," he said, "two facts. First, even though my mother has physical afflictions, she bears up under it all from the support that she receives from her Bible and prayer. Second, I see that she has a secret spring of comfort of which I know nothing. I spend myself on the world and am empty. She has boundless resources. If this secret is in religion, why may I not attain it as well as my mother? I will seek it immediately of God."

What would happen, if mothers everywhere would let their light so shine that men would see their good works and glorify their Father.

PRAYER: *For the faith of our parents, Lord, we give You thanks. For the light that shone out of their lives to bless us, we are grateful. Holy Spirit of God, give us grace to do the same for our children. In Jesus' name. Amen.*

I Love to Steal Awhile Away

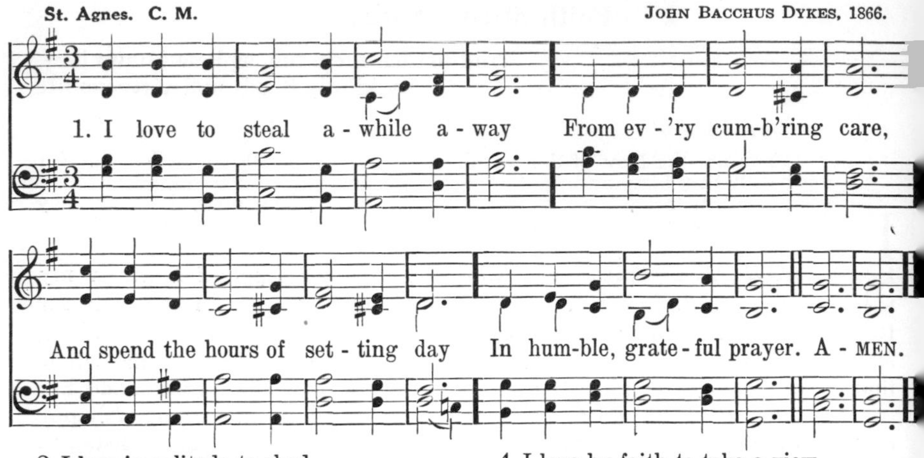

2 I love in solitude to shed
The penitential tear,
And all His promises to plead
Where none but God can hear.

3 I love to think of mercies past,
And future good implore,
And all my cares and sorrows cast
On Him whom I adore.

4 I love by faith to take a view
Of brighter scenes in heaven;
The prospect doth my strength renew,
While here by tempests driven.

5 Thus when life's toilsome day is o'er,
May its departing ray
Be calm as this impressive hour,
And lead to endless day.

Phoebe (Hinsdale) Brown, 1824.

I Love to Steal Awhile Away

From every cumb'ring care

Matthew 6:6

"But when you pray, go into your room and shut the door and pray to your Father who is in secret; and your Father who sees in secret will reward you."

IN HIS book, *The Story of Our Hymns,* Dr. E. E. Ryden tells the significant life story of the author of our hymn for this week. Born in 1783, she was orphaned before she was two years old. Her childhood was spent in the home of an older sister who was married to a jail keeper. Her son wrote later that the stories of deprivation revealed in his mother's diary were enough to break his heart when he read them. Her only schooling was at the age of eighteen, when she attended for three months.

After her marriage to Timothy Brown, life became a little more livable, for he was a good man, though very poor. In not many years, the capacity of their home was stretched, for besides the four children born to them, Mrs. Brown took care of her sick sister, who had the only finished room in the house. It was during these days that our hymn was born. Finding no place in her crowded home where she could retire with God, Mrs. Brown would slip out at eventide, when her household tasks were done, to a beautiful estate where there was a lovely garden. Here she found sweet communion with her Lord. The woman owning the estate had observed her, and one day in the presence of others, cruelly asked, "Mrs. Brown, why do you come up at evening so near our house, and then go back without coming in? If you want anything, why don't you come in and ask for it?"

Humiliated, she went home that night, and when the older children were all in bed, and only the baby in her arms, she took her pen in hand, and with a heart bursting with grief, wrote her explanation and apology to the woman in verse. This is the hymn we love. It began with the lines:

Yes, when the toilsome day is gone,
And night with banners gray,
Steals silently the glade along
In twilight's soft array,

I love to steal awhile away
From little ones and care,
And spend the hours of setting day,
In gratitude and prayer.

Mrs. Brown was following the example of One she loved. The Lord knew the need of retiring alone to commune with His heavenly Father. He went into the hills to pray.

PRAYER: *Thank You, Lord, for the strength that comes from drawing apart with You. Thank You that this privilege is open to everyone. Thank You that the resources of heaven are ours to draw from. Thank You for quiet times. In Jesus' name. Amen.*

I Love to Steal Awhile Away

I love to think of mercies past,
And future good implore

Lamentations 3:22-24

The steadfast love of the Lord never ceases, his mercies never come to an end, they are new every morning; great is thy faithfulness.
"The Lord is my portion," says my soul, "therefore I will hope in him."

THE WRITER of Lamentations in the verses previous to those quoted here speaks of remembering the affliction and gall, and of a bowed down soul because of them. But then he says, "But this I call to mind, and therefore I have hope: The steadfast love of the Lord never ceases."

What a gloom chaser is at our disposal! We awaken in the morning and think, "Another day, with all its work and problems and frustrations! Wish I could just stay in bed!" Then we would turn our thinking to all the good things with which God has filled our lives; to the beautiful things we have been privileged to see; to the expressions of love we have been shown; to the amazing opportunities that have been ours. We would recount that, no matter how hard the task has been, His grace has been sufficient.

The writer of our Scripture for today recalls some pretty bitter things that had happened to him. He speaks of having become "the laughing stock of all peoples," whose "teeth grind on gravel," who has "forgotten what happiness is." He speaks of being walled about and having heavy chains put upon him. After such an accounting he comes through with the glorious witness:

The steadfast love of the Lord never ceases . . .
his mercies . . . are new every morning.

This month marks the birthdays of our daughters. I would be remiss did I not think of mercies past. Today I think of the older one. First I would acknowledge the joy when this little lady was put in my arms. Then in humble gratitude, I would recount the gifts she has been given by her Creator. There were times when she was marvelously spared in one kind of accident or another. At three, her suit caught fire, and her little brother beat it out. A scar on her knee to this day attests to the narrowness of her escape. At five she fell out of an automobile that was going forty miles an hour. The lines in her forehead are but a remnant of the swollen, scarred face that she lived with so many months. At two, in her quick eagerness, she slipped as she was getting out of the car, and tore open her lip. There is still a faint trace of the stitches that were taken. On her seventh birthday, her brothers were launching their canoe and she fell out. Her kicking and swimming brought her safely to land. At eleven she had rheumatic fever. Her heart today gives no evidence of it.

Forgive me. I have been thinking of "mercies past."

PRAYER: *Thank You, Lord, for the mercies that are new every morning. Help us daily to take account of them. In Jesus' name. Amen.*

I Love to Steal Awhile Away

I love in solitude to shed
The penitential tear

Joel 2:12, 13

"Yet even now," says the Lord, "return to me with all your heart, with fasting, with weeping, and with mourning; and rend your hearts and not your garments." Return to the Lord, your God, for he is gracious and merciful, slow to anger, and abounding in steadfast love.

HOW VERY much we need to take a look at ourselves, and see ourselves as God sees us! There is so much of pretense and hypocrisy in our living. There is so much making of alibis and excuses. It is only in the quietness of God's presence, and with the revealing light of His Word, that we can get anything of an accurate evaluation of ourselves. Surely the world has nothing to offer in this respect. It is a ready aid in the business of glossing over. Alone with God, it is different. In the light of His judgment, His values, we get to see ourselves.

Surely the picture does not make us happy! Even the good that we do by His grace is often tainted with ego and pride. We return love for love, but how often do we return good for evil? In the matter of the efforts expended on any given day, how much of them are not selfish! As mothers, what a temptation there is for us to think that when we wear ourselves out for our children we are being nobly unselfish!

Or there is the matter of the pattern of our thoughts. Is yours such that it does not flinch under the white scrutiny of God's all-seeing eye? Are you generous with your judgment of your neighbor, and stern with yourself?

As for me, the catharsis of the penitential tear I need daily. And it does not come when I am with people, nor even so much in group devotions. This spiritual exercise is best accomplished when a soul is alone with his Maker.

A sliver caught underneath the skin will fester and become sore and a source of infection, if it is not removed. So it is with the health of our souls. Little sins burrow in. Sometimes they are so small that we are hardly aware of them. We feel the pain of infection, and wonder what its source is. Only the discerning eye of a practiced physician and the amplified eye of his instruments can detect the cause of the poison that is giving us pain and endangering our health.

Our souls need to withdraw into the quiet presence of the Great Physician. There His instruments, conscience, and the Sword of the Spirit, will detect and expose the sins that we have hardly seen and much less confessed. Then the penitential tear will bring cleansing and healing.

PRAYER: *Help me now, this day, Lord, to be quiet in Your presence. Show me my sins. Forgive me, Lord, and daily by Your grace help me to walk and talk and think more as befits a daughter of the King. In Jesus' Name. Amen.*

I Love to Steal Awhile Away

And all His promises to plead

2 Peter 1:3, 4

His divine power has granted to us all things that pertain to life and godliness, through the knowledge of him who called us to his own glory and excellence, by which he has granted to us his precious and very great promises, that through these you may escape from the corruption that is in the world because of passion, and become partakers of the divine nature.

CAN YOU imagine the promises that the writer of this hymn would plead before God in the hour when she was alone with Him? Desperately weary after a day of ministering to her sick sister and taking care of the needs of her children and her husband; frustrated because of the insufficient funds to supply the wherewithal for the many under her care; burdened with her own unworthiness and sin, she came to God in this quiet place to ask Him to make good His promises. Can you hear her repeating: "Call upon me in the day of trouble; I will deliver you, and you shall glorify me"? Or, "My God will supply every need of yours"?

Can you see her lips move with the magnetic words: "My grace is sufficient for you" or, "I can do all things in him who strengthens me"?

Can you see her shoulders straighten and the glisten in her eye as she pleads His promise, "If we confess our sins, he is faithful and just, and will forgive our sins and cleanse us from all unrighteousness"?

Can you feel the empowering that must have come to her soul as she claimed His promise, "As your days, so shall your strength be"?

Yes, through these promises, any one of us can "escape from the corruption that is in the world" and "become partakers of the divine nature." That is, we can if we, like her, know the Yes that Paul writes of in 2 Corinthians. For, as the apostle writes, it is because of Christ and what He did for us, that all the promises of God find their divine Yes. He is the deposit on our check of eternal life. His everlasting riches are ours for the claiming. They are for everyone who will be His child.

Phoebe Brown found every promise valid, and the consequent empowering adequate. I would like to speak my personal word in this regard, too. Never have I found Him to fail. In every hour the promises of Scripture have "lifted up my head," have "set my feet upon a rock," have been to me "a high tower." To help in other people's needs, these travelers' checks from God have been my only real recourse. My own spiritual checks must too often be marked, "insufficient funds." But the drafts I draw on the Bank of Heaven, the eternal "Yes" for my soul, these have never failed. Try them and see for yourself.

PRAYER: *For Your promises, Lord, I thank You. I thank You that they are adequate for every situation and all of life's needs. Help me to make them mine, and to claim them. In Jesus' name. Amen.*

THURSDAY

I Love to Steal Awhile Away

And all my cares and sorrows cast
On Him whom I adore

1 Peter 5:6, 7

Humble yourselves therefore under the mighty hand of God, that in due time he may exalt you. Cast all your anxieties on him, for he cares about you.

IN A missionary hymn that Mrs. Brown wrote later, she expresses the compulsion of sharing the experience that she speaks of in our lines for today.

Go, messenger of love, and bear
Upon thy gentle wing
The song which seraphs love to hear,
The angels joy to sing.

Go to the heart with sin oppressed,
And dry the sorrowing tear;
Extract the thorn that wounds the breast,
The drooping spirit cheer.

What is the secret of casting your anxieties upon Him? I think it is to be found in the line: "On Him whom I adore." The degree to which you love the Lord is the degree to which you trust Him. You cannot love Him, and then distrust Him.

A physician diagnoses a patient's illness by the symptoms that are evident. Pain in certain areas is evidence of trouble there. The discharge of blood is cause for alarm. Worry and fret and complaining are symptoms of sick souls. If these are present, we had better look to what is our first love; we had better check on ourselves to see if our affirmation of love for Christ is merely a matter of lip service. You see, loving Him makes it possible for you to say to whatever happens, "So what!" Is He not always with you? Is anything too hard for Him? Has He ever failed you? If you know Him in these capacities, how then, can you ever doubt Him?

Had we better take another look at Him? Is it that we do not know Him well enough? Go to your Bible. Read the Gospels again and again. Walk with Him down the highways and byways of Galilee. See the multitudes who came to Him. Talk with the people He cured. Witness the transformation in the life of Mary of Magdala. Go to Calvary and assay the price He paid to be your burden bearer!

And then, as your love grows, release yourself into His presence. Tell Him all your need and trust Him for the supplying. It is a glorious experience!

PRAYER: *So many times, Lord, I have come to You with my burden and continued to carry it with me through the day. That is no way to trust You. Forgive me. Give me the joy of a released soul that has a great burden bearer. Amen.*

I Love to Steal Awhile Away

**I love by faith to take a view
Of brighter scenes in heaven**

Revelation 21:22-27

And I saw no temple in the city, for its temple is the Lord God the Almighty and the Lamb. And the city has no need of sun or moon to shine upon it, for the glory of God is its light, and its lamp is the Lamb. By its light shall the nations walk; and the kings of the earth shall bring their glory into it, and its gates shall never be shut by day—and there shall be no night there; they shall bring into it the glory and the honor of the nations. But nothing unclean shall enter it, nor any one who practices abomination or falsehood, but only those who are written in the Lamb's book of life.

READ THIS Scripture again. Need anything more be said? With such a prospect, anything that we must endure in this life surely is not too significant. I hold no brief for those who live solely for "pie in the sky, by and by," for as I have said before, if you are to know heaven in the tomorrow, heaven will be in you here on earth, too. Heaven is Christ, more of Him; and if you can say, "for to me to live is Christ," then you have a foretaste of the home He has gone to prepare.

I think that as Christians we miss something, however, if we do not take a look at what that home is like. The prospect will give spring to our steps on this journey, and the long look will reflect the anticipation of the sunrise in our faces. No sin, no tears, no death, no parting, no injustices, no falsehood, no pain—these are a part of the "brighter scenes in heaven."

A woman was told that she was going to lose her eyesight in a short time. She decided that she would absorb as much of sight as she could while any of it remained to her. Each morning, she went outside of her house and gazed at the hills that she loved. She strained to see them, that they might be indelibly printed on her memory when her sight was gone. After six months she went back to the doctor to have her eyes checked again. He stood back in utter amazement after the examination. "What have you done?" he asked, "Something has happened." She searched her mind for what he might mean. "Why," she said, "all that I have done is to go out each morning and look at the hills." The doctor came to realize that it was this exercise that had strengthened her sight.

Daily we need to remind ourselves that we have here no abiding city. We need the long look into that other country. It would clarify our values, and give us renewed hope. The "brighter scenes" reflection would help to transform our day. The tread of our feet would have in it the victorious rhythm of the onward, upward march.

PRAYER: *We are on the homeward trail, Lord. Give us enough glimpses of Home at the end of the trail, to reflect faith and love in our daily lives. In the name of the Trail Blazer. Amen.*

I Love to Steal Awhile Away

Be calm as this impressive hour

Acts 6, 7

And Stephen, full of grace and power, did great wonders and signs among the people. . . . And gazing at him, all who sat in the council saw that his face was like the face of an angel. . . . But he, full of the Holy Spirit, gazed into heaven and saw the glory of God, and Jesus standing at the right hand of God; and he said, "Behold, I see the heavens opened, and the Son of man standing at the right hand of God." . . . And as they were stoning Stephen, he prayed, "Lord Jesus, receive my spirit." And he knelt down and cried with a loud voice, "Lord, do not hold this sin against them." And when he had said this, he fell asleep.

WHAT A way to die! It is the glorious way of the cross. There are those who think that contemplating death is morbid. Not to a Christian! Instead, the contemplation is an empowering. It will either be a witness of supreme faith, or it will evidence the doubt with which we lived. The attitude that you have toward death now will condition you for your release from life. For the Christian, it is a glorious anticipation.

A lover brings to his loved one an album of photographs of the home he has prepared for her in a far country. When he is with her, he opens its pages and shows her some of the things that she has to anticipate. What joy and eagerness swell in her breast at the thought of sharing these with him. And he who loves her, has been there before to get all these things ready! He can speak firsthand to her of what the country is like. She can hardly wait until she can make that journey with him to their home.

Should a Christian's anticipation be less, when the Christ has gone before to prepare?

In the parsonage experience we are privileged to share in many a home-going. I think of one bedside in a hospital that left its indelible impression upon me. A young thirty-two-year-old mother lay waiting for her Lord to take her home. Her family was gathered about her bedside, that is, her adult family. Her little boy and girls were being taken care of by relatives. The aged mother was there, with stooped shoulders, symbolic of the burden she had carried in this girl's marriage. It had not been too happy a union, and the grandmother had borne the brunt of the wayward husband's thoughtlessness. She had cared for the children while the mother worked to provide for them. Often she had spoken bitter words about the man her daughter had married. The husband was there, sobbing out his grief and remorse. Then the young mother's eyes opened, and her lips moved. The pastor bent low to hear what she had to say. Her last words were: "I have nothing but forgiveness for everybody," and with that she won through to her home.

Stephen went home like that, calmly, impressively, because he walked with his Lord here on earth.

PRAYER: *Lord Christ, let our walk be so close to You this day that, should our final summons come ere the setting of the sun, we will witness to the everlastingness of our faith. In Your name. Amen.*

O for a Closer Walk with God

Devereux. C. M.

L. DEVEREUX.
Arranged by GEORGE KINGSLEY, 1839.

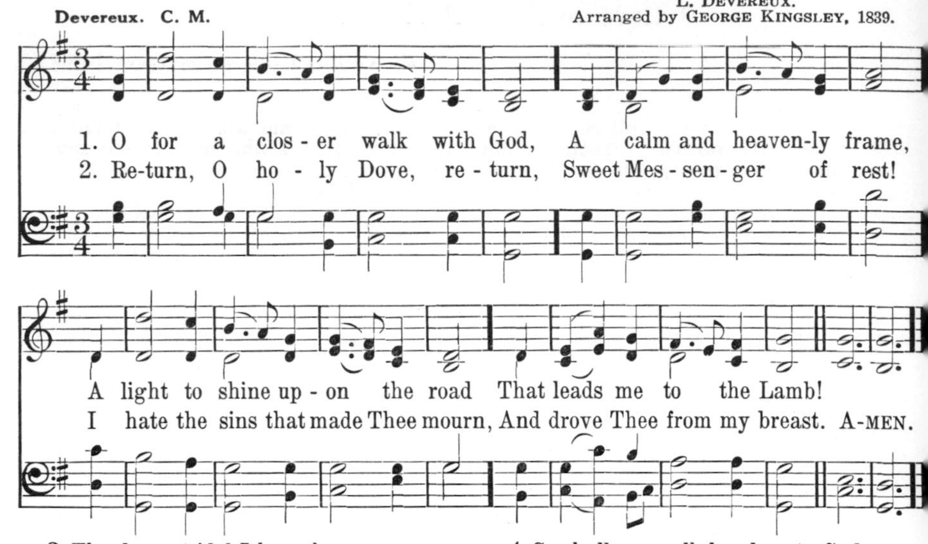

3 The dearest idol I have known,
Whate'er that idol be,
Help me to tear it from Thy throne,
And worship only Thee.

4 So shall my walk be close to God,
Calm and serene my frame;
And purer light shall mark the road
That leads me to the Lamb.

William Cowper, 1772, a.

O for a Closer Walk with God

Return, O holy Dove, return
Sweet messenger of rest

Ezekiel 36:26-28

"A new heart I will give you, and a new spirit I will put within you; and I will take out of your flesh the heart of stone and give you a heart of flesh. And I will put my spirit within you, and cause you to walk in my statutes and be careful to observe my ordinances. You shall dwell in the land which I gave to your fathers; and you shall be my people and I will be your God."

THE STORY of the children of Israel is, in many ways, the story of man's walk through life. Their being called to be set apart, their disobedience to the high calling, their resultant suffering and wandering in the wilderness, their repeated repentance, and the merciful forgiveness of God—all these find their counterpart in the life of most of us. The restless wanderings of our hearts and minds will be stilled only when the Holy Spirit of God finds His dwelling place within us.

The Bible repeats the formula for this experience again and again. The first step is to repent. And of course, before you repent, you must see your own sins. As you are quiet now in the presence of God, what things do you have to confess? The Holy Spirit can find no room in your heart, if there is enmity toward anyone there; or if there is jealousy or envy; or if you are wallowing in the slough of hurt feelings. He can find no room, if you have spoken ill of a brother, and have not confessed it and grieved over it. If your plans are all for self and your circle of loved ones, if you are putting other things before God (good though these things may be), you need a new inventory, and a willingness to acknowledge your sins.

I love Saturday nights at our house. Saturday is the day I change the sheets on all the beds. Saturday is the day the house has a thorough cleaning. The cobwebs are swept away, and the corners are dusted, and the waste paper baskets are all emptied, along with the scrubbing of the floors, and the dusting, and the washing of windows that all make up the cleaning of a house. When at the end of the day I, too, am scrubbed, and get into clean night clothes, and slip in between clean sheets, I have the physical sensation that the soul has, when all the dirt of sin has been removed by the forgiveness of God, and I know the fresh fragrance of the indwelling of His Holy Spirit. Spiritually, we need not have that experience only on a Saturday night. It is ours daily for the asking.

The prayer life of our youngest daughter has been a real inspiration to me. She is the one who prayed about the clean blackboard. It never rains but that she will pray: "Wash me clean, Lord, even as Your rain has washed the earth." Showers of Blessings?

PRAYER: *I want Your Spirit to dwell within my heart, Lord. Show me my sin, and do a thorough housecleaning job on it. In Jesus' name. Amen.*

O for a Closer Walk with God

A calm and heavenly frame

Job 22:21

"Agree with God, and be at peace; thereby good will come to you."

Isaiah 26:3

"Thou dost keep him in perfect peace, whose mind is stayed on thee, because he trusts in thee."

ALL THE literature on peace of mind that floods our book market today is an evidence of the deep longing of human hearts for this quality. It is a priceless jewel for which men are ever seeking. Too often their seeking is down one blind alley after the other. The writer of this hymn, William Cowper, had gone through terrific turmoil, to the point, you will remember, where he tried to take his own life. It was twenty-seven years later that he wrote this beautiful hymn. He had learned that the only way to have a calm and heavenly frame was to have a closer walk with God.

How can we follow this pattern that seems so simple? First of all we must acknowledge that it is not so simple. The devil is constantly about us, disturbing, planting seeds of suspicion and strife and distrust. We are daily in a battle of the spirit, and unless we are aware of this, we succumb to his wiles. But God has provided armor. If we are willing to discipline ourselves to using these gifts of His providence, we can have this calm and heavenly frame, this peace and joy in the Holy Spirit.

There is the helmet of salvation. In Christ, you can know that your sins are forgiven and that eternal life is yours. There is the breastplate of righteousness. This follows your acceptance of Christ. It is the fruit of the Spirit. There is the sword of the Spirit which is the Word of God. Here is a tangible weapon that you can draw to rout any enemy. Discipline yourself to memorizing God's Word, so that within you there is this constant resource. When turbulent, distressing thoughts enter your mind, recall these words of God's undergirding, claim His promises, and you will sense the peace of His presence pervading your soul.

Dr. Laubach has a clever little pamphlet called "A Game with Minutes." Here he suggests that we, minute by minute, try to be aware of the presence of Christ within us. Maybe it will be as we sing a hymn while we are working; or as we recall Scripture in the midst of our duties; or as we pray for whoever comes to our mind. It is a very revealing game, for it evidences how often our thoughts are far from Him.

Christ is your peace!

PRAYER: *Lord, this day stay my mind on You. In Your presence is this calm and heavenly frame. I want that closer walk. In Jesus' name. Amen.*

O for a Closer Walk with God

A light to shine upon the road

2 Samuel 22:29, 30

"Yea thou art my lamp, O Lord, and my God lightens my darkness. Yea, by thee I can crush a troop, and by my God I can leap over a wall. This God——his way is perfect; the promise of the Lord proves true; he is a shield for all those who take refuge in him."

Psalm 119:105

Thy word is a lamp to my feet and a light to my path.

HOW RICH is the Word of God in figures of speech! Yesterday we spoke of the sword of the Spirit, and today we have the figure of a lamp. These are right from out the everyday necessities of people's lives. The kind of lamps we use from age to age may vary; but the need of lamps in darkness is the same in any age. The lamp that the writer of the psalm had in mind was one that was very essential for his safety. There were no street lights in his day, nor headlights from automobiles. When he stepped into the night, there was blackness, except for the light of the stars. Then it was that he would put on sandals that had at the toe an oiled wick. This wick would be lighted, and as the wearer would step into the darkness of the night, his way would be illumined, one step at a time.

God's Word is a light that will shine upon the road of life—one step at a time. Many of us run into difficulty, and fret, because there are no headlights that show the path far ahead. We forget that headlights sometimes create illusions and a distorted concept of what is to come. Not so the step by step lighting. You put your foot forward and that way is lighted, and so with the next, one step at a time.

In the Book of Revelation we are told that in heaven there is no need of sun or moon or stars, because the Lamb is all the light. In my finite mind, I am unable to visualize this, but I do know that Christ is the light of my soul, and that without Him, I am in darkness indeed! I would witness to the fact that the closer my walk with Him, the more radiant is my living. So often my chimney is smoky and my oil is not pure. My light is pretty putrid for leading others, then. You see, it follows that when He is your light, and His word becomes your lamp, you in turn become a light to others. It could be that you might be the light that would lead somebody else to the Lamb. He works in that kind of wonderful way.

PRAYER: *Let Your Word so shine in my home today, that those who dwell herein will carry with them something of Your radiance. Illumine my heart that I may reflect Your love. In Jesus' name. Amen.*

O for a Closer Walk with God

So shall my walk be close to God,
Calm and serene my frame;
And purer light shall mark the road
That leads me to the Lamb

Micah 6:8

He has showed you, O man, what is good; and what does the Lord require of you but to do justice, and to love kindness, and to walk humbly with your God?

Colossians 2:6

As therefore you received Christ Jesus the Lord, so live in him, rooted and built up in him and established in the faith, just as you were taught, abounding in thanksgiving.

THE WALK with God that produces calmness and serenity is a humble walk, for it follows the step of the One who sought out lowly, needy people, it involves willingness to take a towel to wash people's feet; it may mean that you will not have a place to lay your head; it must mean that you are willing to carry a cross. So often we reduce Christianity to some sugar-coated thing. To walk with the Christ is to need courage, though everyone else be against you; to walk with the Christ is to return good for evil; to walk with the Christ is to love even your enemies; to walk with the Christ is to forget your own comforts, and to find your joy in serving others. Of this we must remind ourselves, again and again.

This is the month of my husband's birth. Forgive me, if I pause to pay tribute. It is only to witness to the glory of this kind of walk, as I have seen him live it. Earlier in our married life I was irked by the fact that nothing we ever planned as a family was so important but that it could be foregone, if there was someone that needed him at that time. Many nights I have sat up waiting, while he was trying to serve as a real undershepherd in an area of need. Lots of times people have disappointed him, people to whom he has given hours of his time and days of effort. But that makes him no less eager to help when the next call comes. His greatest joy is when he has been able to see the transforming power of the Holy Spirit in a person's life.

It is wonderful to grow together in such a walk. The road that stretches ahead is lighted by the One who made hearts burn on the Emmaus Road. And always the Christ is ahead, clearing the way.

To walk with Him is a daily experience. It is to see in every human being a soul to be saved. It is to be filled with thanksgiving; it is for your life to show forth His praise.

PRAYER: *Keep me walking so close to You, O Lord, that I will be on Your errands and will reflect the joy of Your Presence through everything I do this day. In Jesus' name. Amen.*

O for a Closer Walk with God

I hate the sins that made Thee mourn

Psalm 51:1,2

Have mercy upon me, O God, according to thy steadfast love;
according to thy abundant mercy blot out my transgressions.
Wash me thoroughly from my iniquity, and cleanse me from my sin!

Psalm 51:17

The sacrifice acceptable to God is a broken spirit;
a broken and contrite heart, O God, thou wilt not despise.

YESTERDAY WE were reminded that the way to open the door of our hearts for the Holy Spirit of God was to acknowledge our sins and repent of them. The hymn line that we are considering today has in it a word that gives character to repentance. That little word is hate. There are people who have an attitude of almost boasting of their sins. There are others who try to hide them. Then there is a large group who are sorry for the consequences of sin, but have no real remorse about the sin itself. They are sorry they "got caught," but as to any sense of the wrong they have done, this they do not comprehend. In all honesty, have there not been times like this in your life?

As a school teacher, I found that this was so often true in the classroom. A student committing the sin of lack of preparation, was not fazed by the fact that he was cheating himself of wonderful learning opportunities; his regret was that the teacher had called on him, and so found him out.

You see, there is a difference between conviction and repentance. As someone has so aptly put it: "It is one thing to be awakened at five o'clock in the morning, and it is another thing to get up." There is, too, the sham kind of repentance that is illustrated by the man who was robbed of one hundred dollars. A long time afterwards, he received this letter: "Dear Sir: Five years ago, I robbed you of one hundred dollars. I am filled with remorse that I could have done such a thing. I send you a dollar and a half to ease my conscience."

Children have a wonderful way of coming to the point. In a Church school class the question was raised as to what repentance meant. One bright little lad raised his hand and said, "It is to be sorry for your sins." A girl in the back seat was not quite satisfied. She raised her hand. "I think it's being sorry enough to quit."

We can glibly say we are sorry for our temper, or our stubbornness, or our deceit; but if we are not sorry enough to ask the Holy Spirit to help us quit these habits, and earnestly cooperate with Him, then we are not repentant.

PRAYER: *In this closer walk, Lord, let Your presence be so real, that I shall see my sins as they really are. Help me to hate them, and to know Your forgiveness. Strengthen my weak will, that I may not repeat the sins that separate me from You, and that are such a poor witness to others. In Jesus' name. Amen.*

O for a Closer Walk with God

The dearest idol I have known, . . .
Help me to tear from its throne

Isaiah 2:7, 8

Their land is filled with silver and gold, and there is no end to their treasures; their land is filled with horses, and there is no end to their chariots. . . . Their land is filled with idols; they bow down to the work of their hands, to what their own fingers have made.

Isaiah 2:17, 18

And the haughtiness of man shall be humbled, and the pride of men shall be brought low; and the Lord alone will be exalted in that day. . . . And the idols shall utterly pass away.

THE UTTER realism of the words, "there is no end to their chariots," I could speak of at this moment. I have just come home from treading through Washington traffic. After the headache of finding a parking place for one of the multitudinous "chariots" of our day, there is the anticipation of moving in a bumper to bumper line of similar conveyances, to wiggle your way home. Yet the kind of car he owns, or whether or not it is the latest model, is often a man's greatest concern. It is a "first" in his life.

Some folks think that idols are only images made of stone or wood; those horrid looking things that the faraway heathen worship! America had better look to its own idolatry. What is the passion of many people? Is it not to get rich—and quick? Is not our judgment of the importance of people often governed by the amount of money they have? There are those who make learning their idol. Learning is a wonderful thing, especially if it begins with the fear of the Lord. But to worship at the throne of the mind is to commit spiritual suicide. There are those who give the major devotion of their lives to these two, because they think that they are a means to prominence. That becomes their idol, the desire for recognition and adulation.

Those of us who are homemakers have our peculiar and subtle struggle with idols, too. One's cooking ability can become the first passion of one's life, or the achievement of one's children, or their appearance. I have known women so inoculated with the collecting bug that they had no time to help in the furtherance of the kingdom work; no time to give a cup of cold water in the name of the Christ. I have seen young people make athletics their idol, or romance has been on the throne in their hearts, or pleasure.

None of these things is a sin in itself. All of them are gifts to us in God's wonderful world. What place they have in your heart, that is the important question. Daily, it is to hear Christ say to you, "Seek first the kingdom."

PRAYER: *"The dearest idol I have known, whate'er that idol be, Help me to tear it from Thy throne, and worship only Thee." Amen.*

O for a Closer Walk with God

The dearest idol I have known, . . .
Help me to tear it from Thy throne

Galatians 2:20

I have been crucified with Christ; it is no longer I who live, but Christ who lives in me; and the life I now live in the flesh, I live by faith in the Son of God, who loved me and gave himself for me.

AN OLD boatman, who was fixing his nets at the end of a pier, was asked by a bystander: "If anybody fell from this pier into the water, would he be drowned?" With a quizzical smile, he gave the answer: "No, it is not falling into the water that drowns a man." "What then, is it?" And his significant answer was: "Staying there." It is not falling into sin that damns a man. It is refusing to return to the Father in penitence and contrition. Succinctly this same thought has been put into these lines:

When the fight begins within himself,
A man's worth something. God stoops o'er his head,
Satan looks up between his feet—both tug—
He's left, himself, i' the middle: the soul wakes
And grows. Prolong that battle through his life!
Never leave growing till the life to come!

ROBERT BROWNING

This tearing the sin from the throne is the difficult process. Some of us have embraced our sins so long that we are in bondage. On the castle grounds in England there are trees that are dwarfed because ivy vines have so encircled their trunks as to stunt their growth. Only the axe of the woodsman can avail to break the enslavement. Yet at one time those strong heavy vines were no more than ivy tendrils. So it is with sin. So subtly does it entwine us that before we know it, its attachment is too strong for us to break. The songwriter speaks of tearing the idol from the throne. That process suggests pain and discomfort. So it will be, if you really want to give up your darling sin. Is it a temper? Is it indifference? Or is it that all-encompassing one, *self?* Even as a tree will only know freedom when the woodsman comes with his axe, so you in your own power will never be able to free yourself. I have an idea you have already learned this. Only by the power of the Holy Spirit of God can you know victory. Each one of us who has tried to remove the obstacles between us and God in our own strength will witness that it cannot be done without Him. But with Him anything is possible; no sin is too tough! That is why we need this closer walk; it is why we should be aware of Him every minute; it is why we need to keep the channels of His Word and prayer constantly open. It is hard to give up yourself to God; but it is the most glorious surrender in all the world. It is the surrender that is victory.

PRAYER: *Live in me, Lord! By the power of Your Holy Spirit, tear the idols from the throne of my heart. Dethrone self! Let those about me today see Your presence in me. In Jesus' name. Amen.*

Onward, Christian Soldiers

Onward, Christian Soldiers

Marching as to war

Revelation 6:2

And I saw, and behold, a white horse, and its rider had a bow; and a crown was given to him, and he went out conquering and to conquer.

1 Timothy 6:12

Fight the good fight of the faith; take hold of the eternal life to which you were called when you made the good confession in the presence of many witnesses.

TOO MANY people who call themselves Christians think of their religion as an escape rather than an encounter; they want to enjoy a siesta rather than to participate in a siege. Christ never minced matters in regard to what His followers had to expect. He made it very plain that it would be a constant struggle, with the odds often appearing to be pitted against you. He emphasized the fact that it would be going against the stream.

Paul, too, in his letters uses the figures of speech that indicate competition and a struggle. "Fight the good fight of the faith," "run a race," "press on to the goal"— these are the terms he uses to describe the Christian life. Could it be that we have lost this sense of commission in the Christian Church today?

It is Bishop McDowell who tells the story of an old soldier who, in recounting his army life, stated that he had received three wounds, one of which he showed the listener. "Where are the other two?" he was asked. "Oh, they were only insignificant, for they were made by spent balls." There are Christians who remain so far away from the scene of battle that the only wounds they ever receive are from spent balls; they literally "bring up the rear." Yet in the Christian battle there can be no rear. Jesus again and again emphasized this fact. Of His disciples it was said, "They left everything and followed him." No halfway measure, this; no "maybe," or "if," or "but"! It is as basic as, "Are you with Him, or are you not?

Each day we need to face ourselves with the choice. Do we want to join Him who went out conquering and to conquer? It is the willy-nilly type of discipleship that is most irritating to the Lord. The Bible uses pretty strong language to describe His reaction: "I know your works: you are neither cold nor hot! Would that you were cold or hot! So because you are lukewarm, and neither cold nor hot, I will spew you out of my mouth!"

Are you willing to face battle for the Christ today? That means forgetting what you want to do, and running His errands. It means that you will be willing to forego your own comforts, if this will make you a better soldier of His. It means that in the planning of this day, you will follow His marching orders!

PRAYER: *Too often, Lord, we have wanted a bed of roses, when You needed us in the dugout. Give us a sense of the glory of the battle for eternity. Make us good soldiers! In Jesus' name. Amen.*

Onward, Christian Soldiers

**With the Cross of Jesus
Going on before**

Matthew 16:24-26

> Then Jesus told his disciples, "If any man would come after me, let him deny himself and take up his cross and follow me. For whoever would save his life will lose it, and whoever loses his life for my sake will find it. For what will it profit a man, if he gains the whole world and forfeits his life?"

THESE ARE hard words. Maybe this soldiering business is not what you want, after all. The rich young ruler, when faced with it, could not take it. In his mind there must have continued the question: "Is there not an easier way?" Down through all the centuries men have flinched at this point. This is symbolically illustrated in the story of a European who some years ago was captured and held captive by a Mohammedan tribe in North Africa. He devoted the time at his disposal to sketching, and many of the natives were delighted at his skill. They determined to use it to the benefit of both: he was to help them by drawing the plans of a mosque; in turn, he would receive his freedom for this work. So he set about to fulfill his part of the bargain. It was finally done, and considered quite excellent, until one of the natives discovered that the building was in the form of a cross. So angry were they that they immediately put the architect to death. The rich young ruler, too, admired the *plan* of salvation, but objected to the cross.

Yet it is only in this cross that we have our power. Its message is victory over death and the promise of everlasting life. Omit the cross from your theology, and you have a humanism that, in the final analysis, is helpless to save a man. A Scotch fisherman, who was something of an amateur bait maker, on one expedition noticed that he was losing all the fish that nibbled. Upon investigation, he found that by some accident, the barb had been broken from the hook. In his quaint philosophy, he said this is exactly what happens when people preached the love of God to men, but left out the essential truth that it is in the Christ on the cross, that God's love is revealed. Jesus said, "And I, when I am lifted up from the earth, will draw all men to myself."

Could it be that our Christian witness has been ineffective because we have balked at the cross? Is there the denying of self in your life? Is it more important that you should be comfortable in your community than that you should stand for the things that you know are right?

Dwight L. Moody has said, "The way to get rid of a cross is to die upon it. Jesus bore no cross in the resurrection." This victory is ahead for every Christian soldier who bears the cross of Jesus.

PRAYER: *So much of our Christian living is soft, Lord. True us up to the kind of soldiering that will be a mighty witness to Your presence in us. Amen.*

Onward, Christian Soldiers

At the sign of triumph,
Satan's armies flee

Luke 4:2-4

And he ate nothing in those days; and when they were ended, he was hungry. The devil said to him, "If you are the Son of God, command this stone to become bread!" And Jesus answered him, "It is written, 'Man shall not live by bread alone.'"

James 1:12

Blessed is the man who endures trial, for when he has stood the test he will receive the crown of life which God has promised to those who love him.

IS THERE anything more exhilarating than by the power of the Holy Spirit to put to rout the enemy of our soul? And is there anything more asinine, or that fills you more with chagrin, than to have to acknowledge that you were weak and gave in? In the discipline of dieting, one has a little of this experience. When you are strong enough to say "no" to the dessert that is oozing with whipped cream and that, incidentally, is your favorite, there is an exhilaration that amply repays you for the denying yourself the physical enjoyment the dessert would have given. And the more times that you can smilingly say "no," the easier the process becomes.

Jesus has set for us the pattern of meeting the onslaughts of the evil one. With every temptation, His weapon was: "It is written." Today, people know so little of the "Writing" that they are ill equipped to meet the enemy. Try Christ's method the next time temptation hits you. Maybe it will be the temptation of your tongue. You will be on the brink of saying something unkind about someone. From your heart let there come the prayer: "Lord, keep a watch over my lips!" Or maybe the temptation will be the one of discouragement. You will be possessed by a spirit of "What's the use?" Then take out of the "Writing" which you have stored up in your heart, "In the world you have tribulation; but be of good cheer, I have overcome the world." Martin Luther wrote it, and it really works! "One little word o'erthrows him." That little Word is Christ! There is no temptation but can be met by the breathing of His name in prayer.

There is the delightful story of the converted miser, to whom a neighbor in distress appealed for help. The miser decided to prove the genuineness of his conversion by giving him a ham. On his way to get it, the tempter whispered: "Give him the smallest one you have." A mental struggle ensued, and finally the miser took down the largest one that he had. "You are a fool," the devil said. The farmer replied, "If you don't keep still, I'll give him every ham in the smokehouse."

PRAYER: *For every temptation, Lord Christ, You have supplied the strength and the wherewithal to meet it. Make me so diligent to know Your Word, that I will be well fortified. Help me this day to make some new portion mine. In Your name. Amen.*

Onward, Christian Soldiers

**But the Church of Jesus
Constant will remain**

Matthew 16:15-18

He said to them, "But who do you say that I am?" Simon Peter replied, "You are the Christ, the Son of the living God." And Jesus answered him, ". . . And I tell you, you are Peter, and on this rock I will build my church, and the powers of death shall not prevail against it."

SURELY IT is inconsistent with the wisdom of God to think that on Peter the church was to be built; Peter, even in the Book of Acts, showing himself to be very human at times, and needing the constant tempering of the Holy Spirit! But to build a church on Peter's confession of faith—that is another thing! And wherever this same confession is made by anyone, there the Church of Jesus Christ is built. The constancy of the Lord can never be questioned. It is only the inconstancy of His followers that is very difficult for the world to understand. The church will know constancy, will be able to convey this sense of eternal stability and dependability, only as you and I, members of that Church, build on Jesus Christ. He is the same, yesterday, today, and for ever. He is a rock and a refuge, and the lifter up of the head to me, as He was to my grandmother and to my mother. He will be the same for our children and their children, if they will put their trust in Him.

Through the dark ages, through persecution, and over above tyrants, though it sometimes had to go underground, the Church of Jesus Christ has conquered in every age. Is there not an exhilaration in being on the winning side? Is this the tone of your church work?

This same victory applies to our personal lives, if our confession is the rock of faith in Christ. We can then say that the Lord is our helper, and we will not fear what man shall do to us.

In the month of May is Memorial Day. Across this great land of ours we honor those who have fought under the banner of the Stars and Stripes. I would pause to think with love about the thousands who could have brought so much to living. Most of them had no desire to fight. They hated it. They hated to be separated from their loved ones and their homes. What can we do to prevent this kind of mass murder from happening again?

You really know the answer down deep in your heart. If we are truly in earnest, we will want to bend every effort to extend the kingdom of Christ on earth. We will want to give our first, our best, and our all for this greatest of all life's causes. We will want to be soldiers in the kingdom of which there shall be no end.

PRAYER: *Thank You, Lord, for the constancy of Your Church. Thank You that it is not built on man's puny efforts. Thank You that in our daily life we need have no fear, when You are our God and Savior. In Jesus' name. Amen.*

Onward, Christian Soldiers

Hell's foundations quiver
At the shout of praise

Psalm 89:1, 2

I will sing of thy steadfast love, O Lord, for ever;
with my mouth I will proclaim thy faithfulness to all generations.
For thy steadfast love was established for ever,
thy faithfulness is firm as the heavens.

Acts 16:25, 26

But about midnight Paul and Silas were praying and singing hymns to God, and the prisoners were listening to them, and suddenly there was a great earthquake, so that the foundations were shaken; and immediately all the doors were opened and every one's fetters were unfastened.

YES, HELL'S foundations quiver at the shout of praise! That is what happened in the prison when Paul and Silas used even their imprisonment to witness to the victory that they knew in Christ. They were singing their hymns to God and prisoners were listening to them. Today as Christians, we need to give the witness of a shout of praise. To acknowledge God, to proclaim His steadfast love and faithfulness; to show that, no matter how tough the going, His empowering is sure—this kind of witness puts Satan to running so fast that you will hardly be able to see his tracks.

The shout of praise in the refrain of a hymn was the gunshot that defeated Satan in the heart of what was Brazil's most notorious gunman. This is the story as told by Pastor Mosely, a missionary in that area. This gunman was the official killer in those parts. If anybody wanted someone bumped off, he hired this man to do it. He carried a knife on one hip and a valuable gun on the other. (Guns were contraband there!) An evangelist heard that this man was driving into a section of the interior where he very much wanted to go. His faith in God's keeping care was such that he asked if he might have a ride. He wanted to conduct a meeting in one of the towns. The gunman acquiesced to his going, but announced to him that in this town he would eat his lunch and drink his home-brew, and when he was through, regardless of the meeting, they were moving on—or else! The evangelist immediately conceived of the idea of announcing a hymn to draw his meeting to a close when the gunman would be approaching. In Brazil they would not think of ever omitting a stanza of a hymn. To them that would be sacrilege. The hymn had thirteen stanzas. The gunman, however, was intrigued by the singing, and rather than interrupting, he listened through them all. Each one ended with a refrain that told of the wonderful love of Jesus. They started on their journey again, but the gunman found that he was haunted by this refrain. He began to inquire about what it meant. Pastor Mosely was sent for, and this brilliant but illiterate man, who was such a destructive tool in the hands of the devil, has now memorized a good portion of Scripture, and is one of the most effective preachers of the gospel in Brazil.

PRAYER: *Put praise on my lips and a song of rejoicing in my heart, O God. In Jesus' name. Amen.*

Onward, Christian Soldiers

Crowns and thrones may perish,
Kingdoms rise and wane

Psalm 46:6-9

The nations rage, the kingdoms totter;
he utters his voice, the earth melts.
The Lord of hosts is with us;
the God of Jacob is our refuge. *Selah.*

HOW SLOW are we to learn and how blind are we when we read! The writing on the pages of the history of our time is a very dramatic story of the tottering kingdoms and perishing thrones. Think of what a series of such events you and I have witnessed in the last fifty years. (You may not be fifty, but you will have read about them!) Earlier there had been a Herod and a Nero and a Caesar. Then there was a Napoleon and a Bismarck. Then there came upon the scene a Hitler and a Mussolini. And a Lenin and a Stalin! Yet people wonder, what the outcome will be, and live in fear and trepidation of all the "isms" that are a part of this generation. Kingdoms rise and wane! How we need to rid ourselves of this terrible fear defensive, whose atmosphere of suspicion is deadly to Christian democracy and to faith! How we need to revive the "gay, unconquerable courage of the early church" that "feared not those who harmed the body, but rather those who harmed the soul." Most often the latter disintegration is within our own hearts and is not from without at all.

When Hitler was riding roughshod over Europe, the places that gave way readily were those where there was interior dissolution. Someone in the home base played traitor. We best serve our country, the world, and our God when we bend every effort to make our Christian profession so real in its daily life, and so applicable in our relations to our neighbors, that the seeds of distrust and dissatisfaction find no soil in which to take root. We need to read our history and hear again the thundering voice of the Old Testament prophet, "Righteousness exalts a nation, but sin is a reproach to any people."

Christian Soldier (even though you may be wearing a house dress), take heart. The only things that are sure and constant and changeless are the precepts of the Lord. Here is the foundation on which to build.

Look to your faith. Live it in your home. Let its fragrance spread to your neighborhood. It is needed desperately "across the tracks." Yes, the call of seeking hearts for a foundation that is sure comes from around the world. Spend your energies and your gifts on building the kingdom. This kind of soldiering makes living abundant!

PRAYER: *Give us such a discernment, Lord, that we may know what the real enemies of our soul are. Help us to battle against pride and prejudice and selfishness and smugness in our lives. We rejoice in the victory that we can know through the empowering of Your Holy Spirit. Thank You, again, that we can walk through life unafraid! Amen!*

Onward, Christian Soldiers

**Onward, then, ye faithful,
Join our happy throng**

Psalm 147: 1-6

Praise the Lord! For it is good to sing praises to our God; for he is gracious, and a song of praise is seemly. The Lord builds up Jerusalem; he gathers the outcasts of Israel. He heals the brokenhearted, and binds up their wounds. He determines the number of the stars, he gives to all of them their names. Great is our Lord, and abundant in power; his understanding is beyond measure. The Lord lifts up the downtrodden, he casts the wicked to the ground.

CHRISTIAN SOLDIERS make a joyful noise unto the Lord. They join with all creation. The psalmist exhorts the latter to praise: "Praise him, sun and moon, praise him, all you shining stars!" How much more ought we who know His redemptive power in Christ Jesus praise Him. A French infidel said to a peasant: "We will pull down your churches, and destroy everything that reminds you of God and Christ." The peasant replied, "But you will leave us the stars, and as long as the stars revolve and shine, so long the heavens will be a sign unto us of the glory of God."

It is not just the vocal singing that is evidence of Christ in the heart. There are those who may not have the gift of voice. But the song of a life is undeniable. A poor widow could neither sing nor lead in prayer, but she was always in her place, encouraging the pastor with her faithfulness. She was not able to contribute much, but she sent flowers to the pastor's study. An invalid who, though detained at home, always wanted to know the pastor's theme, always prayed for the service, and always kept him laden with messages of love for others in the church. Hers was the song of a life.

An English journal quoted the headmaster of a Scottish school: "The wonder is that the church holds its own as it does. Here is a minister. He preaches ten, twenty, thirty, or even forty years, and never lacks someone to listen. He has little help. Look at the theatres. See the staff, the advertisements, and so forth. And yet they must change their bill of fare every week. There must be something divine in the church, otherwise it could never continue."

Mr. Schoolmaster, there is Someone divine in the church. Those of us who know Him have a song in our hearts. We would like to share it. It is too good, too great, to keep. Join us in the happy throng. Look to a Sabbath morning when around the globe the line forms to the temple. See the fruits of compassion and love that Christian lives are sharing around the world. Visit a Christian home and know its hospitality. Yes, onward Christian soldiers! Lift the banner of love around the world; live it in your concern for every person Christ died to save.

PRAYER: *Make us conveyors of Your invitation, Lord. Help us to extend Your fellowship to everyone we meet. Make our soldiering to be a thing of every day and wherever we are. In Jesus' name. Amen.*

Come, Holy Spirit, Heavenly Dove

Belmont. C. M. WILLIAM GARDINER, 1812.

Or: Nun danket all' und bringet Ehr (Störl), No. 66.

3 In vain we tune our lifeless songs,
In vain we strive to rise;
Hosannas languish on our tongues,
And our devotion dies.

4 Come, Holy Spirit, heavenly Dove,
With all Thy quickening powers,
Come, shed abroad a Saviour's love,
And that shall kindle ours.

Isaac Watts, 1709.

SUNDAY

Come, Holy Spirit, Heavenly Dove

With all Thy quickening powers

Joel 2:28, 29

"And it shall come to pass afterward, that I will pour out my spirit on all flesh; and your sons and your daughters shall prophesy, your old men shall dream dreams, and your young men shall see visions. Even upon the menservants and maidservants in those days, I will pour out my spirit."

THE PROMISE in the Book of Joel was given in expectancy of the coming of the day of the Lord. It was fulfilled when God made His personal visitation to this earth in the person of Jesus Christ. When He was about to ascend to His Father, He picked up the promise and reiterated it with His signature that was notarized by the cross. As we are in these commemorative Pentecost days, it would be well for us to consider Pentecost preparations. What did the disciples do while they waited for the outpouring of the Holy Spirit?

Read the first chapter of the Book of the Acts. The disciples had asked Christ, just before His ascension, when they could expect all the things He had promised. Like little children—and like us—they were asking, "when?" Listen to His reply, "It is not for you to know times or seasons which the Father has fixed by his own authority. But you shall receive power . . . ." Then they experienced the ascension and proceeded to carry out His orders. They returned to Jerusalem, went to the upper room and, "All these with one accord devoted themselves to prayer."

What a pattern for the church to follow! "With one accord," "devoted to prayer"—— are these the characteristics of today's church? of your church? Or more specifically (because the church is not different from its individual members), do these two phrases describe your personal life? You will say, " 'with one accord,' how can you say that about me? I am only one person." You are only one person, but there are many parts of you. Is the total of you integrated into the Christ? Does everything you do glorify Him? Think through your calendar for this day, your plans for the week. Could there be written above them, "This one thing I do; . . . I press on toward the goal for the prize of the upward care of God in Christ Jesus"?

And then there is the characteristic, "devoted themselves to prayers." Would that describe your prayer life? Or is it a mechanical process that you go through, thinking that it is some kind of magic that will keep evil from befalling you?

How much do you want a Pentecost in your life? Here are the directions for the preparation. This week as we think about the Holy Spirit, it could happen. Are you willing to pray?

PRAYER: *Holy Spirit of God, prepare my heart for an outpouring of Your presence. Remove the blocks of self-will and indifference. This week, Lord, let me feel the breeze. In Christ's name. Amen.*

Come, Holy Spirit, Heavenly Dove

And light a flame of sacred love
In these cold hearts of ours

Jeremiah 7:13

"And now, because you have done all these things, says the Lord, and when I spoke to you, persistently you did not listen, and when I called you, you did not answer."

Proverbs 29:1

He who is often reproved, yet stiffens his neck will suddenly be broken beyond healing.

PERHAPS IT would be profitable to define the Holy Spirit. He is not so named because He is holier than the other Persons of the Godhead; rather, it is because His special function is to sanctify us, to cultivate holiness in us. Someone has well described Him in these words: "The Spirit is the abiding representative of the Godhead in the heart of the believer." In Martin Luther's explanation to the Third Article of the Apostles' Creed, he says that the Holy Ghost "has called (us) through the gospel, (there is our need of the Bible in our lives again!) enlightened (me) with His gifts, and sanctified and preserved (us)."

Do you remember when, on a given Sunday, you returned from the sanctuary with a stirring within you to renewed Christian living? In the glow of the Holy Spirit's calling, you may even have made some promises to God as to how different some things in your life would be. Then came Monday and the rush of material plans. Somehow or other, the breeze that had stirred was now stilled by the stifling air of the world.

When you say you "meant" to do good things you are only saying that the Holy Spirit called you and you hardened your heart. You know what happens if you hear a voice and go on and on, with no intervening action in response to the voice. You become immune to it. You do not even hear it after a while.

I have visited in a home that was built close to the railroad tracks. The thundering trains that roared by deafened my ears. I have asked my hostess if the noise did not bother. "Why," has been the response, "we don't even hear it!" If the Holy Spirit tugs at your heart again and again, and you do not respond, you will come to the place where you will no longer hear Him. Jesus said, "Why do you call me 'Lord, Lord,' and do not do what I tell you?"

PRAYER: *Lord, again and again, I have said "no" to You, because I have not done what You have told me to. I have not loved my neighbor as myself; I have not gone the second mile very often. And I have complained plenty! Forgive me, and cleanse me through Jesus Christ. And now today, Lord, so dwell in me with Your Spirit, that I shall not miss Your leading. Stir me, Lord. Amen.*

Come, Holy Spirit, Heavenly Dove

See how we grovel here below

Psalm 90:9

For all our days pass away under thy wrath, our years come to an end like a sigh.

Isaiah 55:2

"Why do you spend your money for that which is not bread, and your labor for that which does not satisfy?"

WHAT A description the psalmist gives us with the line: "Our years come to an end like a sigh!" That is a simple picture of a life that has not responded to the Holy Spirit and has groveled in the things of this earth. In Isaiah the contrast is very effectively made between a life spent with material values and one that responds to the call of the Lord. He speaks of spending money "for that which is not bread." In the same chapter, the antithesis is given: "Seek the Lord while he may be found, call upon him while he is near."

Jesus classifies our grovelings into three groups. It is amazing how apropos they are today. What woman has not asked the question, "What shall we have to eat?" And how many women do not make recipes and the setting of voluptuous tables the major concern of their lives? Do not misunderstand me. I, too, love to cook—and how I enjoy eating! Maybe it is because I realize how easily I could spend the major portion of my day doing just these two things that I am so aware of what the Lord meant. The harvest of the earth is for our enjoyment—yes, and well-balanced meals are what every good housekeeper and homemaker should provide for her family. But if these are your major concern, then the Lord is now talking to you.

Surely most of the folks who will be reading this will not have trouble with "What shall we drink?" But the city of Washington's consumption of alcohol would make you realize that for many people this is the burning question of the day. Exhibit "A" is the man for whom we are praying at this moment; gifted and educated, yet sousing himself with alcohol, so that he is ruining not only his own life, but that of his family as well.

Then there is the third question, "What shall we wear?" Here is a vulnerable point with women. When did you last say that? As a mother, are you more concerned that your daughter should look pretty than that she should be "a King's daughter, all glorious within"? Have you worn yourself out shopping for her or for yourself, or slaving over the sewing machine, until you were so short-tempered, you were fit to be tied? What has all this to do with the Holy Spirit?

Our groveling here below is the obstacle for His working in our hearts. Our distorted sense of values is the lock that keeps Him out. What was Jesus' positive addition? "But seek first his kingdom and his righteousness."

PRAYER: *Lord, we spend so much of our lives on things that perish. Come, Holy Spirit, and teach us eternal values. Amen.*

Come, Holy Spirit, Heavenly Dove

**See how we grovel here below
Fond of these trifling toys**

Proverbs 23:4, 5

Do not toil to acquire wealth; be wise enough to desist.
When your eyes light upon it, it is gone;
for suddenly it takes to itself wings, flying like an eagle toward heaven.

Matthew 6:19-21

"Do not lay up for yourselves treasures on earth, where moth and rust consume and where thieves break in and steal, but lay up for yourselves treasures in heaven, where neither moth nor rust consumes and where thieves do not break in and steal. For where your treasure is, there will your heart be also."

A REAL BLOCK to the outpouring of the Holy Spirit in our lives is our concern with things. The materialism of our age insidiously engulfs us, and before we know it, we are caught up in the swirl of wearing away our lives for the things that perish. Jesus pointed out the significance of the importance of our possessions to us, when He said: "Where your treasure is, there will your heart be also."

We were sitting in a jet-turbine plane, flying from Athens to London. My sister-in-law and I were expressing our disgust that our men folks had kept us so busy sight-seeing, that we did not have any chance to shop. The seats were in threes, and the third woman sitting with us joined in our conversation. After she had introduced herself she said, "I couldn't help but hear what you were saying. I'd like to tell you my experience. My husband has been in foreign service for many years. As we traveled from place to place, I gathered many beautiful things, and was very proud of them. Then one day at the outbreak of the last war, I had a telephone call from my husband in which he said: 'Gather whatever you can into one suitcase. We are going to have to flee, quickly. I'll be right home for you.' Well, in those next minutes I did some tall thinking. What were the things that would mean the most in this emergency? I assure you that they were not the baubles that had been my pride and joy. They are gone, and never again will I concern myself too much about anything material."

We sat quietly for some time after that. I remembered having to sort out things after the passing of loved ones. We cannot take material possessions with us, when the call comes to make the last great journey. Why should we become so fond, then, of these trifling toys?

Christ gives us the positive word. "But lay up for yourselves treasures in heaven." A cup of cold water, given in His name; a stranger given hospitality; a call on some aged, forgotten person; a witnessing to someone for the Lord—you add to the list.

PRAYER: *Dear Lord, so much of our life is spent in pursuit of perishing things. Give us again a sense of values that has the long look of eternity. In Jesus' name. Amen.*

THURSDAY

Come, Holy Spirit, Heavenly Dove

Our souls, how heavily they go,
To reach eternal joys

Psalm 42:2, 3, 5, 8

My soul thirsts for God, for the living God.
When shall I come and behold the face of God?
My tears have been my food day and night,
while men say to me continually, "Where is your God?" . . .
Why are you cast down, O my soul,
and why are you disquieted within me?
Hope in God; for I shall again praise him, my help and my God. . . .
By day the Lord commands his steadfast love; and at night his song is with me.

HOW WE need an injection of the Holy Spirit to lift our lagging feet and our drooping shoulders! In his introduction to his modern translation of the Book of Acts *(The Young Church in Action)*, Dr. Phillips sums up the characteristics of the first century Christians. He speaks of their "gay, unconquerable courage" as contrasted to today's church, fat and immobile with opulence, and "muscle-bound with over-organization." What has happened to the gay unconquerable courage in our own lives?

Jews in the Old Testament dispensation have the many burdens of the law to bear; they are weighed down with rules and regulations about their eating and their living. Not so should it be for New Testament Christians. We are forever free from such enslavements. If heaven is what Christ promised, there should be a spring in the ongoing walk of the soul. Why should one be cast down and joyless on the road that leads home? God is always with you, even to a song in the night. Why, then, should your soul go heavily?

How many witnesses have come from bedsides! A young college girl related the memories of her mother's last days in a bout with cancer that had spread throughout the woman's abdomen. What a heritage those memories were for a girl to have! Here was no cringing coward facing the heartache of leaving this lovely daughter, two sons, and a devoted husband! Here was a story of a valiant warrior who lived life abundantly to her last breath and who faced eternity with great expectation through her faith in her Savior. The daughter told of preserving fruits and vegetables as the mother called instructions from the bedroom. She told how her mother wanted life to move right along, and so sent son and daughter back to college, knowing that she was making her final flight. How shameful it is in the face of such courage and faith that we who are in health should ever permit our souls to go heavily. With what trivia we have been burdened!

PRAYER: *Release my spirit, Lord, from the things that weigh it down, and that make my walk lag. Help me to be honest with myself about it. Amen.*

Come, Holy Spirit, Heavenly Dove

In vain we tune our lifeless songs, . . .
Hosannas languish on our tongues

Acts 2:46, 47

And day by day, attending the temple together and breaking bread in their homes, they partook of food with glad and generous hearts, praising God and having favor with all the people.

Acts 4:31, 32

And when they had prayed, the place in which they were gathered together was shaken; and they were all filled with the Holy Spirit and spoke the word of God with boldness. Now the company of those who believed were of one heart and soul.

THE STORY of the early church is a thrilling one. Something of the drama of it is found in the words: "Now when they saw the boldness of Peter and John, and perceived that they were uneducated, common men, they wondered; and they recognized that they had been with Jesus." Is it not in these very words that we have the answer to our languishing hosannas and our lifeless songs? We have been too little with Jesus. Notice again the preliminary to the outpouring of the Holy Spirit: "And they prayed." What is the prayer life of your congregation like? And what about your personal life?

I like the illustration that Dr. S. D. Gordon uses. He tells of a boy in school, puzzling over an arithmetic problem. It will not "come out." He figures away, and his brow is all knitted and worried, but he cannot seem to get it right. Then the teacher comes and sits down at his side. "How are you coming?" she asks. "It won't come out right," he replies. "Let me see, did you subtract here, and carry over here?" "Oh, I forgot that!" Little by little the teacher shows how it is to be done. She did not do the problem for him; she pointed out the places where he was wrong, and gave the right direction. That is the way the Holy Spirit works in our lives.

We are not puppets that He will manipulate around. But He will guide and direct us into the way of Christ's love, if we will but turn to Him and follow His leading. "If we will but turn to Him," aye, there's the rub! We are back at our prayer life again. Your receiving the empowering of the Holy Spirit will be in direct proportion to the health of your prayers. There will be no languishing hosannas or lifeless songs on the lips of those who daily meet the Lord in earnest petition. Rather there will be the evidence of the glad and generous heart that praises God.

PRAYER:

Come, Holy Spirit, come;
Come with Your fire and burn;
Come with Your wind and cleanse;
Come with Your light and illumine.
Convict, convert, consecrate
Until we are wholly Thine. Amen.

NILS FERRÉ

SATURDAY

Come, Holy Spirit, Heavenly Dove

Come, shed abroad a Saviour's love,
And that shall kindle ours

Acts 3:19, 20

"Repent therefore, and turn again, that your sins may be blotted out, that times of refreshing may come from the presence of the Lord, and that he may send the Christ appointed for you, Jesus."

Acts 5:41, 42

Then they left the presence of the council, rejoicing that they were counted worthy to suffer dishonor for the name. And every day in the temple and at home they did not cease teaching and preaching Jesus as the Christ.

IT IS significant that the Holy Spirit is spoken of as a dove in Scripture. You remember that at the baptism of Christ, the Holy Spirit descended in the form of a dove. Of all birds, the dove is the most easily alarmed and put to flight at hearing a shot fired. Could it be that we have frightened away the Holy Spirit with our bickerings and dissensions; with our quarrelings and suspicions? I want to confess that that is surely the truth in my life. The times of conflict and disunity in our home are those times when we have slammed thc door on the gentle bird.

Did you notice in the Scripture passage, that we are told the early Christians "in the temple and at home they did not cease teaching and preaching Jesus as the Christ." They must have lived Him, too. Of Stephen it is said, "And gazing at him (Stephen), all who sat in the council saw that his face was like the face of an angel." There it is again! They could tell that he had been with Jesus.

What could we not do, if we made the invitation of our hymn today vital and sincere! The early Christians healed the sick, they dispelled the evil spirits, they changed the course of history. The hand of the Lord is not shortened today. It is only that we have closed the door on the Holy Spirit. We do not want to be disturbed. But life is dead without the Christ, and there is no purpose in living. We have had enough of Him to be blessed, but our fires have been burning low. Let us fervently pray for the Holy Spirit to rekindle Christians everywhere, and to begin with us.

An allegory is told about the bellows and the hearth. The former seemed dejected and sad, and so the hearth asked what was the matter. "I have toiled to no purpose," was the reply, "for I have not succeeded in kindling the fire. In fact, the more I blow, the darker it appears." "Perhaps," said the hearth, "it requires something more than your blowing to quicken it. Let someone kindle a fire and then your blowing will make it brighter."

PRAYER: *Holy Spirit of God, kindle a fire in our hearts. Show us our sins, so that by the grace of Christ we may remove the ashes that choke the draft. You have provided the fuel through prayer and the Word. Set us on fire. Amen.*

Jesus Shall Reign Where'er the Sun

Duke Street. L. M. JOHN HATTON, 1790.

3 People and realms of every tongue
Dwell on His love with sweetest song;
And infant voices shall proclaim
Their early blessings on His Name.

4 Blessings abound where'er He reigns;
The prisoner leaps to lose his chains;
The weary find eternal rest,
And all the sons of want are blest.

5 Where He displays His healing power,
Death and the curse are known no more;
In Him the tribes of Adam boast
More blessings than their father lost.

6 Let every creature rise and bring
Peculiar honors to our King;
Angels descend with songs again,
And earth repeat the loud Amen.

Isaac Watts, 1719. Abridged.

SUNDAY

Jesus Shall Reign Where'er the Sun

Does his successive journeys run

Psalm 93:1

The Lord reigns; he is robed in majesty; the Lord is robed, he is girded with strength. Yea, the world is established; it shall never be moved.

Psalm 96:10

Say among the nations, "The Lord reigns! Yea, the world is established, it shall never be moved; he will judge the peoples with equity."

ALL THE way through this group of psalms there is the exultant, jubilant note of the victorious reign of the Lord. All of nature is challenged to join with mortals in raising the song to acknowledge the glory of this reign. Here is a missing note in our Christian living today. So often where groups of Christians are gathered, in church organizations or informally, all the problems loom so large that almost a spirit of defeat obsesses people. "What's the use?" or "What can the few of us do?" is the cry. Shame on us! We deny the power of the very One whose cause we claim to follow. You will find no such note recorded of the early Christians. No obstacle was too hard, no suffering too great to endure for these intrepid souls who had been with Jesus and were *sure* of the One they followed.

You ask a person if he is a Christian, and often his response will be, "Well, I think I am," or "I try to be." But this is not enough. We must know! What a wobbly foundation is ours, if it is built on a maybe! In response to Christ's question as to who the disciples thought He was, what if Peter had said, "We hope you are the Messiah"? It was the sureness of his witness that won for him such commendation from the Lord. "I *know* that my Redeemer lives" is the most vital source of strength that a Christian has.

If you do not have this certainty, how do you get it? And if you have it, how do you keep it? Live in God's Word, and claim for yourself every promise of God. There is no wish-washiness about them. They are for you. Move out in faith on these promises and try them. Begin where you are in your home, and take one promise and live with it. Through the power of the Holy Spirit as He works in the Word, there will be a new sense of strength.

All the electrical power in the world is no good if you do not turn it on. I trust its efficacy when I go to my stove and turn the knob. I never question but that it will work, even though there have been times when it has failed. No one who has honestly tried the power of God in his life can say that He has ever failed him.

PRAYER: *Give me, O Lord, this sense of Your conquering power. Let others know in me the sureness of Your sufficiency. Forgive me for my whimperings and whinings, when I have focused only on the problem, and not on Your resources. Make me a tower of strength to others! In Jesus' name. Amen.*

Jesus Shall Reign Where'er the Sun

His kingdom stretch from shore to shore

Psalm 22: 27, 28

All the ends of the earth shall remember and turn to the Lord;
and all the families of the nations shall worship before him.
For dominion belongs to the Lord, and he rules over the nations.

Matthew 24:14

"And this gospel of the kingdom will be preached throughout the whole world, as a testimony to all nations; and then will the end come."

HOW GRATEFUL I am to the Lord that His salvation is for every one who will receive it! Otherwise I might have been excluded! It could be I, as well as anyone else!

The extent of His kingdom was brought more clearly home to me through the acquaintance of Pastor John Havea of the Tonga Islands. With a twinkle in his eye, he asked us if we knew in what a remarkable age we were living. Then he told us that four months after he had come to the United States to study, his wife, in Tonga, had a new baby girl. She wanted to get word to the father quickly, so she telegraphed John the news. He received the telegram six hours *before* the baby was born! United Church Women know well that Tonga is where World Day of Prayer begins, for while we are yet sleeping, it is morning there, and the Queen of Tonga begins the first link, whose chain follows the course of the sun, and encircles the globe.

The promise of Scripture is that the love of Christ will be preached to every land, before He will return in glory. It is happening—and fast! It is a thrilling story, this spreading of the kingdom. There comes to my mind the little woman from the Belgian Congo who spoke to the Women's Society of Christian Service of the Methodist Church in Florida. Her face bore the marks of welts where her father had permitted the witch doctor to use the knife in order to let out the evil spirits! But in spite of this distortion, there was a beauty and glow about her that was unmistakable. She knew Jesus, and she did not want to miss an opportunity of telling others what He meant to her. She told us how her father had promised her as a young child to a chief to be his fortieth wife. In her broken English (she had never been to school a day of her life!) she said, "I no want to be fortieth wife of the chief. I no want to go live with him." Then she related how she came in contact with a mission station and the miraculous change that followed in the pattern of her life. Now she is married to a fine Christian, who was here in the U. S. studying, so that he could go back to his people and translate the Bible into their dialects. "His kingdom stretch from shore to shore."

PRAYER: *Make us mindful this day, Lord, of the peoples of the world. You want all to be saved, and to come to the knowledge of what You have done for us. Amen.*

TUESDAY

Jesus Shall Reign Where'er the Sun

Till moons shall wax and wane no more

Isaiah 9:7

Of the increase of his government and of peace there will be no end, upon the throne of David, and over his kingdom, to establish it, and to uphold it with justice and with righteousness from this time forth and for evermore. The zeal of the Lord of hosts will do this.

Revelation 11:15

". . . . The kingdom of the world has become the kingdom of our Lord and of his Christ, and he shall reign for ever and ever."

THIS TRUTH of the eternity of the kingdom to which Christ calls us, was gloriously prophesied in Isaiah, and runs like a gold thread throughout the Bible. It was reiterated at the birth of Christ, and is reaffirmed in Revelation in connection with the foretelling of His coming again. Life has many beautiful moments, but always they are overshadowed by the realization that they must come to an end. I think about this when the young folks come home for Christmas, and the joy of our being together seems almost more than I can contain. Then all too soon comes the day when their grips are packed again into the car, and the lunch boxes are placed on the back shelf of the vehicle. I wonder if this latter gesture of mine (sending lunch with them to be enjoyed along the way), is not in part a desire to prolong our being together?

So it is with all of life. It is a series of beginnings and endings. Not so the kingdom of our Lord. The Bible uses every possible word to reiterate this truth: endless, everlasting, eternal, forever, without end—you fill out the list as you read Scripture. Is it not thrilling to be a part of such a kingdom?

Surely to such a cause we will want to give our best, our first, and our all! But do we? The answer is so self-evident as to be painful. The work of the Christian Church would not lag, as it so often does, if those who claim to be Christ's followers gave such fealty. Had we sent a thousand missionaries into the Far East fifty years ago, the enslavement that China knows today might never have been. Had we through these years following the Civil War treated people as human beings, instead of as inferior because of their color, we would not be knowing the unchristian tensions that we have today. If we do not today step in and use the open doors of Africa, and some parts of South America, for the Lord Jesus Christ, we may have lost our opportunity. If we do not live Him where we are, in relationship to our concern for our fellow men whoever they be, we are not worthy to be a part of His kingdom.

PRAYER: *We thank You, Lord, that in a world where things are always terminating and changing, we can have the joy of knowing that we are investing in an everlasting enterprise. By the indwelling of Your Holy Spirit, help us to give our best. Amen.*

WEDNESDAY

Jesus Shall Reign Where'er the Sun

People and realms of ev'ry tongue
Dwell on His love with sweetest song

Isaiah 42: 10-12

Sing to the Lord a new song, his praise from the end of the earth! . . . Let the desert and its cities lift up their voice, the villages that Kedar inhabits; let the inhabitants of Sela sing for joy, let them shout from the top of the mountains. Let them give glory to the Lord, and declare his praise in the coastlands.

AS I HAVE been copying this Scripture, the remembrance of guests who have shared our home and who have come from around the world, comes to mind. Around our dinner table there have been these folks from the ends of the earth that have lifted their voices in praise to God for Jesus Christ. It has been as if it were a foretaste of heaven, when from every people and every tribe shall come those who will praise the Lamb.

There was Peter Poonan, now chief bridge engineer under Nehru for the Indian government. His parting is unforgettable for he had come to be like a member of our family. He stood at the door, and with moist eyes said, "We will meet again; if we do not meet in this life, we will in the life to come."

How we enjoyed the sense of humor that Dr. Mary Moses had, and what a thrill it was to hear of the miracles of faith and prayer that she was experiencing in her hospital. I loved what she wrote when my brother visited her in Bhimavarum. He stands six feet and two inches tall, and is a great big Viking. She is not much more than four feet. She told how thrilling his visit was, and then said, "Why, it was just like having my own family with me; he was just like a brother would be!" And the chorus echoes, "Yes, a brother in Christ."

What rich African voices blend theirs with ours in praise to the Christ! No Christmas was richer than the one when Sanga (he said we could simply call him that) from Tanganyika was introduced to America by Christmas in an American home. How beautifully he sang the carols for us in his native tongue. It was to hear afresh the angel chorus. Added to all of these are the friends from Pakistan, from Nigeria, from China, from the Philippines, from India, from Japan. Dr. Kagawa's radiant young daughter was one of these. Not least are our fellow Americans, different color though they be. How they have enriched our lives! I just do not see color of skin any more; I just see eyes—eyes that are windows into souls, precious in the sight of the Lord. People and realms of every tongue . . . dwell on His love!

PRAYER: *Thank You, Lord, for the inclusive universality of Your love. Thank You for the rich contribution every people makes. Thank You that we are all children of the King. Forgive any superiority or snobbery that we may have shown. In Jesus' name. Amen.*

THURSDAY

Jesus Shall Reign Where'er the Sun

And infant voices shall proclaim
Their early blessings on His Name

Matthew 21: 15, 16

But when the chief priests and the scribes saw the wonderful things that he did, and the children crying out in the temple, "Hosanna to the Son of David!" they were indignant; and they said to him, "Do you hear what these are saying?" And Jesus said to them, "Yes, have you never read,
'Out of the mouths of babes and sucklings
thou hast brought perfect praise'?"

AS A mother, how grateful I have been for the pictures that the Bible gives us of God's relationship and love for children. When I was carrying a little one under my heart, it was such a joy to recount the words, "He will feed his flock like a shepherd, he will gather the lambs in his arms, he will carry them in his bosom, and gently lead those that are with young." Children and Jesus belong together. He enjoined us to have a faith like theirs, if we would enter the kingdom of heaven. Wherever His love has gone, children have been blessed.

In the Far East, a woman came to a missionary one day with a baby that had been found in the ditch. The poor child had been cast out by its own father, because it was only a girl. In begging the missionary to take care of the poor little object, (it was covered with mud), the woman said, "Please do take this little thing; your God is the only God that teaches us to be good to children." And it is the God we know in Christ who says that in Him there is neither male, nor female, but that each is as precious in His sight.

What faith children have! When our Aunt Ruth had T.B., and was in a sanatorium, she was the subject of our family prayers every night. It seemed that everybody around the circle would remember her. On this one night, for some unaccountable reason (except that we had been so engrossed by the pressing need of our neighbor), Aunt Ruth's name was omitted. I shall never forget how Biz came to me at the end of our prayers almost in tears and said, "Mother, we haven't helped Aunt Ruth yet." To her, praying was synonymous with helping. And her faith was rewarded, for in a year's time Aunt Ruth was restored to her family and has been living a rich, full life ever since.

Sometimes there are burdens connected with our work, and obstacles that seem almost insurmountable. How many times, then, when I must have appeared downcast, one of the children has come to me and said, "We've prayed about it, haven't we? What are you worried about then?"

PRAYER: *For little children everywhere around the world, we would pray, O Lord. Give us such tender hearts that we will respond to the cry of a needy child anywhere. And O God, help us so to walk, that in following us, they will find You. In Jesus' name. Amen.*

Jesus Shall Reign Where'er the Sun

Blessings abound where'er He reigns

Galatians 5:22

But the fruit of the Spirit is love, joy, peace, patience, kindness, goodness, faithfulness, gentleness, self-control: against such there is no law.

Luke 4:18

"The Spirit of the Lord is upon me, because he has anointed me to preach good news to the poor. He has sent me to proclaim release to the captives and recovering of sight to the blind; to set at liberty those who are oppressed, to proclaim the acceptable year of the Lord."

YES, BLESSINGS abound where'er He reigns. First of all, as our hymn suggests, there is liberty for the prisoner. The worst bondage of all is the bondage of sin. There is only one release from that, and it is through the Lord Christ. Everywhere that Christ has come in His truth and power, physical slavery has had to go, too. It is only where men have called themselves by His name, but really have not known Him, that it has persisted.

Then there is rest for the weary when Christ enters in. As a mother, how I wish I could adequately share this with every mother the world around. For in Him, there is both spiritual and physical rest. Weary souls get an injection of new life after time spent in His presence. What a difference it makes to have Him at a bedside, or by an operating table!

The story is told of a little girl who had to have an emergency appendectomy. When the nurse came to give her an anesthesia, she protested. Then the nurse said, "Don't be afraid. This will just put you to sleep." Brightening up, the little girl replied, "Oh, then I want to say my prayers first." And kneeling at the side of the operating table, while the nurses and surgeon waited, the lass prayed: "Now I lay me down to sleep . . ." And with that she blithely returned to the operating table, and permitted the nurse to put her to sleep. The doctor was so moved at the appropriateness of her prayer, that when he went the round of his wards that day, he shared with his patients the story of the little girl who was not afraid to go to sleep on an operating table, after she had committed herself into God's good hands.

Freedom, rest, healing, release from death—these and many more are the blessings that abound where the Lord Christ reigns.

PRAYER: *Lord, we find that words are so inadequate to express our gratitude for all Your blessings. Wherever You come, You bring life, and peace, and joy. Thank You. In Jesus' name. Amen.*

Jesus Shall Reign Where'er the Sun

Let every creature rise and bring
Peculiar honors to our King

Hebrews 13:15, 16

Through him then let us continually offer up a sacrifice of praise to God, that is, the fruit of lips that acknowledge his name. Do not neglect to do good and to share what you have, for such sacrifices are pleasing to God.

Matthew 25:40

And the King will answer them, "Truly, I say to you, as you did it to one of the least of these my brethren, you did it to me."

EACH OF us will have her own way of showing homage to the King. In Africa a woman may bring an egg or two; and compared to our gifts, that will indeed be great, for it will be out of her necessity. In India a man was found to be plowing with himself in the place where the oxen should be. His gratitude for this new story that he had heard of the love of God in sending His Son to be a Savior, prompted his selling his oxen, that he might give a worthy gift. Even in our contemporary life, here in America, our gifts will vary. To some, God has given a voice to sing His praises; to others He has given nimble hands and feet to serve Him; to some, He has given great intellects and administrative ability. The gifts may vary, but the heart that prompts their dedication is the same. It is a heart wherein Jesus Christ reigns as King.

In certain things the pattern is the same for all of us, regardless of our gifts. Our Scripture speaks of the fruit of our lips, acknowledging His name. It also tells us about something that each one of us is expected to do: "to do good and to share what we have." If Christ lives in you, your heart will beat with compassion for every needy soul in the world. Every injustice will become your concern; every tragedy will find a responsive compassion in your heart. These are the peculiar honors that delight the King.

In one of our missions in Africa, they were bringing their gifts. A little girl stayed over in the corner until everyone had left but the pastor. Then she slipped up to the table and threw a handful of coins down. The pastor was alarmed, because he knew that she did not have resources like that. He was afraid that she might have stolen the money, not knowing any better. So he said to her, "Please tell me where you got that money." She pleaded with him not to press her. Finally he won her confidence and she said, "I love the Lord so, I wanted to bring a worthy gift. Yesterday, I sold myself into slavery, and this is the price I received."

"What shall I give Him?
Give Him my heart."

PRAYER: *How miserly we have been, Lord, in showing our appreciation to You, the King of glory. So often, we have withheld from serving our fellow men, from bearing their burdens. Help us to bring this gift of concern. In Your name. Amen.*

Where Cross the Crowded Ways of Life

En främling klappar på din dörr. L. M. **German.**

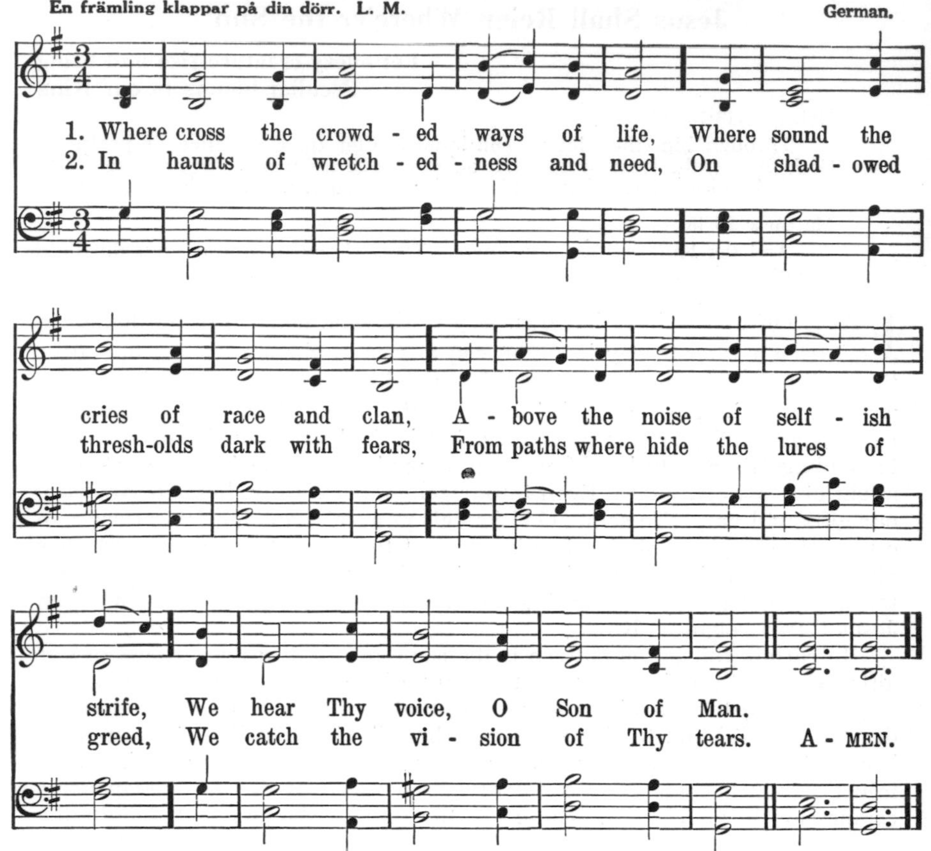

3 From tender childhood's helplessness,
From woman's grief, man's burdened toil,
From famished souls, from sorrow's stress,
Thy heart has never known recoil.

4 The cup of water given for Thee
Still holds the freshness of Thy grace;
Yet long these multitudes to see
The sweet compassion of Thy face.

5 O Master, from the mountain side
Make haste to hear these hearts of pain;
Among these restless throngs abide,
O tread the city's streets again;

6 Till sons of men shall learn Thy love,
And follow where Thy feet have trod;
Till glorious from Thy heaven above
Shall come the City of our God.

Frank Mason North, 1905.

SUNDAY

Where Cross the Crowded Ways of Life

Where sound the cries of race or clan

Acts 17:24-26

"The God who made the world and everything in it, being Lord of heaven and earth, does not live in shrines made by man, nor is he served by human hands, as though he needed anything, since he himself gives to all men life and breath and everything. And he made from one every nation of men to live on all the face of the earth."

HOW DESPERATELY America needs to stop today to hear the voice of the Son of Man, "Where sound the cries of race or clan." If every Christian in America would honestly examine his own heart in regard to his racial attitudes, or whatever his bigotry is, and then would search the Scripture as to the will of God, our race problem would know such a wonderful answer that it would be a witness to all the world. God wants all men to live together as brothers. Every soul is as precious as any other in His sight. We each have special gifts to bring to the world, and no one has a monopoly on God and His blessings. He has told us, that if we say that we love Him and do not love our neighbors, we are liars. Christians everywhere, arise to this hour, and put into practice the presence of Christ within you in regard to your attitude toward race. What would Christ want us to do? How would He want us to act?

What we call our problem is really our opportunity. The untapped resources of races that have been held under by white domination are a great potential in a world on the brink of an atomic age. An aged Negro woman, who was roughly ordered to the back of the bus, was heard to mutter as she stood in the aisle back there, when the front of the bus was practically empty: "God is getting mighty tired of this business." I can well agree with her.

Christians everywhere, will you not go to God in prayer about your attitude toward your fellow men? If we all seek His throne and His will, disunity will be gone. Are you willing to say, "Thy will be done"? Can you not see what would happen, if Christians would pray this? What a witness to godless Communism this would be.

Besides the injuries we do to our brothers in not including them in our fellowship, we do injury to our own souls. There can be no real inner peace when we have aught against our brother. There can be no sense of the universality of Christ's fellowship, when we are not willing to worship with all peoples in the house of God, when we are not willing to bear their burdens, and permit them to be a part of our fellowship. Here is a chance for Christianity to walk down the street and on the highways of the nations by the directive of their Great Commander who walks where cross the crowded ways of life.

PRAYER: *Search us, O Lord, and reveal the hidden bigotries and inconsistencies of our lives. Give us the daring to expose them to Your Word. Help our country in this great hour. In Jesus' name. Amen.*

Where Cross the Crowded Ways of Life

Above the noise of selfish strife

Numbers 11:5

"We remember the fish we ate in Egypt for nothing, the cucumbers, the melons, the leeks, the onions, and the garlic."

Ecclesiastes 6:7

All the toil of man is for his mouth, yet his appetite is not satisfied.

WERE ONE to conduct a poll of passers-by on the street, and ask them for what they were striving, what their goal in life was, I wonder what the majority of replies would be. The tensions that there are between management and labor, the gigantic lobbying interests that hound our congressmen, what are these but evidence of the material goals of men. Listen to some of the situations that obtain in many offices, and you will find that there is an atmosphere of "dog eat dog." Into these crowded ways, where there is such selfish strife, our Lord walks. As we stood by the Sea of Galilee our guide reminded us that in the time of Christ the little country of Palestine was the crossroads of the world. Caravans from the East and West passed there, and commerce flourished. Through the marketplaces and into places of business our Lord here walked.

And where is He today? Sadly He looks at us, as He sees our selfish striving. The downfall of the children of Israel was their constantly remembering the fleshpots of Egypt. This remembrance was what kept them from reaching the Promised Land. Is it not so with too many of us today? Worldly possessions mean more to us than anything else. We are so busy in their accumulation, that our ears are deaf to the voice of the Son of Man above the strife.

What would happen if He would sit down at the bargaining table with men whose goal seemed to be to get as much out of the other as they could. In places where this has been tried, there have been wonderful results. Management has been concerned about working conditions, about adequate salaries, about rightful protections for the workers, when Jesus Christ has directed the thinking. And under these same circumstances, labor has been eager to do a good job, to become a part of a team. There are such plants in the United States. They should be exhibit "A" for every manufacturer and labor official to follow. The degree of productivity, the contentment of the workers, and their loyalty, are a joy to behold.

How about your personal living? Do you hear the voice of the Son of man above the strivings of each day? Dr. Spurgeon has well put a warning: "A Christian making money fast is just a man in a cloud of dust; it will fill his eyes if he be not careful."

PRAYER: *Lord Christ, remind us constantly that You are not a God living on a high mountain, or sitting on the clouds. Your walk is with men into the busy streets of their every day living. Help us by Your Holy Spirit to be aware of Your Presence and to hear Your voice. Amen.*

Where Cross the Crowded Ways of Life

In haunts of wretchedness and need

Proverbs 21:13

He who closes his ear to the cry of the poor will himself cry out and not be heard.

Ezekiel 34:3, 4

"You eat the fat, you clothe yourselves with the wool, you slaughter the fatlings; but you do not feed the sheep. The weak you have not strengthened, the sick you have not healed, the crippled you have not bound up, the strayed you have not brought back, the lost you have not sought, and with force and harshness you have ruled them."

MANY PEOPLE do not want to know about the wretchedness and need that there is in the world. They live within the circle of their own little clique, and are horrified if some account of starvation or sorrow should come their way. They are like a contemporary newspaper magnate, who insisted that any mention of death should be deleted from his papers; he wished to avoid facing its inevitability. You react irritably to his caprice, but how aware are you of the conditions in your own community; the conditions "across the track"; of your next door neighbor; of your prisons; of your courts; of your mental hospitals? If aware, how great is your concern, and what are you doing, about these people whom to serve is to be ministering to the Christ, whose name you bear?

Where did Christ walk when He visited this earth? Read your Gospels, searching out this one fact. Truly you will find Him in haunts of wretchedness and need. Where there were folks who were lost, there He was; where there was sickness, there He came with His healing; where there were evil spirits and demon possession, He brought release and His peace; where there was prostitution and dissipation, there He came with His purity, and cleansed and renewed; where there was greed, as in the case of Matthew, He came and redirected the life. He came to save the lost, to serve the least, and to teach us that if we would be first, we must then be last.

In one of the prisons was an educated man who was a thorough agnostic. Nothing seemed to be able to penetrate his shell. While the chaplain was talking with him one day, he noticed that the convict had a wounded foot. It was evidently a source of pain and the chaplain left off speaking, bent down and examined it, and then bound it more comfortably. As he did so, he felt a great tear upon his head. The little act of kindness had done more than all his pleading. There it is again: "A cup of cold water, given in my name . . ."

PRAYER: *By our willful ignorance, Lord, we are unaware of the needs of people about us and around the world; by our desire to be comfortable, we protect ourselves from this awareness. O Great Galilean, arouse us from our ease, so that we may truly follow in Your steps. Amen.*

Where Cross the Crowded Ways of Life

On shadowed thresholds dark with fears

Proverbs 29:25

The fear of man lays a snare, but he who trusts in the Lord is safe.

2 Timothy 1:7

For God did not give us a spirit of timidity but a spirit of power and love and self-control.

Matthew 10:28

"And do not fear those who kill the body but cannot kill the soul; rather fear him who can destroy both soul and body in hell."

SOME YEARS back, the late Franklin Delano Roosevelt made the classic statement during a critical era, that we have nothing to fear, save fear itself. There is no marauder of health, no destroyer of human relations, no foe more insidious than fear. The Lord was well aware of this when He gave us so many "fear nots." "Fear not, I am with you," "Fear not, I have redeemed you," "Fear not, you will not be ashamed" and countless others are the Christian's securities. Yet today's world is obsessed with fear. Where are we, as Christians, failing?

First, we must recognize that fear is the antithesis of faith. The two cannot live together. The one dispels the other. I am not unaware that we are told to have one basic fear, the fear of the Lord. This is not a cringing, disintegrating kind of thing. It is a fear born of love, and the desire not to displease the One we love. It is a positive thing, and instead of crippling us, enables us to bless others. But the fears that are the deadly foes of men are born of the devil. They deny our dependence on God and our complete trust in Him. They cast a shadow not only on us, but on all we meet as well.

Take a look at some of the basic fears. There is the one about your health which, when extended, is really a fear of death. What do you believe about the hereafter, and what Christ accomplished with His crucifixion and resurrection? Do not the words mean anything to you, "O death, where is thy victory? O death, where is thy sting?" In regard to illness, do you not remember that He has promised that "as your days, so shall your strength be," and that His grace will be sufficient for you? Take out each one of your fears and look at them in the light of God's promises. We cannot be a means of dispelling fear on the dark thresholds of the world, if we are in its deadly grasp ourselves. The world, over its roaring waves, so desperately needs to hear His voice through you say, "It is I, be not afraid."

PRAYER: *Give us such a faith, Christ, as to dispel all fear. Help us to be a source of hope and assurance to our fellow men. May our lives witness to the Rock on which they are built. In Your name who made such a faith possible. Amen.*

THURSDAY

Where Cross the Crowded Ways of Life

From paths where hide the lures of greed

Ecclesiastes 5:10, 11, 13

He who loves money will not be satisfied with money; nor he who loves wealth, with gain; this also is vanity. When goods increase, they increase who eat them; and what gain has their owner but to see them with his eyes? . . . There is a grievous evil which I have seen under the sun; riches were kept by their owner to his hurt, and those riches were lost in a bad venture.

THERE IS a very telling little verse that reads,

"It is well to be prudent
And thrifty—who wouldn't?
And quite self-supporting, 'tis true;
But in getting your money
(Now this may sound funny)
Oh, don't let your money get you!"

"For the love of money is the root of all evil." Basically it comes right back to what is first in our lives. Paul is saying again that, if your sense of values is determined by what happened on the cross, these other things can never possess you. Someone has said that money is the largest slaveholder in the world. Its slavery is often so subtle that we are hardly aware of its encroachments until we are caught in its grip. In Algeria, when a peasant wants to catch a monkey, he attaches a gourd to a tree. Having made an opening large enough for the monkey's hand, the native places some nuts or rice inside. In the night, the monkey goes to the gourd, thrusts in his hand, and grabs the delicacy but cannot withdraw his clenched hand. As he will not let go his booty he is captured. How many foolish monkeys walk the streets of our cities today!

It is a disconcerting thing in a community to see how difficult it is to get money for things that are worth while. Greedy men waste it while our schools, our welfare work, our institutions of mercy, go begging.

I like the action the faculty of Union Theological Seminary took. They asked their Board of Directors to scrutinize their endowments. If any of their income came from slum tenements, or places where the lifeblood of women and children was coined, or from factories where safety devices were missing because of the cost, they asked that these investments be changed. They promised to stand a decrease in salary, if a decreased investment on this account made it necessary.

Through a printer's mistake, a line of a hymn was inadvertently made to read: "Land my safe on Canaan's shore." But you cannot take it with you!

PRAYER: *From the vice of greed, deliver us, O Lord. Help our entire stewardship of life to bear the mark of the cross. Give us the courage to oppose the forces of avarice that are leeches on the lives of men. Make us good stewards of our own pocketbooks. In Jesus' name. Amen.*

Where Cross the Crowded Ways of Life

From famished souls, from sorrows stress

Amos 8:11, 12

"Behold, the days are coming," says the Lord God, "when I will send a famine on the land; not a famine of bread, nor a thirst for water, but of hearing the words of the Lord. They shall wander from sea to sea and from north to east; they shall run to and fro, to seek the word of the Lord, but they shall not find it."

Matthew 5:4, 6

"Blessed are those who mourn, for they shall be comforted." . . "Blessed are those who hunger and thirst for righteousness, for they shall be satisfied."

FROM AROUND the world there comes the word of people hungry. Little children and grownups, in many areas of the world, drag their weary bodies around on a starvation diet. We cannot dismiss this fact with a shrug of our shoulders. As Christians, this must be our concern, our burden, if we truly follow the One who walks the crowded ways of life and knows man's infirmities. The same is true of injustices and enslavements. As Christians in America, we cannot be disinterested bystanders with regard to the perpetuation of colonial slavery as it is being practiced in South Africa. If we are the Christ's, we must face it as our challenge, too. All things that degrade men, and make them less than sons of the King, we should fight with all the strength that is in us.

But the world is filled with another hunger. Really, the two are very close together, and as we satisfy the one, we have the marvelous opportunity to present the food that satisfies the other. Soul hunger is less obvious sometimes. It may exist under the beautiful clothes of your well-groomed neighbor; it may be hiding under a gay exterior in your own household; it often sits in high places; sometimes it is drowned at the bar or night club. People with whom you rub elbows every day may be hungering and thirsting for righteousness. Are you able to share the Bread of Life with them? Can you lead them to the fountain wherein there is Living Water?

It isn't in the words you say, nor is it in your deeds confessed;
But in the most unconscious way is Christ expressed.
Is it a beatific smile, a holy light upon your brow?
Oh no! I felt His presence when you laughed just now.

It isn't in the truth you taught: to you so clear, to me so dim;
But when you came to me you brought a sense of Him.
And from your eyes He beckons me, and from your heart His
love is shed,
'Til I lose sight of you and see the Christ instead.

PRAYER: *Use us, O Lord, as baskets that carry bread to hungry souls. Resupply us daily, and give us such a faith as to know that You will multiply the loaves, if we will but present what we have to You. Let our everyday lives be nourishment to others. In Jesus' name. Amen.*

SATURDAY

Where Cross the Crowded Ways of Life

We hear Thy voice, O Son of Man

John 7:37, 38

On the last day of the feast, the great day, Jesus stood up and proclaimed: "If anyone thirst, let him come to me and drink. He who believes in me, as the scripture has said, 'Out of his heart shall flow rivers of water.'"

Revelation 3:20

"Behold, I stand at the door and knock; if any one hears my voice and opens the door, I will come in to him and eat with him, and he with me."

THROUGH this week we have walked in the places that Jesus walks with His compassionate heart and His healing for every wound. We acknowledge Him as Lord, and claim to be His followers. His commands and directions are unmistakable. What now? Are you ready for a new consecration? Are you really willing to say, "We hear thy voice, O Son of Man"? That can mean great things for the aching heart of the world. The Holy Spirit of the Lord works wonders with one willing soul. And remember that He will begin right where you are! And now!

Some years ago, a Christian Chinaman, moved with compassion for the coolies in South American mines, sold himself as a slave for five years, and so carried the gospel to his countrymen working there.

Recently in Nigeria there were riots, and some native Christians along with others who were guilty, were thrown into prison for a year. During that time, I was told by the young missionary that serves the field, the Christian prisoners made sixteen converts. How easy it would have been for them to have said, "If you release us from prison, Lord, we will be your witnesses." In their first-century trust, they simply used for Him the opportunity they had where they were.

It is much more comfortable for Christians to enjoy the loving atmosphere of the company of like-minded people than to hear the voice of the Son of man in the inexorable command to go into the highways and byways and constrain people to come to the feast of the Lord. If you want to be undisturbed and to continue in your protected circle of friends, do not listen to the voice of God! He breaks down the walls of partition; He upsets personal plans; He demands that you have no anxiety for the things of the world. He expects you to share your brother's burden. Have you stuffed your ears with the cotton of comfort? Down the corridors of time in every age and to each individual He speaks. Are you listening to what He is saying to you? He says, "Behold, I stand at the door and knock." Will you be a part of His extending the invitation to the world?

PRAYER: *Lord, there are multitudinous voices that clamor at the door of our hearts. Give us an ear to hear Yours each day. Then give us the courage to do Your bidding. Amen.*

For the Beauty of the Earth

God of Hosts. 7 7, 7 7, 7 7. EDWARD JOHN HOPKINS, (1818–1901).

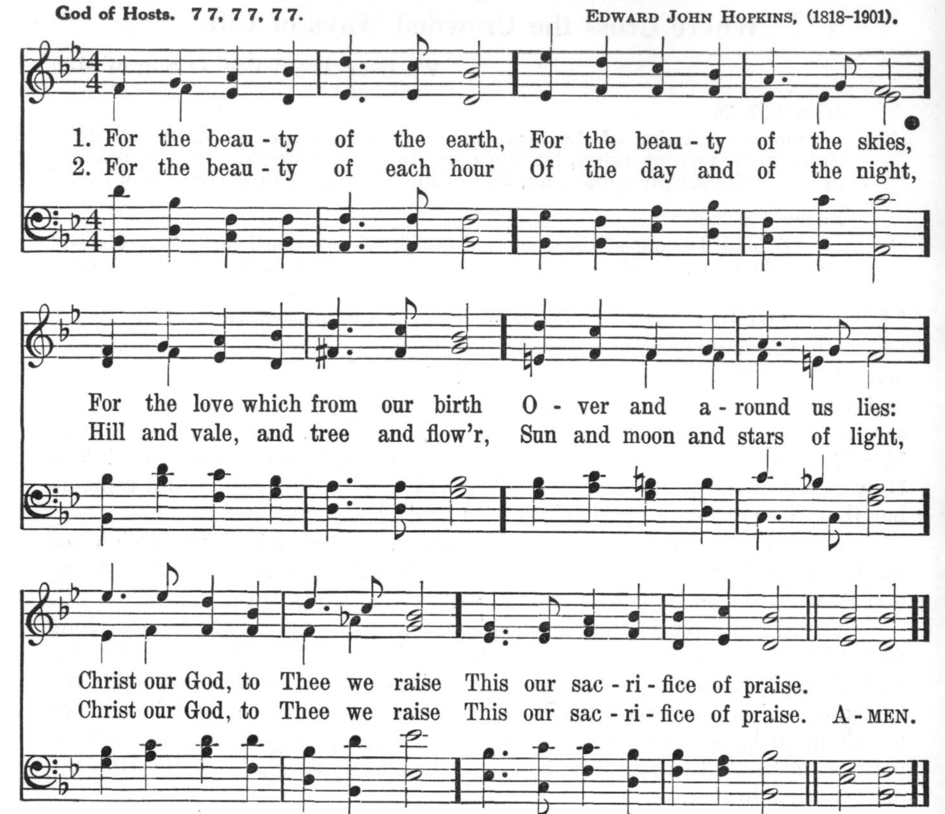

3 For the joy of ear and eye,
For the heart and mind's delight,
For the mystic harmony
Linking sense to sound and sight,
Christ our God, to Thee we raise
This our sacrifice of praise.

4 For Thyself, best Gift divine!
To our race so freely given,
For that great, great love of Thine,
Peace on earth and joy in heaven,
Christ our God, to Thee we raise
This our sacrifice of praise.

Folliott Sandford Pierpoint, 1864.

For the Beauty of the Earth

For the glory of the skies

Job 37:15-17

"Do you know how God lays his command upon them, and causes the lightning of his cloud to shine? Do you know the balancings of the clouds, the wondrous works of him who is perfect in knowledge, you whose garments are hot when the earth is still because of the south wind? Can you, like him, spread out the skies, hard as a molten mirror?"

Psalm 19:1

The heavens are telling the glory of God; and the firmament proclaims his handiwork.

THERE ARE daytime skies and nighttime skies, there are clear skies and cloudy skies. I love the way the color of a sky reflects itself in a lake. I have seen Lake Superior all shades of blue, ominous green, gunmetal grey, aqua, and silver, and then molten lead. The same body of water was there all the time. The difference in its color was the kind of sky it reflected.

How different it is with us! Our variability is due to our own inconstancy. The One whom we should mirror remains ever the same. Our moods change; He is constant.

Then there are the skies at night. To comprehend their distance and number is beyond our finite capacity. What we can see with the naked eye is enough to make us marvel at the mind of the Creator, and want to worship Him. There is a real challenge in the thought that Dr. Phillips presents in his book, "New Testament Christianity." That God should have chosen the little planet, the Earth, as the place to make His divine visitation certainly is noteworthy. In size, it is one of the lesser planets. Whether or not there may be human beings on other spheres, we yet do not know. But we do know that it was in the little country of Palestine, in Asia, on the planet, the Earth, that Christ, God's Son, was born and lived and carved out a pattern of eternity for us. No matter what is found on other planets, this unique experience to the inhabitants of the Earth remains. We are set apart.

Gazing up into the skies, one can be made to feel very insignificant. Jesus must have known how this would be, when again and again He emphasized our individual worth. Even in the face of the magnitude of the heavens, each one of us is precious in His sight.

"His eye is on the sparrow,
And I know He watches me."

PRAYER: *Creator of this beautiful world, we would worship and adore You. The heavens, by day or night; the scudding clouds so heavy with rain to replenish the earth; the stars and moon and sun—all are the work of Your Hand. We thank You for Your amazing providence. Amen.*

For the Beauty of the Earth

For the love which from our birth
Over and around us lies

1 John 4:16

So we know and believe the love God has for us. God is love, and he who abides in love abides in God, and God abides in him.

Jeremiah 31:3

"I have loved you with an everlasting love; therefore I have continued my faithfulness to you."

THE TIMELESSNESS of God's love for us is cause for gratitude. The miracle of creation in the birth of a child, and the protective provisions for this being even before it is born, are evidences of God's love. Then the concomitant care, as He provides it in the love of parents through the stages of infancy and adolescence; yes, His continuing care for us through maturity even to hoary old age—these make us aware of the wonder of His love.

Is there a day in your life that goes by without some visible evidence of God's love? In the material blessings that are yours alone, there are more witnesses to His loving providence than you can even list. Over and beyond these, there are invisible expressions of His care for us that we do not even recognize.

Have you ever been in a place where the air was so stifling that you could hardly take a breath? Yet how often have you thanked God for the good air that daily surrounds you as an evidence of His love?

I am sure that you have complained when you could not sleep, but after a good night of rest, do you express your gratitude for the renewal of your powers through the relaxation of the night?

Maybe you are suffering from ill health, and these things I have spoken about are not yours to enjoy. Has not His grace always been sufficient for you, and do you not have the prospect of a perfect life with Him forever?

Dr. Spurgeon has well described this give and take of love between the Lord and us. He says: "A needle will move toward a magnet when once a magnet has moved near to it. It is ours to run to Jesus as if all the running were ours; but the secret truth is that the Lord runs toward us, and this is the very heart of the business."

"Nearer is He than breathing;
Closer than hands and feet!'"

Yes, His love "over and around us lies"!

PRAYER: *Thank You, Lord, for the asbestos of Your love that is a sure protection from all the fires of the world. Forgive me for so often taking it for granted. Let my gratitude find expression in everyday deeds. In Jesus' name. Amen.*

For the Beauty of the Earth

For the beauty of each hour,
Of the day and of the night

Genesis 8:22

"While the earth remains, seedtime and harvest, cold and heat, summer and winter, day and night, shall not cease."

Romans 13:11, 12

Besides this you know what hour it is, how it is full time now for you to wake from sleep. For salvation is nearer to us now than when we first believed; the night is far gone, the day is at hand. Let us then cast off the works of darkness and put on the armor of light.

Ephesians 5:15, 16

Look carefully then how you walk, not as unwise men but as wise, making the most of the time, because the days are evil.

IGNATIUS, WHEN he heard a clock strike, was accustomed to say, "Now I have one more hour to answer for." Time is a remarkable thing. Here there is no preferential treatment in regard to hours. For each there are twenty-four in the day, whether you are king or hod carrier, scientist or housewife. Night comes to each alike; no human being stops the sun. Each has its own purpose: daytime for working and nighttime for resting. (Some of us have them all mixed up!) A day is beautiful, depending on the quality of each hour. Even so, one bad hour can spoil a day. What would not some of us give to erase ugly memories! Yet they were made in an hour such as is at hand today.

As we enjoy this marvelous plan of the Creator for day and night, and as we appreciate the beauties peculiar to each, we are sobered by the writer of Scripture when he says: "The night is far gone, the day is at hand. Let us then cast off the works of darkness and put on the armor of light." Again we are told to be "making the most of the time, because the days are evil." The older we grow, the faster time flies. What are we doing with our time, this wonderful gift from God?

You can fritter it away, wondering what to do; you can fill it with inconsequential things; you can waste it by worrying about the tasks at hand (I have seen more housewives do this!); or you can use it to the glory of God, and live abundantly. "Time is like money; the less we have of it, the further we make it go." Is that why we always say, "If you want a thing done, ask a busy person to do it"?

"Your date book is your creed. What you believe in, you have time for."

PRAYER: *The days fly so swiftly, Lord, and there is so much to be done, so much beauty to be enjoyed. Give me a discerning mind and receptive heart, that sloth may not overtake me. Thank You for the shining beauty of the day, and the quiet loveliness of the night. Your plan is best. Amen.*

For the Beauty of the Earth

Hill and vale . . .

Genesis 49:26

The blessings of your father are mighty beyond the blessings of the eternal mountains, the bounties of the everlasting hills.

Psalm 65: 12, 13

The pastures of the wilderness drip, the hills gird themselves with joy, the meadows clothe themselves with flocks, the valleys deck themselves with grain, they shout and sing together for joy.

WHICH DO you like better, hills or valleys, mountains or flatlands? It seems to me that each has a beauty all of its own. When I taught in Miller, South Dakota, out on the prairies, I loved them. At night, you could see the lights almost fifty miles away, and the stars seemed to hang almost as close as chandeliers. I have never seen stars quite like that since then, except maybe on the desert in Palestine. They were beautiful.

But I love the hills, too, and the mountains. There is something in a hill that has in it a sense of expectancy—something beyond. And when hill after hill lifts itself higher and higher against the evening sky, you have a feeling of Jacob's ladder, and an approach to heaven. Hills are beautiful.

One stops to worship when one thinks of what the hills contain. What wealth has already been extracted from them! And many are the secrets in the scientific realm that men are only just beginning to probe.

I love hills because so much has happened on them. It was on a hillside that Christ shared the Sermon on the Mount; it was in the mountains that He was tempted; it was up a hill that He traveled with His cross; it was on a hill that He was crucified. Every hill I ever see is a mute reminder to me of that "green hill far away," and what the cataclysmic event that took place there means to my life. I love hills.

I shall never forget the experience we had in entering Jerusalem. It was evening, and the world was veiled in rose and tawny gold. We had been traveling on the desert from Amman to Jerusalem, and we were hot and dirty and tired. The car started climbing the hill up to the ancient city that has been destroyed so many times. Past the little town of Bethany, where the Lord loved to stop with Mary and Martha and Lazarus, and on up the road to the city set among the mountains. Our guide had told us that we would find relief there, but we had not anticipated the tremendous refreshment that cool mountain air would be. My husband took out his Bible, and read for us, "As the mountains are round about Jerusalem, so the Lord is round about his people, from this time forth and for evermore."

PRAYER: *Lord Christ, for the beauty of mountain and valley, for the beauty of hillside and dale, we thank You. For Your willingness to walk up a hill to accomplish our salvation, we thank You. Every hill is a reminder of Your love. Amen.*

For the Beauty of the Earth

And tree and flower

Isaiah 35:1, 2

The wilderness and the dry land shall be glad, the desert shall rejoice and blossom; like the crocus it shall blossom abundantly, and rejoice with joy and singing.

Matthew 6:28

"Consider the lilies of the field, how they grow; they neither toil nor spin; yet I tell you, even Solomon in all his glory was not arrayed like one of these."

FOR THE beauty of trees and flowers—volumes have been written about it, and more could be written! God's world is beautiful, and every time you see a flower, every time you find shelter in the shade of a tree, you should be reminded to give Him thanks.

It is interesting to think about the flowers Jesus saw when He used them as an illustration of God's providence. When the rainy season comes in Palestine, flowers seem to spring up over night where before there had been desert. Anemones of many colors are in profusion; crocuses are everywhere. The rose spoken of in the Bible is thought to be like our moss rose. The symbol of the rose that you see often in churches is patterned after this form. The gladiola is known as the sword lily, and has its blossoms on only one side of its stem.

I like what one Church school class did. They found a little plot on their church lot, and received permission to make that into a flower garden. Then they studied in their Bibles about the flowers of Palestine. The fruition of their study was to plant the kind of garden that would be growing in the Holy Land. Their project did not end here, for when their flowers bloomed, they provided beauty for the altar each Sabbath, and then were taken to the homes of the aged and the ill, to witness to the love of the Lord. Would it not be wonderful if there were flower gardens like this in church yards all over the United States?

The Bible uses trees as an illustration of what God expects of a man in terms of rooting and growing. The First Psalm carries the figure aptly. In speaking of a righteous man, it says: He is like a tree planted by streams of water."

When the writers of Scripture wanted a name to describe the One "altogether lovely," they resorted to flowers. Of Christ it is said: "He is the rose of Sharon, the lily of the valley." All things beautiful belong with Christ, and nothing is truly beautiful apart from Him. I thank Him for flowers and trees.

PRAYER: *In every flower, Lord, there is the wonder of Your creation. How beautiful heaven must be when You have made the earth so fair. Let me, like the flowers and trees, reflect some of Your beauty. In Jesus' name. Amen.*

For the Beauty of the Earth

For the joy of ear and eye,
For the heart and mind's delight

Proverbs 20:12

The hearing ear and the seeing eye, the Lord has made them both.

1 Corinthians 2:9

"What no eye has seen, nor ear heard, nor the heart of man conceived, what God has prepared for those who love him," God has revealed to us through the Spirit.

HAVE YOU ever tried closing your eyes to imagine what it would be like to be blind; or plugged your ears in order not to hear a summoning voice? When you read a book, or see a picture, or hear a concert; when you experience the stimulus of exchange of mind with mind, or know the communion of heart with heart, do you remember to thank God and acknowledge Him? The One who gave us these gifts expects a stewardship from us. Out of what kind of eyes do you see, and to what kind of talk do you give a ready ear?

We are told to have in us the mind that is in Christ Jesus! What a difference it makes, if you see men through His eyes! Eyes wearing the optics of love have far more discernment; they are not satisfied with only a partial picture. The eyes of Christ see what has gone before and what is to come, and they judge what is now from where we have come. How superficial much of our sight is! John Trumbull has put it into verse:

For any man with half an eye,
What stands before him may espy;
But optics sharp it needs I ween,
To see what is not to be seen.

This is what Paul is saying as he quotes Isaiah in his letter to the Corinthians. There is a spiritual eye, given by God, that discerns the things of eternity. Physical blindness is sad; at least, it seems so to us. Yet many who ooze sympathy for the physically blind are themselves living in spiritual darkness. Here it is just as it is with liberty; one may be behind iron bars, and be free as a bird in soul.

What will your ears and eyes record for your mind to retain today? You will see what you are looking for! If it is in search of faults you go, faults you will find. If you are looking for dirt, you will find it. If your ears itch for gossip, that is what they will hear. Dr. Phillips modern translation of Paul's letters, uses the term: "Itching Ears."

There is a still, small Voice that would like your ear. There is a Heart pierced by a cross that would give you discerning eyes. Will you not learn of Him?

PRAYER: *Lord, I would dedicate anew my eyes, my ears, my mind, and my heart to You. And my tongue, Lord, desperately needs the reins of Your Spirit. Make me wholly Yours! Amen.*

For the Beauty of the Earth

For Thyself, best Gift divine! . . .
For that great, great love of Thine, . . .
Christ our God, to Thee we raise
This our sacrifice of praise

2 Corinthians 9:15
Thanks be to God for his inexpressible gift!

THIS WEEK we have been having a sort of summer thanksgiving. We should have a daily one. We have thanked God for heaven and earth, for time and tide, for flower and tree, and hill and vale; we have thanked Him for our senses, and our minds and hearts. Our final "Thank you" is the biggest one of all. In an overwhelming togetherness of all that we are and see and experience, we thank Him for the inexpressible gift of himself in His Son, Jesus Christ, our Lord.

There is a lovely story told about the most beautiful rose in the world. In a faraway country there was a queen who loved roses. She became very ill. "There is but one thing that can save her," said the wise men, "and that is the loveliest rose in the world, the rose that is the symbol of the purest and brightest love." So from all over her realm, roses were brought. The rose of the love of youth and of heroes was brought, but the wise men shook their heads. One mother brought her little baby to the bedside of the queen, claiming that in its rosy cheeks was this flower of love. "It's lovely," said the wise men, "but there is a lovelier still." Even the Bishop came to call upon the ill queen. "The loveliest rose in the world I saw at the altar of the Lord," he said, "the young maidens that went to the Lord's Table. Roses were shining on their cheeks. A young girl stood there. With the love and purity of her spirit, she looked up to heaven. That was the expression of highest and purest love."

But still the wise men shook their heads. "May she be blessed," said one of them, "but still you have not named the loveliest rose of the world."

Then a child came running into the room. It was the queen's little son. "Mother," cried the boy, "only hear what I have read." The child sat at his mother's bedside, and read from *the Book:* "Greater love has no man than this, that a man lay down his life for his friends."

A rosy glow spread over the cheeks of the queen. In the leaves of the Bible there bloomed the loveliest rose which sprang from the shed blood of Jesus Christ. "Now I see," the queen exclaimed, "he who beholds this, the loveliest rose on earth, shall never die, but have eternal life." God's great perennial!

PRAYER: *Beautiful Savior, our hearts cannot contain the gratitude and love for this Gift of yourself. All of life has new meaning because of the fragrance of Your presence. With all our being we would thank You. Amen.*

My Country, 'Tis of Thee

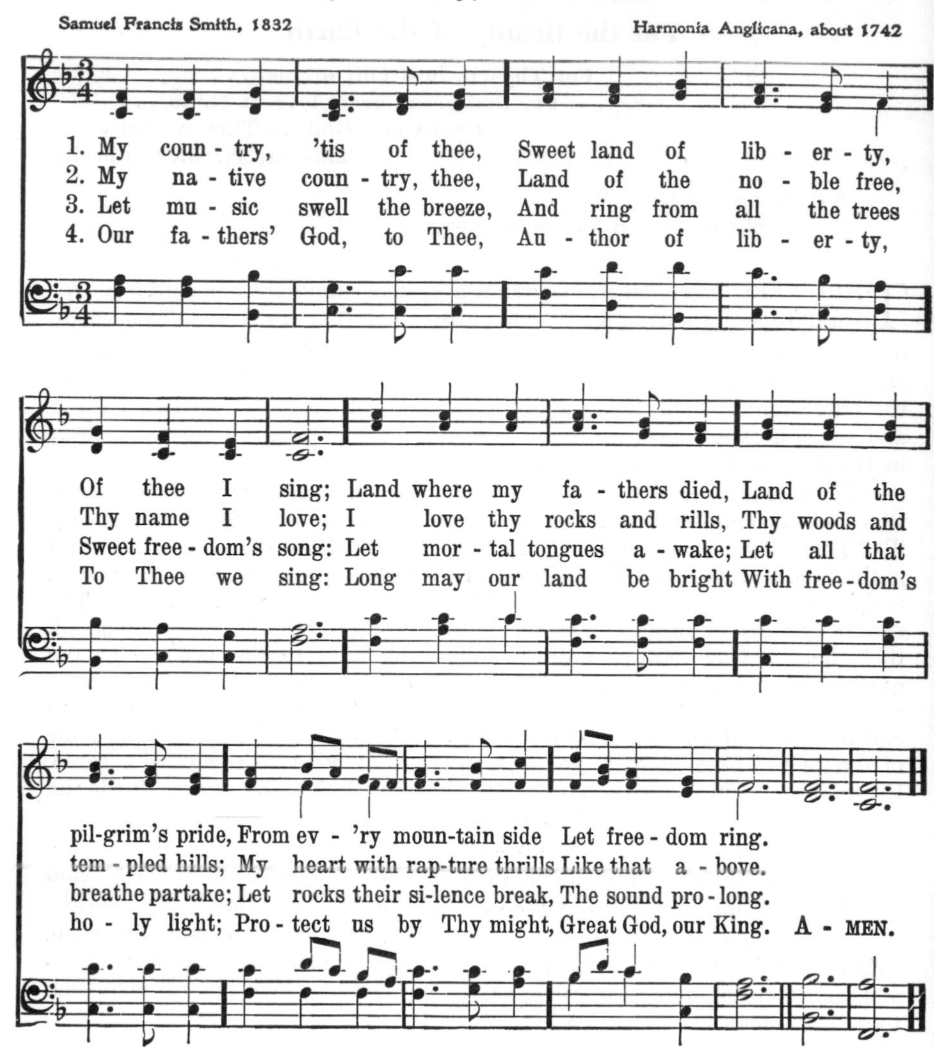

My Country, 'Tis of Thee

Sweet land of liberty

Isaiah 9:2, 3

The people who walked in darkness have seen a great light;
those who dwelt in a land of deep darkness,
on them has light shined.
Thou hast multiplied the nation, thou hast increased its joy.

1 Corinthians 7:22, 23

For he who was called in the Lord as a slave is a freedman of the Lord. Likewise he who was free when called is a slave of Christ. You were bought with a price; do not become slaves of men.

HOW BLITHELY the words, "Sweet land of liberty," trip over our tongues! We need to stop and consider what our heritage cost, and what it ought to mean in action as well as in word. In the next few days there will be firecrackers and flag raising; there will be picnics and accidents; there will be oratory and song. But living in a land of liberty has to mean more than all of that. It, like our Christianity, must be part and parcel of our every day. It must live in relationship to our neighbor, to every person who makes his way to our shores.

As Christians, we should be aware of the roots of freedom. Scripture puts it very simply, "Where the Spirit of the Lord is, there is freedom." Everywhere that real Christianity has come, it has brought with it this fruit, freedom. There is a tremendous danger, in thinking of our own freedom, that we forget that it carries with it responsibilities as well as opportunities. If in a home the principles of individual freedom are practiced, they must always be tempered with Christian thoughtfulness, or there will be strife. How often we hear young people, and older ones too, fling out the words, "Well, I'm free to do as I choose. I won't hurt anybody but myself." But here is the rub. The kind of freedom that finds expression in the divorce court is false, and injures innocent little children who did not ask to be born. Never is it just the parties involved that pay the price. Such so-called freedom is born of selfishness and does injury to all of society.

The freedom that has made America great is not only the freedom of opportunity, but more especially the freedom of responsibility. Our country will be what we are.

So it is with Christianity; so it is with the church. What you bring to them of Christian living, what vital faith, what virile prayer life, what consecration of talents—these will determine what power in your community and in the world Christianity and the church will have.

Sweet land of liberty—to serve the world!

PRAYER: *What blessings are ours, Lord, as a nation! What a responsibility is mine as a citizen. True me up, and help me to assay anew how you would have me serve. In the name of Christ, the great freedom giver. Amen.*

MONDAY

My Country, 'Tis of Thee

Of thee I sing

Isaiah 54:14

"In righteousness you shall be established; you shall be far from oppression, for you shall not fear; and from terror, for it shall not come near you."

Isaiah 66:10

"Rejoice with Jerusalem, and be glad for her, all you who love her; rejoice with her in joy, all you who mourn over her."

SOMEBODY HAS said that our nation is fast becoming a nation of gripers. I am sure you, too, have found yourself criticizing the slow processes of democracy. I have been guilty of that. Yet in that very process is something of our safeguard. A contemporary historian has said that a Fascist form of government is like a highly-geared ship. It expertly sweeps into the ocean, and makes tremendous headway. But when it hits an iceberg, everybody on board is drowned. A democracy, on the other hand, is like a raft. Your feet are wet all the time, and you make very slow progress, but it is impossible to sink it. As we think in terms of lifting a song to the land we love, surely one of our causes for thanksgiving is this system of government in which every man has a voice. Trite, but true, is the statement that you will have the kind of government that you are willing to work for.

Our country is said to be "the land of the free, and the home of the brave." Someone has very aptly said, "It is the home of the free, only as it is the home of the brave." How brave are you in your citizenship? Do you dare speak out against the things that are wrong in your community, even when it is not the popular thing to do? Besides speaking, do you roll up your sleeves and go to work to right the wrong?

If Christian people everywhere really took their citizenship seriously, as God means them to, the social injustices of which you and I are a part would not be able to flourish as they do. I think of the slums, of real estate lobbies, and of the kind of working conditions that have necessitated labor unions. I think of licensed dens of vice in the very neighborhoods where our children are growing up; I think of the slavery we accept in regard to the comic-book mentality that is forced on our bookstands in wholesale lots. I think of the liquor advertisements on television, preliminary to the televising of sports events, as well as in spots during the events. These are not the things about which you want to sing. But these are some of the things that you can change, if you are a responsible citizen.

What have you done about them? The Christ whose name you bear again and again castigates those who are hearers of the word only, and not doers.

PRAYER: *Let there be such a note of sincerity in the singing of this song of the love of our country, Lord, that it will find fruition in action. Use us. In Jesus' name. Amen.*

My Country, 'Tis of Thee

Land where my fathers died

Exodus 23:9

"You shall not oppress a stranger; you know the heart of a stranger, for you were strangers in the land of Egypt."

Leviticus 19:33, 34

"When a stranger sojourns with you in your land, you shall not do him wrong. The stranger who sojourns with you shall be to you as the native among you, and you shall love him as yourself; for you were strangers in the land of Egypt: I am the Lord your God."

MANY OF us cannot sing in truth, "Land where my fathers died," for our forefathers have come from other shores and have found in this great country opportunities that never would have been theirs anywhere else. Is this, then, to say that we are not Americans? Those who put so much stress on tracing their lineage back to the *Mayflower* must acknowledge that, eventually in their history, they arrived at the time when they also came from somewhere else. A sure part of America's greatness has been that in the melting pot process has been this Christian concern about which our Scripture speaks, the concern for the stranger. America will continue to be great only as long as she remembers that what is hers is from God to steward and not to hoard; and only as long as she has a concern and a responsibility for the millions of refugees around the world. When the words engraved on the Statue of Liberty become a mockery, America had best look to her inner decay, for then she will be going against her God who has so abundantly blessed her. Are you familiar with those words? In them is the invitation: "Come, ye tempest-tossed from other shores . . . ."

Remembering, then, that your claims on America are no more legitimate than those of anyone else, what is your responsibility? Scripture tells you in no uncertain terms to show kindness to strangers, to accept them as natives, and to share with them the great opportunities that are yours. Do you know the blessing of having opened your heart and home to some of these refugees?

A friend in Washington told the story of an eleven-year-old Latvian boy who had come to America with his refugee parents. His father's sponsor told the boy that he might go in to one of our ten-cent stores (so-called) and pick out any one article that he would like, and it would be his. Can you imagine what an American ten-cent store would look like to a boy who had known nothing but refugee camps? He passed down the aisle of the store from one counter to another, and came out with an American flag! This symbolized to him new life, new opportunities—freedom! This was the gift he received from Americans of the centuries past, who had been willing to give even their lives that freedom might be maintained.

PRAYER: *Lord, help us not to hold lightly the cost of the freedom that we so quickly take for granted. Make us aware that we will keep it only as we share it. Give us a heart for the stranger. In Jesus' name. Amen.*

My Country, 'Tis of Thee

Let mortal tongues awake;
Let all that breathe partake

Deuteronomy 8:7-10

"For the Lord your God is bringing you into a good land, a land of brooks of water, of fountains and springs, flowing forth in valleys and hills, a land of wheat and barley, of vines and fig trees and pomegranates, a land of olive trees and honey, a land in which you will eat bread without scarcity, in which you will lack nothing, a land whose stones are iron, and out of whose hills you can dig copper. And you shall eat and be full, and you shall bless the Lord your God for the good land he has given you."

ACROSS OUR land this month there will be celebrations of one kind or another. These supposedly are to commemorate the signing of the Declaration of Independence. At the time of the adoption of the Declaration, John Adams wrote his wife a letter which reads like a prophecy: "I am apt to believe," he said, "that it (the day) will be celebrated by succeeding generations as the great anniversary festival. It ought to be solemnized with pomp and parade, with shows, games, sports, guns, balls, bonfires, and illuminations from one end of this continent to the other." In more respects than one we have pretty accurately followed his advice, too many times throwing discretion to the winds to the extent that many lives have been lost. I do not believe that was John Adams' idea. To remind us of the importance and influence of this document is indeed worthy. Many of us have happy Fourth of July remembrances when, as a family, our attention was called to the purpose of the celebration.

What do these words mean to you: "We hold these truths to be self-evident: that all men are created equal; that they are endowed by their Creator with certain unalienable rights; that among these are life, liberty, and the pursuit of happiness"?

Never was the meaning more clearly brought home to me than when I was conducting a sight-seeing tour for one of our Christians from Africa. He was very quiet as he walked from one monument to the other and read the inscriptions. That night at the dinner table, this was his astute contribution: "Now I understand America better. In Europe this summer they showed me their monuments. They are raised to men who go out and conquer other lands. Not so here in America. You raise yours to the men who fight for liberty and freedom for every individual person. You do not want one inch of colony. Now I understand America better."

How thankful I was that Pastor Stephani Moshi would return to his school of boys in Tanganyika, Africa, and give them this picture of America, for this is the message of the Fourth of July. It is the Christian message.

PRAYER: *Even as we lift up our hearts in gratitude to You, O Lord, for this great principle of freedom on which our country was built, we also pray Your forgiveness that too often we have not lived it in relationship to our fellow men. In Jesus' name. Amen.*

THURSDAY

My Country, 'Tis of Thee

Land of the pilgrim's pride

Hebrews 11:8-10, 14-16

By faith Abraham obeyed when he was called to go out to a place which he was to receive as an inheritance; and he went out, not knowing where he was to go. By faith he sojourned in the land of promise, as in a foreign land, living in tents. . . . For he looked forward to the city which has foundations, whose builder and maker is God. . . . For people who speak thus make it clear that they are seeking a homeland. If they had been thinking of that land from which they had gone out, they would have had opportunity to return. But as it is, they desire a better country, that is, a heavenly one. Therefore God is not ashamed to be called their God, for he has prepared for them a city.

BETWEEN THE pilgrims of Israel and the Pilgrims of America there are some very striking similarities. Abraham, at the command of God, started out for an unknown country. Only his faith, and his readiness to listen to God, were his directives. The Pilgrims were feeling in the Old World a restraint on their freedom of religious worship. They, too, heard the voice of God through their consciences, and so decided in faith to seek this other country. The greatest defense they carried with them was the Bible, and their recourse to prayer. Both groups believed that, as God directed, He would also empower; and both of them had the long look to "the other city" of God's promise. Neither of them was ashamed to acknowledge Him as their God.

There are critics of Christianity who would have us think that to carry in our hearts the anticipation of that "other city" is to make us poor citizens of this world. Nothing could be farther from the truth; for when you are aware of eternity in your heart, the nearness of God transforms your person in part, here and now, and you have a daring to put into practice the pattern He has shown. Pilgrims of faith have courage and fortitude, and a song in their hearts, even through the worst vicissitudes, because always there is this onward look and confidence in the One who is ever with them and who has made such a faith possible.

Where are the pilgrims of the twentieth century? Would those early pioneers be proud of what has happened to our country? Would they not marvel at the technical achievement and mechanistic development? Can you see one of them standing on a street corner in New York with the traffic whizzing by, and the rumble of the subway underneath, as well as the roar of the airplane overhead? Yes, great things have happened, but what about the soul of man? Has it proportionately grown in stature?

PRAYER: *Give us the courage of these intrepid souls who sought our land, Lord, and invested their very lives to make this a nation "under God." Give us the faith of Abraham, as we venture forth with You into the land of human relations and values. In Jesus' name. Amen.*

My Country, 'Tis of Thee

I love thy rocks and rills

Psalm 148:9-13

Mountains and all hills, fruit trees and all cedars!
Beasts and all cattle, creeping things and flying birds!
Kings of the earth and all peoples, princes and all rulers of the earth!
Young men and maidens together, old men and children!
Let them praise the name of the Lord, for his name alone is exalted;
his glory is above earth and heaven.

WHEN WE speak of the grandeur and resources of America, we often speak of them as though they were something that we personally were responsible for, as if they were of our making. God could well say to us, as He does so forcibly to Job, "Where were you when I laid the foundations of the earth?" Take your Bible and read this entire thirty-eighth chapter of Job. The result will be, I am sure, a solemn realization of whom credit should be given for the beauty of rock and rill, the glory of lake and forest, the wonder of winter and summer.

How America has been blessed! As you pause in these moments today, call to memory the loveliness that you have seen in this fair land of ours. No matter where you live, and even though you may not have traveled far, you will yet have quite a list.

Who can count the streams and brooks and rivers, so enticingly peopled with fish for fun to those who will pursue them? Or who can adequately describe the forests, some part of which is to be found in every state: forests of birch and pine from the North, and palm and pine from the South, with all the other varieties in between? How ineffective words are, as you contemplate the difference between the Blue Ridge Mountains of Virginia, or the Smokys of Tennessee, or the Alleghenies of Pennsylvania as compared with the Green Horn Mountains of Wyoming or the Tetons and the Rockies of the West.

We have not even mentioned the lakes; there are the Great Lakes, and the thousands of lesser ones, with their lacy tree borders and their wonderful opportunities for swimming and boating and fishing.

Do you like flatlands? There is the beauty of a waving grainfield in the middle west, or the mystic aura of the desert land as you move toward the Pacific. But I do not want to sound like a Chamber of Commerce folder. You take inventory of the beauty you have seen in America. As you find yourself swelling with pride that such a land you can call your own, will you not pray for the humility of spirit that is pleasing to its Creator? Pray for our leaders that they might bring to the world leadership worthy ot a nation born "under God."

PRAYER: *There are no words, Lord, adequate to express the beauty of our land, and our gratitude for it. Help us to be instruments in Your hands to bring healing, the healing of Your generous love, to the ends of the earth. In Jesus' name. Amen.*

SATURDAY

My Country, 'Tis of Thee

Long may our land be bright
With freedom's holy light

Isaiah 9:3, 4

Thou hast multiplied the nation, thou hast increased its joy;
they rejoice before thee as with joy at the harvest,
as men rejoice when they divide the spoil.
For the yoke of his burden, and the staff for his shoulder,
the rod of his oppressor, thou hast broken as on the day of Midian.

FREEDOM was born of God, and finds its fulfillment in Christ, who broke the enslavement by man's enemies, sin and death. Since the time our Lord walked on this earth, this concept of individual liberty has swept from nation to nation. We should acknowledge it as being of God.

In one of the first speeches he made after he was elected president, Dwight Eisenhower quoted from the speech of a European visitor to our shores. This man had come in search of the key to America's greatness. He told of his visits to factories and to schoolhouses; he spoke of the great rolling wheat fields and of the bounty of natural resources. "But in none of these did I find the real secret of America's greatness. Then I went to its churches. Here I heard the directives from God spoken fearlessly and with power. America is great because America is good. When it ceases to be good, it will cease to be great. As long as the men in America's pulpits dare to speak freely and without fear, America will be strong."

Have we been sleeping? There have been insidious forces in our country that would curtail such freedom; that judge a man guilty by association; that want to forget that our system of justice is built on the assumption that a man is innocent until he has been proved guilty. We need to pray:

"Long may our land be bright
With freedom's holy light."

One of our girls had to make a speech on citizenship. She ran across this little anonymous poem which she chose to use for her outline:

I know three things must ever be
To make a nation strong and free;
One is a hearthstone bright and dear,
With busy, happy loved ones near;
One is a quick and ready hand
To love and serve and keep the land;
One is a worn and beaten way
To where the people go to pray.
As long as these are kept alive,
Nation and people will survive.

PRAYER: *God keep them always, everywhere:*
The hearth, the flag, the place of prayer.
Amen.

Samuel M. Miller
Jesus Only
Samuel M. Miller
MELODY
1. Je - sus on - ly on the moun-tain, Je - sus on - ly on the
2. Je - sus on - ly in life's eve - ning, Je - sus on - ly gives me
sea, Je - sus on - ly in the val - ley, There in
rest, Je - sus on - ly can sup - port me, When the
2d stanza-crescendo to end.
dark Geth - sem - a - ne. Je - sus on - ly up to
sun sinks in the west. Je - sus on - ly in the
1st stanza
Cal - v'ry, Je - sus on - ly on the cross, Je - sus
morn - ing Of that vast e - ter - ni - ty, There re -
on - ly in all suff'ring, All things else are emp - ty dross.
veal'd in glo-rious splen-dor, In the home He won for me.
Copyright by Samuel M. Miller. Used by permission of the author.

Jesus Only

On the mountain

Matthew 17:1, 2, 5-8

And after six days Jesus took with him Peter and James and John his brother, and led them up a high mountain apart. And he was transfigured before them, and his face shone like the sun, and his garments became white as light. . . . A bright cloud overshadowed them, and a voice from the cloud said, "This is my beloved Son, with whom I am well pleased; listen to him." When the disciples heard this, they fell on their faces, and were filled with awe. But Jesus came and touched them, saying, "Rise, and have no fear." And when they lifted up their eyes, they saw no one but Jesus only.

IN THE lives of all of us there are high times and low; there are moments of ecstatic jubilation which spiritually are like a glimpse into heaven; then there are low times when the memory of the reality of faith that was ours is so dim that we wonder if the experience was real. The disciples witnessed in the Transfiguration a glimpse of the glory of Christ, the Son of God.

One wonders what they had expected as they climbed the mount with the Lord. They went apart with Christ to pray; then this unforgettable thing happened. Whenever a soul draws apart with the Lord, he can expect great things to happen. But how often do we come into His presence with that kind of anticipation? The wonderful part of such an experience is that the more we focus on Him, the more we become like Him. Something of the luminous light of His presence should rub off on us. Do you remember how they said of the disciples that they could tell they had been with Jesus?

It is good for us to take a look at the disciples' reaction after this glorious experience. They were filled with awe and fell on their faces. But Jesus came and touched them saying, "Rise, have no fear." Whenever we have had a revelation of who He is, there is something of the disciples' response. We are filled with awe at the wonder of being in the presence of such holiness. Then the Christ, who helped every one who came to Him, stops by us and gently says, "Rise, and have no fear."

An old Chinese woman was asked many hard questions during her examination for Christian baptism. At last, she became impatient at some of the puzzling things that were asked her. She turned to her questioners and said, "I am only an old ignorant woman, blind, deaf, and cannot read. How do you suppose that I can answer such things? I just believe in Jesus with all my mind and that is all I want. Isn't that enough?"

PRAYER: *Give me the single look, Lord, that sees You in the center of all of my life. Help me to see the divine possibilities in every one I meet. Amen.*

Jesus Only

On the sea

Matthew 8:23-27

And when he got into the boat, his disciples followed him. And behold, there rose a great storm on the sea, so that the boat was being swamped by the waves; but he was asleep. And they went and woke him, saying, "Save, Lord; we are perishing." And he said to them, "Why are you afraid, O men of little faith?" Then he rose and rebuked the winds and the sea; and there was a great calm. And the men marveled, saying, "What sort of man is this, that even the winds and the sea obey him?"

IN THE Old Testament, too, we are told of the Lord's power over the storm. In Psalm 89:9 we read: "Thou dost rule the raging of the sea; when its waves rise, thou stillest them." And again in Psalm 107: "He made the storm be still, and the waves of the sea were hushed."

In regard to the sea of our spiritual lives, the same thing is true. So often we go along blithely in our little boats, until there is a tempest. The waves rise high, and we see how utterly helpless we are. Then in desperation we call for the "stiller of storms." And He will come, even as He has promised. But when Jesus says to His disciples, "Why are you afraid, O men of little faith?" is He not as much as saying, "Didn't you know I was here all the time, and that when I am with you, you need have no fear?" Is it that we are aware of His presence only when we are desperately in need? That is not His desire for our lives. How many times He speaks of being with us always, of never leaving us, or forsaking us.

There is a parable of a great king who employed his people to weave for him. He was very indulgent and told them that when any difficulty arose they should send for him. Among the men and women busy at their looms, was one little child whom the king did not think too young to work. One day when the men and the women were distressed at their failures—the silks were all tangled and the weaving very much unlike the pattern—they gathered around the child and said, "Tell us how it is that you are so happy in your work? We are always in difficulty." "If you are in difficulty, then why do you not send for the king?" asked the child. "Did he not say that we should send for him when we are in any trouble?" "Oh, we do send for him every morning and evening," they all answered. "Ah," said the child, "but I send for him as often as I have a little tangle."

Better yet it is to abide in His presence so that nothing really seems like a tangle. This is what the Apostle Paul meant when he spoke of the peace of God guarding our hearts and our minds.

PRAYER: *How wonderful it is to know, Lord, that no matter how turbulent the tempest, You will handle the storm. Help me to be aware daily that You are in the boat of my life. In Your name. Amen.*

Jesus Only

In the valley
There in dark Gethsemane

Matthew 26:36-39

Then Jesus went with them to a place called Gethsemane, and he said to his disciples, "Sit here while I go yonder to pray." And taking with him Peter and the two sons of Zebedee, he began to be sorrowful and troubled. Then he said to them, "My soul is very sorrowful, even to death; remain here, and watch with me." And going a little farther he fell on his face and prayed, "My Father, if it be possible, let this cup pass from me; nevertheless, not as I will, but as thou wilt."

YOU REMEMBER the rest of this passage—how the Lord found His disciples sleeping when He came to them after He had struggled with this prayer. In this great hour of His need, He was alone. But His victory in the Garden is the signature to us that we need never be alone in our great hours of decision. The One who never slumbers nor sleeps will be with us.

There are those who wonder why there must be these struggles in life. "If God is love," they say, "why doesn't He make it easier for His children?" It is because He is love, that He does not. There is much to be learned from the story of the naturalist who was watching an emperor moth slowly make its laborious way from the chrysalis stage. Day by day it struggled and squirmed its way, trying to emerge from the cocoon. The opening of the cocoon was so narrow, that this man thought that he would help things along a little bit, so he took his pen knife and cut into the narrow end of the cocoon, so that the opening would be larger and the exit easier. It seemed to him so harsh a struggle ought to be ended quickly. The butterfly emerged, but its wings were imperfect. It could only flutter feebly to the ground. It was feeble and frail, and before night its natural ground enemies ate it. It could not battle its own way in its environment, because its wings had not gone through the long hard struggle which is necessary to develop large, strong wings.

The Gethsemanes in our lives are our empowering for wings that will make us soar, if we have the Lord in our Gethsemane with us. To pray for His will through each day of your life, to struggle for His will in all your decisions, this is the recipe for abundant living.

We knelt there in the place they say is the Garden where our Lord knew such agony. A church has been built in that Garden, and right before its altar is this huge stone, presumably where Christ had prayed His immortal prayer. As we knelt, the lives of our loved ones came before us. As parents, we would so like to protect our children from struggle; we want so to make it easy for them. But as we spoke their names in prayer, we asked that in their lives, as in ours, there might be only one direction: "That God's will might be done."

PRAYER: *Across the threshold of this day, Lord, my prayer is, "May Your will be done." Amen.*

Jesus Only

Up to Calvary,
Jesus only on the cross

John 19:16-19

Then he [Pilate] handed him over to them to be crucified. So they took Jesus, and he went out, bearing his own cross, to the place called the place of the skull, which is called in Hebrew Golgotha. There they crucified him, and with him two others, one on either side, and Jesus between them. Pilate also wrote a title and put it on the cross; it read, "Jesus of Nazareth, the King of the Jews."

THE GOSPEL of John speaks of Jesus bearing His own cross. You and I who have known God's forgiving love in what Jesus did for us on Calvary, know that it was really our cross that He bore. He was without sin, so it would not have been necessary for Him to die at all. We need to think about this, because it seems to me that often we look at Calvary so lightly. This latter conclusion is accurate if we are to judge by our gifts, by our stewardship of life, by our joy in service. What a sense of joyous compulsion there would be, if we really comprehended the magnitude of this gift of God! We would want to say with Dr. E. Stanley Jones, "I wish I had a thousand lives with which to serve Him."

Is that the attitude most people have in your church about serving? Are they glad for the opportunities; or when the church calls, are they full of a million excuses? How do these look in the presence of Calvary?

What about the measure of your gratitude, the evidences of it in your life? It will not be difficult for the children around you to discover what you hold dear, and how dear you hold it. Will their conclusions from your life draw them to the path that leads to eternal life?

There is a marker on the east coast of our country that tells a significant story. It commemorates a sixteen-year-old lad, and on it is the inscription, "Greater love hath no man than this, that he lay down his life for his friends." The boy's father was captain of a ship that plied the ocean. On a very rough voyage, a leak was sprung in the boat. The captain had the men below bailing out the water. It was all to no avail. The water came in faster than they could get it out. Finally he called all the men together and announced to them that it would be necessary for one of them to go in and plug the hole. He bluntly told them it would mean the life of the one who would do it. He asked for volunteers. There was no response. Then his young son came bounding forward. "Let me do it, Dad; please let me do it." "No, no, not you! It can't be you!" was the dismayed father's response. But the boy's winning ways persuaded the father and so the lad gave his life that those on board that ship might safely reach the other shore. Another Father gave His only Son . . . .

PRAYER: *Only You, Christ, God's holy Son, would suffice on the cross to save me. How can I thank You, dearest Friend! Amen.*

Jesus Only

In all suffering;
All things else are empty dross

Job 23:10

"But he knows the way that I take; when he has tried me, I shall come forth as gold."

1 Peter 1:6, 7

In this you rejoice, though now for a little while you may have to suffer various trials, so that the genuineness of your faith, more precious than gold which though perishable is tested by fire, may redound to praise and glory and honor at the revelation of Jesus Christ.

AS I have copied these lines of Scripture, there has come to me anew an overwhelming sense of what it means to have a Savior who was willing to experience every kind of human affliction and suffering, in order understandably to share ours with us. "But he knows the way that I take!" What a comfort those words are for my soul!

It is Matthew Henry who has said, "Sanctified afflictions are spiritual promotions." How do you take suffering when it is your lot? Are you a whiner or a refiner? Your answer will depend upon whether or not you have Jesus with you in that suffering. His presence is the refining process that produces the gold.

The story is told of Queen Victoria that during one of her visits to Scotland she heard of a poor woman whose child was stricken by a sad accident. It melted her heart, and she went to the hut of the peasant. Her visit gave new life to the woman, so that the neighbors marveled at her resignation. They asked her the reason for it. She replied, "The Queen's visit lifted me above my sorrows." Then she was asked: "What did the Queen say? What did she give? What did she do?" Her answer was: "The Queen said nothing; the Queen gave nothing; the Queen did nothing. She was so broken down that she cried with me as though her heart would break." There is One who was willing to bear the feeling of our infirmities, so that He might share our deepest sorrow, our severest affliction.

What a witness Christians give when they invite Christ in at such times. When I was in high school (I attended a Christian Academy supported by our Church), I had for my course in Christianity a teacher who left a very deep impression on my life. There was something about the glow that one saw from behind her eyes that first drew me. But the exclamation point to her influence in the life of this adolescent was, when at the passing of her own mother, she sang at her funeral. Without a waver, she witnessed in her song: "My faith looks up to Thee." Since then I have come to know that this is the way that it ought to be at every Christian homegoing, for, "we sorrow not as those who have no hope."

PRAYER: *You have taken our afflictions, Lord, and made them steppingstones to victory. Help us not to grovel in the mire of our own despair, but to look up and see You. Amen.*

Jesus Only

In life's evening
Jesus only gives me rest

Exodus 33:14

And he said, "My presence will go with you, and I will give you rest."

Isaiah 46:4

"Even to your old age, I am He, and to gray hairs I will carry you. I have made, and I will bear; I will carry and will save."

Matthew 11:28-30

"Come to me, all who labor and are heavy-laden, and I will give you rest. Take my yoke upon you, and learn from me; for I am gentle and lowly in heart, and you will find rest for your souls."

JESUS ONLY in life's evening! What glorious home goings are those, when souls have heard the foregoing invitation, and have accepted it. The only qualitative stipulation is "all who labor and are heavy-laden." The promise is without reservation: "I will give you rest." Possibly to every person rest is a different picture. Two artists tried to illustrate their conception of rest. The first one chose a still, lone lake in the mountains as his idea of a symbol of rest. The second painted a thundering waterfall, with a fragile birch tree bending over the foam. At the fork of the branch, almost wet with the cataract's spray, a robin sat on its nest. The latter painter had a real point. Christ's life was one of the most tempestuous that has ever been lived, ending in the explosion that was the cross. But His inner life was like a sea of glass. Always there was that calm that was born in eternity. Even when His enemies were dogging His feet in the streets of Jerusalem, He turned to His disciples and offered them, as a last legacy: "My peace."

When you have walked through life knowing this inner calm, no matter how distressing the outward circumstances may be; when through all that has befallen you, the sense of His sureness was like a mighty rock; then, when you come to life's evening, you will also know the wonderful companionship of the One who has lighted the way, and there will be no fear.

The world is full of weary people; the world is full of restless souls. They are chasing up one road and down the other, wildly seeking a will-o'-the-wisp of one kind or another. They pass your door; they live in your neighborhood; they may even live in your home. In the midst of all the turmoil, is there that in your life which will make them pause? From your own experience, can you speak a word of faith and calm to them? Yours may be the sign on the road that will make them leave the detour, and plant their feet on the road that leads Home.

PRAYER: *You know how busy life is, Lord, and how quickly confusion and despair set in. O help me to live so close to You that the steady beat of Your eternal heart may find its echo in mine. In Jesus' name. Amen.*

SATURDAY

Jesus Only

In life's morning
In that home He's won for me

Revelation 22:12-14

"Behold, I am coming soon, bringing my recompense, to repay every one for what he has done. I am the Alpha and the Omega, the first and the last, the beginning and the end." Blessed are those who wash their robes, that they may have the right to the tree of life and that they may enter the city by the gates.

DO YOU remember when you were a little child, how you anticipated an outing or a party or maybe a trip? You waited and waited for the day to come! (How long a week seemed then!) When the morning finally arrived, you were so excited, you could hardly get dressed! Some of our earthly anticipations can be very disappointing. Maybe you remember about such an anticipated time, when it rained and everything seemed to go all wrong. Your dreams burst like a bubble!

Never will it be so to a child of God who anticipates eternity's morning. Scripture gives us to know that our wildest anticipations are utterly inadequate.

Does it not seem very inconsistent, then, for us to wail and moan when a Christian has passed through the night into that morning? How pagan our funerals often are! Death is not the end, it is the beginning of a wonderful life with the Savior who has walked with you here. It is to His home you are going. We ought so to walk, then, as to witness to people that we are pilgrims going home.

A minister tells of an experience he had when a doctor asked him to go with him to a house where a woman was dying. Reaching the house, the doctor said, "The friends have done all they could. I will go in first and make her as comfortable as I can. Then I will call you to talk with her." After a time, the minister was summoned. He took the woman's hand and asked if she knew the Lord, and trusted in His grace. She indicated that she did. Then she whispered: "I'm going through the valley." "Is there anyone with you in the valley?" the minister asked. She pressed his hand and there came a peaceful smile over her face as she whispered, "Yes." That was her last word.

The physician and the minister rode home together. The doctor said, "It has been a joy for me to be with you today. I have been brought to realize something as never before." "And what is that?" asked the minister. "I have seen that when friends and loved ones have gone as far as they could go with their Christian dear one," said he, "there is Someone from the other side who takes them up. That woman was not alone as she went through the valley."

PRAYER: *Thank You, Lord, for Your providential care that includes this life and that other morning. In every day we would see Jesus only. Amen.*

O God! How Wonderful Thou Art

Beatitudo. C. M. JOHN BACCHUS DYKES, 1875.

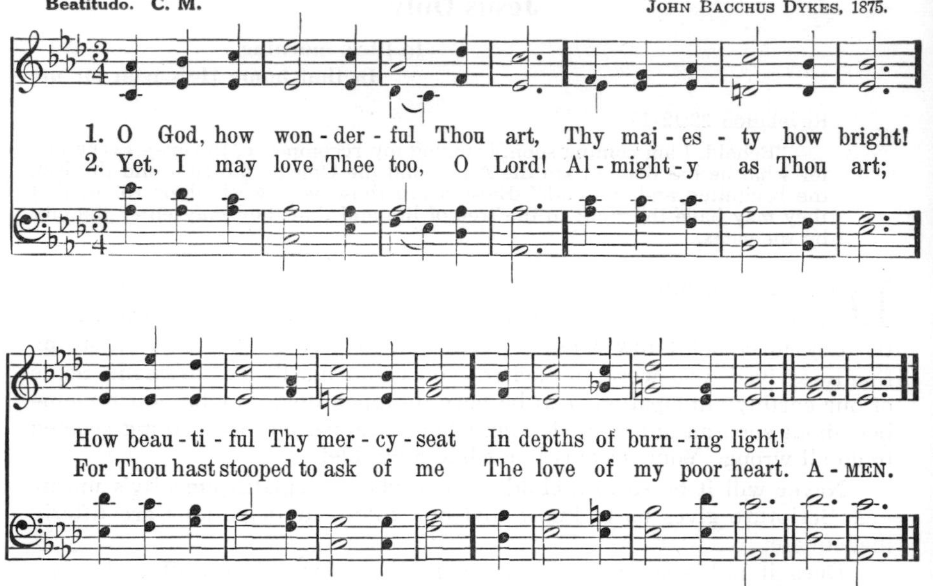

3 No earthly father loves like Thee,
No mother e'er so mild
Bears and forbears as Thou hast done
With me, Thy sinful child.

4 O God, how wonderful Thou art,
Thou everlasting Friend!
On Thee I stay my trusting heart
Till faith and vision end.

Frederick William Faber, 1849.

O God, How Wonderful Thou Art

Thy majesty how bright

1 Chronicles 29:11-13

"Thine, O Lord, is the greatness, and the power, and the glory, and the victory, and the majesty; for all that is in the heavens and in the earth is thine; thine is the kingdom, O Lord, and thou art exalted as head above all. Both riches and honor come from thee, and thou rulest over all. In thy hand are power and might; and in thy hand it is to make great and to give strength to all. And now we thank thee, our God, and praise thy glorious name."

THIS AGE is often accused by its critics of holding too frivolous a concept of God. Such popular songs as "The Man Upstairs," and "He" seem a rather light way of approaching the King of creation and the Ruler of the world. Yet in these very titles is expressed the hunger of our times for Someone outside of oneself, Someone upon whom we can depend. The danger is that this Someone comes to be "The Great Whatever," and the realization of *who* He is never comes to fulfillment.

It is good for us to consider the majesty of God, because the wonder of His love becomes more apparent. To the people of Israel He was so holy that they hardly dared to speak His name. They remembered when He spoke to Moses, and His glory was so great that Moses had to cover his face. Their history was a succession of witnessing to God's omniscience and omnipresence and power. They knew that He was not One to be held lightly.

We have gone the other extreme in our day. The carelessness of our speech is good evidence of that. The slang that so many good church people use so readily has its derivation in the names that should be the most revered and holy in their vocabulary. "Gee" is a shortening of Jesus, and "gosh" and "darn" are modified forms of God and damn. Oh, I know that people do not think about this when they use them, but is not this, too, an evidence of our carelessness, as well as of the poverty of our speech?

Do we need our attention called again to the bright majesty of God? As our Scripture says, "All that is in the heavens and the earth is thine." It is amazing how we kowtow to people of wealth or position. How honored we are to receive an invitation from someone who is a V.I.P.! Have we lost the sense of who God is, that we treat His invitations so lightly?

Let us pray for a renewed consciousness of the majesty and power of God. And our response will be that of the writer of Scripture: "And now we thank thee, our God, and praise thy glorious name."

PRAYER: *Forgive us God, that too often we have been unmindful of who You are. This day, in the evidences of Your handiwork all about us, help us to be aware of Your Majesty. Amen.*

O God, How Wonderful Thou Art

**Yet, I may love Thee too, O Lord,
Almighty as Thou art**

Deuteronomy 7:8

"It is because the Lord loves you, and is keeping the oath which he swore to your fathers, that the Lord has brought you out with a mighty hand, and redeemed you from the house of bondage, from the hand of Pharaoh, king of Egypt."

1 John 3:1

See what love the Father has given us, that we should be called children of God; and so we are. The reason why the world does not know us is that it did not know him.

THE STORY is related of how Henry George and Cardinal Manning were one time talking together. The cardinal said, "I love men because they love God." To which the great economist replied, "And I love God because He loves men." Really both of the men were right. Scripture tells us, "We love, because he first loved us." God, almighty as He is, will never force anyone to love Him. The wonder is that God should even want our love; that it should make any difference to Him whether or not we respond to Him.

This love for God is different from earthly love, yet within its full scope it has all the qualities of the various loves combined. There is "eros," the love of a man for a maid. There is "filios," the love of child to parent. Then there is "agape," the love that is God. As we return His outpouring upon us, there is something of the romance and expectancy of the first; there is the devotion and gratitude of the second; plus this almost indefinable quality, that by the grace of the Holy Spirit makes one willing to lose one's identity in the beautiful love of God.

It is a healthy exercise for us to examine our hearts and assay the quality of our love for the Lord. With the intimate personal relationship that we are able to have because of God's revealing himself in Jesus, is there this quality of worship and adoration that befits the King of kings?

Dr. Phillips in his book, *Your God Is Too Small,* pictures various modern concepts of God. He speaks of the "jack-in-the-box" attitude, where we believe we can push a button and God will jump out. There is the "handy man" attitude that treats God as something like a plumber's helper. There is the "no god" attitude, where in actuality we worship things rather than the Creator.

Yes, we need to examine the picture of God that we have in our hearts. As we do, there will be the response of wonder that He seeks our love.

PRAYER: *Thank You, Lord, that You want my love. When I think of Your majesty I am awed; then I remember Your divine visitation to earth. Thank You for this. For as You walked among people, You lived with them and were touched with the feeling of their infirmities. You have done that for me too, and I thank You. Amen.*

O God, How Wonderful Thou Art

For Thou hast stooped to ask of me
The love of my poor heart

Jeremiah 24:7

"I will give them a heart to know that I am the Lord; and they shall be my people and I will be their God, for they shall return to me with their whole heart."

Jeremiah 31:3

"I have loved you with an everlasting love; therefore I have continued my faithfulness to you."

THROUGH THE Book of Jeremiah there runs the refrain: "and they shall be my people and I shall be their God." Something of the yearning heart of God is revealed here. The entire history of the children of Israel is a revelation of the infinitely patient seeking of Almighty God for the love of His children. It is not different today. Jesus' very purpose on earth finds its fulfillment in this. It is why He left His heavenly home; it is why He suffered ignominy, shame, and death. These all are a part of the price of His seeking. The hymn writer has rightly used the word "stooped." From the throne of heaven to the lowliest place a man could ever come, the God of creation stoops to ask for your poor heart.

Many years ago the tears of a slave girl about to be sold drew the attention of a man as he passed through a southern slave mart. The kind man stopped to ask why she wept. Her attitude was in such contrast to the other slaves, who seemed to be rather indifferent to the whole procedure. This girl, however, had been reared by a very kind owner, and she was terrified to think of who might buy her. The man asked her price. He hesitated when he learned how much it was, yet so deeply touched was he, that he paid it, and then gave her papers of freedom. Yet no joy seemed to come to the slave's face when she was told that she was free. She had been born a slave, and knew not what freedom meant. Finally, however, he was able to make her understand that she was beholden to no one, and could do as she pleased. When this realization dawned on her, she exclaimed with her first breath, "I will follow him. I must serve him with my life." To every reason given her against it by her friends, she responded with, "He redeemed me! He redeemed me!" She insisted on going to his home to work. People visiting that home noticed the extraordinary devotion of the girl and would inquire about it. Her response would be "He redeemed me!"

There is One who finds us enslaved by sin and, though He is King of glory, He stooped to redeem us. What is our response?

PRAYER: *Like this little slave girl, Lord, I want to give my whole life to serve You. Take my heart, my mind, all that I am and have, and use them that others might know this matchless love. Amen.*

O God, How Wonderful Thou Art

No earthly father loves like Thee

Psalm 27:10

For my father and my mother have forsaken me, but the Lord will take me up.

Matthew 7:9-11

"Or what man of you, if a son asks for a loaf, will give him a stone? Or if he asks for a fish, will give him a serpent? If you, then, who are evil, know how to give good gifts to your children, how much more will your Father who is in heaven give good gifts to those who ask him?"

IN CONTRAST to our thinking of God in His majesty is this picture of Him as a father. It is true that there have been some fathers who have been unworthy to be called such, but by and large, our fathers have commanded not only our respect, but our love as well. They have provided for us, they have worked hard to give us opportunities; they have found their joy in the fulfillment of our lives. In his explanation to the salutation of the Lord's Prayer, Luther says of this pattern that Christ gave: "God would thereby affectionately encourage us to believe that He is truly our Father, and that we are His children indeed . . ."

I remember my own dad. We were ten children, and dad worked plenty hard in order that opportunities that he never had might be ours. He wanted us all to have the opportunities of an education. For thirty years he never took a day's vacation except the Sabbath and the national holidays. He was willing to forget his own need that we might be provided for. Often he went without buying a new suit, because his strapping boys needed suits and shoes so constantly; and his girls had a way of growing, too. He never was absent from his church on the Sabbath, and the first fruits of his income, all of his time outside of working hours, whatever talent he had, were given to the extension of the kingdom. I said all of his time outside of working hours. That really is not accurate, because in his work he was constantly witnessing to the Lord that he loved. He taught a Bible Class of young people, and I can remember him many evenings sitting with the Book, preparing his lesson. To understand the love of God, as exemplified in my father, is not at all difficult for me. This is what Jesus is saying to the fishermen. If your children are hungry and ask for some bread, you do not give them a stone. Or if when you pull your nets in, they come running and ask for a little fish, you do not give them the snake that has been caught. "How much more will your Father who is in heaven give good gifts . . . ?"

I am so grateful that the Lord did not give us a picture of himself only as King and Creator. I am grateful that He revealed this father heart.

PRAYER: *Heavenly Father, how thankful I am for all Your loving care and provision for my life. You are interested in everything I do and am. Your resources are sufficient for all my needs. Keep me ever aware that I am Your child. Amen.*

O God, How Wonderful Thou Art

No mother e'er so mild
Bears and forbears as Thou hast done

Isaiah 49:15, 16

"Can a woman forget her sucking child, that she should have no compassion on the son of her womb?" Even these may forget, yet I will not forget you. Behold I have graven you on the palms of my hands; your walls are continually before me.

I SUPPOSE if there is one sentimental word in our language over and above any other in regard to our human relations, it is the word "mother." Neither sweetheart nor wife begin to convey what the name mother does. Here is embodied the remembrance of a refuge. Can you recall the wonderful feeling of your mother's arms about you as you sat in her lap? Here is the synonym for sympathy, the kind that helped to make things right. In our home, Mother was also our mediator. When we knew that our requests might be a little difficult of fulfillment, we used Mother as a buffer to Dad, because we knew that she had a way that might make the difference. Here was generosity that was utterly self-effacing, that knew its greatest joy in giving. Here was patience with our repeated mistakes and transgressions. And here was love, lived in every deed of every day on our behalf.

But no matter how many wonderful things you can say about your mother, they are not adequate to describe God. He is all these, and much more. His patience knows no end. He has graven us on the palms of His hands. He has died for us!

No wonder we want to sing: "O God how wonderful Thou art." As you learn these words this week, will you not try to be more aware of the magnitude and love of God? In our materialistic world it is so easy for us to take them for granted.

Dan Crawford tells of an experience he had in his work in Africa. Five times he redeemed one mother from slavery. Five times she had sold herself into slavery, because her little boy who changed bondmasters was a slave. Each time she followed up her son, gladly enduring bondage under her five slave owners to be near her boy. That boy grew up to be one of the earliest converts on Lake Mweru. Could it not be that it was easy for him to understand something of the love of God and the price He paid for our freedom because of the pattern of his mother's life?

"Even these may forget, yet I will not forget you."

PRAYER: *Even as we thank You again, Lord, for the love of our mothers, we acknowledge Your greater love. How can we show our gratitude? Make us channels into the lives of others of all we have received. In Jesus' name. Amen*

FRIDAY

O God, How Wonderful Thou Art

Thou everlasting Friend

John 15:15

"No longer do I call you servants, for the servant does not know what his master is doing; but I have called you friends, for all that I have heard from my Father I have made known to you."

A PRIZE was offered some years ago for the best definition of a friend This is the one that won: "A friend is a person who comes in when every other person has gone out." What is your definition of a friend? Make it whatever you will, include every possible attribute that you hold dear, and I will wager that Christ will be adequate to every definition.

A friend is loyal. In the finest of human friendships, there are times when one wonders. Is it so of the One who stays closer than any brother?

A friend sees the best in you, all the while he is aware of the worst. How else would the Christ have been willing to die for us, sinners that we are?

A friend is good company. There is no one who gives life zest as the Giver of abundant life. To be in His presence is to know joy.

A friend forgives. But what a hard time he has to forget! Not so with the Friend of friends. When He forgives, He remembers your mistakes no more. They are gone.

A friend understands. Jesus was touched with the feeling of our infirmities; He came to earth to live as a man; to know hunger and weariness; to know hatred and disappointment; to know rejection and contumely, in order to be to us an everlasting Friend.

To have Him as your Friend is never to need to be dismayed.

In today's world there is a great deal of moving about. The old pattern of growing up with people in one town is fast disappearing. The result is that our friendships also are much more ephemeral. As we move about from place to place, there are very few friends who remain close and true. But there is One who will go with you wherever you go; who will face with you any situation; who will give you the wisest counsel to be had.

God is Before me, He will be my guide,
God is Behind me, no ill can betide;
God is Beside me, to comfort and cheer,
God is Around me, so why should I fear?

ANON.

PRAYER: *For a friendship that is everlasting life to me, I thank You, God. Help me to share Your friendship with others. In Jesus' name. Amen.*

O God, How Wonderful Thou Art

On Thee I stay my trusting heart
Till faith and vision end

Psalm 37:5
Commit your way to the Lord; trust in him, and he will act.

Isaiah 26:4
"Trust in the Lord for ever, for the Lord God is an everlasting rock."

TO COMMIT your life into the hands of God, the almighty God, the majestic God, the everlasting Father, the wonderful Friend, is to give yourself a protection from any of the hurts and harms of life. Truly, a Christian can say, "So what!" Not flippantly does he say this, but in the wonderful faith that knows that no matter what happens to him, he has a powerful Friend who is sufficient for any and all exigencies. God's love is like a great asbestos that envelops us and protects us from the fire of the world. We may still be right in the midst of that fire, mind you; may even feel the heat thereof; but we will never be consumed because of His enveloping love.

The following humorous story illustrates this point somewhat. It is told by a former governor of New Jersey. One day a chauffeur driving a car came out of Trenton at about seventy miles an hour. A trooper chased him and apprehended him. "What's the big idea? Don't you know you were going seventy miles an hour?" "Was I?" was the chauffeur's reply, "that's all right with me." The trooper looked at him for a moment and said, "You're sort of fresh, aren't you?" "No," replied the man, "give me two or three tickets if you like." That was too much for the trooper, so he took him to jail.

When the chauffeur appeared before the judge, the judge heard the case and said, "I'm going to fine you twenty-five dollars." "Oh, that's all right, Judge," said the man, "make it one hundred dollars if you like." The judge was somewhat nonplussed, but he said, "I'm going to make it twenty-five dollars and a year in jail besides." "Oh, I like that fine. Make it two or three years if you would like." Finally the judge said, "What's wrong with you? Who are you anyway?" "Well," said the fellow, "I'm the chauffeur for the warden of the penitentiary and I'm in for life."

In a wonderful way there comes a time of faith in your Christian life when nothing can really touch you. You are so sure of the hand that guides you, to which you are clinging, that no matter how rocky the path or how dark the way, you know you are going Home. You are "in" for life.

PRAYER: *It is impossible in mere words to tell you, Lord, what it means for me to put my trust in You. What a difference it makes in how I greet each morning! Nothing this day may bring can possibly harm me when You are at my side. Everything that happens this day will work toward good when I meet it with You. Thank You for Your presence. Amen.*

Name of Jesus, Softly Stealing

Beatrice. 8 7, 8 7. WILLIAM WALLACE COE, 1895.

2 Name of Jesus, Heaven of gladness,
Cause our doubts and fears to cease;
Soothe away the aching sadness;
Name of Jesus, give us peace.

Unknown.

Name of Jesus, Softly Stealing

O'er a world of strife and shame

Philippians 2:9, 10

Therefore God has highly exalted him and bestowed on him the name which is above every name, that at the name of Jesus every knee should bow, in heaven and on earth and under the earth, and every tongue confess that Jesus Christ is Lord, to the glory of God the Father.

WHAT IS in a name? These past months we have been listening to a ludicrous advertisement over radio that enjoins every prospective parent to send for this booklet to help them name their child. It is interesting to note the things that influence parents in this respect. Of course, we have all heard about wealthy relatives for whom aspiring babies are named. Or sometimes the ambitions of the parents for their offspring find their expression in the name they give to the child. In one of his much quoted passages, Shakespeare said, "What's in a name? A rose by any other name would smell as sweet!" That may be true of the names we mortals give. My parents had such high hopes for their children that they gave us each a Bible name, a historical name, and then a common name. Such names as Lincoln, Ferdinand, Mathias, Augustine, Nathaniel, Victoria embellish the family roster if the bearers are not too timid to acknowledge their full nomenclature! I cannot believe that these names really made any difference in our aspirations.

But there is a Name that was announced years before the birth took place. It was reiterated to the mother before her baby was born. It is the last name on the lips of people who leave this earth for the Other Country. It is the most powerful name in all the world. It is the bridge, and the only bridge, to heaven. What a message Mary received! "And you shall call his name Jesus, for he will save his people from their sins."

Into what kind of world does that name come today? This may well be evidenced by the fact that so often this name is taken in vain.

Surely we are living in a world of strife and shame today. There are wars and rumors of wars on all sides. I have the feeling that, if only we were bold to witness to the power of this name in our own lives, we could be a help to the world. I know that in our own home, when there is strife, the one sure surcease for it is to acknowledge the sovereignty of this Name, and to seek the guidance of the One to whom it belongs.

Is there a significance in that the hymn writer speaks of the Name softly stealing over the world? Is it evidence of how timid Christ's followers are? Of the early Christians we are told they witnessed boldly.

PRAYER: *Lord Christ, empower us anew with the knowledge that in Your name there is healing for the nations. Wherever Your name has come in its full power, there has come peace. Help us to be ready witnesses. Amen.*

Name of Jesus, Softly Stealing

Thou canst bring us heavenly healing

Psalm 41:4

As for me, I said, "O Lord, be gracious to me;
heal me, for I have sinned against thee!"

Isaiah 53:5

But he was wounded for our transgressions, he was bruised for our iniquities; upon him was the chastisement that made us whole, and with his stripes we are healed.

IN MEDICAL circles today there is a great deal of unanimity about the effect of the mind on the body. Where a patient is at peace with God, the chances of physical healing are much greater. This is basically true in the cure of T. B. It is true in every other disease, too. You know how your sewing machine acts when there is too much tension. The thread breaks and gives you much trouble. When you are able to release the thread so that it feeds easily through the needle, then the machine functions properly.

So quickly in this age of tensions we get all tied up inside. The speed with which we live, and the many diversions beckoning on all hands, are not conducive to relaxing. As Christians we must discipline ourselves to do this. The world needs desperately our witness in this respect. What good is it for us to talk about the peace of God, if our own lives are all in a snarl, if we are a bundle of nerves? On the other hand, if His peace is in us, we will bring healing into every situation by His resources that we may command.

We should take note that preliminary to the healing of the soul, there is confession of sin. Is this the place where the world balks? Is this why the name of Jesus must come softly stealing? Speaking that name might not make some people too comfortable. Maybe speaking it makes us squirm. He sees everything. He knows our duplicity and our hypocrisy. Are we willing to come confessing, so that we may know the balm there is in Gilead?

In this field of God's power to heal both mind and body, there is a vast ocean to be explored. For you today the point is this: the fret that you carry, the ill will that you harbor, the uncertainty as to the future that you feel—bring these all to the One who has heavenly healing. From Him will flow such peace as to be a new empowering, for from Him is forgiveness of all past sins, a new page, and a chance to begin again.

PRAYER: *Lord, You know how sick the world is with distrust and hatred and sinning and forgetting You. You know how quickly these things creep into our lives. Help us to go to the medicine chest of Your Word, and find therein that which will heal. We thank You that, as we believe in You, Your name will have such power. Amen.*

Name of Jesus, Softly Stealing

O Thou all-restoring name

Psalm 51:10-12

Create in me a clean heart, O God, and put a new and right spirit within me. Cast me not away from thy presence, and take not thy holy Spirit from me. Restore to me the joy of thy salvation, and uphold me with a willing spirit.

Acts 4:12

"And there is salvation in no one else, for there is no other name under heaven given among men by which we must be saved."

RESTORING HAS in it the suggestion of refueling. What a difference it would make to any one of our days, if in the hurly-burly schedule we keep, there would be refueling places. The Jews practiced the three-hour prayer schedule. Too often, however, it became a mere mechanical process. Kept vital in the faith of the Name that restores, it could be a powerhouse for abundant living. We have a friend who keeps these hours: 6, 9, 12, 3, 6, 9. Wherever he is, whether in a crowd or where, he makes his tryst with the One whose name has this restoring power. It trues him up to the value of the thing at hand. It makes him aware of his resources in Christ.

For souls that are dying in sin, there is restorative power in this Name. As our Scripture points out, "there is no other name under heaven . . . by which we must be saved." The efficacy of this Name did not come by any magic. It was purchased with a life, the holy life of the Son of God. You and I may be restored to spiritual health, as we acknowledge the power in this Name and our need of it.

In the Alps mountains, large St. Bernard dogs are trained to trail lost persons and save their lives. The dogs are taught to scratch snow from the body, and then to lie down upon it. Often the heat from the dog revives the person, and a flask tied about the dog's neck contains liquor to revive him. One beautiful dog had found his sixty-ninth man. He had worked to remove the snow from the man's body and then had placed his own warm one on top of the victim. The man began to stir and seeing the animal on top of him, thought that he was about to be devoured by a wolf. He was able to reach for his dagger and quickly plunged it into the animal's side. Without a sound, the dog crept away to his master's cabin to bleed to death at the doorstep. A few days later mountaineers learned the full story.

There is something that is reminiscent of the Calvary experience in this story. How often we cruelly stab our Savior by blaspheming His name, with rejection of His proffered hand!

PRAYER: *For the restoring power that is in Your name; for the whole effect of Calvary that is behind it, we thank You, O Lord. May there be a reviving of our ebbing spirits through the warm contact of Your life. Amen.*

Name of Jesus, Softly Stealing

Heaven of Gladness

Psalm 4:7

Thou hast put more joy in my heart than they have when their grain and their wine abound.

Psalm 34:4, 5

I sought the Lord, and he answered me, and delivered me from all my fears. Look to him, and be radiant; so your faces shall never be ashamed.

2 Corinthians 3:18

And we all, with unveiled face, beholding the glory of the Lord, are being changed into his likeness from one degree of glory to another; for this comes from the Lord who is the Spirit.

HAVE YOU ever noticed the difference that there is when people enter a room? When certain ones enter, there is a feeling of exuberance and joy, there is a lift; when others enter, there is a sag, a feeling of depression. I am not speaking about "Pollyanna" stuff, a superficial smile plastered on the face. This does not give the lift, because in it there is a feeling of hollow mockery. I am speaking of the sensing of an indwelling Spirit whose very presence is joy. What atmosphere do you bring with you, when you enter a group?

The psalmist puts it so simply. "Look to him, and be radiant." Here is the "heaven of gladness." The world that does not know Christ is not going to study theology first to find Him. They are going to observe His effect on you. In large measure that will determine whether or not they will be intrigued to go in search of the source of your gladness.

Young folks have been repelled often, because our Christian living has lacked the flavor of joy. So they have sipped the wine of the world with its glamorous promise. We stand convicted as Christians because there is not enough of gladness in us. A minister coming to a new parish asked a boy outside the church, "Do these people enjoy their religion?" His significant reply was: "Them that has it, does."

The wife of a preacher on Cape Cod relates a significant Church school experience, which Dr. Stidger tells in one of his books. In her class of ten-year-olds, one Sunday, their conversation about Jesus was interrupted by one girl who asked, "Mrs. Hutchinson, do you think that Jesus really had a halo like you see in all the pictures of Him?" The teacher turned to the girls and said, "What do you think about it? Have you ever seen anyone whose face was all radiant with sunshine?" Much to the teacher's embarrassment and amazement, they all chorused, "Yes, you, Mrs. Hutchinson." Momentarily the pastor's wife was struck dumb. Before she could add anything, another little girl spoke up. "Perhaps I ought not to say this," she said, "but I lived with Mrs. Hutchinson for a week while my mother was away, and I never saw her halo."

PRAYER: *It is only when we are unwilling to expose ourselves to You that our spirits lag, Lord. Help us to live the joy of salvation. Amen.*

Name of Jesus, Softly Stealing

Cause our doubts and fears to cease

Matthew 14: 30, 31

But when he [Peter] saw the wind, he was afraid, and beginning to sink, he cried out, "Lord, save me." Jesus immediately reached out his hand and caught him, saying to him, "O man of little faith, why did you doubt?"

JESUS CHRIST is the true antidote for fear. There is no other like it. How many times a day could the Lord say to you, "O man of little faith!"? Sometimes I think people prefer to concentrate on their troubles, rather than on the solution. There is a certain wallowing in despair that we almost enjoy. A Christian does not deny the existence of obstacles and difficulties. But he also takes stock of the resources that are his with which to meet them.

He finds his ammunition for the battle of life in God's Word. He repeatedly takes inventory, in order to be aware of his strength. His stock list reads like this:

> "Fear not, I am with you." "Fear not, I have redeemed you." "Fear not, you shall not be ashamed." "Fear not those who harm the body." "Fear not, little flock, it is your Father's good pleasure to give you the kingdom."

The Lord showed holy impatience with the disciples when they evidenced doubt. Do you remember how He said to them, "How is it that you have been with me so long, and yet you doubt?" There are times for all of us when He well might say, "O foolish men, and slow of heart to believe!" Is it that we do not realize that doubt is sin, because it is lack of faith? This I have said before, and I think we could well stand to have it repeated each day. The inefficacy of the Christian Church today is not due to the battle waged by atheists. That would hardly make a ripple. Our weakness is our own lack of faith; our not daring to attempt great things for the Lord; our trusting only in the resources that are material, that we can see with the eye; our failure to believe that when God gives a directive, He also provides the empowering. I have sat at business meetings of congregations and groaned in spirit at the excuses and obstacles offered for the slow progress of the work. What is true for the church is just as true for our individual lives.

As Christ was discouraged at the lack of faith, so was He encouraged when He found it. The centurion who wanted his servant healed rejoiced the heart of the Lord with his faith; the Syrophoenician woman who asked for only the crumbs (figuratively speaking), caused the Lord to exclaim about her faith.

The living, vital name of Jesus can cause our doubts and fears to cease.

PRAYER: *Forgive us, Lord, that we piddle along in our own strength, when the power of Your name is there for us to use. Increase our faith. In Jesus' name. Amen.*

Name of Jesus, Softly Stealing

Soothe away the aching sadness

Isaiah 24:1-3

> Behold, the Lord will lay waste the earth and make it desolate,
> and he will twist its surface and scatter its inhabitants.
> And it shall be, as with the people, so with the priest;
> as with the slave, so with his master; as with the maid, so with her mistress;
> as with the buyer, so with the seller; as with the lender so with the borrower;
> as with the creditor, so with the debtor.
> The earth shall be utterly laid waste and utterly despoiled;
> for the Lord has spoken this word.

THIS FIRST part of the twenty-fourth chapter of Isaiah is a pretty woeful picture. The continuance of the above passage speaks of the earth, and the heavens, and the world languishing and withering. There are sections here that it seems to me could well be a description of what the earth would be like in atomic explosion. Certainly the catastrophic results pictured here are comparable to what was known at Hiroshima. There is something of a summation of sorrows in a line of the eleventh verse: "All joy has reached its eventide; the gladness of the earth is banished. Desolation is left in the city, the gates are battered into ruins."

Reading thus far, you think that you could just as well fold up and be done with it. The aching sadness that comes from the desolation of sin permeates to the innermost chamber of the heart. But, thank God, we do not have to end here. For even as sin and sadness go together, so also do God and gladness.

Then again there is a picture of the desolation of the wicked: "The earth staggers like a drunken man." This is followed by the glorious victory of salvation in the twenty-fifth chapter: "O Lord, thou art my God; I will exalt thee, I will praise thy name. . . . For thou hast been a stronghold to the poor, a stronghold to the needy in his distress, a shelter from the storm and a shade from the heat. . . . This is the Lord; we have waited for him; let us be glad and rejoice in his salvation."

Reading the Book of Isaiah one almost has the feeling of a teeter-totter. You are up and you are down. Only the sustaining sureness of God's everlasting love can be the balance that will hold steady. With all its picture of sin and devastation and destruction, the Book of Isaiah has the theme of salvation. Isaiah is pre-eminently the prophet of redemption.

The aching sadness that comes from the picture of the world about us, madly manufacturing its own destruction; the soreness of heart one feels at the rejection of Christ for materialism—all of this is dispelled in the wonderful knowledge of the victory that there is in this Name of Jesus.

PRAYER: *We are often caught in the grip of defeat and hopelessness, Lord. Holy Spirit of God, come with Your power and give us light. In Jesus' name. Amen.*

SATURDAY

Name of Jesus, Softly Stealing

Name of Jesus, give us peace

Psalm 29:11
May the Lord give strength to his people! May the Lord bless his people with peace!

John 16:33
"I have said this to you, that in me you may have peace. In the world you have tribulation; but be of good cheer, I have overcome the world."

PERHAPS THERE is no single word on the lips of as many people today as the word peace. We mouth it much, yet the reality is far from us. This is true both internationally and individually. Our Scripture suggests that peace may be had in the midst of struggle; that it is the result of an indwelling spirit. To have this is to have life's richest gifts; to be without it is to be poor indeed. How can one possess it?

In words it is so simple. It is to give up to God; it is to give over your life to Him. It is not so much a struggle as it is a yielding. It is not something you attain; it is something you accept. What is so simple in words often becomes exceedingly difficult of realization because there are roadblocks in our lives to prevent the entry of the Prince of peace. We want peace, but according to our blueprints, not God's. Self is the biggest obstacle.

For yourself and for the whole world, there is but one road to any peace that will last. This is the Bethlehem road. It is to bow in adoration and love before the One who humbled himself to be born in a manger, that the way of peace might be opened to all men.

Many books on peace fill our bookstores today. People frantically buy them, hoping for some sugar-coated pill that will be easy to take. The disillusioning that follows is often devastating. Our hymn gives us the guide in our search. It is only in the name of Jesus that we find peace.

A middle-aged man in Boston tells the story of how he found it. When his wife went out one night, he was alone with his little niece. Snuggling up to her uncle, she said, "Uncle, tell me something about Jesus. Mother always does on Sunday nights." He tried to evade it, but she would not be put off. Opening her eyes wide, she said, "Why, you know about Jesus, don't you?" The man was overcome with a sense of ignorance and guilt, and went to his Bible with an anxious and inquiring heart. He found his Savior there in the Book, and that great find brought a wonderful peace to his soul.

What your age, or station, or condition is, does not really make any difference. The fruit of the Spirit is peace. The name of Jesus, effective and alive in your heart, spells it out.

PRAYER: *In a world where the rumblings of war never seem to cease; into my life where there are so many conflicts, come, Lord Christ, with the power of Your name, and the peace of Your presence. Give me the grace to walk by the Spirit, Your Spirit of peace. Amen.*

Thou Art My Shepherd

Elsie Thalheimer, 1800 Thuringian Folk Song

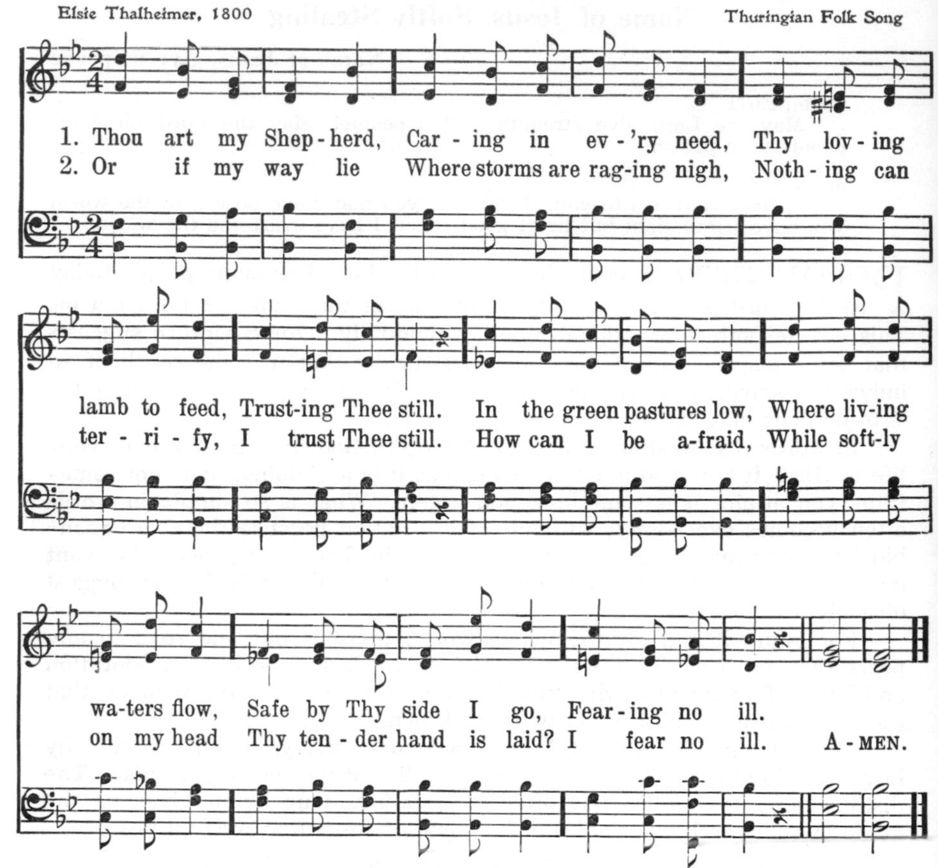

SUNDAY

Thou Art My Shepherd

Caring in every need
Thy loving lamb to feed

Psalm 23:1

The Lord is my shepherd; I shall not want.

1 Peter 2:25

For you were straying like sheep, but have now returned to the Shepherd and Guardian of your souls.

ACROSS THE pages of the Bible, from the early Genesis narratives to the mention of Christ as the Lamb in the Book of Revelation, there walk the shepherd and his flock. Practically all the lands where most of the scenes of the Bible are laid are pastoral country. There is one exception to this, and that is Egypt. Delta farm folk found the Hebrew sheep herders "an abomination." They detested the boorish ways of the shepherds, and knew that sheep-raising and agriculture were incompatible.

In his own society, however, the shepherd held an honorable position. To the good shepherd of the community the people always turned for his wise advice. They felt that his nearness to God equipped him to counsel them. The writer of the Psalm found a very natural figure of speech, then, in the shepherd, for here was a calling that every one knew.

The loneliness of the shepherd's life, those long months when he was away from his community in order that the sheep might find pasture, was compensated for by the loyal love of the sheep, which is in contrast to the heartless attitude of the camel and his driver. There was a devotion of the flock to its shepherd akin to that of a dog to its master.

Another compensation for the shepherd was the joy of God's out-of-doors. The revolving seasons he came to know intimately, and was able to see in each its peculiar beauty. The shepherd was ingenious about his own entertainment, too. With a homemade pipe he made his music, to the rhythm of which he sometimes trained the accompanying goats to dance.

Can you see this shepherd, living with his sheep night and day, knowing each one personally, calling each by name? Can you sense the intimate relationship that such an experience would create?

When I was a little girl, I used to sing "I Am Jesus' Little Lamb." When I came to the line, "Even calls me by my name," I would often pause and speak my own name, "Ruth, Ruth," as if it were the Savior calling. The wonder of that personal relationship has never left me.

In Jeremiah our attention is called to the wicked shepherds that lead their sheep astray; and the Bible speaks of the wolves that come in sheep's clothing. The Shepherd and Guardian of your soul, the real Shepherd, wants to provide for your every need this day.

PRAYER: *Good Shepherd, thank You that I may be in Your fold. Thank You that there is no want of mind, body, or soul that You cannot fill. Walk with me this day. Amen.*

MONDAY

Thou Art My Shepherd

In the green pastures low
Where living waters flow

Psalm 23:2, 3

He makes me lie down in green pastures.
He leads me beside the still waters; he restores my soul.

THE PSALMIST knew both the shepherd and the pasture. Below the hills of Bethlehem, just below the terraced farms, are some of these green pastures. In the summer of 1953, when we were privileged to walk the road above those hills on the outskirts of Bethlehem, we saw sheep and shepherds in much the same manner as that described in the psalmist's picture. Their very garb was like that which was worn in Old Testament times.

The Eastern shepherd, unlike those we have in our country, walks ahead of his sheep. He leads them. To the still waters he would lead them, for the torrential streams that rushed to join the Jordan, or the other rivers to the sea, would be disastrous watering places for the sheep. The "still waters" known to the Psalmist were the wells, pools, and quiet rivulets or sheltered sand bars, such as you can see where the Dog River enters the Mediterranean in the summer. There, under a bridge, we saw drinking flocks watched by Syrian shepherds who had led them from the highlands. Can you sense the devotion engendered in the sheep when, panting for want of water, they were led to a place where there was a cool, refreshing drink?

There is another Shepherd who this day would lead you. If in your soul there is some unsatisfied longing, a thirst that the world can never quench, He has that which will assuage your thirst, and set your soul at peace. He spoke of it to the Samaritan woman, as He sat with her at the well. "Whoever drinks of the water that I shall give him, will never thirst." Why is it that people will try every other watering place first? The wells of the world are polluted and, besides, never satisfying. They often carry germs that are the source of disintegration and disease. What fools we are! Here is offered freely, for just believing, the kind of refreshment that is an elixir for all of life. Yet we get ourselves sick by trying everything else first.

There is another wonderful thing about drinking this water of life. We are told about it in John 7:38, "He who believes in me, as the scripture has said, 'Out of his heart shall flow rivers of living water.'" As we follow the shepherd and drink of the water He provides, we become channels for this same life-giving liquid to flow into the lives of others.

In your daily living is there the atmosphere of thirst quenched "beside the still waters"?

PRAYER: *Why, Lord, have we ever fretted or worried about what a day would hold, when You are leading? Why have we ever been concerned about the wherewithal for what might happen, when You are the Provider? Forgive us, and make us channels of this "living water." In Jesus' name. Amen.*

TUESDAY

Thou Art My Shepherd

Safe by Thy side I go
Fearing no ill

Psalm 23:3

He leads me in the paths of righteousness for his name's sake.

THE PSALMIST follows his metaphor through every detail of his song. The paths of righteousness about which he speaks, referred in shepherd language to the age-old sheep-walk used since the beginnings of the Hebrew people. These were the tried walks, the ones that had proved safe for generations of sheep before.

How many people have found out too late the dangers and pitfalls on the path of the world! That road is so wide, and seems so smooth and easy. It does not climb uphill. Too soon they find that the road becomes soft, and their feet are stuck in the mire. The smoothness and ease were only an alluring beginning of what turned out to be a muddy and disastrous conclusion.

You cannot play with sin, and not get soiled. There are those who have such confidence in themselves that they think they can pick their way daintily through the dirt, and come out unspotted! Let them look to their souls. The paths of righteousness on which the Shepherd guides you may seem to be plain. There may not be glittering lights or mincing music. But stay by that Shepherd, and trust Him on those paths, and there will be the pastures green.

The Psalmist speaks of walking beside the shepherd. Here is the key. Not only can one have complete confidence as to where the path will lead as one walks beside the Shepherd, but the walking is exceedingly wonderful in His presence. You know how it is with certain friends. This is how it is with any one you love. It is not *where* you are with them that makes the going pleasant; it is that you are *with* them. Anywhere in their company is joy, because you love them. So it is with your Shepherd. You can be doing a very menial task, if that is the path He has led you to. Because He is with you, it will take on a glory that no one could ever dream. Yes, this happens to the humdrum, repetitious tasks that face a housekeeper every day. There is an aura on the road of daily toil, because you go safely by His side.

Following the paths of righteousness, one must be aware that outward regulations are not all the answer. The Pharisees were strict observers of the law, but there did not seem to be an ounce of love in their hearts. The path on which our Lord walks with you has but one compulsion, that is the compulsion of love.

PRAYER: *Good Shepherd, walk by my side this day, and put a glory in everything that I do. Amen.*

Thou Art My Shepherd

Or if my way lie
Where storms are raging high

Psalm 23:5

Thou preparest a table before me in the presence of my enemies; thou anointest my head with oil, my cup overflows.

Psalm 18:48

Who delivered me from my enemies; yea, thou dost exalt me above my adversaries; thou didst deliver me from men of violence.

IS THERE anyone who has not felt at some time or another that there were those who were conspiring against him? How often this very fear is a source of irritation that brings ill health. Here the shepherd picture has a word of real comfort again. The "prepared" table of the sheep were the green grassy spots to which the shepherd had led the sheep. Sometimes lurking in the grass were the sheeps' hereditary enemies, venomous snakes which liked to bite the faces of the unsuspecting ones. But the shepherd had gone before to put to rout those who would do injury to any in his fold. So though these very enemies might be in the surrounding area, watching the sheep nibble the grass, they did not molest them because of fear of the shepherd.

The picture of oil is an interesting one, too. In an oxhorn container, the shepherd carried oil or butter to put on the sheep, should anyone have strayed beyond the safe area and been bitten. "Thou anointest my head with oil" is a witness to a second-mile shepherd, who provided even for the animal injured because of its own willfulness.

"My cup overflows" takes on new significance when you see the Wise Men's Well on the northern outskirts of Bethlehem. The well is too deep for the sheep to profit by, so there is provided a stone "cup," or trough, next to it. The shepherd dips the water out of the well into the cup for the sheep to drink. When the water overflows in the cup it is most accessible to the sheep.

Such a Shepherd is our Savior. You have not a need that He cannot supply; there is no difficulty that you face but that He is adequate for it; there are no enemies that you have that He cannot overcome.

When the storm is raging high, a good shepherd is at his best. Then he proves his love and devotion to his sheep. In the presence of lurking enemies, the shepherd's true qualities are put to the test. A good shepherd will even lay down his life for his sheep.

PRAYER: *Our thanks are so inadequate, Lord, for Your protecting, providing, abundant care. Forgive us that we are ever anxious. We would pray for our enemies, Lord. Help us to win them for you! In Jesus' name. Amen.*

Thou Art My Shepherd

Nothing can terrify;
I trust Thee still

Psalm 23:4

Even though I walk through the valley of the shadow of death, I fear no evil.

Isaiah 25:8

He will swallow up death for ever, and the Lord God will wipe away tears from all faces, and the reproach of his people he will take away from all the earth; for the Lord has spoken.

MOST OF the things that people fear in life are related to death. The tragedy is that the death of the body is considered the most awful thing that can happen to you. Most people are unaware of the real tragedy, the death of the soul. As we have said before, to a Christian the death of the body is the going home of the soul; it is to put on a more glorious body; to begin a more wonderful life. It is true that we pass through the valley from one life to the other. But the psalmist makes us to know that only the shadow of death is here. Who is afraid of a shadow, when your hand is in the hand of One who has walked this way before, and faced the enemy, and once and for all defeated him?

"The valley of the shadow" in this shepherd's parlance was the deep rock-cleft passage where serpents lurked, and where the sheep were in complete dependence on their watchful, tender shepherd. But the shepherd was adequate and prepared, and so the journey was made without harm.

One of the most beautiful stories that Jesus ever told was the story of the lost lamb. How hard our Lord is trying to teach us that each one is important; that He knows when anyone is missing; that He cares for each. Knowing and believing this is a part of our not being afraid of anything; of our trusting Him.

In Syria, in certain sections, there still remains the custom of calling sheep by name. An American doubted that the sheep would respond, so he challenged the shepherd to show him. The shepherd called "Carl." The sheep came and looked up into the shepherd's face. He called another and another, and they each responded. To the American they all looked alike. "How can you tell them apart?" he asked. "Oh, there are no two alike," said the shepherd, and then he went on to point out the black mark on one nose, the toes turned in on another, and so forth.

So the Lord must distinguish us: the man who is covetous and has grasping hands; the woman who stirs up the whole neighborhood with her gossiping. Each one of us needs the Shepherd. And He walks with every one who will take His hand, even "through the valley of the shadow."

PRAYER: *Thank You, Lord, that we can say with the song writer, "Nothing can terrify." Thank You that You have swallowed up death forever. Amen.*

FRIDAY

Thou Art My Shepherd

How can I be afraid,
While softly on my head
Thy tender hand is laid?

Psalm 23:4

For thou art with me; thy rod and thy staff they comfort me.

Proverbs 13:24

He who spares the rod hates his son, but he who loves him is diligent to discipline him.

Mark 6:8

He charged them to take nothing for their journey except a staff.

IN THE Bible the staff is spoken of as an instrument of support: "one that leans on a staff"; "they trust on the staff"; "for with only my staff I crossed the Jordan." The rod, on the other hand, is an instrument of correction. To the sheep, the rod was a short stick that the shepherd did not hesitate to use on them when they would stray and get into dangerous paths. He "rodded" them into the sheepfold when they were headed the other way. The staff with its crooked handle was the instrument that he used as a support, and also to lift them out of difficult places.

Every life needs to know the rod and the staff. The use of the rod is often the means of saving a life, even though at the time what is done seems hurtful. This is well illustrated in the incident that happened in a Pennsylvania town. The broken end of a high voltage wire was lying upon the pavement along which the engineer was walking. A friend saw the danger and yelled to warn him, but the noises in the street drowned out his voice. Quickly he picked up a stone, and threw it at his friend so that it hit him in the chest. The engineer looked up and avoided the wire just as he was about to step on it. With tears streaming down his face, he thanked his friend for saving his life.

Some use of the rod in your life may be God's way of keeping you from some greater harm. Remember it is always the long look, the direction of the soul, that He has in mind. When His tender hand is laid softly on your head, need you be afraid?

There is a picture showing a boat laden with cattle, being ferried across an angry, swollen river in time of storm. Judging from the threatening clouds and the play of the treacherous lightning, one would think that the cattle were marked for destruction. But the title of the painting is simply: "Changing Pastures." When it seems that the rod is heavy in your life, remember there is the staff to lean upon, and maybe in the process you will be simply changing pastures! It may be His "tender hand."

PRAYER: *For the rod and the staff, we thank You, Lord. Give us a faith that is willing and glad to follow the Shepherd all the way. In Jesus' name. Amen.*

SATURDAY

Thou Art My Shepherd

I fear no ill

Psalm 23:6

Surely goodness and mercy shall follow me all the days of my life; and I shall dwell in the house of the Lord for ever.

Psalm 27:5

For he will hide me in his shelter, in the day of trouble; he will conceal me under the cover of his tent, he will set me high upon a rock.

TO THOSE of us who have known a real home, the word is synonymous with haven. Home is a refuge from the battering of the world. Home is the place you are loved and safe. To go home is the happiest thing we can do. At least that is the way it ought to be. It is home as God means it for us.

The dwelling "in the house of the Lord" with which our psalm ends, is a reflection of the shepherd's return to the village, where joyous families get ready after the summer grazing period to go up to the house of God, in mended garments and new-made shoes, to thank Him for all His loving-kindness, and entreat Him to let these blessings follow the family forever.

Every Christian has this prospect of home going and the attendant being in the house of the Lord forever; and therefore with assurance he can say, "I fear no evil." Historically there is the feeling of God's house as a sanctuary from harm, for during the middle ages, there were countries in which, if a man was able to get into a church, pursuers could not touch him as long as he remained in the sanctuary. This practice is what gives meaning to this latter name that we use so often in connection with the house of God.

For every sinner there is sanctuary in the heart of God, and there is a glorious home-coming. When you rest in Him, you bid fear out; when you accept His gift of salvation, you can say with the psalmist: "He will hide me in his shelter in the day of trouble; he will conceal me under the cover of his tent, he will set me high upon a rock."

Many people depend upon their feelings, and so are alternately high and low. One day they walk in confidence, and the next in fear. Your feelings are shifting sands on which to build—and there is a Rock. A dear old Christian, on hearing people speak of their feelings, used to say "Feelings! Feelings! Don't bother about your feelings. I just stick to the old truth that Christ died for me, and He is my surety right on to eternity, and I'll stick to that like a limpet to a rock."

"Be my feelings what they will,
Jesus is my Savior still."

PRAYER: *Because You have gone before and opened the way, we may walk through life unafraid. We thank You for the prospect of summer's end, and going home. It is good to know we will be with You there, too. Amen.*

What a Friend We Have in Jesus

What a friend. 8 7, 8 7. D. CHARLES CROZAT CONVERSE, 1868.

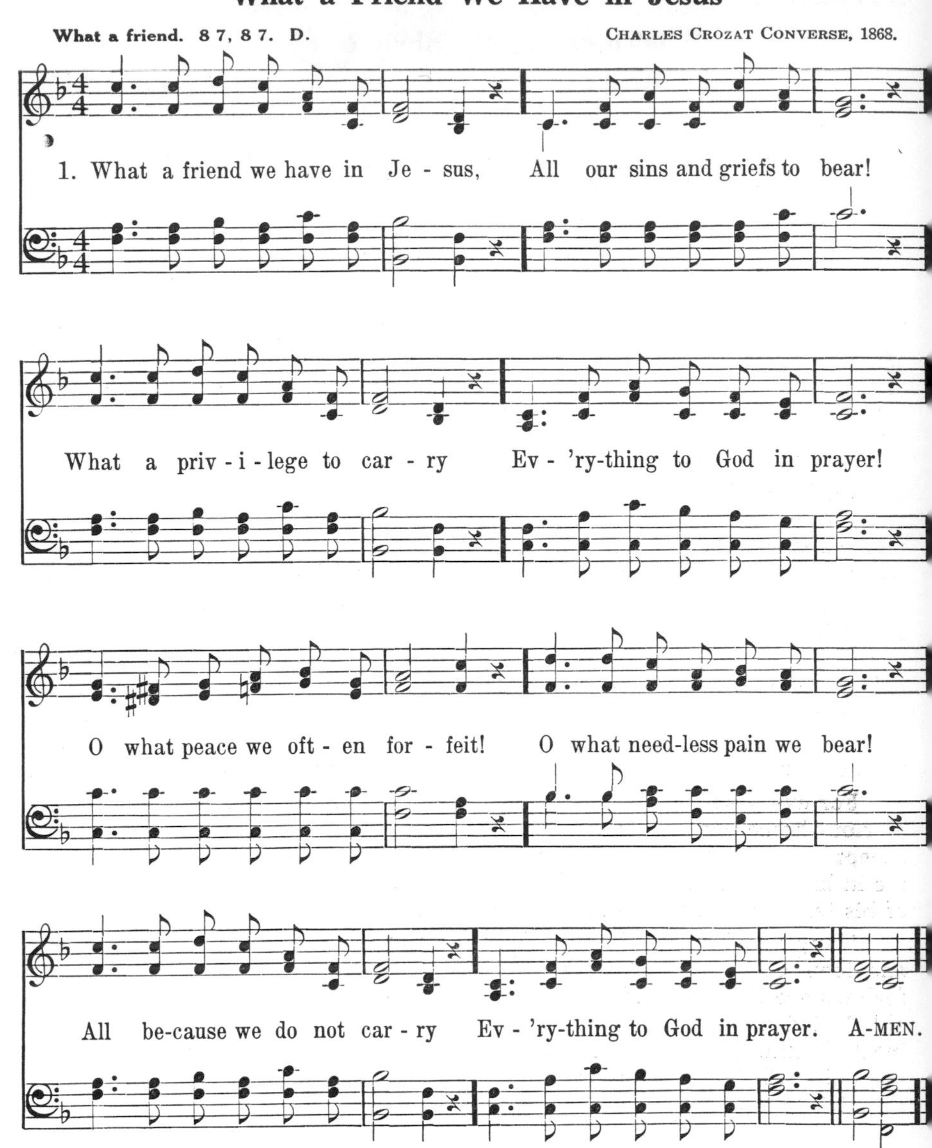

2 Have we trials and temptations?
Is there trouble anywhere?
We should never be discouraged,
Take it to the Lord in prayer.
Can we find a friend so faithful,
Who will all our sorrows share?
Jesus knows our every weakness,
Take it to the Lord in prayer.

3 Are we weak and heavy laden,
Cumbered with a load of care?
Precious Saviour, still our refuge,—
Take it to the Lord in prayer.
Do thy friends despise, forsake thee?
Take it to the Lord in prayer;
In His arms He'll take and shield thee,
Thou wilt find a solace there.

Joseph Scriven, 1855.

What a Friend We Have in Jesus

What a privilege to carry everything to God in prayer

Ecclesiastes 5:2

Be not rash with your mouth, nor let your heart be hasty to utter a word before God, for God is in heaven, and you upon earth; therefore let your words be few.

Revelation 3:8

"Behold, I have set before you an open door, which no one is able to shut; I know that you have little power, and yet you have kept my word and have not denied my name."

JOSEPH SCRIVEN, the writer of our hymn for the week, had a life of such sorrow, that he well might have prayed: "Out of the depths have I cried to thee, O Lord!" He was engaged to be married, but his fiancee was drowned a day or two before the wedding. This tragedy induced a melancholia that followed him all through his life. Born in Ireland, he migrated to Canada, and there in Port Hope lived as something of an eccentric. However, the presence of God in his life was evidenced in that he was a philanthropist, and devoutly religious. He was known as the man "who saws wood for poor widows and sick people who are unable to pay." Something of the Friend that he found in Jesus, he became to other people.

Ira Sankey, the gospel singer, tells this story of how he came to write this hymn. A neighbor, sitting up with Mr. Scriven during an illness, came upon the manuscript, and asked him about it. The writer said that he had composed it for his mother to comfort her in a time of special sorrow, not intending that anybody but she should ever see it. When a neighbor asked him some time later if it was true that he had composed it, he said, "The Lord and I did it between us."

It is interesting to note that, though the writer was a graduate of Trinity College in Dublin, in very simple terms he expresses his faith. The wisest of men have access to the throne of God through the same childlike faith that the humblest do. God is no respecter of persons. And to every soul He offers this wonderful privilege of prayer.

When the hymn writer suggests that we carry everything to God in prayer, he is being consistent with the Bible. Paul in his Letter to the Philippians enjoins us to be anxious about nothing, and in everything to let our supplications be made known to God. Christians who grow in grace find that less and less do they have to spell out to God their needs. More and more they yearn for His will and this, then, becomes the channel for their prayers.

The most wonderful privilege in the world means nothing if it is not used.

PRAYER: *For the wonderful privilege of prayer, we thank You. Lord, teach us to pray aright. In Jesus' name. Amen.*

What a Friend We Have in Jesus

O what peace we often forfeit

Isaiah 48: 17, 18

Thus says the Lord, your Redeemer, the Holy One of Israel:
"I am the Lord your God, who teaches you to profit,
who leads you in the way you should go.
O that you had hearkened to my commandments!
Then your peace would have been like a river,
and your righteousness like the waves of the sea."

Psalm 119:165

Great peace have those who love thy law; nothing can make them stumble.

OFTEN WE feel like crying out with Jeremiah, "They have healed the wound of my people lightly, saying, 'Peace, peace,' when there is no peace." What is the secret of this search of the heart for peace?

Today's Scripture is helpful in our search. The Lord says in the Book of Isaiah, "O that you had hearkened to my commandments!" And again, the psalmist writes: "Great peace have those who love thy law." Lack of peace, then, comes from breaking God's law. Consider this truth in your own life. When you have been very close to the Lord, and walked in His love, have not these times been your periods of greatest peace? Possibly they have been the most hectic from the outward viewpoint; but because you knew that you were in the will of God, you have had an inner calm that could not be disturbed. On the other hand, when you knew in your innermost heart that what you were doing was contrary to His will, no exterior pretense could disguise your fret and dissatisfaction. There is the key: "to hearken to His commandments"; to love God with *all* your heart, and your neighbor as yourself.

"But," you say, "who is sufficient for this? Can anyone meet this requirement of God?" And from Scripture we answer, "No, not one. All have fallen short." "Aha," you conclude, "just what I thought. There is no such thing as peace."

Right here is where we so often forfeit the peace we are seeking. We fail to turn to the Friend who is the answer. If we are repentant of our wrong-doing and confess it to Him, He is faithful to forgive us, to remember it no more, and to give us the very peace we are seeking.

Why, then, do we go groveling, and fretting? Why are we dissatisfied and restless? That which our souls want most is free to us for the taking; free because this wonderful Friend was willing to die that we might have peace. When next you are restless, and your heart is filled with longing, turn to Him, call upon Him, tell Him all, and you will receive the gift of love, His peace.

PRAYER: *We have not known peace, Lord, because we have not kept Your commandments. But we thank You for the forgiving love we know in Christ. Come, then, and reign in our hearts with Your peace! Amen.*

TUESDAY

What a Friend We Have in Jesus

Have we trials and temptations?
Is there trouble anywhere?

2 Corinthians 4:16-18

So we do not lose heart. Though our outer nature is wasting away, our inner nature is being renewed every day. For this slight momentary affliction is preparing for us an eternal weight of glory beyond all comparison, because we look not to the things that are seen but to the things that are unseen; for the things that are seen are transient, but the things that are unseen are eternal.

HENRY WARD BEECHER has said, "Find out what your temptations are, and you will find out largely what you are yourself." We need to take a clean, honest look at our temptations. To Christians, often, they are so subtle as even to go under the guise of piety. Too many people, when they think of temptations, think only of drunkenness, or prostitution, or burglary. The temptation to pride, which is right at their elbow when they think of these obvious sins, they do not recognize.

Do you have a quick tongue that is ready to pass along to others some half-truth, or, "have you heard"? Do you readily sit in judgment of the other fellow, and sanctimoniously draw your skirts about you? Are you easily hurt at some lack of attention or neglect from a dear one or an acquaintance? As subtle and insidious as these temptations are, they find their match in our peerless Christ. What a word for us: "For because he himself has suffered and been tempted, he is able to help those who are tempted." Take a look at yourself, and then take what you find to Him in prayer. A whole host of angels will fortify you, and you will rise from your knees strong in His strength.

Is there trouble anywhere? What a question! "Where isn't there trouble?" would be more to the point. No matter how sheltered a life may look to you, there is no one in this world that does not have some kind of trouble. The great Dr. Spurgeon said, "Trials teach us what we are." It is not what happens to a man that is important, it is how he takes it. A jeweler gives as one of the surest tests for diamonds the "water test." If you are unable to tell a real diamond from an imitation, put the stones under water. The imitation is practically extinguished, while a genuine diamond sparkles under water and is distinctly visible. It is when the waters of sorrow and trials overtake a Christian that he will shine by the grace of God as a star in the night. Of the members of the early church, the pagan observers said, "See how these Christians bear their sorrow!"

You know the secret, be it the meeting of temptation, or sorrow, or trial of any kind. "Take it to the Lord in prayer!"

PRAYER: *We have been weak, O Lord, at those times when we have tried to go it alone. Forgive our conceit. We have been discouraged, when our faith has faltered. Forgive our lack of trust. Help our prayer-lines to be in such good repair, that power will flow constantly from Your boundless resources to our immediate needs. In Jesus' name. Amen.*

WEDNESDAY

What a Friend We Have in Jesus

Can we find a friend so faithful?

Proverbs 17:17

A friend loves at all times, and a brother is born for adversity.

John 15:13

"Greater love has no man than this, that a man lay down his life for his friends. You are my friends if you do what I command you."

IN THE will of a late associate Justice of the Supreme Court there is an unusual legacy. The testator leaves to his family "his friendships, many and numerous, in the hope that they will be cherished and continued." Earthly friends are wonderful, and enrich our lives beyond computation, but the friendship of the Lord makes life; makes it abundant and rich beyond the describing. There are parents who try to will to their children their friendship with God. They can only be introducers! Friendship must be a first-hand relationship between the two parties involved.

In the Book of Proverbs we read that a friend loves at all times. We remember the classic example of the friendship of Jonathan and David and how "soul was knit to soul." One finds very few friends like this in today's world. Our friends are mostly casual, and we have lost from life the richness of friendships where there is a soul relationship.

More tragic than this situation is the fact that too many people are too busy to develop a friendship with God. I say "develop" advisedly. No friendship that is lasting is static. A real relationship grows in enrichment.

What is the "know how" of this attainment? Talk to the Lord in prayer. Listen to Him through His Word. Accept the gifts that He offers, and thank Him for His generous love. Between real friends there can be speech or silence; for there is such an understanding that it reaches beyond words.

In his splendid book, *An Autobiography of Prayer,* Dr. Albert Day, in sharing his experiences as he searched for a vital relationship with God, speaks about how we need to feel that we are God's associates; this means that we do not just call upon Him in time of need; it means that prayer is a part of our vital breath, and that our association with our heavenly Father is a continuous one, not to be turned off and on at will. It is a fellowship that is sufficient for any exigency, and that is constant, no matter what the fluctuations of our lives may be.

The richest experience one can have is the direct, immediate relationship with God. He wants to be your everlasting Friend.

PRAYER: *For human friendship, Lord, that puts a glow into living, we thank You. But most of all we thank You for the kind of Friend You are! Every moment spent with You is blessed. Help us so that there will be fewer and fewer moments without You. This day, be very close, eternal Friend. Amen.*

THURSDAY

What a Friend We Have in Jesus

Are we weak and heavy-laden?

Lamentations 3:19, 22

Remember my affliction and my bitterness, the wormwood and the gall! My soul continually thinks of it and is bowed down within me. . . . But this I call to mind, and therefore I have hope: The steadfast love of the Lord never ceases, his mercies never come to an end.

IN A world where psychology and psychiatry are on everybody's lips, the term "self-examination" is not a new one. Yet who is really honest with himself? Professor Overstreet has said, "It takes us a thousand years to get within shouting distance of ourselves." We employ the most childish ways of kidding ourselves as to what we are, and why we do certain unpredictable things. God knows the need for a man to come clean with himself, to examine himself. God knows the very intent of our hearts before we even express it. If our friendship with Him is to be vital, we must honestly acknowledge to Him what we really are. "If we say that we have no sin, we deceive ourselves."

What has this to do with being weak and heavy-laden? Most of our burdens are self-imposed. When we acknowledge this, we have come a long way. Besides, to stay weak is lack of faith, when for the asking there are the resources of the strength of the eternal Son of God at your command. To whimper about a situation in which you find yourself is to acknowledge that you do not rely upon Him.

O that we could tear away the subterfuges in our living! O that we might have that wonderful feeling of having "come clean" before God. Then indeed our burdens will roll away, and for weakness there will be strength, and the strong shoulders of Christ will carry whatever burden there might be.

Over television the other night we saw a very thought-provoking play. There were portrayed before us the eight or nine different personalities of one man, and his reactions under varying circumstances. In one's reflections, one was aware of these conglomerate people within one's own personality, and how contrary and difficult such a combination can be.

Our greatest burden is ourself. If we are disintegrated and find ourselves going in all directions, we are indeed heavy-laden and miserable. If we are full of aches and pains, of complaints and whinings, we need a thorough self-examination. And right at hand is the great antidote. Scripture speaks to it: "Test yourselves . . . . and see whether you are holding to your faith." Do you not realize that Jesus Christ is in you?

The steadfast love of the Lord is new every morning. It is offered to you today with all its sufficiency. It guarantees strength for the weak.

PRAYER: *By the power of Your Holy Spirit, give me grace, Lord, to give up myself. I have been the block in the channel of my life for Your power to flow through. I would, even now, release myself into Your love. In Jesus' name. Amen.*

FRIDAY

What a Friend We Have in Jesus

Do thy friends despise, forsake thee?

Psalm 38:9-11

Lord, all my longing is known to thee, my sighing is not hidden from thee. My heart throbs, my strength fails me; and the light of my eyes—it also has gone from me. My friends and my companions stand aloof from my plague, and my kinsmen stand afar off.

2 Timothy 4:16, 17

At my first defense no one took my part; all deserted me. May it not be charged against them! But the Lord stood by me and gave me strength to proclaim the word fully, that all the Gentiles might hear it. So I was rescued from the lion's mouth.

I AM constantly amazed at the wonder of Scripture. I have lived with it all my life, and yet the more I study it, the more meat there is for the soul. There is no situation in life for which it is not adequate. Poor starved people who do not know what a table is spread before them! And woe is me, if I do not do all in my power to lead a hungry world to the banquet feast of the Lord.

Have there been times in your life when you felt like the loneliest person in all the world; felt that even your best friends and your family had deserted you? Scripture speaks of this lonely longing again and again. In the Thirty-eighth Psalm there is recorded the heartache of one whose friends and family "stand afar off." Paul knew desertion of human help when he took a stand about sharing Christ with the Gentiles. If he had not been fearless and bold in following this directive of the Lord, you and I might never have known salvation in Jesus Christ.

Whenever a man dares to take a stand, the price that he pays is loneliness. When he is bold about putting into practice the directives of the Lord, he will often find himself alone. It has been so through all the ages.

The Apostle Paul speaks the great "but." "But the Lord stood by me and gave me strength." What a friend we have in Jesus! There is no loneliness that He cannot fill; there is no one that ever needs to be completely forsaken.

"God pity all the lonely Folk
With Griefs they cannot tell
Women waking in the night
And men dissembling well."

Here is your challenge! To share with others this Friend of friends who is sufficient for the loneliest hour; who will never leave you nor forsake you; who will empower you to do great and wonderful things. Here is your opportunity to share with others how God answers prayer.

PRAYER: *Thank You, wonderful Friend, that You will never forsake anybody who turns to You. Thank You that You are sufficient for every circumstance. Help me to share this Divine Friendship with all the world. In Jesus' name. Amen.*

SATURDAY

What a Friend We Have in Jesus

In His arms He'll take and shield thee,
Thou wilt find a solace there

Deuteronomy 33:27

"The eternal God is your dwelling place, and underneath are the everlasting arms."

Isaiah 25:4

For thou hast been a stronghold to the poor, a stronghold to the needy in his distress, a shelter from the storm and a shade from the heat.

A POET has sung:

" 'Tis man's perdition to be safe,
When for the truth he ought to die."

If one is seeking an escape from life, if one is concerned only about his own welfare and security, let him not come to the Lord. I do not say this with my tongue in my cheek. I recognize that the crying need of every individual is for security, whether it be for old age, or youth, or the "dangerous" middle years. Security is imperative for every individual, whether he be the snob or the pauper; the V. I. P. or the common man. But security needs to be defined. The solace and shield that the hymn writer speaks about is not the egocentric desire for your protection on the battlefield, when your neighbor is getting shot; it is not the call for guardian angels on the highway, when others are being demolished in accidents; it is not the asking for special protection from God in a business crisis, when other men's business is failing; it is not the pleading for a protective enclosure for your children, when other children are being exposed to the onslaughts of the world. If these are the content of your prayers, they are too small.

The psalmist says about one who finds friendship with God, "He is not afraid of evil tidings; his heart is firm, trusting in the Lord." Here, then, is the security about which the Bible speaks. It is not an outward protection, it is an inner resource. It is most noticeable when outward circumstances seem most difficult. It defies trouble because of the adequacy of the One who is its source. There is no security that can be won by oneself. There is nothing but security when one gives one's self to God.

Here is the secret of real prayer. It is not taking a shopping list to God's warehouse, and getting all the items supplied; it is saying to a Father: "You know my needs!" It is a security begotten by the indwelling of Jesus Christ, of which we are made aware through constant communication with Him.

Sometimes we need to die for the truth, in order that our souls may be safe.

PRAYER: *What a gift, Lord, is the security of Your presence! What confidence is ours in Your power. Help us to witness to this inner resource to others. In Jesus' name. Amen.*

Jesus, Saviour, Pilot Me

Pilot. 7 7, 7 7, 7 7. JOHN EDGAR GOULD, 1871.

2 As a mother stills her child,
Thou canst hush the ocean wild;
Boisterous waves obey Thy will
When Thou say'st to them, "Be still."
Wondrous Sovereign of the sea,
Jesus, Saviour, pilot me.

3 When at last I near the shore,
And the fearful breakers roar
'Twixt me and the peaceful rest,
Then, while leaning on Thy breast,
May I hear Thee say to me,
"Fear not, I will pilot thee."

Edward Hopper, 1871.

Jesus, Saviour, Pilot Me

Over life's tempestuous sea

Psalm 124:1, 2, 4, 5

If it had not been the Lord who was on our side, let Israel now say—if it had not been the Lord who was on our side, when men rose up against us, . . . then the flood would have swept us away, the torrent would have gone over us; then over us would have gone the raging waters.

AS I write this, I am sitting beside a lake where the wind is tearing at the waters, and raising turbulent white caps. The waves pound in upon the shore, one upon the other. Yesterday, when the storm first blew up so suddenly, many a frail fishing craft strained at the oars to get the boats safely ashore. Only one who knows the sea, and knows how to handle a boat, would dare venture out today.

Watching the stormy upheaval, I realize anew how apt the figure is that the song writer uses. The writer of the hymn, Rev. Edward Hopper, was pastor of the Church of the Sea and Land, established as a mission for seamen. It was originally a six-stanza hymn, but only three verses have survived. It was first published anonymously in "The Sailor's Magazine." The writer used such terminology in the hymn as would best appeal to his sea-going audience. The theology that this man had learned in his seminary might be difficult for some of them to understand, but here was their language, and the implications of faith they could not avoid. Our Lord employed this same method of teaching people. From the familiar things about them, He chose His illustrations, so that there was no mistaking the meaning for their lives. How we need to remember this, as we share the things of the kingdom with our children, and with other people. The Gospel of Jesus Christ is not merely something in a book for theologians to ponder over; it is a life to be lived, that effects everything we do. It is a recipe for abundant living.

It does not take a sailor, however, to acknowledge that the "sea of life" is tempestuous. Any one of us would witness to the sense of being tossed to and fro. To what degree we are tossed, depends in large measure to what we are tied.

During a frightful storm in the Georgian Bay of Canada years ago, a ship was wrecked. Many perished. The mate, with six strong men and one timid girl, escaped in a boat, but the waves were so high that the boat turned over and over, and one after the other the men lost their hold. The girl, however, had been lashed to the prow of the boat by the mate, and so she drifted ashore and was found by an Indian. She lived many years after this experience. She did not escape by her skill and wisdom. She escaped because she was fastened firmly to that which could not sink.

There is a Pilot who is unsinkable. To be fastened to Him in the stormy sea of life today is to be safe.

PRAYER: *Dear Savior, the sea of life is riotous, and my craft is so small. Let me be so bound to You that I may face the sailing unafraid. Amen.*

Jesus, Saviour, Pilot Me

Unknown waves before me roll

Psalm 65:5, 7

O God of our salvation, . . . who dost still the roaring of the waves, the tumult of the peoples.

James 4:14

Whereas you do not know about tomorrow. What is your life? For you are a mist that appears for a little time and then vanishes.

IN EVERY age, in every man's heart, there is the wonder, "What of tomorrow?" It is by faith we are to walk with the One who doth "still the roaring of the waves, the tumult of the peoples." Walking with Him makes the morrow's uncertainty of no concern.

Balzac, in his tale, "The Christ of Flanders" tells of the passage of a ship from Cadzant to Ostend on the Flanders coast. Just before the ship cast off, a bareheaded stranger of plain attire boarded the vessel. The rich and fashionable passengers in the rear of the ship hastened to sit down, so that there would be no seat left for the stranger. But the poor who sat in the bow moved over to make room for him. After the ship had been out to sea a bit, a hurricane struck with terrific force. In the light that came from a break in the clouds, the passengers saw this newcomer in a new light. On his face was a sublime gentleness illuminated by radiant love. The other passengers were in a dither of fear, because of the tempestuous waves. In turn, the stranger spoke a word of faith to each one.

Almost in sight of Ostend, the ship began to sink, The stranger stood up and walked with firm steps on the waves, saying as he did so, "Those that have faith shall be saved. Let them follow me." A young mother took up her child and followed; then came a soldier, a prostitute, and two peasants. Last of all, came a sailor. The merchant went down with his gold; the man of science who had mocked, was swallowed up by the sea. Others went down in the sea with their sins, but those who had faith followed the stranger and trod with firm, dry feet on the raging waters. When they reached the shore, the stranger led them to a fisherman's cabin, where a light flickered in the window. When they had all gathered in, the Savior disappeared. Something of this kind of an experience the poet writes about:

Faith and Sight

So I go on, not knowing,
—I would not, if I might—
I would rather walk in the dark with God
Than go alone in the light;
I would rather walk with Him by faith
Than walk alone by sight.

MARY GARDNER BRAINERD

PRAYER: *Wondrous Sovereign of the sea, reign over my life. Whatever unknown waves there may be, I shall be able to ride them with You at my side. In Your name. Amen.*

Jesus, Saviour, Pilot Me

Hiding rocks and treacherous shoal

Psalm 91:1-6

He who dwells in the shelter of the Most High,
who abides in the shadow of the Almighty,
will say to the Lord, "My refuge and my fortress;
my God, in whom I trust."

For he will deliver you from the snare of the fowler and from the deadly pestilence; he will cover you with his pinions, and under his wings you will find refuge; his faithfulness is a shield and buckler. You will not fear the terror of the night, nor the arrow that flies by day, nor the pestilence that stalks in darkness, nor the destruction that wastes at noonday.

THE FIGURES of speech that the psalmist uses are not nautical, but the conclusions they arrive at might well be applied to sailing. The Bible does not hesitate about mixing figures, for in this very passage different likenesses are used. Here you have the figure of the protection offered by the wings of a bird in the same line of thinking as the protection from warfare. It all relates to God's wonderful deliverance in time of trouble.

Our song for the week speaks of the unknown waves that hide the rocks, and the dangerous shallows. To point up the dangers of life is only to cause you to take inventory of your resources. What can keep your boat from going on the rocks? Are you not sufficiently aware and responsible to set your own course?

The Titanic is exhibit "A" in voyaging with such a self-sufficient attitude. On the very night in which it was frantically calling for help, because it had hit an iceberg and was sinking, the New York papers were full of the glory and wonder of this palatial boat whose passenger list included so many "names." But the Titanic hit an iceberg and went down, taking hundreds of its passengers with it. Something of the human element had crept into all the provisions for the passengers' safety.

There is but one guarantee against the treacherous rocks of life. There is but one adequate resource to direct away from the treacherous shoal. That is to have Jesus as your pilot. You need not fear the terror by night, nor the arrow that flies by day. His resources are sufficient for any circumstances that may arrive. His judgment is without fault.

With such a help at our command, why do we so often flounder and hit the rocks before we seek Him? O yes, He will help us even then. He will never turn a deaf ear to anybody who calls upon Him. But He rejoices when His children turn to Him for guidance before the unnecessary cost of shipwreck. We need to witness to the joy of a life directed by the great Pilot. It is paradoxical to find perfect shelter as you live dangerously!

PRAYER: *You know, Lord, how often the rocks and the shoals are hidden. Pilot us over every treacherous place. Help us to be ever mindful that the real danger is to our souls. Set their sails for everlasting life with You. In Your name. Amen.*

Jesus, Saviour, Pilot Me

Chart and compass came from Thee

Psalm 37: 23

The steps of a man are from the Lord, and he establishes him in whose way he delights; though he fall, he shall not be cast headlong, for the Lord is the stay of his hand.

FOR EVERY person the Lord has a plan. That plan is that each one should be saved. The Lord wants all men to come to the knowledge of salvation. Whether or not we follow His plan, is our choice. To those who choose to walk His way, the chart is made clear, one step at a time. But the Lord will not force anybody to love Him. The chart is His, the choice to follow it is ours.

Often as a mother, I have stood by and watched our young people make decisions that were life changing. How desperately I yearned to make the decision for them! Yet, it had to be their choice. I could only stand by and pray. I am sure in some such manner the Lord yearns over us. He is praying for us; praying that we will be willing to trust Him to lead the way.

On the day in 1874 that David Livingstone was to be buried in Westminster Abbey (that is, all but the heart of him; that was left in Africa) the streets were lined with thousands seeking to pay their respects to the great pioneer. In the crowd was a poor old man, weeping. Someone inquired as to the cause. "I'll tell you why," the old man replied. "David Livingstone and I were born in the same village, brought up in the same school and Sunday school, worked together in the same room. But David went that way, and I went this. I have nothing to look forward to but a drunkard's grave." Such is the difference in one's choosing to follow God's chart for one's life, or one's own.

In New England, some years ago, a young lad was making his way westward—leaving home to face the world. He felt lonely and homesick and sad. He was also troubled about his future. Just then he happened to see a waterfowl winging its way southward. In the contemplation of from where it had come, and to where it was going, and the miracle of its direction and surety of purpose, William Cullen Bryant, the lonely young man, wrote these lines:

He who, from zone to zone,
Guides through the boundless sky thy certain flight,
In the long way that I must tread alone,
Will lead my steps aright.

"One becomes a God-trusting, God-expectant, God-co-operative person."

PRAYER: *We thank You, Lord, that we do not need to depend upon our own poor plans. Your chart for our lives is best. By the grace of Your Holy Spirit, may we follow it. Eternal salvation is the harbor. In Jesus' name. Amen.*

Jesus, Saviour, Pilot Me

Chart and compass came from Thee

Isaiah 42:6, 16

"I am the Lord, I have called you in righteousness,
I have taken you by the hand and kept you." . . .
And I will lead the blind in a way that they know not,
in paths that they have not known I will guide them.
I will turn the darkness before them into light,
the rough places into level ground.

YESTERDAY WE considered the chart that the Pilot has made for us; today, as we think of Him, let us consider the compass. It is one thing to have a trip planned; it is another to be able to follow the plan. In the old days when a ship set sail, it had no way of knowing where it was going. Often it landed on the rocks and was demolished. Then the compass was discovered. When the ship was equipped with one, those manning it could tell the direction they were going even when it was night.

Within us God has put a compass, the voice of our conscience. If this is set by the Sun of Righteousness, it will be a never-failing guide on our voyage. It will keep us from shipwreck.

An Eastern legend tells the story of a great magician who gave his prince a wonderful ring studded with priceless gems. But what gave the ring its chief value was, that so long as the prince was doing right the ring was comfortable to wear; but whenever he cherished evil thought in his heart or did anything wrong, it suddenly contracted and pressed painfully on his finger. Our conscience is our soul's sentinel; it is the compass within us trueing us up to going God's way.

In our Scripture there is a beautiful evidence of the compass' working. The Lord speaks of leading "the blind in a way that they know not"; of turning "the darkness before them into light." He enjoins us to choose His "instruction instead of silver, and knowledge rather than choice gold." The compass of the Lord leads to everlasting life.

Sometimes we do not hear the "still, small voice"! There are too many other voices that drown it out. Travelers tell us that there are rivers flowing beneath the ancient city of Schechem. During the hours of day you cannot hear them because of the noise of the streets and the merchants at their bazaars. But wait until night comes, and the clamor dies away. Then, quite audibly, in the hush of the night, you can hear the sound of the buried stream.

A man speaking of certain things which other people sometimes practice said, "I cannot do such things. If I do, there is someone inside of me who talks to me nights."

The voice of God within us is the compass that can steer our ship in the right course.

PRAYER: *Quiet my heart, Lord, that I may hear Your voice. Make me sensitive to Your leading. In Jesus' name. Amen.*

Jesus, Saviour, Pilot Me

**As a mother stills her child
Thou canst hush the ocean wild**

Psalm 107: 29, 30

He made the storm be still, and the waves of the sea were hushed. Then they were glad because they had quiet, and he brought them to their desired haven.

Matthew 8:23-27

And when he got into the boat, his disciples followed him. And behold, there arose a great storm on the sea, so that the boat was being swamped by the waves; but he was asleep. And they went and woke him, saying, "Save, Lord; we are perishing." And he said to them, "Why are you afraid, O men of little faith?" Then he arose and rebuked the winds and the sea; and there was a great calm. And the men marveled saying, "What sort of man is this, that even winds and sea obey him?"

WOULD YOU not have liked to watch the expression on the disciples' face when, at the command of Jesus, the waves were stilled? It seemed so simple the way that He did it. Yes, says our song writer, as simple as a mother stilling her child. In Church school I teach the very youngest children, from little babies to the age of four. Sometimes, after the mother has slipped out to go to church, the little ones' underlip will begin to pucker, and slowly the storm comes up, until it is full-fledged, rain and all. I have tried every trick in the bag with some of the children, only to have momentary respite. A little lull, and then the storm again. By this time, we send for the mother. Hardly is she in the door, when the sobbing of her little one ceases, and the sunshine of a smile breaks through the rain.

I have seen couples in tumultuous conflict pause in the presence of the the parsonage, torn by the storms of life, battered and bewildered in the wild ocean of a great city. Their bodies witness to the wear and tear of the storm, for they are restless; they find it very difficult even to sit still to share their distress. Then I have heard the word of the "Stiller of the Storm" read—read in faith, because the pastor knows its power. The storm begins to lose its intensity. Then there is prayer. Because the one who prays has seen the miracle of calm again and again through the power of prayer, he prays with complete confidence. It happens! The storm-tossed soul arises from his knees with a new outlook. There is awareness of a resource of strength that he had either never been conscious of before, or that he had forgotten about.

I have seen couples in tumultuous conflict pause in the presence of the "Stiller of Storms," and find such a perspective as to resolve their differences. There is no disturbance that the Christ cannot calm.

PRAYER: *For the calming influence of Your presence in times of stress, we thank YOU, O Savior. Give us such a faith as to know that no storm is too rough for You to calm. In Your name. Amen.*

Jesus, Saviour, Pilot Me

May I hear Thee say to me,
"Fear not, I will pilot thee"

Isaiah 25:8

He will swallow up death for ever, and the Lord God will wipe away tears from all faces, and the reproach of his people he will take away from all the earth; for the Lord has spoken.

OUR HYMN writer says: "When at last I near the shore." The most certain thing in all of life is death. Yet there are people who studiously avoid facing it. That is being unreal. Facing it in the fellowship of the victorious Pilot is to anticipate gloriously what is ahead. Have you noticed how often the hymn writers mention it?

There is a condition in the hymn that is significant to hearing the "fear not." We find this in the words: "Then, while leaning on Thy breast." You will not know this assurance, unless you are very close to the Master. In fact, it is doubtful that you will hear Him, unless you are really leaning on Him, and trusting Him to support and guide you.

From out of the horrors of the last war comes a glowing witness of one who trusted the Pilot through all the shoals and rocks of resisting an evil government, and daring to preach the love of Christ in spite of the state. Pastor Dietrich Bonhoeffer knew the Pilot personally, so he was fearless in life as he was in death. Listen to the account of an English officer with whom he had spent those last months of imprisonment:

> Bonhoeffer always seemed to me to spread an atmosphere of happiness and joy over the least incident and profound gratitude for the mere fact that he was alive. . . . He was one of the very few persons I ever met for whom God was real and very near. . . . On Sunday, April 8, 1945, he conducted a little service of worship and spoke to us in a way that went to the heart of all of us. He found just the right words to express the spirit of our imprisonment, the thoughts and resolutions it had brought us. He had hardly ended his last prayer when the door opened and two civilians entered. They said, "Prisoner Bonhoeffer, come with us." That had only one meaning for all prisoners—the gallows. We said good-bye to him. He took me aside. "This is the end, but for me it is the beginning of life." The next day he was hanged.*

The text on which he spoke that last day was "With His stripes we are healed."

PRAYER: *Strong Deliverer, sure Pilot, help me in my daily living so to lean upon You that I will bear testimony to the Port for which I am heading. Let the set of my sails be a witness to the direction in which I am going. In Your name. Amen.*

---

* From *Life Together* by Bonhoeffer. Introduction by John W. Doberstein. Harper Brothers. Used by permission.

Open Mine Eyes

Clarence A. Johnson | Clarence A. Johnson

1. Open mine eyes, O Lord, Open mine eyes;
Into my darkened heart Let Thy light arise.
Show me myself, O Lord, Show me Thyself, O Lord,
Show me Thy truth, O Lord, Open mine eyes!

*2. Open mine eyes, O Lord, Open mine eyes.
Thy Word and Sacrament Let me ne'er despise!
Thou art the Way, O Lord, Thou art the Truth, O Lord,
Thou art the Life, O Lord, Open mine eyes!

Second stanza by T. E. Conrad.

Open My Eyes, O Lord

Into my darkened heart

Jeremiah 17:9, 10

The heart is deceitful above all things, and desperately corrupt; who can understand it? "I the Lord search the mind and try the heart, to give to every man according to his ways, according to the fruit of his doings."

THE STORY that inspired the writing of this little prayer indicates the necessity of our being willing to admit the darkness of our hearts. One of our missionaries from India related the experience of a Bible woman visiting a native home to recruit children for the mission school. When the mother was asked if there were any children living there, she sent for a young boy. After the Bible woman's interrogation, it was agreed that he should come to school the next day. She knew that there was another child in the house, however, so she persisted in pressing the mother on this point. Finally the mother said, "Oh, we have a girl, but she's too dumb to learn anything. There is no use in your talking to her. She's too dumb!" However, she was persuaded to bring the little one out. The child came in cringing, and repeating the words of the mother: "I am too dumb to learn anything."

In loving patience, the Bible woman took the child on her knee and said, "I'm going to teach you a prayer." Then she taught her to say, "Jesus, teach me to see myself." To the girl's amazement, she was able to learn the prayer, and happily promised to come to school. She came for a couple of days and then was absent. The Bible woman was about to go to the home to find out what the trouble was, when outside the mission she came across the boy with his sister. They were standing in front of a picture of Jesus on the cross. The girl was crying, and the boy was pointing to the Christ.

The Bible woman came up to them and said to the little girl; "We've been missing you from school. What's happened?" The little girl blurted out, "You taught me to say that prayer. I don't want to say that prayer any more. I saw how I stole egg money and lied to my mother. I don't want to say that prayer any more." Gently the Bible woman said, "Now I am going to teach you to say another prayer: 'Jesus, teach me to see Thyself.'" The lass learned this prayer, and by the power of the presence of Christ is today one of the most effective workers in the Christian mission.

If the miracle-working power of Christ is to be effective in us, we must first admit the darkness of our hearts. We must be able to say with the Apostle Paul, "I know that nothing good dwells within me, that is, in my flesh."

PRAYER: *Search our hearts, Lord, and clean out all the debris of self that blocks the way for Your presence. Help us to examine our motives, even in the good that we do. Dig deep, Lord, and clean out the corners. In Jesus' name. Amen.*

Open My Eyes, O Lord

Let Thy light arise

Isaiah 9:2

The people who walked in darkness have seen a great light; those who dwelt in a land of deep darkness, on them has the light shined.

John 8:12

Again Jesus spoke to them saying, "I am the light of the world; he who follows me will not walk in darkness, but will have the light of life."

JUST TO admit the darkness of our hearts is no virtue in itself, if we do not move on out. Remember the parable Jesus told of the house that was emptied of an evil spirit, but because it remained empty, seven more evil spirits came and possessed it? Often you hear people belittle themselves. They will even pour out an account of their sins; they will reveal the utter darkness of their hearts. There are those who almost boastfully will say, "Well, that is the way I am, and I can't help it." Even people who call themselves Christian have been known to utter words like this. There is no virtue in darkness, unless it is to admit the need of a light. And to say that you can't help it is to deny God.

From the beginning of time people have sought for a light to lead in the dark ways of the world. The world has its lights that emblazon the streets of our cities. Blinking, glaring, winking lights that so often are an invitation to inner darkness! Let a storm come, however, that breaks the connecting wires to power, and in a single flash you will have complete darkness. The darkness seems heavier because of the glare that preceded it. The sun and the moon and the stars, on the other hand, never fail of their light. O yes, there may be clouds to hide it, but day follows night as surely as we live.

If our inner light is dependent upon the battery of the world, upon the "good time" that we have, upon the wealth that is ours, upon the attention people give us, it is pretty fragile and uncertain. Not only will there be stumbling and blunders here, but it will be totally inadequate in the "valley of the shadow."

But there is a Light. To know Him is to have a resource of inner illumination that is sufficient for any darkness. He sheds light on every problem; He enlightens every relationship; His light is completely adequate for whatever the future may hold.

The lamp of faith is the means of walking in the way of the One who is eternal Light. It is Augustine who said, "Faith is to believe what we do not see, and the reward of this faith is to see what we believe."

How good are your eyes of faith?

PRAYER: *Into my darkened heart, let Your light arise, O Lord. Give me such a lamp of faith as will shed light on the path for others. In Jesus' name. Amen.*

Open My Eyes, O Lord

Show me myself, O Lord

Psalm 36:1-3

Transgression speaks to the wicked deep in his heart;
there is no fear of God before his eyes.
For he flatters himself in his own eyes
that his iniquity cannot be found and hated.
The words of his mouth are mischief and deceit;
He has ceased to act wisely and do good.

Revelation 3:17

"For you say, I am rich, I have prospered, and I need nothing; not knowing that you are wretched, pitiable, poor, blind, naked."

THERE IS one thing on which the saints of all time are unanimously agreed: that there must be an annihilation of self before there can be a continuous and full revelation of God. In *Theologia Germanica* we read: "All self-hood and I-hood and nature must be forsaken and lost and die altogether." St. John of the Cross put it starkly when he said: "The road to God consists not in a multiplicity of meditations . . . but in the ability to deny one's self truly . . . all other methods are so much wandering in a maze." Jesus used the significant figure: "Unless a grain of wheat falls into the earth and dies, it remains alone . . ."

Here, then, is the crux: to be willing to crucify ourselves. It would not be so bad, if one could do it once and for all, and be done with the agony. But as Martin Luther so well puts it, there must be "daily sorrow and repentance"; the fight is on into eternity; the crucifixion is daily.

Here is where the devil works so effectively. With his cloak of spiritual pride, he crawls into a Christian's heart, and causes him to think he is pretty good. It is so easy to point out the prostitute and the drunkard. Dr. Day tells about his little daughter who when she had been very naughty said, "I asked God to make me good. Why doesn't He then?" She knew in her heart that it was not God who had failed, but that she was not willing to accept what God wanted to do for her.

Today, when you look at yourself through the eyes of God, what do you see? Does not your family appreciate you enough, or make over you sufficiently? When you are in a crowd, is your concern whether they are noticing you, admiring you?

As I write these lines, how convicted I am! I remember the many times I held the center of conversation; in fact, was so eager to make my contribution that I interrupted others and hardly heard what they had to offer. I remember the times when even what I have offered to the Lord in the work of the kingdom has been tainted with the desire for the approbation of people. Seeing myself has been miserable—but healthful.

PRAYER: *The cry of my heart, Lord, is to be merciful to me a sinner! My ego has more than seven lives. And it is so deceptive. Even the good that I do is tainted. Come with Your grace and the power of Your Holy Spirit, that self may constantly be crucified. In Jesus' name. Amen.*

Open My Eyes, O Lord

Show me Thyself, O Lord

2 Corinthians 4:5-7

For what we preach is not ourselves, but Jesus Christ as Lord, with ourselves as your servants for Jesus' sake. For it is God who said, "Let light shine out of darkness," who has shone in our hearts to give the light of the knowledge of the glory of God in the face of Christ.

HAVE YOU not often wondered what your reaction would be, were you to see Jesus in the flesh? Would you recognize Him? How would it feel to have His eyes turned upon you?

Again and again I am overwhelmed by the marvel of God's love that was willing to come to earth in the form of man, and reveal to us His heart in a way that our finite minds could understand. To see Jesus is to blot out the picture of self, for He fills the frame completely.

What do you see in Jesus? You see incarnate love that was willing to die to save. You see compassion that seeks the last and the least. You see justice that hates deception. You see forgiveness that knows no limit. To see Him is to see a new beginning for your life; a going from glory to glory in His strength.

Vignettes from Christ's life flash across the mind: His presence at the marriage of Cana made that an unforgettable experience; His passing by the road where Bartimeus sat changed the latter's life from one of darkness to light: His stopping at a well in Samaria revolutionized the life of the woman whom He met there, as well as the lives of a great number of her fellow-villagers; He paused at a lake where men were fishing, and the course of their entire lives was changed; He stopped at a tax-collector's table, and the man's sense of values was turned right side up; He found a woman in the sin of adultery, and so transformed her that today her name is revered among women. Whatever situation He came into, He changed things: sickness to healing; sorrow to joy; oppression to freedom; slavery to liberty; inequality to justice. What a picture! And finally the cross changed defeat to victory! Take your eyes off yourself, and look to Him. All through this day seek to see Him in the work that is at hand, in the people you meet. Seek to see what He would do in the circumstances in which you find yourself.

The world about you needs to see Jesus. Everybody you meet needs to see Him. Will they see Him in you? "And we all, with unveiled face, beholding the glory of the Lord, are being changed into His likeness from one degree of glory to another."

PRAYER: *Throughout this entire day, Lord, keep my eyes fixed on You. Help me to see opportunities for You in every situation in which I find myself. And O please, Lord, perform in my life the miracle of my growing more like You. In Jesus' name. Amen.*

THURSDAY

Open My Eyes, O Lord

Show me Thy truth, O Lord

John 8:31, 32

Jesus then said to the Jews who had believed in him, "If you continue in my word, you are truly my disciples, and you will know the truth, and the truth will make you free."

THROUGHOUT ALL ages, wise men of all nations have sought to know the truth. Great controversies have arisen, and competitive schools of thought have sprung up. In too many instances, the Source of all truth has been completely ignored, or at best, given nothing more than a nod. So men keep seeking, up one blind alley and down another, to quench the thirst of the human heart for truth.

As in days gone by, so it is today. New instruments have been devised, new areas discovered, in this relentless pursuit of the fountain of truth. Today, too, most seekers look everywhere else but to the place where their thirst can be satisfied. Check on the results of Bible knowledge tests given to university students even in the post-graduate schools, and you will find an appalling lack of any intimate acquaintance with the Book that through all the ages has held to the claim that it contains the truth for this life as well as the life to come. One would think that scientifically one would not be permitted to discard as inconsequential, a way that makes claims to being The Way, without the scientist's having given it a try. It is difficult to understand this inconsistent quirk in the pattern of modern scientific search.

All that Christ asks of any seeking soul is that he tries Him. All He requires is that they come to a knowledge of Him through the Book where He is revealed. Further, that they check on the way He works in people's lives; check as to whether or not what He claims will be does happen, if the conditions of the experiment are accurately fulfilled. Is not this the right procedure in checking any truth? Yet in our universities and secular colleges everything is done to tear down a man's faith in too many instances, and nothing is done to challenge the student to seek for himself. So we have an increasing rate of suicide, of mental illness, of debauchery, because without the Truth life has no meaning that is worth while.

Any time anyone earnestly seeks he finds. In Christ there is the truth for every age. In Him is the journey's end. Could it be that we have been such poor advertisement for His indwelling truth that we have discouraged others?

PRAYER: *Lord, how can it be that in our search, we so readily pass You by? Open our eyes to see the Truth, and quicken our heart and mind to share it. In Jesus' name. Amen.*

Open My Eyes, O Lord

Thy Word and Sacrament
Let me ne'er despise

John 5:38, 39

"And you do not have his word abiding in you, for you do not believe him whom he has sent. You search the scriptures, because you think that in them you have eternal life; and it is they that bear witness to me."

2 Timothy 3:16, 17

All scripture is inspired by God and profitable for teaching, for reproof, for correction, and for training in righteousness, that the man of God may be complete, equipped for every good work.

IN LUTHER'S explanation of the Third Commandment, "Remember the Sabbath day to keep it holy," he includes as a part of the meaning of this commandment, that "we should not despise the Word, and the preaching of the same, but deem it holy, and willingly hear and learn it." The Old Testament history is a record of repeated instances when God's chosen people slipped into the idolatrous ways of the people around them, ignored and neglected their covenant with God and His commands, and consequently suffered repeated exile, slavery, and defeat. What holds for this people is true also in our individual lives.

Too often it is that our "despising" takes the very polite form of ignoring. We are not deliberately antagonistic against it; we just do not pay any attention to it. In too many homes the experience that a certain clergyman had could well be true. He was invited to a house in the country to perform a marriage ceremony. They searched everywhere for a Bible, but could not find one. Finally some member of the family went up into the attic to search. There in an old sea-chest they found one. On the outside of the chest was written: "Not wanted on the voyage."

It is amazing that intelligent people can so quickly fall into the pattern of ignoring this Book. From a literary standpoint alone, you would think that their curiosity would be aroused. When Charles Dickens was asked for the most pathetic story in literature, he answered, the Prodigal Son; when Coleridge was asked for the richest passage in literature, he pointed to the first sixteen verses in the fifth chapter of Matthew; when Daniel Webster was consulted about the greatest legal statute on the brotherhood of man, he said it was the Sermon on the Mount. From an intellectual viewpoint alone, it should be pretty hard to ignore such a book.

But knowing the Bible intellectually is not enough. Jesus speaks to the Scribes and Pharisees about their searching the Scriptures, and yet refusing to acknowledge that they bore witness of Him. Besides searching, one must try them, put them to work to test their claims. Of a Chinese convert it was said, "There is no difference between him and the Book."

PRAYER: *Lord, so often I have ignored Your Word. Open my eyes to the wonderful truths that are to be found in it. Speak to me through it, Lord, and help me in turn to share it with others. In Jesus' name. Amen.*

Open My Eyes, O Lord

Thou art the Way, O Lord

John 14:4-6

"And you know the way where I am going." Thomas said to him, "Lord, we do not know where you are going; how can we know the way?" Jesus said to him, "I am the way, and the truth, and the life; no one comes to the Father, but by me."

HOW SIGNIFICANT is the article in front of the word "way." Jesus does not say a way, one of the ways. He makes it very specific and exclusive: "I am the way." An Indian friend argued this point one day in our home. She spoke of her Hindu friends who were seeking God, and living lives of sacrifice that would put many of us Christians to shame. She questioned the validity of the Gospel of John because of the forthright claims that are made for the Christ. But then, we pointed out to her, to be consistent, she would have to reject the whole Bible. And further than that, she would have to call Jesus an imposter and a liar, if the claims that He made for himself were so grossly untrue. There is no mistaking the certainty and exclusion in the declarations, "for there is no other name under heaven given among men by which we must be saved," and, "You shall call his name Jesus, for he will save his people from their sins."

The contrast of idol worship and the worship of God becomes very sharp when you realize that the heathen must always carry their idols; they are burdens which weigh them down. God lifts His people; He carries them. And Christ, God's revelation of himself to us, becomes the great Burden Bearer of the world.

In the Book of Hebrews we are reminded of what happened at the crucifixion. Before this, no one but the priest could enter the Holy of Holies to approach God. But on that great day, the veil of the temple was rent, and a new and living way was opened to every one who is willing to accept Christ. He is the great Trail Blazer who bridged eternity with His love, and now beckons us to follow Him. How we need to pray: "Open our eyes!"

The world sits at the feet of Christ,
Unknowing, blind and unconsoled;
It yet shall touch His garment's fold,
And feel the heavenly Alchemist
Transform its very dust to gold.

John Greenleaf Whittier

PRAYER: *Lord, we would acknowledge that there is no one else who has the sure word of eternal life. You are the Way for our lives. But we cannot be content to keep the knowledge of this way for ourselves. The wonder of it we must share. Use us to guide others to find it. In Jesus' name. Amen.*

Day by Day Thy Mercies

Carolina V. (Sandell) Berg, (1832-1903)
Tr. Ernest Edwin Ryden, 1928

Oskar Ahnfelt, (1813-1882

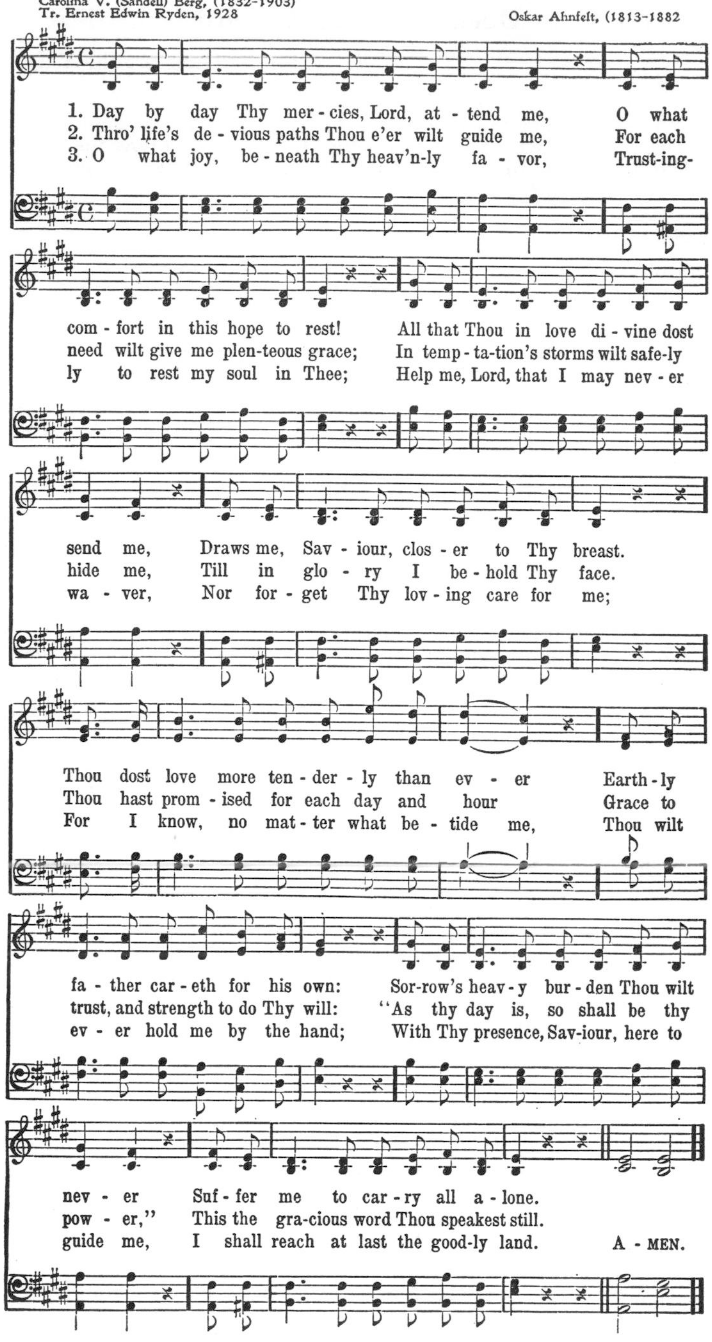

SUNDAY

Day by Day Thy Mercies, Lord, Attend Me

O what comfort in this hope to rest

Exodus 16:4

Then the Lord said to Moses, "Behold, I will rain bread from heaven for you; and the people shall go out and gather a day's portion every day, that I may prove them, whether they will walk in my law or not."

SOME OF the children of Israel learned the hard way that the Lord meant they should gather manna one day at a time, except on the day that preceded the Sabbath. They thought they would put one over on God, and take it easy the second day, by gathering enough today to last for tomorrow. Perhaps they reasoned: "Who knows that it will rain manna tomorrow? We'd better be safe, and play it our way." But they found their food worm-eaten when they arose on the next day.

All through Scripture God gives us this day-by-day pattern. In the Lord's Prayer we have it: "Give us this day our daily bread." In the Book of Lamentations we read that the steadfast love of the Lord is new every morning. How we need to take this day as out of God's hands, and fill it with the goodness of living in His love and serving Him! What a life we would then have, a succession of days lived in the sufficiency of Christ's presence, and in the expectancy of His wonder-working love!

What hang-over from yesterday is spoiling your today? This day is fresh and new from out of God's hand. Meet it in faith, knowing that whatever happens, He will be sufficient for it.

In a magazine the story is told of a great preacher who returned one night to his home from a very stormy session with his church board. It had been the most disappointing meeting that he had ever attended. He dropped disconsolately into a big chair in the living room, feeling that everything was hopeless. His wife did her best to console him, but her every effort failed. He finally retired, feeling whipped.

The next morning his wife, good mate that she was, arose early, and slipped down the hall intending to urge her husband to stay in bed and let her bring him his breakfast. To her complete surprise, she heard her husband going through his morning exercises, singing a hymn at the same time. "Why, Samuel," she said, "what about the terrible meeting that you had last night and all the trouble you were in when you came home? I thought you would be used up today." As he continued his exercise without a pause, he replied, "That was yesterday."

Friend, do not bring with you into today any burden of the past. Rest in the comforting hope that God's mercies are new every morning.

PRAYER: *Thank You, Lord, that in Your wonderful plan, each day is fresh and new. Give me grace to make this a good day for all those around me. In Jesus' name. Amen.*

Day by Day Thy Mercies, Lord, Attend Me

All that Thou in love divine dost send me,
Draws me, Saviour, closer to Thy breast.

Romans 8:28, 35

We know that in everything God works for good with those who love him, who are called according to his purpose. . . . Who shall separate us from the love of Christ? Shall tribulation, or distress, or persecution, or famine, or nakedness, or peril or sword?

WHILE YOU are learning your hymn this week, it would be wonderful for you to learn this passage of Scripture, too. These are great words, and give one the sense of pillars of God in a tottering world. They have special meaning for me tonight as I type this, for my writing was interrupted this afternoon by the news of the sudden passing of the sister of a dear friend and neighbor. We have just returned from visiting the home where sorrow struck so suddenly, and witnessed again how Christians meet whatever happens to them in a day, with the empowering of the Holy Spirit of God. Here was a young, nineteen-year-old daughter, facing life without the widowed mother who had been both father and mother to her through all the years; facing life with the faith of the mother that had so suddenly been taken away with a heart attack as she was driving her car. There was a real sense of this tribulation in the life of this girl, necessitating her leaning more heavily on the everlasting arms. "No, in all these things we are more than conquerors through him who loved us." The word "conqueror" was not spoken tonight, but it was there in the room, in the smile through the tears, in the meeting of the many responsibilities of the moment, in the calm assurance of a loved one's having won through to her home.

How do you take your vicissitudes? What witness do you give in times of stress?

Dr. Wilfred Grenfell tells an incident in connection with his experiences in Labrador. He said a paralyzed patient, who for years had lain prostrate in one of the wards asked him one day, "What can I do, Doctor, that is worth anything?" "Be an angel, dear lad; just be one, so that nurses and all of us shall love to come to your bedside." He was an angel. His patience, his courage, his sensitivity to other people's needs made his corner a little bit of heaven. People would seek him out to be strengthened to face their lot.

In everything God works for our eternal good, if we love Him. That means that sometimes He says "no" to your request, because it would not be for the good of your soul. Your heavenly Father knows your daily needs, and sees the effect of what happens to you in the light of everlasting life. As you accept what He sends in mercy, let it also be the means of your leaning more heavily upon Him.

PRAYER: *Thank You, Lord, for the strength to bear whatever any day may bring. Thank You for the witness of Christians in emergencies. Thank You that You are a haven for my soul. In Jesus' name. Amen.*

TUESDAY

Day by Day Thy Mercies, Lord, Attend Me

Sorrow's heavy burden Thou wilt never
Suffer me to carry all alone

Isaiah 41:8-10

But you, Israel, my servant, Jacob, whom I have chosen, the offspring of Abraham, my friend; you whom I took from the ends of the earth, and called from its farthest corners, saying to you, "You are my servant, I have chosen you and not cast you off"; fear not, for I am with you, be not dismayed, for I am your God; I will strengthen you, I will help you, I will uphold you with my victorious right hand.

Hebrews 13:5, 6

Keep your life free from love of money, and be content with what you have; for he has said, "I will never fail you nor forsake you." Hence we can confidently say, "The Lord is my helper, I will not be afraid; what can man do to me?"

WE SPOKE yesterday of the witness of one who faced sudden sorrow with the undergirding of her Christian faith, so that instead of hysteria and confusion, there was calm and order. The basic thing is that if our hearts are fixed on Christ our Savior, we never have to bear a burden all alone; His strong shoulders are always there to take the heaviest part of the load. Physically, you know what this experience means. You are carrying something that is too heavy for you. You think you cannot go on another step with the load. Along comes a friend and says, "Let me help you. That is much too heavy for you to carry." What a relief it is to have strong arms release the weight from you! Maybe you will even say, "I don't know what I would have done, if you hadn't come along."

That is the kind of friend our Lord is to us. He will never stand by and watch us carry a load that is too heavy for us. He steps in and offers His strong shoulders. So often in the parsonage, as we share in times of sorrow, people will say, "If anybody had told me this would be happening to me, I would have thought that I couldn't bear it. But somehow the strength comes each day. I can only thank the Lord."

Do we then remember to thank the Lord for His sustaining strength, and witness to others what it means to have such a never-failing Friend in time of need? Here is a blessing that your sorrow can bring. You can attest to God's sufficiency for whatever the day may hold.

The Lord will never permit you to carry a heavy burden alone. In turn, He wants you to be His strong shoulders to others. "Bear one another's burdens," is His command. For those who have known His sharing, it is a compulsion that cannot be escaped; a compulsion of compassionate love that makes life rich and abundant.

PRAYER: *We thank You, Lord, for the assurance that You will uphold us with Your victorious right hand. We thank You that in confidence we may say, "The Lord is my helper, I will not be afraid." Amen.*

Day by Day Thy Mercies, Lord, Attend Me

Through life's devious paths Thou e'er wilt guide me

Psalm 16:11

Thou dost show me the path of life; in thy presence there is fullness of joy, in thy right hand are pleasures for evermore.

Psalm 25:4, 10

Make me to know thy ways, O Lord; teach me thy paths.
All the paths of the Lord are steadfast love and faithfulness,
for those who keep his covenant and his testimonies.

OFTEN WHEN we speak of God's leading along life's way, people will say , "But how can you know God's guidance? How can you be sure that He is pointing the way?" Our Scripture today has one of the conditions that we must begin with: "All the paths of the Lord are steadfast love and faithfulness, for those who keep his covenant and his testimonies." To know God's guidance means that you have to be very familiar with His will and mind; it means that the spirit of the Bible will be a natural part of your thinking; that its values will unconsciously be yours. You see, here is the Waterloo for many people. They have not been willing to take time to get their directions straight, and so they get lost. All the maps in the world will do you no good on the trip, if they lie unused in the trunk. But if someone who has gone before has marked the way for you, and you keep the chart in the front seat of your car, and refer to it at each turn in the road, you will safely arrive at your destination—and by the best route. It is what the psalmist is praying when he says: "Make me to know thy ways, O Lord; teach me thy paths."

When you have a decision to make in life about which path to go, how zealous in prayer are you? Folded hands are strong ones, and praying knees have a sure step when they arise to walk the path they have been shown.

The world has many inviting walks. We need to be aware of their destination. A minister was out visiting on a farm, and thought that he would like to take a walk to explore the place. He asked the young lad in the house to go with him. The minister took the lead, and started down a path that looked intriguing as it wound its way in the woods. The lad, however, stopped him and said, "Oh no, let's not go in that path." "Why?" asked the minister, "it looks interesting." "Oh," said the boy, "that is the path that the pigs have made, and it will lead to a slough and mud."

I would like to witness personally to God's guidance each day. So often when I have been on my knees for my morning prayer time, He has put into my mind those I should be remembering through that day; through the fog of many things, He has supplied the right perspective, and placed first things first. To walk His way day by day is to live gloriously.

PRAYER: *Thank You, peerless Pioneer, for breaking the trail for us. Thank You for showing the way. Help us to follow. In Your name. Amen.*

Day by Day Thy Mercies, Lord, Attend Me

For each need wilt give me plenteous grace;
In temptation's storms wilt safely hide me

2 Corinthians 12:9, 10

But he said to me, "My grace is sufficient for you, for my power is made perfect in weakness." I will all the more boast of my weaknesses, that the power of Christ may rest upon me. For the sake of Christ, then, I am content with weakness, insults, hardships, persecutions, and calamities; for when I am weak, then I am strong.

WITH WHAT confidence the Apostle Paul can speak! He is relating what he has experienced. In the previous section of this portion of 2 Corinthians, he tells about how he had prayed for "the thorn in his flesh" to be removed. Just what this thorn was, we are not sure. There are Bible scholars who think it might have been epilepsy. We do know that it was a physical ailment. Could it be that Paul might have said, "Lord, I want to serve you. This is a handicap to my service. You have the power to heal me. Please do." Whatever his prayer was, the answer is unmistakable, and Paul's response to that answer is an example. "For the sake of Christ, then, I am content with weakness. . . ." Notice that he does not say that he will just bear it. There is no feeling of resignation about his response; rather it is resolution. It is not just to have defensive undergirding; it is to have offensive enthusiasm. What words are these: "I am content with my weaknesses"! Many of us with able, strong bodies know very little about being content. What is Paul's secret?

It finds its replica in many lives today. It gives the same glorious witness. It is knowing the Savior so intimately that there is perfect trust; trust that goes forward when it cannot see; trust that smiles when there is pain; trust that is strong when others are weak.

Many of the most beautiful souls we have known have had bodily afflictions for years. Keith Brooks tells the story of Dr. Nathaniel Kendrick, one of the founders, and the first executive head of what is now Colgate University. He was paralyzed in the prime of his life, and lay for many years in bed, unable to move. Those who visited him said that the majesty of his Christian faith made him seem almost divine at times. One related how his son had said to him, "Father, I never loved you as I do now. Oh, if I could only bear your pain for you." But the father replied, "No, my son, I have not one pain to spare. He who allows me to suffer, loves me more than you do and knows just what is best for me. I sometimes think this is the happiest period of my life. His mercies are so great."

Day by day His grace is sufficient, whatever your need, whether it be physical, or spiritual. Can you say with Paul, "I am content"? Is this the witness you bring to your family, to your friends, to the world?

PRAYER: *For the witness of folks like Paul who lived so victoriously, we thank You, God. Help us to know and use their source of strength. In Jesus' name. Amen.*

Day by Day Thy Mercies, Lord, Attend Me

**O what joy beneath Thy heavn'ly favor,
Trustingly to rest my soul in Thee**

Psalm 20: 7, 8

Some boast of chariots, and some of horses; but we boast of the name of the Lord our God. They will collapse and fall; but we shall rise and stand upright.

Psalm 68:4

Sing to God, sing praises to his name; lift up a song to him who rides upon the clouds; his name is the Lord, exult before him!

THE KING JAMES' translation of Psalm 19 uses the word "trust" instead of "boast." Perhaps the latter word has in it something of the little lad who says to his playmate, "My dad can lick your dad." Certainly in either instance the meaning is unmistakable. When the strength of the Lord is yours to command, you are unbeatable.

Today's world is in a dither. The radio constantly reports how one country competes with another in the invention and manufacture of one deadly weapon after the other. The race is on as to who can kill the fastest and most completely. Where are the Christians, and what has happened to their voices? Are these the things in which we trust? Are these the things that have been the defense for the people of God through all the generations? What does the psalmist mean when he says that those who put their trust in chariots "will collapse and fall; but we shall rise and stand upright"? O yes, the Lord could command chariots, if He needed them. His resources are indicated in the "thousands upon thousands." But Jesus told us to put by the sword. He told us to feed our enemies, and pray for them. And the kind of armor that the Apostle Paul enjoins us to have and use is the "sword of the Spirit," the "breastplate of righteousness," the helmet of salvation," the "shield of faith," and the "loin cloth of truth." Then he says our feet should be shod with the "equipment of the gospel of peace." Are these the things that the Christians in today's world are relying upon? Shame on us for claiming one thing with our lips saying that we trust the Lord and His resources, and that He is sufficient for any situation in the world today; and then preparing our measly weapons of defense as if there were no God, frantically following the pattern of our godless enemies who do not seem to know about trusting in Him. No wonder much of our song has been stilled! "Lift up a song to him who rides upon the clouds!"

Do you trust in God? Then live it today, in your home, in your community. Speak the words of faith and assurance and joy! Live the gospel of love.

PRAYER: *Forgive us, Lord that we have said one thing with our lips, and done another thing with our lives. Help us today to bring faith and love to our corner of the world. In Jesus' name. Amen.*

SATURDAY

Day by Day Thy Mercies, Lord, Attend Me

Help me, Lord, that I may never waver,
Nor forget Thy loving care for me

Deuteronomy 8:2

"And you shall remember all the way which the Lord your God has led you these forty years in the wilderness, that he might humble you, testing you to know what was in your heart, whether you would keep his commandments, or not.'

Hebrews 10:23, 24

Let us hold fast the confession of our hope without wavering, for he who has promised is faithful; and let us consider how to stir up one another to love and good works.

HOW HUMAN it is for us to forget what the Lord has done for us! Often when we have called upon Him in trouble, we have made such glib promises of our loyalty and gratitude. So many times, when things have leveled off in our lives, we have forgotten.

Others of us praise Him when it is comfortable; but cringe like cowards, when our witness means that we must face the ignominy of the disapproval of our associates. We marvel at Peter's quick fall after his glib pronouncement of his loyalty to Christ; then we remain silent, in alien circumstances, in regard to our allegiance to Him. The prayer of the hymn writer: "Help me, Lord, that I may never waver, nor forget Thy loving care for me," is one that we need to pray hourly.

It is a good daily exercise to recount the evidences of God's loving care in your life. It might even be good to write them down. It is good to speak of them to your family; it is good to witness of them to your neighbor. Such remembrance is fortification for your loyalty.

He needs you. He needs every Christian to stand up and be counted. Oh, not as a matter of keeping records, of knowing numbers. He needs you to live His love in today's world; He needs you in the Christian army whose purpose is to bring healing rather than destruction; who believe in the power of love. What of your loyalty? Do you give the best of your talents to His kingdom work? Does He get the first fruits of your income? Has He priority on your time?

A native pastor in Central China was offered a salary ten times as large as the small sum which was given him by the Mission Board, but he replied, "Matthew left the customs to follow Christ, and do you think I am going to leave Christ to follow customs?"

He has promised that, if you are faithful, He will give you the crown of life. The glorious part is that while you are faithful, you are really living.

PRAYER: *Today I would remember all your mercies in my life, Lord; I would recount how You have answered prayers, how You have done for us more than we could even ask or think. And then, by the grace of Your Spirit, I would reaffirm my loyalty. Day by day, You take care of me. Day by day, let me live for You. Amen.*

Children of the Heavenly Father

Tryggare kan ingen vara. L. M. Swedish Folksong.

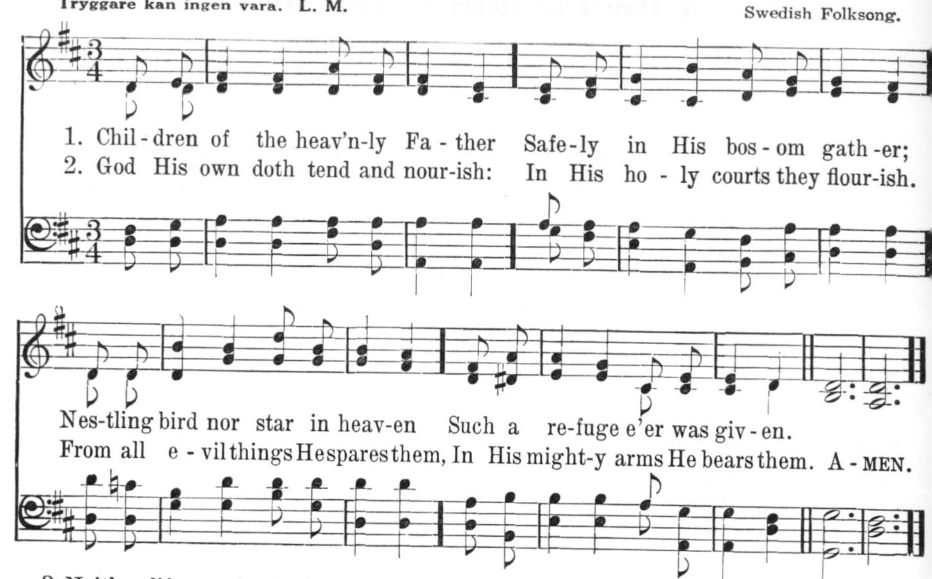

3 Neither life nor death shall ever
From the Lord His children sever;
Unto them His grace He showeth,
And their sorrows all He knoweth.

4 Lo, their very hairs He numbers,
And no daily care encumbers
Them that share His every blessing,
And His help in woes distressing.

5 Praise the Lord in joyful numbers:
Your Protector never slumbers.
At the will of your Defender
Every foeman must surrender.

6 Though He giveth or He taketh,
God His children ne'er forsaketh,
His the loving purpose solely
To preserve them pure and holy.

Carolina Vilhelmina (Sandell) Berg, (1832–1903).

Children of the Heavenly Father

Safely in His bosom gather

Galatians 3:23-26

Now before faith came, we were confined under the law, kept under restraint until faith should be revealed. So that the law was our custodian until Christ came, that we might be justified by faith. But now that faith has come, we are no longer under a custodian; for in Christ Jesus you are all sons of God.

Ephesians 4:4, 5

There is one body and one Spirit, just as you were called to the one hope that belongs to your call, one Lord, one faith, one baptism, one God and Father of us all, who is above all and through all and in all.

WHAT A wonderful way God has of picturing himself! He is our Father, He is our Shepherd. Surely the purpose of these pictures that the Bible gives us is to make clear how intimate God wants the relationship between Him and us to be. What child is afraid of a loving father? What sheep stand in fear of a tender shepherd? The Lord tells us that we bring joy to Him when we call Him Father; we make glad the heart of God when we acknowledge that we are His children.

I love the story told of a deaf boy who had not learned to speak. His parents sent him away to school for four years where he was taught to speak as well as such afflicted people can. The boy was an only son. When he returned home, he stretched out his arms to his father and said with clear, distinct enunciation: "My father!" The latter was almost overwhelmed and said later, in recounting the incident, "If I live to be eighty, I'll never forget the moment when I heard my boy say, 'My father.' "

How do we become children of God? Today's Scripture points out the way. We were under the custodian, the law. Then God sent His Son to be our Savior. He bought us from sin, and through His love we become joint heirs with Him of His Father's kingdom, and He becomes our elder brother. As Paul says, "But now that faith has come, we are no longer under a custodian; for in Christ Jesus you are all sons of God."

God's marvelous provisions for this inheritance begin with baptism. Here by the miracle of His grace we become His children, and our names are written in His family book.

Those who are God's children know the safety of His bosom. They have an abiding place that is a protection from all harm. So often we confuse harm to the body with harm to the real self. It is our souls that are kept in the hollow of God's hand, when we acknowledge Him as our Father, and claim the inheritance of being His children.

PRAYER: *For the intimate relationship that we can know when we call You, our Father, we thank You, Lord. For the privilege and joy of being Your children we sing praises. For the gift of this inheritance in Christ Jesus our Savior, we worship You. Make us to be worthy children of such a Father. Amen.*

Children of the Heavenly Father

Nestling bird nor star in heaven
Such a refuge e'er was given

Luke 12:24

"Consider the ravens: they neither sow nor reap, they have neither storehouse nor barn, and yet God feeds them. Of how much more value are you than the birds!"

Psalm 8:3, 4

When I look at thy heavens, the work of thy fingers,
the moon and the stars which thou hast established;
what is man that thou art mindful of him,
and the son of man that thou dost care for him?

BIBLE WRITERS knew their birds. As fine a piece of bird lore as you can find is contained in the Book of Job in those remarkable nature chapters 28-41. So often the eagle is used as a simile: "As the eagle stirs up her nest," "Riches certainly make themselves wings, like an eagle that flieth toward heaven."

The Book of Proverbs has that classic section:

Three things are too wonderful for me;
four I do not understand:
the way of an eagle in the sky,
the way of a serpent on a rock,
the way of a ship on the high seas,
and the way of a man with a maiden.

Our Lord made several allusions to birds. He compared the little creatures, catching seeds which the hurried sower let fall along a hard path, to evil forces snapping up from wavering disciples the truths they had been taught; He spoke of small birds lodging in the branches of a mustard bush; He contrasted His own homelessness to the birds that had their nests; and He pointed out that, even though a sparrow was sold at the rate of five for two pennies, yet His heavenly Father had concern for them.

Many an agnostic has been made to think of spiritual things through the witness of creation. The story is told of an incident between Robert Ingersoll, the agnostic, and Henry Ward Beecher. In the latter's study was an elaborate celestial globe which had been given to him. On the surface, in delicate workmanship, were raised figures of the constellations and the stars which composed them. The globe struck Ingersoll's fancy. "This is just what I want," he said, "who made it?" "Who made it, did you say, Colonel? Who made it?" was Beecher's reply. "Why nobody, of course. It just happened!"

PRAYER: *The wonder of Your creation, the marvelous plan of it; Your concern about every living thing and, most of all, Your love revealed to us in Christ—these make us bow in adoration and praise. Thank You that we may be Your children. Amen.*

TUESDAY

Children of the Heavenly Father

Praise the Lord in joyful numbers

Psalm 34:1-3

I will bless the Lord at all times; his praise shall continually be in my mouth. My soul makes its boast in the Lord; let the afflicted hear and be glad. O magnify the Lord with me, and let us exalt his name together!

2 Chronicles 20:22

And when they began to sing and praise, the Lord set an ambush against the men of Ammon, Moab, and Mount Seir, who had come against Judah, so that they were routed.

CHRISTIANITY IS a singing religion. Wherever the message of Christ has come, there has accompanied it joyous song. At the birth of Christ the most important news that the world will ever know was announced by the angel's song. Why should Christians sing?

In I Peter 2:9 the reasons are very strongly given: Christians are a chosen race, God's own people. Why? That they may declare the wonderful deeds of Him who called us out of darkness to marvelous light. Is this spirit of praising the Lord in the joy of salvation characteristic of you? As you work about the house, or in an office, or in a schoolroom, or wherever the place might be, is there a song in your heart? It will show in your face, and give nimbleness to fingers, and clarity to mind. With a theme like salvation, if it is really our personal experience, how can we help but rejoice?

In a certain church in Scotland there was a dear old lady, who disturbed her minister by her habit of exclaiming at given intervals in his sermon: "Praise the Lord, Amen." He finally went to her and made her a proposition. "Betty," he said, "I get a little disturbed by your calling out during my sermon. Now if you will stop doing it all this year, I'll give you a couple of woolen blankets at the end of the year." Betty was poor, and the woolen blankets looked like quite a prize. So she agreed to the bargain. Sunday after Sunday she kept her part of it. But one day, a visiting minister was in the pulpit. He bubbled over with the joy of the gospel that he had to share. As he spoke of the blessings of the forgiveness of sins, and the joy that comes from the knowledge of salvation, the visions of the blanket began to fade. At last Betty could stand it no longer. Jumping up she cried, "Blankets or no blankets, Hallelujah!"

In our staid pattern of life, the story may seem a little ludicrous but the point of it is something we could think about. If we know the Lord; if we are aware of what He has done for us, and daily is doing; if we walk in His company; if we are children of the heavenly Father, surely we should be praising the Lord in joyful numbers. Is there a song in your heart today?

PRAYER: *Lord, give us grace to have a song in our living; put words of praise on our lips. Make us daily aware of the privilege of being Your children. In Jesus' name. Amen.*

Children of the Heavenly Father

Your Protector never slumbers

Psalm 121:2-8

My help comes from the Lord, who made heaven and earth. He will not let your foot be moved, he who keeps you will not slumber. Behold, he who keeps Israel will neither slumber nor sleep. The Lord is your keeper; the Lord is your shade on your right hand. The sun shall not smite you by day, nor the moon by night. The Lord will keep you from all evil; he will keep your life; the Lord will keep your going out and your coming in from this time forth and for evermore.

IT IS an interesting thing to hear people talk about their sleep. "Why," one will say, "I hardly slept at all last night." And another one will chime in that she had the same experience. To have sleepless nights can be a gruelling experience. A repetition of these dissipates one's energies and wears down one's resistance.

All sorts of psychological devices are given for insomnia victims. It used to be that they were told to count sheep. Many resort to artificial medicine. The few times when I have found that sleep escaped me, I have had the glorious experience of using that time to converse with my heavenly Father. The conversation may follow different patterns. Sometimes I just listen while He talks through all the Scripture I have memorized. Before I know it, the restfulness of His presence has done the job, and I am deep in slumber. Sometimes I use the pattern of hymns, and recount those that I know. Again, I remember in prayer folks who have been out of mind for a while, and who are recalled in the waking hours of the night. Actually, any one of these methods works so fast that before I know it, on the wings of a prayer I am in slumber.

There is One whose watchful eye is always awake. Can you read Psalm 121, and not thrill to the completeness of God's care for you? Human friends may have areas of failing. But of our Lord we can say, "From this time forth and for evermore."

A gentleman in India paid a servant to fan him through the night. Now the practice was that you fanned your object until he was asleep, and then waited until you saw his eyes open and began fanning again as if you had never stopped. This gentleman had a glass eye, which he took out and laid on the table when he went to sleep. His fanner reported to a friend that he had to fan the gentleman all night, because he had an eye that never went to sleep. The "Eye that never sleeps" is watching over us.

"God is before me, He will be my guide,
God is behind me, no ill can betide;
God is beside me, to comfort and cheer,
God is around me, so why should I fear?"

PRAYER: *It is so good to know, Lord, that our Protector never slumbers. We need fear neither the sun by day nor the moon by night. We thank You. Amen.*

Children of the Heavenly Father

At the will of your Defender
Ev'ry foeman must surrender

Exodus 14:14, 15

"The Lord will fight for you, and you have only to be still." The Lord said to Moses, "Why do you cry to me? Tell the people of Israel to go forward."

1 John 5:4

For whatever is born of God overcomes the world; and this is the victory that overcomes the world, our faith.

IT IS a wonderful thing for children to have confidence in their parents. Such confidence is bred when parents have kept their promises, and in general have shown themselves to be worthy of the confidence. There is something psychologically sturdy in a child's personality, when he has been reared in a home like this. When this confidence is coupled with love, you have the basic formula for an integrated personality. All of this is the inheritance of children of the heavenly Father.

In our excerpt from Genesis we have called to mind the journey of the children of Israel. How often they had to be reminded what their resources were! How much like us they were!

Even the world will stand back in awe, and recognize the power of the Lord, on which they had hitherto not calculated. In America today, we need to take stock of our foundations and look to our roots, so that we may know the spiritual power that should be ours. We need to be much more concerned about our own spiritual integrity than about the strength of the enemy. If our cause is just, why should we fear? Chronicles records that the other countries became fearful when they saw that the Lord was on the side of the Children of Israel.

As it is for the nation, so it is for the individual. The Word that Jesus speaks to us, as recorded in the Gospel of John, is a completely victorious one. Recognizing the difficulties in this present world, our Lord tells us to be of good cheer, because He has overcome the world. And in I John this is reiterated in pointing up what our weapon is in this battle of life against the foes that would overwhelm us: our faith.

The witness of victorious Christians is undeniable. All the preaching of a year of Sabbaths is not as effective as the day by day triumphant living of those who are God's children. What does your attitude toward life, your zest for living, say to your family and to your neighbors?

PRAYER: *For the triumphant victory that is our prospect in Your love, we thank You, O Lord. Forgive the times when our heads have looked downward, and our shoulders have been stooped, and our countenances have been sad. Let the "good cheer" of Your eternal victory be reflected in our lives. Amen.*

Children of the Heavenly Father

Though He giveth or He taketh,
God His children ne'er forsaketh

Job 1:21

And he said, "Naked I came from my mother's womb, and naked shall I return; the Lord gave, and the Lord has taken away; blessed be the name of the Lord."

Psalm 27:10

For my father and my mother have forsaken me, but the Lord will take me up.

HOW VALUES can vary when looked at from different points of view! The law of supply and demand can cause a price fluctuation that is amazing. A thing that is held to be of worth in one country is looked upon as utterly worthless in another. Values of material things change from season to season. It is not so with eternal values. They are invariable, like the One who controls them. In our Christian faith it is essential that we develop this long look, this measuring stick of eternity, if we are to have the peace that our Lord promises.

In this matter of having or losing, for instance, the importance which you give to possessions will depend upon what you believe. It is true of things; it is true of life. In the matter of things, have you not been trued up? "What will it profit a man if he gains the whole world and forfeits his life?" In the matter of life, are you not able to say with the Apostle Paul, "For to me to live is Christ and to die is gain"?

There is a very significant thought in the Book of Chronicles. If we are to be served by a God who will never forsake us, we must not forsake Him. His promise holds only as long as we keep our part of the contract. This would be frightening, recognizing how weak we are, were it not for the fact that He will reinstate us if we, like the prodigal, leave home, but then return. How wonderful to know that our Father's arms are always open to receive us! He rejoices, and all the angels of heaven rejoice with Him, at the return of any of His children.

"But the Lord will take me up," even when my own family forsakes me. To us who have an inheritance of faith from our families, this seems a little farfetched. It is more real than you know. Around the world it is happening, this being forsaken by one's own kin, because one chooses to follow the Christ. Yes, it is happening in America, too. I think of the young Jewish girl whose parents held a funeral for her when she became a Christian. To them she was dead. But the Lord took her up!

PRAYER: *We thank You, Lord that whatever comes from Your hands is good; that Your love to us is invariable. Give us such a trust that we will not doubt even when we cannot understand. Help us never to forsake You. In Jesus' name. Amen.*

SATURDAY

Children of the Heavenly Father

His the loving purpose solely
To preserve them pure and holy

Ephesians 1:3-6

Blessed be the God and Father of our Lord Jesus Christ, who has blessed us in Christ with every spiritual blessing in the heavenly places, even as he chose us in him before the foundation of the world, that we should be holy and blameless before him. He destined us in love to be his sons through Jesus Christ, according to the purpose of his will, to the praise of his glorious grace which he freely bestowed on us in the Beloved.

THE LOVING purpose of God is made very clear to us in the Letter to the Ephesians, namely that the Lord had destined us to be holy and blameless. But because sin entered the picture, He had to reclaim us again. This is the picture that we are given. Now again, His purpose is that we should become His sons through Jesus Christ. It is interesting to notice Paul's language as he tries to describe what Christ has done for us. It is "glorious grace," which "He lavished upon us," and "freely bestowed." One has the feeling so often in Paul's letters that he cannot find words that are adequate to express his own sinfulness, and God's love as revealed in Christ. He is constantly dealing in superlatives.

The experience that the apostle had is the one of every Christian when he comes to the realization of God's grace. The wonder and marvel of a holy God loving a miserable sinner is almost beyond our comprehension. And to know that everything He does, is "to preserve them pure and holy" makes one very humble and grateful to be His child.

An unforgettable Washington experience occurred at a World Day of Prayer observance at the Cathedral. We had prayed much about this meeting that it might be a witness to our oneness in Christ. Mrs. Eisenhower and her mother were along to be a part of the prayer chain that encircled the world. I was to meet the First Lady's party outside. When I greeted Mrs. Doud, her mother, I mentioned that my people had come from Sweden, for I knew that was true of Mrs. Doud's parents. Her eyes lighted up, and she asked me in Swedish if I could speak it? Just then we were in the procession to go in to the service. God richly blessed the gathering and gave us a real sense of His presence. People of all colors and nations were one in Him that day at the Cathedral. Both Mrs. Eisenhower and her mother were deeply moved. As the latter bade me farewell she said, with tears in her eyes, "All I could think of was, 'Tryggare kan ingen vara,'" the Swedish hymn translated as, "Children of the heavenly Father."

Yes, His loving purpose is that we all should be His children!

PRAYER: *For the wonder of your world-wide family, for Your love which is sufficient for all, we thank You. Help our love to be as inclusive as Yours. In Jesus' name. Amen.*

Jesus, Priceless Treasure

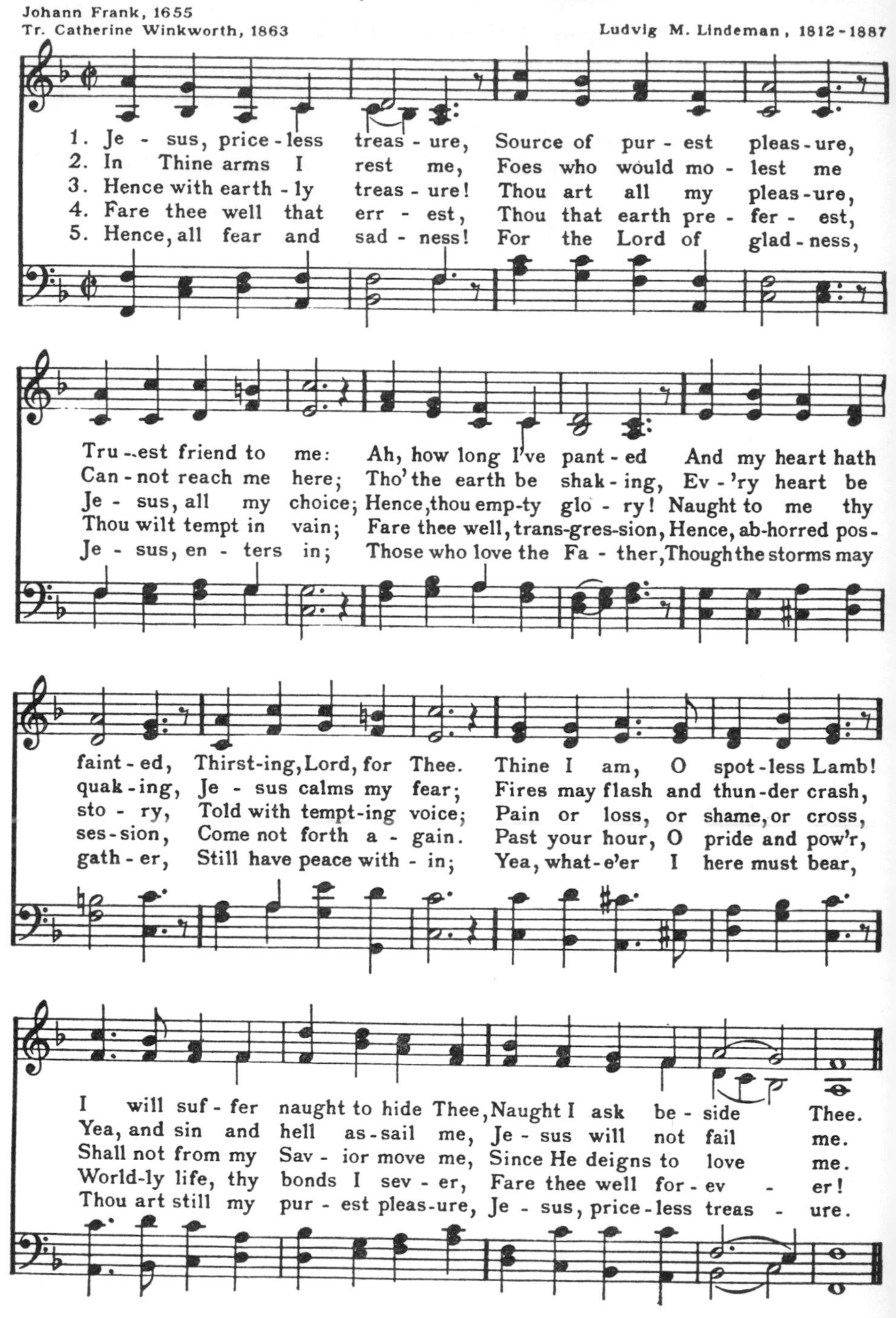

Jesus, Priceless Treasure

Source of purest pleasure,
Truest friend to me

Proverbs 18:24

There are friends who pretend to be friends, but there is a friend who sticks closer than a brother.

1 Peter 1:8

Without having seen him you love him; though you do not now see him you believe in him and rejoice with unutterable and exalted joy.

UPON THE choice of one's friends often hinges the pattern of one's life. Friends can make or break a person. As a friend, you have such power in regard to others. We need to give thoughtful attention to who our friends are. Very often it is the kind of pleasure that we choose that determines our friends.

We are living in a pleasure-mad world; not that pleasure need be sinful in itself. Our hymn writer speaks of Jesus as being the source of purest pleasure. And Christians through the centuries will attest to this. Notice the language in this section of I Peter that you have just read: "rejoice with unutterable and exalted joy." There is nothing very long-faced or dejected about that, is there?

In the Book of Proverbs we are told about friends who merely pretend to be friends. The prodigal son must have experienced this kind of friendship. When his money was gone, he found himself very much alone. And the kind of pleasure such friends want you to share will leave you sullied. Have you had the experience of coming home from some questionable entertainment, and feeling that you had a bad taste in your mouth?

There are those who claim that they can do anything, and remain clean. The experience that a woman going into a mine had is very apropos. She had on a white dress, and turned to the miner as he was about to lead the way and said: "Can't I wear a white dress down into the mine?" "Yes, mum," returned the old man "there is nothing to keep you from wearing a white frock down there, but there will be considerable to keep you from wearing one back."

Another woman who loved the world was defending her practices and said, "I can take Jesus with me anywhere I go!" To which the pastor quietly replied, "Oh, is that so? You can take Jesus with you. I did not know that was the order—that it was yours to lead, and His to follow."

To be with some friends is just joy; you do not have to be doing anything necessarily; just to be with them is joy. The companionship of the Friend of friends is unutterable, exalted joy. Such a friendship keeps any experience from ever becoming commonplace; it keeps any day from just becoming another. Here is the purest pleasure for which every soul longs.

PRAYER: *For Your friendship, which is life and pleasure and the fulfillment of every longing, I thank You, dearest Friend. Help me to share Your friendship with others. Amen.*

Jesus, Priceless Treasure

My soul had fainted,
Thirsting, Lord for Thee

Psalm 63:1

O God, thou art my God, I seek thee, my soul thirsts for thee; my flesh faints for thee, as in a dry and weary land where no water is.

Revelation 7:16, 17

"They shall hunger no more, neither thirst any more; the sun shall not strike them, nor any scorching heat. For the Lamb in the midst of the throne will be their shepherd, and he will guide them to springs of living water; and God will wipe away every tear from their eyes."

IS THERE anything worse than being thirsty? The human body can live much longer without food than it can without water. Have you not said when you have been thirsty, and a variety of fruit juices or other drinks were at your disposal, "There is nothing that quenches the thirst like water." And so it is. No wonder, then, that we find in the Bible again and again the figure of thirst used to describe the soul's longing for God. It is interesting to note the progression of the satisfying of this thirst as the Bible records it. In the Old Testament it is mostly spoken of as a longing with the hope of fulfillment in the future. In the New Testament Jesus asserted the great "I am" when He said, "If any one thirst, let him come to me and drink."

To say that the world is thirsty for such a drink is to put it mildly. People are trying to slake the thirst of their souls by drowning the voice of conscience in a mad race for the slough of despond. Every day each one of us undoubtedly meets souls that are thirsty for the Living Word. If someone about you were parched physically, you would go to no end of trouble to supply that which would quench his thirst. Yet we pass by unheeding this far more important need.

As Christians we are enjoined to be the salt of the earth. Besides adding zest to food, salt does other things. A Bible study group of college girls was discussing the passage that includes the statement about salt from the Sermon on the Mount. The preservative qualities of salt were the ones most of the girls thought about. Then a Chinese girl in the group quietly suggested, "Salt creates thirst." "You are the salt of the earth" means then that, besides preserving righteousness, you should be creating a thirst in others for the Living Water. This is what evangelism is; this is what witnessing means; this is to follow the command of the One who alone has that which can satisfy a human soul. How savory a salt are you?

PRAYER: *Lord, how can I keep to myself the riches of the Fountain that has so wondrously satisfied the longing of my soul? Give me such a compulsion to share You this day, as will make me a blessing in the lives of others. In Jesus' name. Amen.*

Jesus, Priceless Treasure

I would suffer nought to hide Thee

Psalm 89:46

How long, O Lord? Wilt thou hide thyself for ever? How long will thy wrath burn like fire?

Psalm 10:1

Why dost thou stand afar off, O Lord?
Why dost thou hide thyself in times of trouble?

Job 23:3, 8, 9

"Oh, that I knew where I might find him, that I might come even to his seat! . . . Behold, I go forward, but he is not there; and backward, but I cannot perceive him; on the left hand I seek him, but I cannot behold him; I turn to the right hand, but I cannot see him."

OVER THE story of the Book of Job there could be written the title "When God Hides." This hiding experience for Job, however, was a testing, a polishing of the gold of his faith. It was not of Job's making nor desire. It produced that glorious profession of faith: "Though he slay me, yet will I trust in him" (K.J.V.). Perhaps it is something of this that the hymn writer has in mind. It is the content of the verse the Apostle Paul gave us, which we have had occasion to use again and again: "Who shall separate us from the love of Christ . . . ?" God may seem to be hiding himself temporarily, in order to bring your faith into clearer focus. When I have been gone from home for a season, and the children have had to hold forth without me, then it is they best witness to my presence, if during my absence they do those things which I have tried to teach them. So God may seem to withdraw for a bit, to let our witness stand out in clearer focus. But do we sometimes try to raise a smoke screen between ourselves and God?

There was Lot's wife who let worldly allurements come between her and God, and was destroyed; discouraged men opposed the building of the wall of Jerusalem; unbelief hindered Christ's work in Nazareth; worldly possessions kept the rich young man from seeing who Christ was, and following Him; family ties prevented a man from accepting an invitation, and so hid God from him; and in Hebrews we are told that weights as well as closely clinging sin are a hindrance to God's revelation to us.

There you have a list of things that can hide God from us: worldly allurements, discouragement and lack of faith, worldly possessions, human ties, and sin.

Two Christians were visiting mission stations in China. From time to time, one of these men asked the Christian converts what, in their opinion, was the greatest barrier to the spread of Christianity in China. Almost invariably the answer that came back was, "Ourselves."

PRAYER: *Lord, You see into the innermost parts of my heart. Clear away from my life that which hinders full view of You. I do not want anything to hide You. In Jesus' name. Amen.*

Jesus, Priceless Treasure

Naught I ask beside Thee

Joshua 24:15

"And if you be unwilling to serve the Lord, choose this day whom you will serve, whether the gods your fathers served in the region beyond the River, or the gods of the Amorites in whose land you dwell; but as for me and my house, we will serve the Lord."

Hebrews 11:24, 25

By faith Moses, when he was grown up, refused to be called the son of Pharaoh's daughter, choosing rather to share ill-treatment with the people of God than to enjoy the fleeting pleasures of sin.

LIFE IS one succession of choices: we choose to get up or stay in bed; we choose to eat or not to eat; we choose to stay home or go out; we choose to listen or walk away from what we do not want to hear—well, we could go on indefinitely. The most important choice for this life and for eternity is the one that the hymn writer indicates he has made when he says: "Naught I ask on earth beside Thee." Having found Christ, the priceless treasure, he has made an unqualified and complete choice. It is to such a choice Joshua is calling his people; and he is warning them not to postpone their decision. "Choose this day whom you will serve."

Many people go through life without possessing the greatest Treasure, because of their failure to come to a decision. They stall along from day to day, following this or that, bound by fears and uncertainties, and never know the clean, free feeling of the great choice. One thing is certain: your very failure to choose is a choice of its kind; it is a choice against God. You know how it is with elections. The fellow who does not go to the polls to vote is as good as a vote against a good man who would get his vote, if he voted. Our Lord made it very clear that it is necessary for us to choose. He reminds us that we cannot serve God and mammon.

It is this lackadaisical professing in the church today that is its weakness. It is the forgetting all about the Sunday worship during the following days of the week, that is the blight on the witness in the community.

Really to be in earnest about "naught I ask beside Thee" means to put Christ first and uppermost in everything. It means that the kingdom work has first claims on your time, on your talent, on your energies, on your purse. It means that you crucify the desire for the approval of others; it means that you put to death worldly ambitions; it means that you will not be concerned that you get credit for what you do; it means that you will find your joy in serving, rather than in being served.

Moses made a clean break in his choice. He would rather suffer ill-treatment with the people of God, than to enjoy the fleeting pleasures of sin.

PRAYER: *You know it is not easy, Lord, to come clean with a choice. Give us grace today to choose the things that are first. May Your Holy Spirit guide us during this day. In Jesus' name. Amen.*

Jesus, Priceless Treasure

Hence all fear and sadness
For the Lord of gladness
Jesus, enters in

Ezra 6:22

And they kept the feast of unleavened bread seven days with joy; for the Lord had made them joyful, and had turned the heart of the king of Assyria to them, so that he aided them in the work of the house of God, the God of Israel.

Psalm 126:2, 3

Then our mouth was filled with laughter, and our tongue with shouts of joy; then they said among the nations, "The Lord has done great things for them." The Lord has done great things for us; we are glad.

WE ARE back at the note we have mentioned again and again: the note of joy in our Christian living. Sometimes we feel it is the lost chord. The song writer knows that the entrance of Jesus into a heart is the exit of fear and sadness. The presence of Christ and a mood of depression just do not go together, no matter what the circumstances. Listen to the language of the psalm: "Our mouth was filled with laughter. . . . our tongue with shouts of joy."

Times for rejoicing have been vividly portrayed in Scripture.

In Psalm 30:11: we have recorded the return of divine favor:
Thou hast turned for me my mourning into dancing;
thou hast loosed my sackcloth and girded me with gladness.
Jeremiah records the joy at the deliverance of a nation (30:19):
"Out of them shall come songs of thanksgiving,
and the voices of those who make merry."

The crowning experience of joy comes with the vision of the resurrected Savior as recorded in the Gospel of John: "You will be sorrowful, but your sorrow will turn into joy. . . . So you have sorrow now, but I will see you again and your hearts will rejoice, and no one will take your joy from you."

Because a young lad came whistling into a railroad station, some years ago, and a woman observed the effect on the people who heard, today there is music in half the railroad stations of the U. S. A. A whistling boy—and a changed atmosphere. A risen Savior—and joy that no one can take from you; a contagion that will surely catch.

What of the song in your heart? What kind of melody are you carrying today? What snatches of it will be left in the hearts of the people you meet?

PRAYER: *Please God, let there come from my life the song of gladness that the knowledge of salvation gives me. Forgive me for ever being downcast. Today, let me sing joy into somebody's life. In Jesus' name. Amen.*

Jesus, Priceless Treasure

Though the storms may gather,
Those who love the Father
Still have peace within

Psalm 107:28-30

Then they cried to the Lord in their trouble, and he delivered them from their distress; he made the storm be still and the waves of the sea were hushed. Then they were glad because they had quiet, and he brought them to their desired haven.

READ PSALM 107. It supplies the pattern for the lines of our hymn today. Opening with the note of thanksgiving that should be the first expression of a Christian's tongue, we have the challenge to witness in the summons, "Let the redeemed of the Lord say so." Then in succeeding paragraphs, the psalmist goes on to enumerate the situations from which the people had been redeemed. Talk about storms! Listen to them! There were those who had wandered in desert wastes, hungry and thirsty; there were those who were prisoners and sat in darkness and gloom; there were those who were sick through their sinful ways; there were those who went down to the sea in ships. Then the refrain which caps the beautiful description of these varying situations is the one that should sing in the heart of every child of God:

"Let them thank the Lord for his steadfast love,
for his wonderful works to the sons of men!"

The psalmist with the song writer had experienced that there was no storm in his life but that the Lord was at the center of it; there was no situation that He could not handle; there was no disturbance, but that His peace could be within.

Very often children teach us things wonderfully. William Canton, author of *The Bible and the Anglo-Saxon People,* tells the story of a group of city children who were taken to a country village for an outing. They were to be lodged in an unoccupied house. In the night they were frightened by some unfamiliar noise. They lay terror stricken, until one child suggested that they say their prayers. She had learned at the Mission Sunday school the story of "The Guardian of the Door," a legend of an angel protecting some children. After she told them that story, they all knelt down and repeated after her: "God bless this house from thatch to floor." Then they all went quietly to bed, and slept peacefully until morning. This they repeated each evening, with the result that they had no more disturbed nights.

Those who love the Father have such confidence in His ability to handle any situation that, no matter how rough the storm, they still have peace within.

PRAYER: *Prince of Peace, so dwell within my heart that no storm can really rock the boat of my life. Let me give the witness of Your calm; let there go from me a sense of Your strength. In Your name. Amen.*

Jesus, Priceless Treasure

So whate'er we here must bear,
Thou art still my purest pleasure,
Jesu, Priceless Treasure

Proverbs 10:22

The blessing of the Lord makes rich, and he adds no sorrow with it.

Ephesians 1:18

Having the eyes of your hearts enlightened, that you may know what is the hope to which he has called you, what are the riches of his glorious inheritance in the saints, and what is the immeasurable greatness of his power in us who believe.

MANY FANCIFUL and interesting stories have been written about people's search for treasures. Many have lost their lives in some wild gold rush, or in search of some diamond mine. This overwhelming thirst for the riches of the world is well illustrated in the life of King Midas who, when told he could make one wish, desired that everything that he touched should turn into gold. It was fun at first to touch a chair and have it become gold. But it lost a little of its ping when he touched a rose and its fragrance was exchanged for the metal it became; it was something of a problem when he went to eat, and the food became gold; and it turned into stark tragedy when his little daughter came running into his arms and her warm little body became hard gold. The riches of the world have their price, and they can never buy happiness, peace, or salvation.

But a child of God inherits the kind of riches that last for eternity. In no uncertain terms, the Apostle Paul says that everything else is loss to him, in comparison with the surpassing worth of knowing Christ Jesus as Lord. Yet many people have this gift within sight, and everybody who has heard the gospel has it within reach. How few claim it as their own! They grovel along in life as spiritual paupers, when all the while the inheritance of the King might be theirs.

In southwest Virginia are the Pocahontas coal fields. These have been considered the wealthiest in the world. This land was once owned by a farmer, who was barely able to eke out an existence for himself and his family on the miserable land. One day some men from the North came down and examined the fields. They were convinced that there was coal there, so they offered him a thousand dollars for the ground. Immediately he accepted it, and moved on down into the village. These men got possession of those coal fields, and today you could not buy them for millions of dollars.

Within the grasp of everyone who hears God's Word is the inheritance that is a priceless Treasure. Countless people are letting it slip right through their fingers.

PRAYER: *Truest friend, purest pleasure, priceless treasure—all these You are to me, O Lord. Help me to share the "priceless pearl" of Your presence with others. Amen.*

Sweet Hour of Prayer

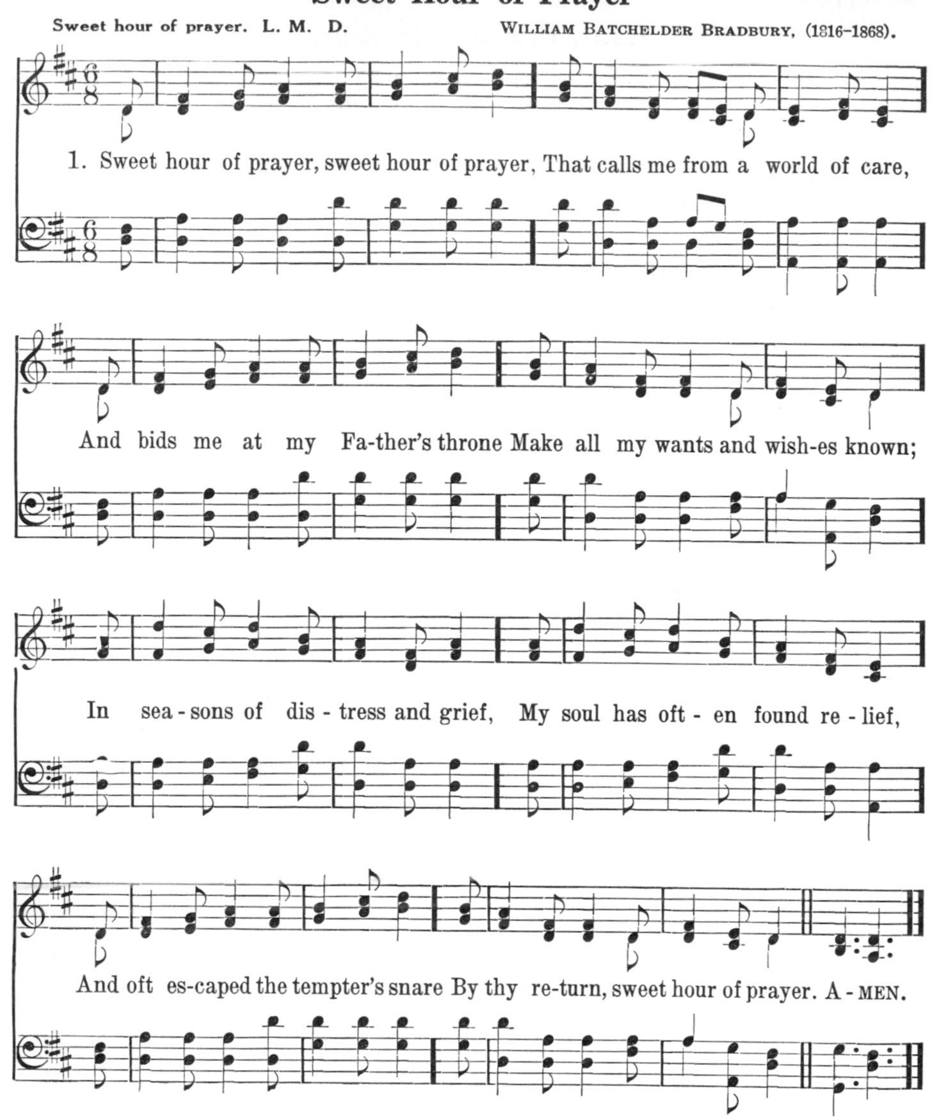

2 Sweet hour of prayer, sweet hour of prayer,
Thy wings shall my petitions bear
To Him whose truth and faithfulness
Engage the waiting soul to bless;
And since He bids me seek His face,
Believe His Word, and trust His grace,
I'll cast on Him my every care,
And wait for thee, sweet hour of prayer.

3 Sweet hour of prayer, sweet hour of prayer,
May I thy consolation share;
Till from Mount Pisgah's lofty height
I view my home and take my flight;
This robe of flesh I'll drop, and rise
To seize the everlasting prize;
And shout, while passing through the air,
Farewell, farewell, sweet hour of prayer.

Frances Jane (Crosby) Van Alstyne, 1861.

Sweet Hour of Prayer

That calls me from a world of care

Matthew 6:5-6

"And when you pray, you must not be like the hypocrites; for they love to stand and pray in the synagogues and at the street corners, that they may be seen by men. Truly, I say to you, they have their reward. But when you pray, go into your room and shut the door and pray to your Father who is in secret; and your Father who sees in secret will reward you."

THIS HAS been the beginning of fall school in millions of homes across our country. Maybe it would be good for each of us in our own private way to go to school this week. I should like to share with you in a school of prayer. Your teacher will be learning right along with you, and will constantly be consulting the Master Teacher. How about having a report at the end of the week, too? Why not keep a daily record of your progress? Possibly you could have such divisions as: Prayer Time, Thought Control, Disposition, Service. Each day mark yourself in these categories as you are reviewing your lessons in prayer.

I like to call my prayer time by the caption of a modern advertising slogan: "The Stop That Keeps You Going." Such I have found it to be in a wonderful way. The time when I am alone with God in His Word and in prayer is my empowering time for any tasks the day may hold.

Where should it be, and what might be a helpful setting? The place each one must determine for himself. That you have a specific place is important, because then it takes on the aspect of which Christ spoke, "go into your room and shut the door." I have a certain chair in the living room that is my prayer corner. Here, daily, I draw aside with the Lord, and reaffirm our relationship, and get my marching orders for the day. It is a precious spot, for many battles of the soul have been fought here.

What should your posture be? The postures mentioned in the Bible include bowing. Genesis 24:26, "The man bowed his head and worshiped the Lord"; on the face before God, Joshua 5:14, "And Joshua fell on his face to the earth, and worshiped and said to him, 'What does my Lord say to his servant?' "; standing, Luke 18:11, "The Pharisee stood and prayed thus. . . ."; and kneeling, Psalm 95:6, "O come, let us worship and bow down, let us kneel before the Lord, our Maker!" The Bible portrays Stephen kneeling to pray his final prayer. It tells us that Peter knelt, and Paul, and many of the prophets and other disciples. We are told that "every knee should bow and . . . every tongue confess that Jesus Christ is Lord." Possibly this is why I like the latter posture best. It is an acknowledgment of my adoration of Christ.

In what position you are is not of vital importance. That you have a place and time for prayer is.

PRAYER: *Great Teacher, open up for us this week the wonders of God's listening to man. School us in the ways of prayer. Give us hearts quick to learn and open to the things You would teach us. Amen.*

Sweet Hour of Prayer

And bids me at my Father's throne
Make all my wants and wishes known

1 Kings 9:3

And the Lord said to him, "I have heard your prayer and your supplication, which you have made before me; I have consecrated this house which you have built, and put my name there for ever; my eyes and my heart will be there for all time."

TODAY WE are going to consider the content of our prayers. In Ecclesiastes 5:2 we read: "Be not rash with your mouth, nor let your heart be hasty to utter a word before God, for God is in heaven and you upon earth; therefore let your words be few." And Jesus told us that we should not use vain repetitions "as the Gentiles do; for they think that they will be heard for their many words." He also spoke in condemnation of the Pharisees who "for a pretence make long prayers." So one thing we are sure of in the beginning is that to have prayers long and involved is both unnecessary and undesirable.

What then, should be the content of our prayers? Notice in The Book of Kings what the prophet had asked for. It was for a spiritual blessing for the house of God. So it is our Lord says, "I have heard your prayer. . . ." In the prayer that the Lord taught us we have our perfect example. In the opening salutation, "Our Father," we have the inclusion of everybody. Next we have an expression of praise, "Hallowed be thy name." There is one petition for the extension of the kingdom and one for the will of God. There is one petition for the necessities of life, "our daily bread," and then the confession of sin in, "forgive us our trespasses. . . ." Next we commit the future into God's hands, "lead us not into temptation," "deliver us from evil," to which the church has added a final word of praise "for Thine is the kingdom. . . ."

Reviewing then this simple analysis, a helpful prayer pattern contains: praise for mercies past and acknowledgment of who God is; an expression of the soul for spiritual growth and enrichment; confession of sin; presentation of needs; supplication for others. How does the content of your prayers check up?

Certainly this is not to say that every time you want an audience with God you must go through any formula. Any soul that earnestly calls upon Him in any way He will hear. Why, we are told that He responds to our groanings and knows our needs before we even speak to Him! But as human parents we love it when our children approach us in gratitude and respect as they come with their petitions.

When prayer time is a series of "gimmies" for physical blessings, it stays right down on earth. When it is a yielding in the presence of God to His all-wise will, it is a foretaste of heaven.

PRAYER: *Lord, teach us to pray aright. So often our prayers have been childish. In childlike faith, we acknowledge Your sovereign will and its blessings for our lives. Make it clear. In Jesus' name. Amen.*

TUESDAY

Sweet Hour of Prayer

In seasons of distress and grief
My soul has often found relief

Psalm 91:15

When he calls to me, I will answer him; I will be with him in trouble, I will rescue him and honor him.

HAVING CONSIDERED the setting and content of prayer, our next question is: When should we pray? It is significant to me, as a mother, that prayer is first mentioned in the Bible after the birth of a child. Genesis 4:26 reads: "To Seth also a son was born, and he called his name Enoch. At that time men began to call upon the name of the Lord." I shall never forget the feeling of holy awe when our firstborn was put into my arms. I needed the help of the Lord in the rearing of this child, and it was the first thing that I wanted to ask for. The same has been true of each child that has followed.

As to the time of day for your private prayer period, that again will have to be a matter of personal choice. The Bible mentions morning and evening prayer, and the Old Testament prayer hours. Our Lord spent a whole night in prayer. *When* you will have your daily appointment with God, will depend upon your occupation and work schedule. The important thing is that you discipline yourself to a specific time.

But you say, is one not praying all the time? Should not the companionship of the Lord be constant? Indeed it should! It is, what the Bible means by saying: "Pray constantly." The joy of a Christian life is always to be in the presence of the Lord. But would you say that Jesus did not so live because He withdrew at given intervals to pray? An illustration that the great Indian Christian, Sadhu Sundar Singh, used, illustrates the point we are trying to make. He spoke of sitting by a river and observing fish come to the surface as if to breathe. Then he was told that the air in the water near the bottom of the river was insufficient for them, and so at intervals they had to come to the surface for an abundance of air. So he said it is in the world where we are working hard and involved in many affairs. The soul must come up into a spiritual atmosphere of prayer and communion with God, or it would die in the depths.

Over and above our regular prayer time there will be times of special need. Who has not hugged to his heart the promise: "Call upon me in the day of trouble; I will deliver you, and you shall glorify me"? It is tragedy, if this is the only time that you call upon God. But those of us who have felt the need of literally spending nights in prayer in time of need, cannot thank Him enough that His ear is ever alert and listening to the cry of His child.

PRAYER: *We thank You, Lord, that Your presence is with us constantly. We thank You, too, for these special hours when we are in Your presence. Help us to keep a daily tryst and to know the empowering such an appointment can give. In Jesus' name. Amen.*

Sweet Hour of Prayer

And oft escaped the tempter's snare
By thy return, sweet hour of prayer

1 Corinthians 10:13

No temptation has overtaken you that is not common to man. God is faithful, and he will not let you be tempted beyond your strength, but with the temptation will also provide the way of escape, that you may be able to endure it.

PRAYER IS a wonderful armor with which to meet the onslaughts of the evil one. Today we would like to consider some of the obstacles to prayer. Rest assured that Satan would like to hinder prayer; that is a weapon stronger than he, and so he will do everything in his power to keep you from it. By the way, how are you coming along on checking up on yourself? The evil one does not like us to do that sort of thing either. His best method is to lull us into an easy lethargy.

What are obstacles to answered prayer? We go to our Textbook and find these: 1. Disobedience. Deuteronomy 1:43: But you rebelled against the command of the Lord.

2. Secret sin. Psalm 66:18:

If I had cherished iniquity in my heart
the Lord would not have listened.

3. Indifference. Proverbs 1:28,29: Then they will call upon me, but I will not answer; they will seek me diligently but will not find me. Because they hated knowledge and did not choose the fear of the Lord.

4. Neglect of mercy. Proverbs 21:13: He who closes his ear to the cry of the poor will himself cry out and not be heard.

5. Iniquity. Isaiah 59:2: But your iniquities have made a separation between you and your God, and your sins have hid his face from you so that he does not hear.

6. Instability. James 1:6 But let him ask in faith, with no doubting, for he who doubts is like a wave of the sea that is driven and tossed by the wind.

7. Self-indulgence. James 4:3: You ask and do not receive, because you ask wrongly, to spend it on your passions.

Were there space, we could continue the list. If you have aught against anyone, carry a grudge in your heart, your prayer cannot ascend to God's throne with such a weight. All these things the devil uses to keep us from knowing God's power in prayer. All manner of distractions he will put in our way to try to divert us. Even when we are on our knees, he does not give up, but puts inconsequential thoughts into our minds to pull them away from God. Prayer demands disciplining yourself.

PRAYER: *Lord, You have been my defense against the onslaughts of the evil one. Make me aware of his subtle maneuverings. So strengthen my prayer life, that my defense will be sure. In Jesus' name. Amen.*

THURSDAY

Sweet Hour of Prayer

Thy wings shall my petitions bear

Romans 8:26, 27

Likewise the Spirit helps us in our weakness; for we do not know how to pray as we ought, but the Spirit himself intercedes for us with sighs too deep for words. And he who searches the hearts of men knows what is the mind of the Spirit, because the Spirit intercedes for the saints according to the will of God.

IT IS interesting to read the witness about prayer that Christians have made through the ages. One says, "Prayer is the voice of faith"; in the Westminster Catechism we read: "Prayer is an offering up of our desires to God, for things agreeable to His will, in the name of Christ, with confession of our sins, and thankful acknowledgment of His mercies." Martin Luther's word is: "Prayer is a powerful thing; for God has bound and tied himself thereto." Phillips Brooks puts it in another way, "Prayer is not conquering God's reluctance but taking hold of God's willingness." Again, the latter preacher says: "A prayer in its simplest definition, is merely a wish turned heavenward." Which brings us to our lesson for today: The Spirit's intercession for us; praying in God's will. Of this fabric are the wings of prayer made.

As Protestants we are grateful that we need not go through a labyrinthian process to have access to the throne of grace. In the crucifixion the veil of the temple was rent, and henceforth every person is a priest before God. But with the gratitude for this freedom from intermediaries, there is a concomitant gratitude for the One who gives our prayers wings. Because He became man, He can interpret our frail desires to the Father. Christ ever lives to make intercession for us. How could we ever have known the wonderful Father heart of God, had it not been revealed in the divine visitation, Christ's coming to earth? So Christ, on our behalf, is the ladder whereby we may ascend to the throne of God. It is why so often we indicate this in words when we conclude our prayers with: "In Jesus' name." Here is the access to God's throne; here are the wings that send our petitions soaring heavenward.

So often we weight down our prayers with our worldly, selfish desires. If our prayers are to be given the lift of Christ, they must submit to the Gethsemane test. There must be in their content, "Thy will be done."

Think through your prayers. Is there in them such a trust in the love and wisdom of God that underneath every petition there is, the attitude, as a child so simply put it, "But You know what is best"? A sure indication of Christian maturity is less and less praying for things, and more and more praying to be in God's will in all that you do. This is to be working for the Master's degree in prayer.

PRAYER: *Thank You Christ, for translating our wishes into terms that are acceptable to the Father. Over the portal of our lives, Lord, we want to have inscribed: "God's will be done." Amen.*

Sweet Hour of Prayer

And since He bids me seek His face

Matthew 26:41

"Watch and pray that you may not enter into temptation; the spirit indeed is willing, but the flesh is weak."

John 16:23, 24

"Truly, truly I say to you, if you ask anything of the Father, he will give it to you in my name. Hitherto you have asked nothing in my name; ask, and you will receive, that your joy may be full."

THE ENTIRE Bible is the story of God's invitation to man to seek Him. It is notarized with the seal of the cross and the shed blood of His only begotten Son. The "comes" of the Bible very simply tell the story: "Come to the waters." "Come, let us return to the Lord." "Come to me, all who labor." "Come into him and eat with him." The yearning arms of the heavenly Father are extended in every page of the Book, for He wants each one to be saved. Yes, even in those pages of His wrath there is mercy in the awful justice.

When He came to earth in Christ, He showed us in human terms the extent and intent of His great invitation. The Gospels reiterate how Christ healed everyone who came to Him. How He loved the experience of those seeking Him.

The three "C's" that you find in the invitation are something of the progression there is in our experience with Him. "Call upon me," "Come to me," "Claim the promises"— this is what happens to anyone who accepts His invitation. "Lord, I believe; help thou my unbelief," may be the first call. The response to this in a person's life will bring about the coming to Him. Then, in the richness of this latter experience, there is the claiming of all the wonderful promises for life abundant and joys unspeakable.

There is a part of the prayer experience that we have not mentioned. This is the listening process. Prayer is a two-way conversation. It is talking to God, yes, but it is also listening to His response. Here is where many of us fail. We carry over into our conversation with God the habit that we exercise with people. We do most of the talking. I speak as one who knows this weakness. After I have been in a group, often I hang my head in shame with the realization that I have done most of the talking. How desperately we need to learn to listen; yes, to each other, and to God. Do you know the rich joy of being quiet before Him? His "still, small voice" is often drowned out with our much speaking. Turn to the Book, for that is His voice to man. Memorize passages, search His heart, and you will find that in the quietness of your prayer time He will be speaking to you.

PRAYER: *For Your supreme invitation, Lord, we thank You. We thank You for taking the initiative on our behalf. We thank You that You are a seeking, searching, saving God. Give us grace to be quiet in Your presence. Give us listening ears. Amen.*

Sweet Hour of Prayer

Believe His Word, and trust His grace

Mark 11:22-24

And Jesus answered them, "Have faith in God. Truly, I say to you, whoever says to this mountain, 'Be taken up and cast into the sea,' and does not doubt in his heart, but believes that what he says will come to pass, it will be done for him. Therefore I tell you, whatever you ask in prayer, believe that you receive it, and you will."

AS THIS week in the school of prayer comes to a close, we have in the words of the hymn the master key to unlock all doors: "Believe His Word, and trust His grace." It is by faith that we are saved; it is by faith that we walk; it is in faith that we pray; it is in faith that we look forward to another city. Faith and love beget hope; and these three are the great trinity for abundant living.

Faith and love are closely intertwined. It is faith in God's love that spells salvation. In this subject, what is your grade? Here is a commodity that has more power than dynamite, more than the atom. Our hearts are the manufacturing plants; our lives are the consumers. Prayer is an instrument used in the manufacturing process; the other indispensable one is the Bible. You are the manpower.

What is the quality of your faith, not to mention the quantity? Do you really believe the promises of the Lord? Do you live expectantly, knowing the answer will come? Does this faith reflect itself in your disposition, in your attitude to your family, in your relations with your neighbors, in your responsibility to the world?

A missionary had to deny a young convert's request to go back to school with her because there were insufficient funds. She told Keo to pray about it, and then started out on her journey alone. When she reached her home, she found in her mail the necessary ten dollars for Keo's maintenance. "Now Keo shall come to school," was her quick response, and she dispatched a man for the little orphan. Starting in the morning, he should be back at night, but at midday he returned and brought Keo with him. "How is this?" asked the missionary. "How could you be here this quickly?" "Oh, Keo will tell you," he replied. "Well teacher," said Keo, "you know you said we must pray. So I thought I would better be ready." She had walked halfway to meet the answer to her prayer. Keo believed His Word and trusted His grace.

Oh there is never sorrow of heart
That shall lack a timely end,
If but to God we turn, and ask
Of Him to be our friend!

William Wordsworth

PRAYER: *Every time, Lord, that we have trusted in You, our faith has been rewarded. Enlarge our faith, school us in prayer, teach us Your Word that our lives may have in them the breath of heaven. In Jesus' name. Amen.*

Break Thou the Bread of Life

Break Thou the Bread of Life

Then shall all bondage cease,
All fetters fall

Romans 8:14, 15, 21

For all who are led by the Spirit of God are sons of God. For you did not receive the spirit of slavery to fall back into fear, but you have received the spirit of sonship. . . . Because the creation itself will be set free from its bondage to decay and obtain the glorious liberty of the children of God.

THE GLORIOUS liberty of the children of God—what a gift! In the nation's capital we are very aware of the documents of freedom. The Magna Charta that set a pattern for our national documents finds its basis in the Christian concept of the worth of every individual; the Declaration of Independence and the Bill of Rights are based on the great democracy of God in which it is each one's inalienable right to life, liberty, and the pursuit of happiness. These precious historical documents are thoroughly guarded in the Archives Building. A sight-seer was riding in a taxicab past this building one day, and he read the inscription to be found there: "The past is prologue." He turned to the cabdriver and said, " 'The past is prologue.' What does that mean?" The cabdriver was quick with his reply: " 'The past is prologue.' . . . that's just government language. What it really means is 'You ain't seen nothing yet.' "

These man-made documents are great with their pronouncements of freedom and liberty, but where is there anything that can break the bonds and fetters like the Word of God? Here is the knife that cuts the ropes of sin that so quickly enslave!

"You ain't seen nothing yet" until you have seen how Christ can set a man free. Here is a man with a vile temper that makes him difficult to live with. Christ takes over that man's heart, and the temper is tamed by its new Master. Here is a young woman selfishly planning her own life, and petulant in the bondage of her own ego. She meets the Christ, and finds freedom from herself and the glorious release there is in serving Him.

In this month is the birthday of our foster daughter. I shall never forget when she first came to our home. When a young adolescent she had lost both father and mother. But the Lord did not forsake her, and the prayers of those parents were answered even after they had gone to their heavenly home. But the uncertainty of what might happen to her had bound this lovely young lady with fear. What a joy to see the bondage broken, and the sense and joy of security come just from being loved. And how she has blessed thousands of lives by passing this love on to others!

There is One who loved us so that He broke the enslavement of death and every fear that is its progeny. Through faith in Him, there is release for every captive soul.

PRAYER: *Often, Lord, we are slaves of our own making. There are habits that bind us; fears that fetter us. Come with the power of Your love this day, and set us free. In Jesus' name. Amen.*

Break Thou the Bread of Life

Dear Lord, to me

Deuteronomy 11:18, 19, 20

"You shall therefore lay up these words of mine in your heart and in your soul; and you shall bind them as a sign upon your hand, and they shall be as frontlets between your eyes. And you shall teach them to your children, talking of them when you are sitting in your house, and when you are walking by the way, and when you lie down, and when you rise. And you shall write them upon the doorposts of your house and upon your gates."

Jeremiah 15:16

Thy words were found, and I ate them, and thy words became to me a joy and the delight of my heart; for I am called by thy name, O Lord, God of Hosts.

IT IS not inappropriate, I think, to follow the school of prayer, with a school of the Word. People find the Bible difficult because they are not enough in prayer as they approach it, and conversely, people's prayers are ineffective, because they do not study the Word enough.

Our hymn was written by Mary Lathbury, who is sometimes called the "lyrist of Chautauqua," for she is the author of the famous Chautauqua hymn, "Day Is Dying in the West." This hymn, too, was written on the shores of beautiful Lake Chautauqua, and was called "A Study Song." It was written for the Chautauqua Literary and Scientific Circle, a group that promoted correspondence courses in the Bible and religious studies. Among its members, were many aged and shut-ins. On the shores of Lake Chautauqua the writer was reminded of the scene from the Gospels of Christ's breaking the bread to feed the multitude. So it is fitting that this hymn should be the framework for our consideration of the hungry souls in the world today, and the food which can satisfy their hunger.

The thing that we must first remember in our consideration of this spiritual food is that it is for us, personally. It is God's personal letter to you, as Dr. Kierkegaard has so simply stated. It must be read with the sense of this intimacy, if the reader is to derive nourishment from it.

Then if it is to become a part of your muscle and flesh and bone, it must be eaten, chewed and digested by you. Any amount of food that someone else eats, even though they may do it in your name, will not keep your body alive. Nor can your soul be kept alive vicariously. It is under this delusion that so many people have been laboring and starving. The Bread of Life must be broken to you, if you are to receive strength from it. The motto that a great philosopher took for his guidance in study is a good one: "Apply thyself wholly to the Scriptures and apply the Scriptures wholly to thyself."

PRAYER: *Lord, by the power of Your Holy Spirit, open up the truths of Scripture for each one of us. Help us to receive the truths personally from You. Help us to "eat them" so that they will become a part of us. In Jesus' name. Amen.*

TUESDAY

Break Thou the Bread of Life

As Thou didst break the loaves
Beside the sea

Matthew 14:17-19

They said to him, "We have only five loaves here and two fish." And he said, "Bring them here to me." Then he ordered the crowds to sit down on the grass; and taking the five loaves and the two fish he looked up to heaven, and blessed, and broke and gave the loaves to the disciples, and the disciples gave them to the crowds.

THE BIBLE is for you personally, and it is multiplied in your life as you share it. Notice in the account of the miracle of the loaves and the fishes that the Lord used the supplies that were on hand. So many people with a shrug of their shoulders, dismiss their reading of the Bible, because they say there are so many things that they do not understand. There are many things in their everyday living that they should eliminate, if they were to follow this same reasoning. Do you understand, and can you explain everything that you handle and use? Christ took what was at hand. Begin where you can understand, begin with the Gospels. If you want to make even these more understandable, read Dr. Phillips' modern translation. Reread them until the word is "near you, on your lips and in your heart." Along with them, as devotional background, read the Psalms. Memorize portions that seem to fit your need. "Hide the word in your heart." Have an attitude of expectancy. You are to have an audience with the King. Come to the experience with the determination to remember everything you can that He says.

During the day, recount what His conversation was. Then share some portion of it with somebody. As the disciples distributed the miraculous multiplication of the Lord, the increase went on and on. The more they shared, the more there was. Begin by taking some very small secton that has meant something to you. Then share this and witness to its effect on your day in the course of your conversation with a friend, the same way you would tell about something nice that a human friend had done for you. What a blessing you will be! Can you not hear this friend going to somebody else and saying, "Jane just told me something that was so very helpful. She said that, as she was reading her Bible today, she came across these words. . . ." Do you see how it would work?

Surely there may be those who will think you a bit queer at first. People do not like to be disturbed from a comfortable pattern; and the religion of Jesus Christ is anything but comfortable. But you will be a blessing in the lives of many, and maybe some heart that does not even know it is hungry will have an awakened appetite.

PRAYER: *Open up the truths of Your word for me in a new and living way, O Lord. Then give me grace to share these truths with others. In Jesus' name. Amen.*

Break Thou the Bread of Life

Beyond the sacred page
I seek Thee, Lord

John 20:31

But these are written that you may believe that Jesus is the Christ, the Son of God, and that believing you may have life in his name.

THERE ARE people who use the Bible in different ways. A Korean gambler bought a copy of the New Testament, thinking that if he sat on it, he would be sure to win. The first night he lost five dollars, and the second night, three dollars, so he decided that the doctrine must be against gambling.

In the Gospel of John we are told in simple terms what the purpose of scripture should be: "That you may believe that Jesus is the Christ, and . . . have life in his name." Every time, then, that you turn to the Scriptures, there should be this seeking for Him, and the resultant instructions for walking His way.

As you become more schooled in Scripture, and learn how to use a concordance, a whole new adventure in learning awaits you. To be able to trace through the Old Testament the prophecies concerning Christ, His birth, His life, and His death, is to find the crimson thread that ties all the books together. To study the history of the Jewish people, as they kept their covenant with God, and as they broke it, and then through the Epistles to learn that we become "children of Abraham and of the promise" through faith in Jesus Christ, is to read the biography of the human race. Are you familiar with Dr. Phillips translation of these Epistles, called *Letters to Young Churches*? Here again is a modern tool to help reveal, in language that is yours, the Christ of whom the apostle wrote, "For to me to live is Christ."

Perhaps you have thought that it is confusing that we speak of Christ as the "Bread of Life," and use the same term for Scripture. But this is as it should be, for these are they which reveal Him. The same interchange is used in the Bible with "the Word."

A father brought home to his family a jigsaw puzzle of the United States. He was amazed at the speed with which the children had put it together. Then they showed him the secret. On the other side of the map was a picture of George Washington. It had been very simple to fit this image together. Turning the puzzle over, they had a map of the United States.

The Bible may seem to one who gives it but a cursory glance to be a conglomerate mixture of poetry and prose, of history and exposition. But go to it seeking the Savior, and you will find the pieces remarkably put together.

PRAYER: *In our search of Scripture, Lord, we would find the revelation of You. Open up the pages to us, and make our hearts ready to receive. In Jesus' name. Amen.*

...k Thou the Bread of Life

My spirit pants for Thee,
O living Word

...ays are coming," says the Lord God, "when I will send a ...d; not a famine of bread, nor a thirst for water, but of ... of the Lord."

...k the Lord for his steadfast love, for his wonderful works ...n! For he satisfies him who is thirsty, and the hungry he ...ngs.

...a man's heart for God is as old as the human race. It ...In every tribe, in every nation, there is ...ce of yearning. In our civilized world, ...neer of secular culture, and the pride of ...ances of life break through this hard ...nting for that which will satisfy. Would ... to the Bread of Life? To open up for ...at I know. I have found my own words ...pirit in God's Word that gives it power. ...g told the story of a man who went to ...vey of the Holy Land. He was a noted ...Testament with him, not because he be...se he believed that it would help him to ...ly Land. While seated on the hillside one ...and, and his eye fell upon the margin referring hi... Psalm and the fifty-third chapter of Isaiah. He re... ...tead of finding out the geography of the Holy Land ...n Sea, he found the holy land of the eternal city, an... ...eatest converts to the true faith among the Jews. He ...eaching the Gospel of Jesus Christ,

If we ...earching the Scriptures, for in them we have eter... ... say that just the mechanical reading is enough. ... to his pastor that he had "gone through" the Bible ...ificantly the pastor said, "The important question i... ...ow many times have you gone through the Bible?' as... the Bible gone through you?' "

For ... ...nest there are so many helps today. There are Bible ... up methods, and there are correspondence Bible cou... thing, too, when friends get together and read the ... our women's groups, some of the very happiest tim... ...een doing just this.

PRAYER: *Why is it, Lord, that the opportunity that is so readily available we so often scorn? Forgive our stubborn obstinacy and our pride. Help us to be true seekers and finders. In Jesus' name. Amen.*

COMES THE DAWN
After a while you learn the subtle difference
Between holding a hand and chaining a soul,
And you learn that love doesn't mean security,
And you begin to learn that kisses aren't contracts
[illegible] aren't promises
And you begin to accept your defeats
With your head up and your eyes open,
With the grace of a woman, not the grief of a child,
And you learn to build all your roads
On today because tomorrow's ground
Is too uncertain. And futures have
A way of falling down in mid-flight,
After a while you learn that even sunshine burns if you get too much.
So you plant your own garden and decorate your own soul, instead of waiting
For someone to bring you flowers.
And you learn that you really can endure . . .
That you really are strong,
And you really do have worth
And you learn and learn
With every goodbye you learn.

Break Thou the Bread of Life

O send Thy Spirit,
Lord, now unto me,
That He may touch my eyes,
And make me see

Luke 24:25, 26, 30, 31, 38, 45-47

And he said to them, "O foolish men, and slow of heart to believe all that the prophets have spoken! Was it not necessary that the Christ should suffer these things and enter into his glory?" . . . When he was at table with them, he took the bread and blessed, and broke it, and gave it to them. And their eyes were opened and they recognized him; and he vanished out of their sight. . . . And he said to them. "Why are you troubled, and why do questionings arise in your hearts?" . . . Then he opened their minds to understand the scriptures, and said to them, "Thus it is written, that the Christ should suffer and on the third day rise from the dead, and that repentance and forgiveness of sins should be preached in his name to all nations, beginning from Jerusalem."

THE EMMAUS story is a beautiful one, for it meets every seeking soul at his place of doubt, and opens a window through which he may see. We rode on the highway that we were told followed the path that Christ and His disciples took on that memorable post-resurrection day. We were carried along speedily in a modern automobile, but even so we passed a man and a woman on donkeys and a caravan of camels with their load. It was not hard to forget the winged mechanism we were in, and be transported to the walk that resulted in eyes opened.

Notice that Christ joined the group when they were talking about Him. To be sure, their talk was unenlightened, but their spirits were open, and so He was with them. This is true wherever there are honest seekers. As a church we have often been harsh and dictatorial in our attitudes to those who are "slow of heart to believe." Our Christ patiently reviewed for them all those things that pointed to who He is.

It is significant to me, too, that it was in the breaking of bread that His identity came into its clear focus. He shares himself with us, as we invite His participation in our everyday lives. In the humblest of duties about the house, I can know His companionship and often when I'm doing some very menial task some new light will come.

Dr. J. R. Miller tells the story of a young lady who purchased a book and read a few pages, yet failed to become interested in it. Some months afterward, she met the author. They became interested in each other, and their friendship ripened into love, leading to marriage. Then the book was no longer dull. Every sentence had a charm for her heart.

PRAYER: *Thank You, Lord, for the revelation that Your Spirit has made to us as we have broken bread with You. There are no limitations to the Holy Spirit, so we pray that this day we may be the means of witnessing to Your presence. Help us to begin in whatever circumstances we find ourselves. In Jesus' name. Amen.*

SATURDAY

Break Thou the Bread of Life

And I shall find my peace,
My all in all

Romans 5:1-5

Therefore, since we are justified by faith, we have peace with God through our Lord Jesus Christ. Through him we have obtained access to this grace in which we stand, and we rejoice in our hope of sharing the glory of God. More than that, we rejoice in our sufferings, knowing that suffering produces endurance, and endurance produces character, and character produces hope, and hope does not disappoint us, because God's love has been poured into our hearts through the Holy Spirit which has been given to us.

IN THE same classroom with the same teacher, there can be two people who will react in completely different ways. One will have a learning experience and be enriched and edified by the course; the other one will be bored and disgruntled and have wasted his time. What is the reason? Basically it is the difference in the attitude in which these persons come into the classroom. In the one, there was the attitude almost of: "I dare you to try to teach me anything!" In the other, the spirit was "This is going to be fun. I think that I am going to enjoy this!" In one instance, the fist was clenched; in the other, the palm was open.

Two people can go to the Bible and have opposite reactions. The one will find peace; the other, problems. The one will be open to the Holy Spirit's working; the other will refuse to respond to the knocking at the door. Amos R. Wells put this experience into a modern parable: "There was once a very foolish wise man who received a letter. He began at once to study it in this way. He measured it accurately; he examined it with a microscope to see the fiber the paper was made of; he analyzed the ink, and the mucilage which was on the flap; he gauged the average slant of the letters. While doing so, a friend came in and glancing at the letter he said, 'Why, that letter is from your father.' 'Is it?' asked the foolish wise man, 'I have not got far enough yet to find out.' "

The peace that is the gift the Bible gives does not depend upon mechanical armaments, or one's own ingenuity, and therefore it is not variable. It is of God, His gift to men of faith. It is free, because once and for all the purchase price was made in the life and the death of His only begotten Son. It is a gift for anyone who will come expecting to receive it; it has a totality about it that is "all in all."

Here again is the place where many wayfarers are deterred. They are unwilling to go all the way. No one will really know the fruits of faith: peace, joy, hope, love, unless there is complete capitulation of himself into the heart of God. To every hungry soul the Bread is there for the taking.

PRAYER: *We thank You, Lord, for the peace that is our joy in Your presence. We thank You that You are truly the Bread of Life, and that the cupboard of Your Book is full. Help us daily to nourish our souls, and to share with others. In Jesus' name. Amen.*

Jesus, Name All Names Above

To my sister Ruth

THEOCTISTUS of the Stadium (b. about 890) — CARL R. YOUNGDAHL

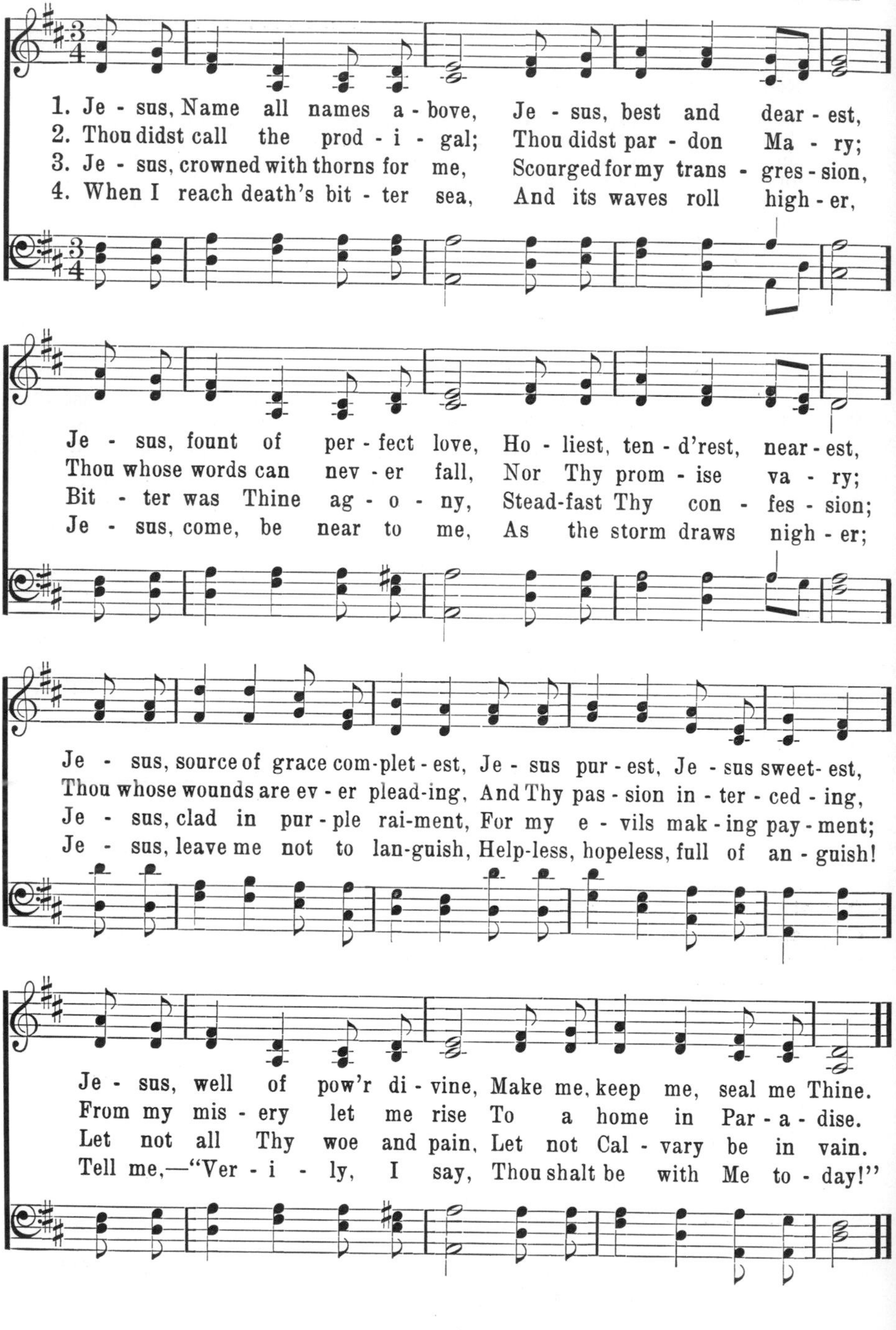

1. Je - sus, Name all names a - bove, Je - sus, best and dear - est,
2. Thou didst call the prod - i - gal; Thou didst par - don Ma - ry;
3. Je - sus, crowned with thorns for me, Scourged for my trans - gres - sion,
4. When I reach death's bit - ter sea, And its waves roll high - er,

Je - sus, fount of per - fect love, Ho - liest, ten - d'rest, near - est,
Thou whose words can nev - er fall, Nor Thy prom - ise va - ry;
Bit - ter was Thine ag - o - ny, Stead-fast Thy con - fes - sion;
Je - sus, come, be near to me, As the storm draws nigh - er;

Je - sus, source of grace com-plet - est, Je - sus pur - est, Je - sus sweet- est,
Thou whose wounds are ev - er plead-ing, And Thy pas - sion in - ter - ced - ing,
Je - sus, clad in pur - ple rai-ment, For my e - vils mak - ing pay - ment;
Je - sus, leave me not to lan-guish, Help-less, hopeless, full of an - guish!

Je - sus, well of pow'r di - vine, Make me, keep me, seal me Thine.
From my mis - ery let me rise To a home in Par - a - dise.
Let not all Thy woe and pain, Let not Cal - vary be in vain.
Tell me,—"Ver - i - ly, I say, Thou shalt be with Me to - day!"

SUNDAY

Jesus, Name All Names Above

Jesus, best and dearest

Acts 4:10-12

"Be it known to you all, and to all the people of Israel, that by the name of Jesus Christ of Nazareth, whom you crucified, whom God raised from the dead, by him this man is standing before you well. This is the stone which was rejected by you builders, but which has become the head of the corner. And there is salvation in no one else, for there is no other name under heaven given among men by which we must be saved."

TO MOST of you this hymn may be new and unfamiliar. I hope that you will be adventuresome enough to learn it. You will be well repaid. The basic content of the words comes to us from way back in the ninth century. Nothing is known of the writer, Theoctistus, except his devotion to the cross of Christ as signalized in his "Suppliant Canon to Jesus." From this Dr. Neale has made one of the most beautiful hymns of adoration in existence. Read it through, thoughtfully, and you will have such a sense of worship as to make you feel that you have truly been in the presence of the Lord. It is an added enrichment to me that my brother has written the musical setting for this hymn.

What does the name Jesus mean to you?

The Bible's variation on the name is amazing. There is one for almost every letter in the alphabet, and for some letters there are many. In 1 Corinthians 15:45, Jesus is spoken of as "the last Adam"; in 4 John 2:1, He is called "Advocate." Revelation 1:8 uses "Almighty," and also, "Alpha and Omega"; Revelation 3:14 calls Him the "Amen"; In Hebrews, He is spoken of as "the apostle and high priest of our profession"; In Isaiah as "the arm of the Lord." Again Hebrews uses the term, "pioneer and perfecter of our faith" and, "source of eternal salvation." Yes, in the name, Jesus, there is a wealth of meaning! But the really important consideration is, What does it mean to you?

To the man whose healing had caused such a furor, as related in our Scripture passage today, the Name meant that, lame though he had been those many years, now he could walk; that though he had been sick, now he was well. To the Jews who were hard of heart to believe, it was the stone which the builders rejected, which had now become the head of the corner. In a book, above an altar, on a sign, or in symbol, the Name may not mean anything to you. What is really basic is, "Is it written in your heart?" "There is no other name under heaven given among men by which we must be saved."

PRAYER: *Jesus Christ, Your name is life to me. You are the Author and Finisher of salvation. Let Your Name, written in my heart, transform my living today. Amen.*

MONDAY

Jesus, Name All Names Above

. . . Fount of perfect love

Psalm 36:9

For with thee is the fountain of life; in thy light do we see light.

Proverbs 14:27

The fear of the Lord is a fountain of life, that one may avoid the snares of death.

Jeremiah 2:13

"For my people have committed two evils: they have forsaken me, the fountain of living waters, and hewn out cisterns for themselves, broken cisterns, that can hold no water."

THAT THE writers of Scripture should have used the figures of speech of both fountains and cistern is readily understandable when one is aware of how dependent they were for these sources of water supply. Fountain and spring are used interchangeably, and refer to the running water which supplied the reserve that the cisterns held. In Psalm 87:7 we read "All my fountains are in thee" (R.S.V. uses the word "springs"). All over Palestine and Lebanon, there are gushing springs, many of which merge to form the sources of the principal rivers. They are a fulfillment of God's promise to Israel recorded in Deuteronomy 8:7, that He would bring them into a land not only of waterbrooks, but of fountains and springs, flowing in valleys and hills. Several of the cities had the word"en" or "ain," meaning "spring" added to their name.

Even today the average village in the Bible lands depends upon the public fountain for its water supply. It was quite an experience to pause by the fountain in Nazareth and watch the women and children come to the watering place to fill their various containers. It was not difficult to turn the pages of history back and see Mary, good housewife and mother that she was, come to fetch for her family the water that is so essential to life. Outside of Jericho we watched the stream of people as they came to and from the well.

Remembering, then, the lifeline that these fountains were to the people of Israel, what this name means in reference to Jesus is clear. He is essential for living!

In the Book of Jeremiah the writer bewails the fact that the people have forsaken God, the fountain of living water, and hewn themselves cisterns, broken cisterns that can hold no water. What a picture of the resources of today's world! And how many people have not spent their lives in the building of broken cisterns! There seems to be a mad rush for wealth, and comfort, and power.

In Christ the hymn writer finds the fount of perfect love.

PRAYER: *There are days, Lord, when life seems to be a "dry and thirsty land." As I drink from the Fountain of Life, and find my thirst quenched, help me to bring others to the Source of Living Water. In Jesus' name. Amen.*

Jesus, Name All Names Above

Well of pow'r divine

John 4:6-15

Jacob's well was there, and so Jesus, wearied as he was with his journey, sat down beside the well. It was about the sixth hour.

There came a woman of Samaria to draw water. Jesus said to her, "Give me a drink." For his disciples had gone away into the city to buy food. The Samaritan woman said to him, "How is it that you, a Jew, ask a drink of me, a woman of Samaria?" For Jews have no dealings with Samaritans. Jesus answered her, "If you knew the gift of God, and who it is that is saying to you, 'Give me a drink,' you would have asked him, and he would have given you living water." The woman said unto him, "Sir, you have nothing to draw with, and the well is deep; where do you get that living water?" . . . Jesus said to her, "Every one who drinks of this water will thirst again, but whoever drinks of the water that I shall give him will become in him a spring of water welling up to eternal life." The woman said to him, "Sir, give me this water, that I may not thirst, nor come here to draw."

IN THE religious and cultural history of Israel wells, or man-curbed springs, have played an important and picturesque role. The digging of a new one was occasion for community singing. In the reclaiming of Israel today, this same tradition has been followed. Then as now, life and comfort depended upon water. Therefore the water supply was always a focal point of contention for competing tribes. (How true that is in the Arab-Israel controversy today!) The oldest water-right contract in the Bible is the covenant of Beersheba between Abraham and Abimelech. Beer means a well, and the name Beersheba, means well of the Oath.

Romance flourished by wells in Bible times. Here Rachel first met Jacob when he "rolled the stone from the well's mouth," and helped her to water Laban's flock. In the courtship of Isaac and Rebekah a well figured prominently.

In our hymn we have the term "Well of power divine." Again the figure calls to mind the fact that Jesus is life; that in Him is the power for this earth and for the life to come. But people have been known to have resources within reach, and yet to have died of thirst. Two things are essential: first, that we know where the source of supply is, and second, that we go to it to draw. A well can produce life-giving water endlessly and help no one, if its supply is not tapped.

A street corner preacher was being heckled by a bystander with the taunt: "This Christ you preach has been talked about for over 1900 years, and look at the wickedness in the world!" The preacher's quick and pertinent retort was: "There's plenty of water available in this city, but look how dirty your face is!"

PRAYER: *Well of living water, fount of perfect love— these, and more, are You, Lord, to our souls. Help us to drink deeply each day, and thereby know the strength that flows on into eternal life. Fill us with Your power. In Jesus' name. Amen.*

Jesus, Name All Names Above

Thou didst call the prodigal

Luke 15:18-24

"'I will arise and go to my father, and I will say to him, "Father, I have sinned against heaven and before you; I am no more worthy to be called your son; treat me as one of your hired servants."' And he arose and came to his father. But while he was yet at a distance, his father saw him and had compassion, and ran and embraced him and kissed him. The son said to him, 'Father, I have sinned against heaven and before you; I am no longer worthy to be called your son.' But the father said to his servants, 'Bring quickly the best robe, and put it on him; and put a ring on his hand, and shoes on his feet; and bring the fatted calf and kill it, and let us eat and make merry; for this my son was dead, and is alive again; he was lost, and is found.'"

THE STORY told of the Prodigal gives this "Name all names above" a new luster, a new beauty. You recall the beginning of the story. The son came to the father to ask for his inheritance, because he wanted to live his own life; he wanted to be free to taste what the world had to offer. When his money was gone, and he was friendless, he determined to seek his father's house again, and ask if he might just be a servant. Then we have the glorious portion that we have quoted, revealing the father heart of God, adding the gift of overwhelming forgiveness to those already contained in that wonderful name. It is as if every time you speak His name, all of these remembrances are blended.

The story of the Prodigal is a story of ruin and reconciliation. A Bible student has devised seven downward steps and seven upward steps, as the story unfolds itself. The steps downward as listed are: self-will, selfishness, separation, sensuality, spiritual destitution, self-abasement, starvation. The upward climb begins with realization, resolution, repentance, return, reconciliation, reclothing, rejoicing. Christ pictures the father placing the ring of reconciliation on the hand of the returning son.

In the name of Jesus, then, there is included all that would make such a reconciliation possible. The father heart as revealed on the cross; the heart that even in agony prayed for its enemies; the heart that showed concern for a penitent thief; that made provisions for a mother. What a name to have included in it the connotations of "Judge of Israel" and "Savior"; of "Almighty" and "Redeemer"; of "King of kings" and "Lamb of God"; "Nazarene" and "Prince of Peace"; of "Man of Sorrows," and "Light of the World." The One about whom all this, and much more, can be said is pictured as the father who ran to meet his renegade son, who opened wide his arms to receive him, who called for the feast at the return of the son, and placed the ring on his finger. For each of us there are the open arms of God.

PRAYER: *The wonder of Your forgiving heart, Lord, makes us bow in adoration. We thank You for this gift that is included in the Name we love. Amen.*

Jesus, Name All Names Above

Thou didst pardon Mary

Luke 8:1, 2

And the twelve were with him, and also some women who had been healed of evil spirits and infirmities: Mary, called Magdalene, from whom seven demons had gone out.

John 20:1, 16, 18

Now on the first day of the week Mary Magdalene came to the tomb early, while it was still dark, and saw that the stone had been taken away from the tomb. . . . Jesus said to her, "Mary." She turned and said to him, "Rabboni!" (which in Hebrew means Teacher). . . . Mary Magdalene went and said to the disciples, "I have seen the Lord"; and she told them that he had said these things to her.

THIS, THEN, is the known biography of Mary of Magdala. It is often assumed that she was a woman who had lived in sin before she met the Lord. However, the Bible statement is that she was "possessed of seven demons." Be that as it may, what the Lord did for her was so wonderful that the remainder of her days was spent in serving and following Him. She was the recipient of a great salvation, so she evidenced a great gratitude. This was coupled by a loyalty that took her even to the foot of the cross, and by a hope that brought her to the tomb when all seemed lost. She was the one to whom the Lord first appeared after the resurrection.

In the story of this meeting, perhaps nothing is more significant to her than His calling her by name. To her was given the revelation of this great victory, and hers was the joy of bringing word of it to the disciples. What a message to carry! "Have you heard that Jesus is not dead? He is risen; I have spoken to Him."

A little boy was asked to give a definition of forgiveness. The one he gave is classic: "It is the scent that flowers give when they are trampled on." This is the kind of forgiveness from God that is embodied in Christ's death.

But you cannot just be a recipient of this great gift, and do nothing about it. Included in the Lord's Prayer is a very telling petition: "Forgive us our trespasses, as we forgive those who trespass against us." There is a charming old legend which says that the angel of mercy was sent to a saint to tell him that he must start for the Celestial City. On his way up, he became perturbed by his sins and said to the angel, "Mercy, where did you bury my sins?" "I only remember I buried them," was the reply, "but I cannot tell you where. As for the Father, He has forgotten that you ever sinned."

PRAYER: *Lord, like Mary, we are indebted to you for a new beginning, for a new life. Each morning Your mercies are new; each day Your love is sufficient. We thank You. Help us to carry no resentment or ill will in our hearts. Help us to reflect Your great heart of love. In Jesus' name. Amen.*

Jesus, Name All Names Above

Jesus, clad in purple raiment
For my evils making payment

Jeremiah 23:5, 6

"Behold, the days are coming, says the Lord, when I will raise up for David a righteous Branch, and he shall reign as king and deal wisely, and shall execute justice and righteousness in the land. In his days Judah will be saved, and Israel will dwell securely. And this is the name by which he will be called: 'The Lord is our righteousness.' "

John 1:49

Nathanael said to him, "Rabbi, you are the Son of God! You are the King of Israel!"

WE NEED in our acts of worship to pause and remember who Jesus is. A never-failing friend, yes; a companion on life's way; an elder brother and Redeemer; yes, but He is also King. The symbol of the purple robe that was ironically put on His shoulders at the cross, and the sign above that crude throne, "Jesus of Nazareth, the King of the Jews" are not things that just happened. When Pilate put to Christ the question, "So you are a king?" Jesus answered in the affirmative in no uncertain terms. Then He explained that His kingdom was not of this world. "And this is the name by which he will be called: 'The Lord is our righteousness.' " That was the prophecy, and of Him, Pilate the judge had to say, "I find no fault in him."

If His kingdom is not of this world, where is it that Christ reigns? A portion of that kingdom is within you, within me. He wants to be King of our hearts. And even as "He must reign until he has put all enemies under his feet," so in your heart, He keeps calling for a total commitment, for a complete yielding to His rule. How we are wont to withhold, to keep some little area for our own selfish purposes! Is it a peeve, or a grudge, or a resentment, or a desire, or an ambition? Is it a prejudice, or a willfulness, or some other sin? The "name which is above every name" takes on new power when it is permitted to take over a new territory. It has a right to the total, for that was the kind of ransom that was paid.

Those who have submitted to this reign have known glorious living. On one of the islands of the Samoan group, a king, some years ago, had to make a choice. He was a good deacon in the church when he was chosen to be chief. There were those who doubted the wisdom of a man's holding the two offices, so the missionary went to him and asked him, "Which do you prefer to be, king or deacon?" "To be deacon" was the immediate response. "But, if you must give up one or the other, which will you do?" "I will at once cease to be king."

Are you choosing to serve the King? Today?

PRAYER: *That our best Friend can also be the King of kings is one of these unfathomable things to us, Lord. Help us never to forget that You are Lord Jesus, and as such should be Lord of our lives. Remove what is unworthy in one of Your followers. Amen.*

SATURDAY

Jesus, Name All Names Above

Jesus, come, be near to me,
As the storm draws nigher

Psalm 103:11, 12

For as the heavens are high above the earth,
so great is his steadfast love toward those who fear him;
as far as the east is from the west,
so far does he remove our transgressions from us.

DESTRUCTIVE STORMS in the Bible follow man's willful disobedience of God. The storm that reigned for forty days and forty nights when only Noah and his family were preserved was the result of debauchery and sin and ignoring the laws and love of God. Every time that I see a rainbow, I am grateful of the reminder that it is a symbol of God's faithfulness in keeping His promise never to send another flood like that one. The storm that swept over Sodom and Gomorrah, raining fire and brimstone was a judgment of the wickedness and rebellion against God of the inhabitants of those cities. The Lord commanded Moses to call for hail to destroy the crops of Egypt, when Pharaoh would not let the children of Israel go.

The song writer must have felt that the day in which he was living was a stormy time. Possibly in his own life, too, there was turbulence and disruption. Whether we are thinking of the gathering storms about us in the world picture, or the sinister events that sometimes overtake us in our personal lives, there is a Name that is like a rock; there is a Name to which we may cling and know a sure refuge. Frances Ridley Havergal has simply and beautifully expressed it in poetry:

Thy Presence

Thou layest Thy hand on the fluttering heart
And sayest, "Be still!"
The shadow and silence are only a part
Of Thy sweet will.
Thy Presence is with me, and where Thou art
I fear no ill.

Every soul has its stormy times; in every life there are the winds of adversity. Whoever draws near to the Savior knows an anchor that will hold. Here is a prize that is priceless.

Of all the prizes
That earth can give,
This is the best:
To find Thee, Lord,
A living Presence near
And in Thee rest.
Author unknown

PRAYER: *Ruler over wind and wave, help me always to find my peace and calm in Your presence. In Your name. Amen.*

In Christ There Is No East or West

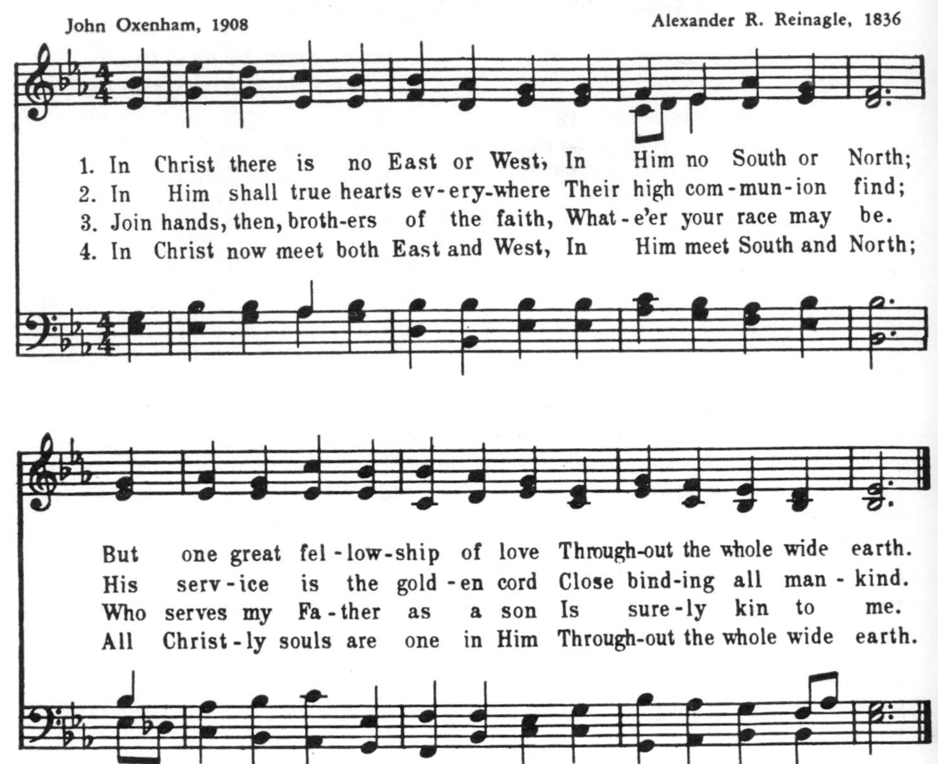

SUNDAY

In Christ There Is No East or West

In Him, no south or north

Matthew 12:46-50

While he was still speaking to the people, behold, his mother and his brothers stood outside, asking to speak to him. But he replied to the man who told him, "Who is my mother, and who are my brothers?" And stretching out his hand toward his disciples, he said, "Here are my mother and my brothers! For whoever does the will of my Father in heaven is my brother, and sister, and mother."

THE DISUNITY of the Christian church is one of the sins that we are going to have to be accountable for to God. If we are all saints and members of the household of God, how can we justify our rivalry, our smug pride, each in his own denomination. Dr. Phillips tries to diagnose the ineffectiveness of the Church today as compared with the Church of the first century. He speaks of "our sinful complacency over a divided church." One thing is sure: In Christ there is no east or west.

Every year as I kneel to participate of the body and blood of Christ on World Communion Sunday, I am electrified by the awareness of Christians together around the world. A couple of years ago in our Church in Washington, we had a real sense of how world-wide was this experience, because at our altar that day there knelt people of the yellow race, of the Negro race, and of the white race; people from South America, from Europe, from the Middle East, and the Far East, and from most of the states in our union.

Each person kneeling at that communion table was a sinner, acknowledging his sin before God and asking for forgiveness. No one had any priorities. We were all cleansed in the same way. When will we who claim to be members of His body get His point of view? It is tragic that in areas of the world where tensions are smoldering to the point of explosion any moment, there are those in leadership who call themselves Christian, but who seem to be the tools of the devil when it comes to race relations.

It is a sobering thing in our own United States to know that there are enough people on the church books, and to spare, to change the whole climate of racial tensions, were they courageous enough to stand up and be counted, courageous enough to go to God's Word and find out what the pattern of Christ is, and then dare to do it, believing that He who gives the command will also give the enabling. This could be America's greatest hour, if Christians, north and south, would join in prayer that they might know the will of God in relation to their attitude toward their fellow men. Whoever might be reading this word, will you pray about that today? As a Christian, will you not join me in prayer for God's will? Do you dare ask Him to begin with you?

PRAYER: *God of all people, Savior of all mankind, forgive our pride and stupid separation. Raise up courageous men and women of faith everywhere, who will witness to Your pattern of one family. In Your name. Amen.*

In Christ There Is No East or West

But one great fellowship of love
Throughout the whole wide earth

1 Corinthians 1:10, 12, 13

I appeal to you, brethren, by the name of our Lord Jesus Christ, that all of you agree that there be no dissensions among you, but that you be united in the same mind and the same judgment. . . . What I mean is that each one of you says "I belong to Paul," or "I belong to Apollos," or "I belong to Cephas," or "I belong to Christ." Is Christ divided? Was Paul crucified for you? Or were you baptized in the name of Paul?

1 John 1:7

If we walk in the light, as he is in the light, we have fellowship with one another, and the blood of Jesus his Son cleanses us from all sin.

PAUL'S DISSERTATION in his Letter to the Corinthians could so easily be paraphrased to fit our modern situation. There have been churches where the people's loyalty to the pastor as a person has superseded their loyalty to Christ. Are you one of these people who dote on a certain preacher, and find it very difficult to take another man's presentation? Do you not know that the Lord uses various vessels?

The plea that the apostle makes surely is the plea that our Lord also makes: that we be united in the same mind and the same judgment. If we turn to Christ as our final authority, how can it be otherwise?

Dr. Oxenham, the writer of this hymn, voiced a universal faith, a glowing ideal for the world to see and pursue. It is in diametric contrast to Kipling's words: "Oh, East is East and West is West, and never the twain shall meet." As Christians we dare to work for the fellowship in Christ that knows no barrier; a fellowship that is a foretaste of how we shall dwell in the home that Christ has gone to prepare.

There is told the story that John Wesley had a vision. In this imaginary world, he found himself at the gates of hell. He knocked and asked who were within. "Are there any Roman Catholics here?" he asked. "Yes," was the answer. "Any Church of England people?" and again the answer was "Yes." "Are there any Presbyterians?" he asked. "Yes, a number." "Are there any Wesleyans here?" "Yes, we have some of those, too," came the answer. Disappointed and dismayed, especially by the last reply, he turned his steps heavenward. Here he repeated the same questions. But here, in each instance the answer was "No." In desperation then he asked, "Whom do you have here?" "We know nothing here of any of the names that you have mentioned," the angel replied. "They are all Christians here —born-again people. Of these we have a great multitude which no man can number, gathered out of all nations and kindreds and peoples and tongues."

PRAYER: *Forgive us, Lord, for the man-made barriers and divisions which are such a poor witness to our fellowship in You. Draw us each closer to Your heart and then we will be together. In Jesus' name. Amen.*

In Christ There Is No East or West

In Him shall true hearts everywhere
Their high communion find

Psalm 119: 63, 64

I am a companion of all who fear thee, of those who keep thy precepts. The earth, O Lord, is full of thy steadfast love; teach me thy statutes!

IN THESE lines of this hymn is the key to real Christian unity. As we are one in Christ, we must fellowship one with another. There are no segregated areas in the heart of Christ.

I like the thought suggested in Psalm 34. The Christian fellowship is the fellowship of the brokenhearted and those of a contrite spirit. It is the fellowship of the forgiven. Anyone who has really known the conviction of sin, and then has known the wonderful release and empowering that there is in Christ, becomes a part of this fellowship. And even as in the organization of Alcoholics Anonymous, the brotherhood is strongly bound together by a common need.

Here there is no mention of economic status. A soul has no color, except that it be crimson or white, depending upon whether or not it is pre- or post-cleansing. There is no language barrier, because the language of the heart—tears and laughter, compassion and love—is the same in any nation. The psalmist puts it well when he says: "I am a companion of all that fear thee!"

Friend, if in your heart there is anything of hatred or ill will or resentment or superiority or building a fence around you and your kind, you had better examine your relationship with the Lord. When He died on Calvary, a Savior for sinners, He broke down all barriers between man and God, and man and man.

Those who know this fellowship in Him know what other people are missing. I love my people and my heritage. But the enrichment I have known in communion with God's people from my own city who do not have the same background as I, as well as with the Christians from around the world, has been priceless. When I meet a group of strangers, and we share our love of Christ and our concern for the work of His kingdom, immediately we are one; and when I have to leave them, I feel as if I am parting from a part of my family. It does not make an ounce of difference whether they are blond Scandinavians, or beautiful brown eyed orientals; it is basically inconsequential whether their hair is straight or curly, or their skin brown or beige, when we meet at the throne of God in prayer. When we share the fellowship that we know in Him, we are one family.

PRAYER: *You know, Lord, how full of divisions the world is; you know the man-made barriers that wall us from each other. O great heart of Love, make our concern drawing near to Your heart, and there find our brothers. In Jesus' name. Amen.*

In Christ There Is No East or West

His service is the golden key
Close-binding all mankind

1 Corinthians 3:9

For we are fellow workmen for God; you are God's field, God's building.

Mark 10:42-45

And Jesus called them to him and said to them, "You know that those who are supposed to rule over the Gentiles lord it over them, and their great men exercise authority over them. But it shall not be so among you; but whoever would be great among you must be your servant, and whoever would be first among you must be slave of all. For the Son of man also came not to be served but to serve, and to give his life a ransom for many."

HAVE YOU never said, "Well, I really didn't get to know her until I started working with her"? Following yesterday's thinking about being in the heart of Christ together, we have this follow up. How did Christ say we were to serve Him? If there is anything that He made very clear, it is this, that in serving the needs of our fellow men, we are serving Him. We quote so glibly the "inasmuch," and then we walk out of the way to avoid those across the tracks, and we shrug our shoulders of any responsibility for them. I have heard Christian people say of unfortunates, "Well, their trouble is of their own making. Now they will have to take the consequences. They are not my responsibility!" Are they not, though? If this had been the attitude of God toward our sin, where would we be?

As we serve the Lord, we lose our own identity in His, and so this togetherness is a natural consequence. Ernestus, Duke of Luneburg, caused a burning lamp to be stamped on his coin, with the initials, A.S.M.C., by which is meant, Aliis Serviens Meipsum Contero (By giving light to others, I consume myself). Observe candles burning. Is their light dependent upon the color of the wax, or the height of the candle, or on whether or not they are new or old, fancy or plain?

Dr. E. Stanley Jones tells the story of a North Dakota farmer whose little five-year-old daughter became lost in a grain field. Frantically everyone set about searching for her. The field stretched over many acres, and hour after hour passed, going into the long hours of the night. Finally one of the neighbors said, "You know some of us find ourselves covering the same territory. Why don't we join hands and make a human rake. Then we won't miss any section." They followed his suggestion, and in a little while, a part of the "rake" came across the little prostrate form. But it was too late. The little girl had died of exhaustion and fright. Mournfully, the father said, "Why didn't we join hands sooner!"

PRAYER: *There is so much that we need to do together, Lord, and the world is so full of need! Give us the joyous fellowship of working shoulder to shoulder with Christians everywhere, in order to show Your love to all mankind. In Jesus' name. Amen.*

In Christ There Is No East or West

**Join hands, then, brothers of the faith,
Whate'er your race may be**

Ephesians 4:11-13

And his gifts were that some should be apostles, some prophets, some evangelists, some pastors and teachers, for the equipment of the saints, for the work of ministry, for building up the body of Christ, until we all attain to the unity of the faith and of the knowledge of the Son of God.

THIS IS a timely word from the apostle to the Christian Church today. As the writer of this great ecumenical book, Ephesians, tells us so well, we all have different gifts; God calls us each to use whatever gifts He has given us for one purpose. I am grateful for this diversity of gifts. I love song, but if everybody were a soloist, I have an idea that I would get pretty fed up on singing. Always I have wished that God might have given me a voice to raise in song for Him; yet what I need to do is to take inventory of the gifts with which He has endowed me, and put them to use for Him.

Notice the conclusion of this strong passage from Ephesians: "We are to grow up in every way into him who is the head, into Christ, from whom the whole body, joined and knit together by every joint with which it is supplied. . . ." Join hands, then, brothers of the faith in America, in Africa, in India, in the Far East, in the Near East. I believe with all my heart that if we can be aware of our oneness in our love for the Christ, we will not look with suspicion at each other, and we will not question motives.

Yes, joining hands together in faith is a wonderful thing! You do not look to see whether the hand you hold is black or white, whether it is masculine or feminine; whether it has a wedding ring or not. The current of the love of Christ flows through any conductor that does not put up a resistance.

We had an unforgettable experience in Washington not many weeks ago. The delegation of Russian Churchmen were guests of the National Council of Churches in our city. There were about seventy of us gathered together in a church parlor to break bread. As they shared with us the concerns of their hearts (through interpreters), and as we, in the same way, poured out the longing of our hearts for peace, we found that in our allegiance to Christ was the answer. Before we parted, we formed a circle around the room, and joined hands, Metropolitan Nicholai, the leader, and all the rest, and sang

"Blest be the tie that binds
Our hearts in Christian love."

There was something electric about that experience, and we all felt what the Estonian clergyman so fervently said, "This is the work of the Holy Spirit of God."

PRAYER: *Yes, Lord, that is what we need, an outpouring of Your Holy Spirit, that the walls of partition might be broken down. Amen.*

In Christ There Is No East or West

Who serves my Father as a son
Is surely kin to me

Isaiah 64:8

Yet, O Lord, thou art our Father; we are the clay, and thou art our potter; we are all the work of thy hand.

Ephesians 3:14, 15

For this reason I bow my knees before the Father, from whom every family in heaven and on earth is named, that according to the riches of his glory he may grant you to be strengthened with might through his Spirit in the inner man .

THE INCONSISTENCY of our practice with our profession must grieve the heart of God. Again and again the Bible reiterates that we are all the work of God's hands. We are all His sons through faith in Him. Surely, then, as the hymnwriter says, if we are all His sons, we must be brothers to each other. What snobs we have been!

As I was copying this Scripture, I came to the realization that Christians should look alike, too. You know how it is with creations of art; one is pretty much able to classify paintings by certain characteristics witnessing to the hand that created them. So we, too, will have the marks of the Master Artist whose image we bear. Christians from every nation and race should give a "look-alike" feeling.

Yes, we will bear on our persons the marks of the Lord Jesus Christ.

Some years ago, a forty-nine-year old missionary died of cancer. The disease first appeared on his left shoulder and then on his right. He had been sky pilot to the lumberjacks, and in order to minister to them had carried a pack sack on his shoulders with some personal necessities and some hymnbooks and Bibles. This weight and the rubbing had caused the cancer to start. Truly he bore on his body the marks of the Lord Jesus Christ.

Around the world this story with variations could be told. Children in the family of God show a likeness, a family resemblance!

Dr. Phillips' translation of the Letter to the Corinthians has in it a vivid presentation of this same thought: "He makes our knowledge of him to spread like a lovely perfume throughout the world. We Christians bear the unmistakable scent of Christ. . . ."

Do you have a sense of this family of God that transcends any division or geographical boundary, or ethnological pattern? When we affirm in our Creed: "I believe in . . . the holy Christian Church, the communion of saints," this is what we are saying. Do you mean it?

PRAYER: *What privileged children we are, Lord, to belong to Your family! Remove any vestiges of snobbery or exclusion. Unite us all in Your great Father heart that revealed itself in Christ, our elder Brother and Lord. Amen.*

In Christ There Is No East or West

All Christly souls are one in Him
Throughout the whole wide earth

Romans 12:4, 5

For as in one body we have many members, and all the members do not have the same function, so we, though many, are one body in Christ, and individually members one of another.

Galatians 3:26, 28

For in Christ Jesus you are all sons of God, through faith. . . . There is neither Jew nor Greek, there is neither slave nor free, there is neither male nor female; for you are all one in Christ Jesus.

THE BIBLE is filled with references to the necessity of this oneness in Christ. Notice that in the Gospel of John Jesus tells why it is so important: "that the world may believe that thou hast sent me." No wonder that Communism has been able to take root; no wonder that Gandhi never came to the place where he would publicly acknowledge Christ as Redeemer! The divisive witness of the Christian churches, the bigotry and lack of love on the part of professing Christians, were to him too great a paradox to understand. Christian friends, the only unanswerable defense against the onslaughts of paganism is the living Christian witness that, because we love God with all our hearts, we love our neighbor as ourselves

From the Tonga Islands comes the most beautiful description of Christian fellowship that I have ever heard. Pastor John Havea personally shared this. He said that when they came to translate the Bible, they did not have an adequate word for fellowship. They searched about for an experience that would convey to the people what was meant in the verse, "If we walk in the light, as he is in the light, we have fellowship with one another, and the blood of Jesus his son cleanses us from all sin." Then one day one of the translators observed a group of women. They were following their customary practice of making a cocoanut lotion. They opened a cocoanut, and mashed the white meat into a pulp. Then they gathered the most fragrant flowers on the island and crushed them. These two ingredients they put into a bowl, and a little group of them sat together under the sun, each stirring the contents of the bowl. They had umbrellas over them, but the bowls were out in the sun, in order that its transforming power might do its work with the cocoanut and the flowers. At the end of the day, a woman would dip her finger into the clear liquid that had formed at the bottom, and then hold it to her nostrils. If in the cocoanut liquid she could smell the fragrance of the bloom, if the two had become fused into one, so that you could no longer tell where one left off and the other began, then you had fellowship.

So works the Sun of Righteousness!

PRAYER: *Arouse Your Church, in our day, Lord, to a unity of spirit that will witness to You. Forgive us our pride that has kept us apart. In Jesus' name. Amen.*

Come, Ye Disconsolate, Where'er Ye Languish

Consolation. 11 10, 11 10. SAMUEL WEBBE, 1792.

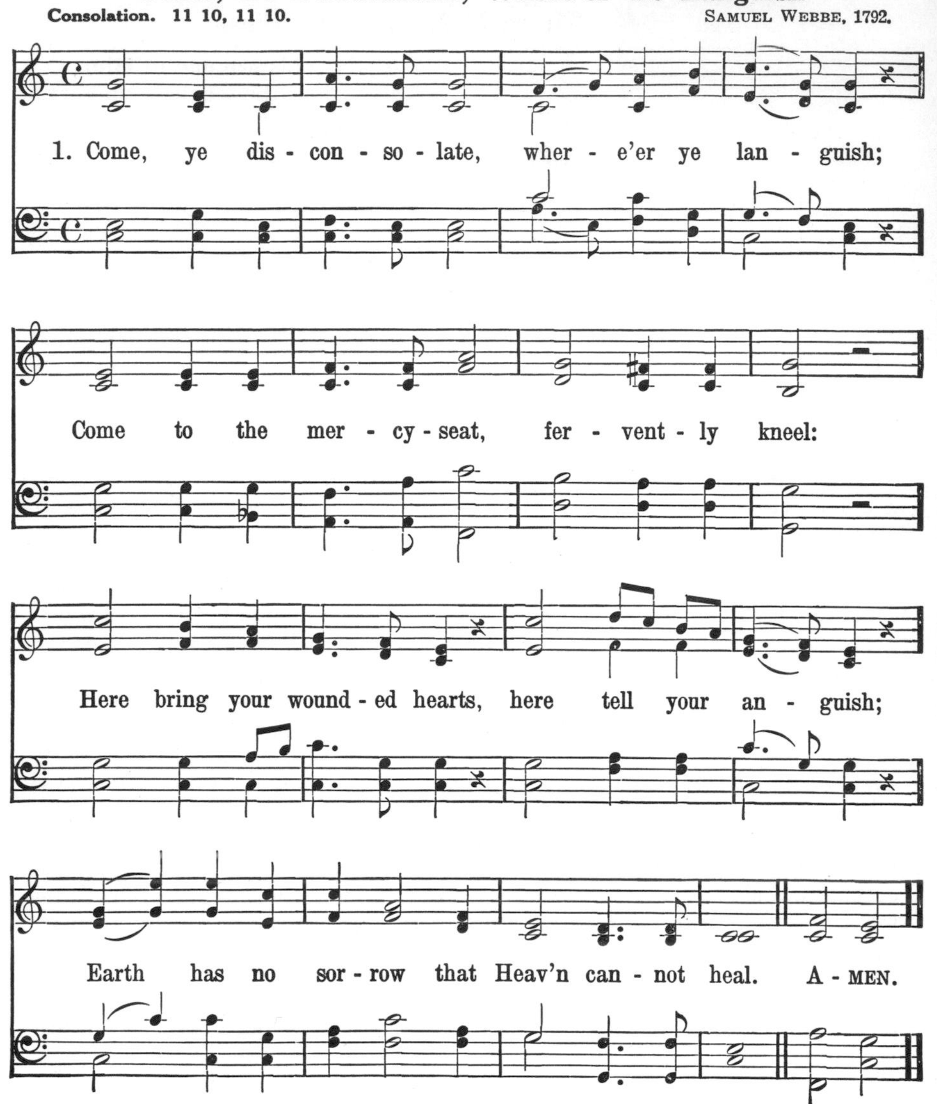

2 Joy of the desolate, light of the straying,
Hope of the penitent, fadeless and pure!
Here speaks the Comforter, tenderly saying,
"Earth has no sorrow that Heaven cannot cure."

3 Here see the Bread of Life; see waters flowing
Forth from the throne of God, pure from above;
Come to the feast of love; come, ever knowing
Earth has no sorrow but Heaven can remove.

St. 1, 2, Thomas Moore, 1816.
St. 3, Thomas Hastings, 1831.

Come, Ye Disconsolate

Come to the mercy seat

Exodus 25:17

"Then you shall make a mercy seat of pure gold . . . ."

Exodus 25:21, 22

"And you shall put the mercy seat on the top of the ark; and in the ark you shall put the testimony that I shall give you. There I will meet with you, and from above the mercy seat, from between the two cherubim that are upon the ark of the testimony, I will speak with you of all that I will give you in commandment for the people of Israel."

Joel 2:13

Return to the Lord your God, for he is gracious and merciful, slow to anger, and abounding in steadfast love.

IN THE instructions for the building of the tabernacle in the Old Testament, the Lord made provisions for this mercy seat, which is the haven for every distressed, sin-harassed soul. It was an object that you could see with the eye, in those times, and was set on top of the ark of the covenant, God's promise to man of salvation. In regard to the mercy seat we have the promise of God, "There I will meet with you. . . ." In the Old Testament tradition and according to the command of God, no one but the priest could stand before this seat in the Holy of Holies. He it was who brought the petitions of the people who would be praying without to this place; he it was who would speak God's answer to them as they awaited it.

But Christ died, and arose. Today you and I and everyone, for that is the expanse of God's great invitation, can come to the mercy seat before the great throne of God, and speak to Him, and He to us. No one need ever carry his load of sin, no one need ever stay burdened.

The condition necessary for coming is really so simple, yet for many people so difficult. In the twelfth and thirteenth verses of the second chapter of Joel the condition is stated very clearly: "Return to me with all your heart, with fasting, with weeping, and with mourning; and rend your hearts and not your garments." John the Baptist said it in very simple words, too, when he was the "voice crying in the wilderness: Prepare ye the way of the Lord." "Repent" was his cry, "for the kingdom of heaven is at hand." Peter too, when after Pentecost he fearlessly preached what rejection of Christ meant in a life and the people, convicted, cried out, "What shall we do?" told them: "Repent, and be baptized." There is no consolation in the mercy seat for one who does not come as a repentant sinner. But for the one that does, there is mercy, and forgiveness, and hope, and everlasting life.

PRAYER: *Thank You for this wonderful invitation, Lord. Thank You for Your love which made salvation possible for all the world. In Jesus' name. Amen.*

Come, Ye Disconsolate

Here bring your wounded hearts

Psalm 131:1, 2

O Lord, my heart is not lifted up, my eyes are not raised too high; I do not occupy myself with things too great and too marvelous for me. But I have calmed and quieted my soul, like a child quieted at its mother's breast; like a child that is quieted is my soul.

Isaiah 35:3, 4

Strengthen the weak hands, and make firm the feeble knees.
Say to those who are of a fearful heart, "Be strong, fear not!"

AT THE mercy seat there is the balm of Gilead for wounded hearts. What makes wounds of the heart? A first answer is self-evident: the wounds in many hearts are self-inflicted; they are the wounds of dissipation, of walking with the world and feeling its disintegration; of compromise, and licentiousness; of selfishness and pride. Sometimes we are even unaware of the injuries that are brought on by these. The destroying chemical is in the atmosphere we breathe, and in the company we keep, and is so subtle that the work has been done before we are aware. I shall never forget standing on a street corner in New York, waiting to get the bus that would take me to my destination, when I happened to glance down at my stockings. To my utter amazement, they were almost like lace; they were filled with holes. They were a new pair that I had put on only that morning. Of course I was chagrined, for I had no reserve pair with me, but more than that, I was puzzled. How did this happen? I picked up the evening paper to read on the bus, and there I found that in the air that day, in the vicinity where I was, there had been an explosion of some kind of chemical that could neither be seen nor smelled, but that disintegrated nylons. Ladies were having trouble with their hose.

Something like this are many of the sins of the world. The heart is wounded almost before it knows that it has been exposed. Be sure, then, of the air you breathe.

Then there are hearts wounded by the misdeeds of others. Parents often know this kind of ache; and in reverse, children suffer at the hands of parents. I am not speaking of physical wounds, but rather of those of the spirit. Scripture speaks of being wounded in the house of a friend. I suppose that there is not one of us but has experienced at one time or another such a wound.

For all—there is a mercy seat. Whatever the wound may be, however it has been made, whether it be by one's own sin and perversity, or at the hands of others, there is healing at the heart of God. No one, then, need ever go unaided; no one need ever carry an injured heart.

PRAYER: *For a source of sure healing, whatever the wound of my heart may be, I thank You, Lord. Help me to give the right directions to others that they might find this gracious station of healing, and know the comfort of the Great Physician. In Jesus' name. Amen.*

TUESDAY

Come, Ye Disconsolate

Here tell your anguish

Job 30:17-19

"The night racks my bones, and the pain that gnaws me takes no rest. With violence it seizes my garment; it binds me about like the collar of my tunic. God has cast me into the mire, and I have become like dust and ashes."

Job 33:29, 30

"Behold, God does all these things twice, three times, with a man, to bring back his soul from the Pit, that he may see the light of life."

HAVE YOU read anywhere a more vivid description of pain than you find in the Book of Job? Vicariously one almost has the physical sensation of agony when one reads that "it binds me about like the collar of my tunic." In spite of all this, and the additional goading of his wife, Job is able to fling out his witness to the sufficiency of God: "Though he slay me, yet will I trust in him. . . . I know that my Redeemer lives. . . ."

As I read the lines from Isaiah, "the twilight I longed for has been turned for me into trembling," I thought of the many old people who have experienced this. One of the most gifted pastors I have ever heard, who has had a brilliant ministry, is experiencing this kind of approach to twilight. From our human values, it seems tragic; yet the witness that his wife and family are giving, as well as the man himself, is such that it must be a tremendous strengthening to the thousands that know them. There is this about such a witness that says: "This life is only a small part. God is sufficient, no matter what happens here. See how He sustains us!" I am sure that there are many times when these souls have gone to the mercy seat and cried out their anguish; I am sure that there have been many times when things have seemed immeasurably dark. Yet the wife, the mother in the home, witnesses constantly to the reality of answered prayer and the subsequent undergirding of God. Their complete confidence is in the One of whom it is promised that, "he will wipe away every tear from their eyes, and death shall be no more, neither shall there be any mourning nor crying nor pain any more, for the former things have passed away."

There are hours of anguish in every life. Some are the result of physical pain; others are caused from burdens of the heart. At the mercy seat there are the open arms of a Savior who can understand, because He became man, that He might "sympathize with our weaknesses." There is a long procession of saints from every age that will attest to His sufficiency. Our hymn writer is one of them. That is why he can say with such confidence: "Earth has no sorrow that Heaven cannot heal."

PRAYER: *Thank You, Lord, for the release that we know as we share with You the anguish in our lives; thank You that You are always sufficient. Forgive us the times that we have groveled with our woes, rather than released them to You. Give us grace to use these experiences as preparation for ministering to others. In Jesus' name. Amen.*

Come, Ye Disconsolate

Joy of the desolate

Romans 5:1-5

Therefore, since we are justified by faith, we have peace with God through our Lord Jesus Christ. Through him we have obtained access to this grace in which we stand, and . . . . we rejoice in our sufferings, knowing that suffering produces endurance, and endurance produces character, and character produces hope, and hope does not disappoint us, because God's love has been poured into our hearts through the Holy Spirit which has been given to us.

Habbakuk 3:17, 18

Though the fig tree do not blossom, nor fruit be on the vines, the produce of the olive fail and the fields yield no food, the flock be cut off from the fold and there be no herd in the stalls, yet I will rejoice in the Lord, I will joy in the God of my salvation.

"JOY OF the desolate" seems to be a paradox of words, and yet it has in it that diversity of experience which indicates that a person is with God, or without Him. There is no human desolation but that a Christian can make it an occasion for some rejoicing, if he will look deeply enough and wait long enough. In the Letter to the Romans Paul lists some of the fruits that can come from "rejoicing in suffering." From such experiences character is produced. Think of your friends. Which ones have the most to offer in terms of rich and abundant living? Is it those who have been protected and have had an easy life? Or is it those who have known the tumultuous experiences of suffering, of disappointment, of adversity, and by the grace of God have risen above all these?

Thomas Moore, the writer of this hymn, was able to speak from first-hand experience. He was an Irishman with a Celtic temper, who had a turbulent life. He was a gifted poet, the author of "The Last Rose of Summer," "Believe Me If All Those Endearing Young Charms," "Oft in the Stilly Night" and so forth. But he was a poor business man, and when he did not lose his resources himself, others absconded with them. It must have been from out of these uncertainties in his life that this hymn was written.

Yes, there is joy for the desolate, if they will come to the mercy seat. A young crippled girl, the youngest in a large family, was feeling very desolate when she happened to pass by a bookstore. She had just inwardly commented, "I'm a cripple and in everybody's way." The book that was being displayed in the window, had over it the advertising caption: "The Lord hath need of him." She carefully remembered that reference, and searched it out at home. "Jesus once needed a donkey," she said, "so perhaps He wants me, a cripple. I'll ask Him." Forty years afterwards, a lame Bible woman died, beloved by hundreds and blessed by God in her work. The Bible woman was once the crippled girl.

PRAYER: *Gladness, joy, rejoicing, these are the words, Lord, that ring through Your Book. Put this note into our lives. In Jesus' name. Amen.*

THURSDAY

Come, Ye Disconsolate

Light of the straying

Hebrews 2:17, 18

Therefore he had to be made like his brethren in every respect, so that he might become a merciful and faithful high priest in the service of God, to make expiation for the sins of the people. For because he himself has suffered and been tempted, he is able to help those who are tempted.

ARE OUR churches becoming too respectable? Is there a desire that sinners should seek a Savior in them? We need to test our Christian practice with the teachings of the Lord! I have heard pastors criticized by their people because they were spending too much time on some drunkard or ne'er-do-well. "He's a no-good; why bother with him?" is often the attitude. God pity us, if we have evolved as a church into a respectable society for well-groomed people. No longer, then, are we the vessel for the light of Christ. We have forfeited the right to be His bride. That church which is out on the streets with the invitation of love, that church which is serving the underprivileged, and the "sinners"—the brand of sinning that is so much more obvious than our kind—that church is Christ's, and will truly know His power.

In our attitudes many of us are like the man who stood on shore when a boy was drowning. The boy had gone beyond his depth. The man heard his cries, and asked him if he could not swim. The boy replied that he could not. "What a foolish boy you are to go into the water without knowing how to swim," replied the man. But the boy called out, "Help me out and scold me afterwards."

He is the "light of the straying," for sin and Christ cannot walk down the same path together. A mother came to college to visit her son. She was a little distressed to find on the walls of his room suggestive pictures that would not be conducive to the kind of thinking the Letter to the Philippians enjoins us to have. She said nothing, but when she returned home, she sent him a lovely picture of the Christ, and asked if he would not hang it on a wall. A few months later she had occasion to visit the campus again, and also his room. She was pleased with what she saw. The walls were clear, except for the picture of Christ. "What happened to the other pictures?" she casually asked. "Oh," was the reply, "when I put this one up, the others just didn't look right."

PRAYER: *Thank You, Lord, that at Your mercy seat there is a place for sinners. Thank You that Your restraining hand on our lives is a light that calls us back. In the life of each soul we meet, help us to shed Your love. Arouse Your Church today to its mission. Use my voice to that end. In Your name. Amen.*

FRIDAY

Come, Ye Disconsolate

Come to the feast of love

Luke 14:15-17; 23

When one of those who sat at table with him heard this, he said to him, "Blessed is he who shall eat bread in the kingdom of God!" But Jesus said to him, "A man once gave a great banquet, and invited many; and at the time for the banquet he sent his servant to say to those who had been invited, 'Come; for all is now ready.' But they all alike began to make excuses. . . . And the master said to the servant, 'Go out to the highways and hedges, and compel people to come in, that my house may be filled. For I tell you, that none of these men who were invited shall taste my banquet.'"

IN THE practice of the early church, the "feast of love" (agape) was a preliminary experience to the Lord's Supper. It was a communal feast in which all shared. How often the Lord used human situations to describe spiritual experiences! In our Scripture portion today there is the story of the rejected invitation. Before we consider the excuses, let us remind ourselves of some of the invitations that God extends to us.

When the Lord said to Noah, "Go into the ark, you and all your household," it was an invitation to safety. Here was a place of refuge, when everything else would be gone. When Moses invited Hobab to join the children of Israel, he said: "We are setting out for the place of which the Lord said, 'I will give it to you'; come with us, and we will do you good; for the Lord has promised good to Israel." Here was an invitation to fellowship. Isaiah records one of the many invitations for cleansing: "Come now, let us reason together, says the Lord: though your sins are like scarlet, they shall be as white as snow; though they are red like crimson, they shall become like wool." There is the "Come to me," for rest to the soul; there is the "Come everyone that thirsts" for a satisfying portion; and there is the threefold invitation of Revelation: everyone who hears, come; everyone who is thirsty, come; and the invitation of the Spirit and the Bride.

No one can say that he is not invited! God has extended the invitation across the community of the world. He has done everything He could do as the great Host, except to force us to come. What about our R.S.V.P.? What is our responase?

Listen to some of the excuses that our Lord tells us about: "I have bought a field," "I have bought five yoke of oxen," "I have married a wife." Possessions, occupation, family—these came first, and so the invitation to the feast was rejected.

Today's church should be out on the highways and byways.

PRAYER: *Lord, we thank You for the invitation to share in Your feast of love. By the grace of the Holy Spirit, we are accepting and already have tasted the life-giving food. Give us grace to break this Bread with others. In Your name. Amen.*

Come, Ye Disconsolate

Earth has no sorrow that heaven cannot heal

Malachi 4:2

"But for you who fear my name the sun of righteousness shall rise, with healing in its wings. You shall go forth leaping like calves from the stall. And you shall tread down the wicked, for they will be ashes under the soles of your feet, on the day when I act, says the Lord of hosts."

Revelation 22:2

And the leaves of the tree were for the healing of the nations.

THE WORD heaven in this last line does not refer to the abode of the blessed. Rather it is a poetic word for God. The writer is wanting to say that there is nothing that the presence of God cannot heal; there is no situation or malady, or difficulty that is too hard for God. In the Book of Malachi there is given, rather succinctly, the condition preliminary to such an experience, what happens, and the result. In the words, "you who fear my name" is the preliminary requisite. This is not a fear born of dread. It is a fear of love. Then there is the effect: "the sun of righteousness shall rise, with healing in its wings." There is the response to your faith, the evidence of God's love, and the witness to hope.

Then what? I wonder if too often we forget this next part, for this is where we come in. "You shall go forth leaping like calves from the stall." Here is what is expected of those who have known the cure, and have been healed. They are to announce it to others. By their very actions, people are to know what has happened. By the power of their living, folks will be able to tell where they have been.

Throughout this entire song, even though the words, "disconsolate," "straying," "anguished," "desolate," "wounded," are used, there is a note of victory and lifting up. From whatever depths we are in, regardless of what our problem may be, no matter how difficult the circumstances, come to the mercy seat, and you will be lifted, your complexities will be simplified, and you will find grace and strength. As you sit quietly now in the presence of God, why do you not mentally write your own little chapter to add to the witness? Recount how, when you called, the Lord heard, and did more for you than you could even ask or think. Go one step further. Some time during the day witness to someone else of God's goodness, and how He helped you. You will have a good day!

PRAYER: *There are not words enough to say thank You, Lord, for Your sufficiency for all my needs. Thank You for Your ready ear that is so willing to listen to my difficulties. Thank You for Your redeeming grace that is life to me. Bless those who are disconsolate. Put it upon my heart to share with someone this day in a way that will be helpful. In Jesus' name. Amen.*

Abide with Me! Fast Falls the Eventide

Eventide (Monk). 10 10, 10 10. WILLIAM HENRY MONK, 1861.

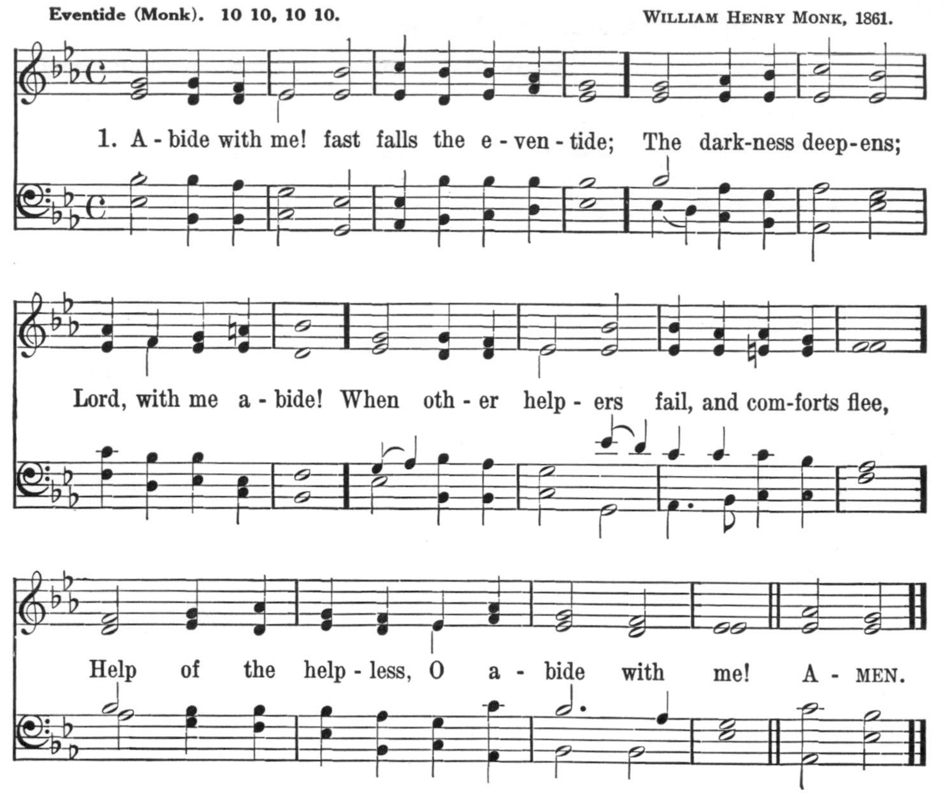

2 Swift to its close ebbs out life's little day;
Earth's joys grow dim, its glories pass away;
Change and decay in all around I see;
O Thou who changest not, abide with me!

3 Not a brief glance I beg, a passing word,
But as Thou dwell'st with Thy disciples, Lord,
Familiar, condescending, patient, free,
Come not to sojourn, but abide with me!

4 I need Thy presence every passing hour:
What but Thy grace can foil the tempter's power?
Who like Thyself my guide and stay can be?
Through cloud and sunshine, O abide with me!

5 I fear no foe, with Thee at hand to bless:
Ills have no weight, and tears no bitterness.
Where is death's sting? where, grave, thy victory?
I triumph still, if Thou abide with me!

6 Hold Thou Thy cross before my closing eyes,
Shine through the gloom, and point me to the skies:
Heaven's morning breaks, and earth's vain shadows flee;
In life, in death, O Lord, abide with me!

Henry Francis Lyte, 1847.

SUNDAY

Abide with Me! Fast Falls the Eventide

The darkness deepens; Lord, with me abide!

Isaiah 5:7

And he looked for justice, but behold, bloodshed; for righteousness, but behold, a cry!

Isaiah 5:21-23

Woe to those who are wise in their own eyes, and shrewd in their own sight! Woe to those who are heroes at drinking wine, and valiant men in mixing strong drink, who acquit the guilty for a bribe, and deprive the innocent of his right!

IF YOU want a challenging experience, read these first chapters of Isaiah, and see what a contemporary picture they paint. As I read about the land "filled with horses," with "no end to the chariots," all I could think about was the multitude of cars that we are contending with in our day, and how impossible it is to find a parking place. Yes, "there is no end to our chariots." Pick up any newspaper, and classify what you read. How much is about war or its incendiary potential? How much about murder or accidents because of drunkenness? How much of divorce and entanglements? How much about the gaining of possessions and wealth? How much about man-made instruments of destruction? "The darkness deepens . . ."

Or in your personal life, has there been a series of disappointments and disillusionments? Have there been misunderstandings and difficulties, parents with children, brother with brother, employer with employee or what have you? Let us take the very worst circumstances out and look at them. Let us dig into every corner of the closet of our hearts and pull out into the light all the debris. We will be realistic and face things as they really are. For the song writer has a word for us in all these circumstances and Scripture has many. Our petition in the worst of all these situations goes up to heaven: "Lord, with me abide." In the fifty-first chapter of Isaiah there is a special word, too: "Look to the rock from which you were hewn, and to the quarry from which you were digged."

And the ransomed of the Lord shall return,
  and come to Zion with singing,
  with everlasting joy upon their heads;
they shall obtain joy and gladness,
and sorrow and sighing shall flee away (Isaiah 35:10).

Even as the early chapters of Isaiah give this realistic and grim time-picture, so the later chapters are full of the promise of the abiding presence of the Almighty with those who love Him.

PRAYER: *With gratitude, O Lord, we lift up our hearts to You. No situation is too dark for Your light to pierce; no snarl is too involved for You to unravel; no gloom so deep, but that Your presence can change. Come now afresh into my life, and shine on the dark places. In Jesus' name. Amen.*

Abide with Me! Fast Falls the Eventide

When other helpers fail, and comforts flee

Psalm 60:11, 12

O grant us help against the foe, for vain is the help of man! With God we shall do valiantly; it is he who will tread down our foes.

Psalm 94:16-19

Who rises up for me against the wicked? Who stands up for me against evildoers? If the Lord had not been my help, my soul would soon have dwelt in the land of silence. When I thought, "My foot slips," thy steadfast love, O Lord, held me up. When the cares of my heart are many, thy consolations cheer my soul.

HAVE YOU had experiences when you felt that the props were just taken from underneath you? Someone upon whom you thought that you could depend a hundred per cent has failed you. In the work of the kingdom, how often this is true. An assigned job that you had written off your shoulders, because you believed it to be in such capable hands, comes bouncing back to you undone, or with complaints about the difficulties. Someone on whom you were sure you could depend proves false. Or you have a vision of what God wants for His kingdom, and so you turn to those you think will be sensitive to the ongoing challenge of God, only to find wet blankets thrown over what you felt was a directive from your Captain. Anybody who deals with human beings knows what it is to have "helpers fail, and comforts flee."

It is interesting to note that the closing refrain in Psalm 60, which is here quoted, is identical with the closing words of Psalm 108. Here the psalmist begins with the explanation: "My heart is ready, O God, my heart is ready!" The King James translation uses the word, "fixed," instead of "ready." The thought, then, is, that a fixed or ready heart is able to say, "With God we shall do valiantly; it is he who will tread down our foes."

"Vain is the help of man." Job had that experience. All the condolences of his wise friends in his times of desperate trouble were to no avail. Only as he struggled in his heart with his faith in God was he victorious.

A lumberman in Louisiana had traveled for hours under a scorching sun. His thirst was terrible. He looked everywhere for water, but found none. His strength was failing, and things looked pretty desperate, when he looked up and saw a ridge, crowned with pine trees, their tops bending to a hollow below. He knew that this meant that there was water in the hollow. Soon he was cooling his parched lips. Often our despair will be changed to rejoicing, if we are willing to look up and receive the help that is at hand. For anyone who turns to Him, the Lord is ready to assist and relieve. Then we, like the pine trees bending to the water, will witness to others where there is help.

PRAYER: *Our disappointments in life, Lord, have been only when we have depended upon men, rather than upon You. Forgive us that so quickly we forget this, and try everything else before we turn to You. Amen.*

Abide with Me! Fast Falls the Eventide

Swift to its close ebbs out life's little day

Ephesians 5:15

Look carefully then how you walk, not as unwise men but as wise, making the most of the time, because the days are evil.

1 Chronicles 29:15

"For we are strangers before thee, and sojourners, as all our fathers were; our days on the earth are like a shadow, and there is no abiding."

HOW MANY times do you hear people say "Doesn't time fly!" We have a little summer cabin in the woods where we vacation together as a family. Every summer as we leave, I think with a feeling of nostalgia that it will be a long time before we will be together again in this blessed spot. Then, almost before I know it, that long time has gone by and we are heading westward. Young folks smile, when this white haired lady says to them that it seems but yesterday that she was a little girl with long pigtails, squealing when her mother was braiding them. I guess some of this oblivion to the fact that time has passed is evidenced in those of us who still call each other "girls" and then say coyly, "Oh well, we are still girls at heart!" "Swift to its close ebbs out life's little day."

In the section from 1 Chronicles that is quoted above, time is spoken of as being a shadow; in the Book of Job we read, "My days are swifter than a weaver's shuttle"; and again in Job, days are spoken of as swift messengers. In one of the Psalms the word "handbreadth" is used. In the Book of Isaiah we read: "My dwelling is plucked up and removed from me like a shepherd's tent; like a weaver I have rolled up my life." And James, the epistle writer, gives a very vivid picture of the uncertainty of life. "Whereas you do not know about tomorrow. What is your life? For you are a mist that appears for a little time and then vanishes." Scripture, then, makes it very clear, that life on this earth is both short and uncertain. James adds the thought after this last quotation that in our plans we should always add, "if the Lord wills."

Seeing then, that time passes so quickly, what are we to do about it? Paul says that we should "make the most of the time" or as the older translation reads, "Redeeming the time." So many of us allow life to slip right through our fingers, because we are always looking to tomorrow for some big opportunity to arrive. It is what you make of life day by day that counts. It is what you make of a day, minute by minute, that determines the quality of your living. Today you can so walk with the Lord as to make it an ongoing part of the eternity you hope to know with Him. Today salvation through the redeeming love of Christ can bring heaven into your living here and now.

PRAYER: *Make us aware, Lord, that today never returns. Give us a sense of stewardship of life that will make us want this day to count for You. Thank You for the blessed hope of eternity. Amen.*

Abide with Me! Fast Falls the Eventide

Come not to sojourn, but abide with me

John 15:4-7

"Abide in me, and I in you. As the branch cannot bear fruit of itself, unless it abides in the vine, neither can you, unless you abide in me. I am the vine, you are the branches. He who abides in me, and I in him, he it is that bears much fruit, for apart from me you can do nothing. If a man does not abide in me, he is cast forth as a branch and withers; and the branches are gathered, thrown into the fire and burned."

I HAVE always been a little disturbed by the motto that hangs in some homes: "Jesus Christ Is Guest in This House." There are two points of disturbance: Often when we have guests, we are on company behavior; and second, a guest does not stay, but sojourns for a while, and then moves on. I should like it better if it read: "Jesus Christ Lives in This House." I have an idea that this is what the motto is supposed to mean. Too often, however, we treat Christ as a guest only.

One is reminded of the Chinese Kitchen God who is supposed to pay a call once a year into each home to check up on it. Believe me, the home is in shipshape on the day in which the call is expected. Pretty much the way some homes are when the preacher is expected! The figure that Jesus used of himself is significant: "I am the vine, you are the branches." Surely the point of the metaphor is that the two are so closely united that the life-giving veins run from one to the other and are the source of furnishing food.

When folks invite the Lord to abide with them, how often are they aware of the implications that ensue? "He who abides in me, and I in him, he it is who bears much fruit." Is it not logical, then, to assume that you can tell whether or not one is abiding in the Lord by the kind of fruit his life produces? This does not mean that you play a game of sitting in judgment on other people. It means that you apply this criterion to your own life. "By their fruits you shall know them," is another plain statement of Scripture. Remember that this means that by the kind of life that you live people will know whether or not you are a living branch in the Lord. All the arguments in the world will not convince some people about the reality of Christ's presence; but seeing Him live in you has no possible refutation.

So it is a dangerous thing to ask Christ to abide with you. Everybody, I suppose, might like to have Him make periodic visits like a rich uncle, in order to get out of Him what you may need. But He is not content with any such relationship. He wants to live in you.

PRAYER: *Thank You, Lord, for Your abiding presence. Thank You for the promise of answered prayer that such a relationship carries with it. Help us, this day, to bring forth fruit that will attest to the kind of a vine to which we belong. In Jesus' name. Amen.*

Abide with Me! Fast Falls the Eventide

I need Thy presence every passing hour

Genesis 28:15

"Behold, I am with you and will keep you wherever you go, and will bring you back to this land; for I will not leave you until I have done that of which I have spoken to you."

Psalm 16:8

I keep the Lord always before me; because he is at my right hand, I shall not be moved.

IN THE previous stanza of this hymn the writer spells out what he means by this abiding presence of the Lord. Not just a glance, a passing word, but the way the Lord dwelt with His disciples, walking and talking with them; eating and sleeping with them; going apart alone to pray. So in this hymn our prayer is for the hourly presence of Christ; for His sharing in every part of our living.

Henry Francis Lyte, the author of this hymn was a parish pastor in Ireland. Even in college he had been something of a poet and expressed in rhyme the wish that some verse of his might bless mankind. That wish came to fulfillment in "Abide with Me," as well as in several other beautiful hymns which he composed.

The death of a neighboring clergyman, and Lyte's part in the preparation for this experience, made a profound impression on his whole life. When he was called to this man's bedside, he discovered that neither he nor his friend had the faith with which to meet death triumphantly. It was quite a blow, for they realized that they had been "blind leaders of the blind." However, they knew where to seek, and in their prayerful search of Scriptures they both came to a firm faith in Christ, so that Lyte was able to write of his friend: "He died happily in the belief that, though he had erred, there was One whose sufferings and death would atone for his delinquencies, and that he was forgiven and accepted for His sake." Of himself after this experience, Lyte says that he had an entirely different attitude toward life, and that he began to study his Bible and preach in a different way. His health was poor, and toward the end of his ministry, he would have to spend the cold months in Italy, being with his congregation only in the summer. On this Sunday he was preaching his farewell sermon before leaving. There was a searching of the hearts, followed by a communion service. On that lovely afternoon he went down to the water and watched the glory of the sunset. Then he came home to his study and wrote the words that have blessed so many lives. A short time later, while in France on his way to Italy, he died. On his lips as he slipped his moorings, were the words: "Joy, peace!"

"I need Thy presence every passing hour."

PRAYER: *Companion of the Way, You who walked with Your disciples on the roads of Galilee, walk with me down the way of life and on into eternity. Amen.*

Abide with Me! Fast Falls the Eventide

Hold Thou Thy cross before my closing eyes

Ephesians 2:13-16

But now in Christ Jesus you who once were far off have been brought near in the blood of Christ. For he is our peace, who has made us both one, and has broken down the dividing wall of hostility, by abolishing in his flesh the law of commandments and ordinances, that he might create in himself one new man in place of the two, so making peace, and might reconcile us both to God in one body through the cross, thereby bringing hostility to an end.

THERE IS but one way for man to bridge the gulf of his sin that separates him from God, and that is the cross of Jesus Christ. Not a wooden cross, or a gold cross; but the cross of His love who died in order that we might live; the cross that canceled the prison sentence caused by our sin. The song writer so beautifully expresses it, when he speaks of the cross as shining through the gloom and pointing to the skies. In the Letter to the Ephesians, Paul says of Christ, "He is our peace," and then goes on to explain how through the cross, Jesus reconciled us to God, abolishing the old laws that condemned us, and bringing hostility to an end. All this accomplishment is in the cross of Christ.

We have witnessed many deaths. To see souls going home to meet God is a beautiful experience. But when there is uncertainty, when the offer of Christ has been ignored, then there is sadness indeed.

Again and again this hymn has blessed people's lives, because in poetry it has so simply put the way of salvation. A dramatic incident is related in connection with the Welsh Chorus. An observer noticed that, even though much of their program was secular, they ended every evening performance with the singing of "Abide with Me." When asked about it, the director told about how they were crossing the Atlantic, when their ship started sinking. Permitting the women and children to use the lifeboats first, they found themselves without any recourse, but to try swimming in the ocean. Night was fast descending, and they realized that chances of being rescued in the fast approaching darkness were pretty slim. They were facing eternity. Then some one of them called out: "Sing, men, let's sing!" And with that the hymn, "Abide with Me" was struck up. One voice after the other joined in. They had not finished the hymn, when they heard the sound of an approaching boat. Here were rescuers even in the darkness. When questioned, the latter related how they were just about ready to give up their search because of the approaching night, when they heard the song, and following the sound were led to the rescue. As an act of gratitude to God, these men closed every program with the hymn.

"Hold Thou Thy cross before my closing eyes."

PRAYER: *Thank You, Lord, that You have shown us how to live and how to die. Thank You that in the cross You have provided the way. Use us to show this way to others. In Your name. Amen.*

SATURDAY

Abide with Me! Fast Falls the Eventide

Earth's joys grow dim, its glories pass away

Ecclesiastes 2:9-11

So I became great and surpassed all who were before me in Jerusalem; also my wisdom remained with me. And whatever my eyes desired I did not keep from them; I kept my heart from no pleasure, for my heart found pleasure in all my toil, and this was reward for all my toil. Then I considered all that my hands had done and the toil I had spent in doing it, and behold, all was vanity and a striving after wind, and there was nothing to be gained under the sun.

IT WOULD be good in this connection to read the entire Book of Ecclesiastes. The writer enlarges in a very edifying way the thought of the hymn writer: "Earth's joys grow dim, its glories pass away." Those of us who keep house and prepare food can easily get a feeling of the futility of our labor. We will spend hours preparing a meal, and in less than no time it will be consumed, and leave nothing but the litter of dirty dishes in its wake. Or we can thoroughly clean a house, only to have a gang descend upon us, and leave it looking as if it had never known either dustcloth or vacuum cleaner. How much of today's striving is after these things that either perish or that "cannot be taken with us."

The writer of Ecclesiastes lists his accomplishments: First, he said that he would make a test of pleasure. His conclusion was that laughter was mad, and pleasure was useless. He tried wine; he built houses and planted vineyards; he developed gardens and parks; he made pools. He bought slaves, and had great possessions of silver and gold. He purchased entertainers, both singers and concubines. He became greater than anyone both in wisdom and possessions, and had whatever his eye desired. And his conclusion is that "all was vanity and a striving after wind, and there was nothing to be gained under the sun."

The amazing thing is that generation after generation repeats this same vain search and arrives at exactly the same conclusion. I know women who think nothing of spending hours in an antique search, but have not time to read their Bibles. I know women who are so busy with their gardens that they cannot have any responsibility in the kingdom work.

In this month is the birthday of our older son. When that little life was placed in my arms, there was a new sense of my own helplessness, and of the values of life from an eternal viewpoint. I wanted one thing more than anything else: that the soul contained in those six pounds and nine ounces of mortal flesh might open its wings and find its way home again to God, and that in its flight, it might bless all those whose lives it touched, and lead the way for others to follow.

PRAYER: *The things that we held so dear yesterday, Lord, our dolls and our toys, are of less than passing importance today. Give us to recognize the baubles of life, and not to spend ourselves in their vain possession. In Jesus' name. Amen.*

Behold a Host, Arrayed in White

Great White Host. 8 8, 8 6. 12 lines.

Norwegian Folksong.
Arranged by EDWARD HAGERUP GRIEG, (1843–1907).

2 Despised and scorned, they sojourned here,
But now, how glorious they appear!
These martyrs stand a priestly band,
God's throne forever near.
So oft, in troubled days gone by,
In anguish they would weep and sigh;
At home above, the God of love
The tears of all shall dry.
They now enjoy their Sabbath rest,
The paschal banquet of the blest;
The Lamb, their Lord, at festal board
Himself is host and guest.

3 Then hail, ye mighty legions, yea,
All hail! now safe and blest for aye;
And praise the Lord, who with His Word
Sustained you on the way.
Ye did the joys of earth disdain,
Ye toiled and sowed in tears and pain;
Farewell, now bring your sheaves, and sing
Salvation's glad refrain.
Swing high your palms, lift up your song,
Yea, make it myriad voices strong:
Eternally shall praise to Thee,
God, and the Lamb, belong!

Hans Adolph Brorson, about 1760

Behold a Host, Arrayed in White

Like thousand snow-clad mountains bright

Revelation 7:9-10

After this I looked, and behold, a great multitude which no man could number, from every nation, from all tribes and peoples and tongues, standing before the throne and before the Lamb, clothed in white robes, with palm branches in their hands, and crying out with a loud voice, "Salvation belongs to our God who sits upon the throne, and to the Lamb!"

IN THE heart of man from the beginning of time there has been the question that Job put into simple words, "If a man die, shall he live again?" As Christians with the resurrection light we say, "O death, where is thy sting? O grave, where is thy victory?" And our lives take their direction from the words of the Savior, "I go and prepare a place for you, . . . that where I am you may be also."

Hans Adolph Brorson, the writer of this hymn, lived in the eighteenth century. He was a Danish Lutheran pastor, but very often the hymn is thought of as being from Norway, because the music to which it is sung is by Grieg. If it is new to you, you will not find it easy; but you will be well repaid any effort you make to memorize it, because it has a haunting, soul-satisfying melody, and the words tie together this world and the next. This hymn was not published until a year after the death of this poet-pastor, in 1765. It was included in a collection entitled: **Adolph Brorson's Swan-song.** All seventy poems in this collection were written in the last year of Pastor Brorson's life.

His word pictures are taken directly from the seventh chapter of Revelation. The white robes are symbolic of the purity that every Christian knows through the cleansing blood of Jesus Christ. The palm branch, which is the emblem of peace, could well stand for the peace that has been made between God and man through the truce of the cross. The united chorus singing and worshiping in adoration are the answer to the prophecy which tells us that before the Lamb "every knee shall bow."

It is good for us to think of the day when we will shed this shell, our body, and stand before our Creator to claim our inheritance in Christ our Lord. It is good to think about going home, for if the prospect in your heart is real, it will cast its radiance over this life, too; the anticipation will cause you to have the upward look instead of being downcast; it will cause you to walk with a sense of victory, instead of defeat; and it will erase from your heart any enmity toward anyone, because you cannot harbor such feelings and anticipate meeting your God. The kind of song that you sing on your journey, will be determined by your destination.

I am glad that I am going Home.

PRAYER: *For our wonderful hope of everlasting life, for the glimpses that You have given us as to the glory of Your home, we thank You, Lord. Let the anticipated sunrise be reflected in our lives each day. In Your name. Amen.*

Behold a Host, Arrayed in White

Who are this band
Before the throne of light?

Revelation 7:13. 14

Then one of the elders addressed me, saying, "Who are these, clothed in white robes, and whence have they come?" I said to him, "Sir, you know." And he said to me, "These are they who have come out of great tribulation; they have washed their robes and made them white in the blood of the Lamb."

"AND THOSE who are wise shall shine," we read in the Book of Daniel. Who are this band before the throne of light? Those who have feared the Lord, and accepted His plan of salvation, and known forgiveness in Jesus Christ. So many people are uncertain about their future. To a Christian who has accepted Christ, there need be no uncertainty, because the future is not dependent on anything we do; it is dependent on what Christ has done for us. Where we are responsible is whether or not we accept this gift. If we do in faith, then we are stamped as His.

In the Letter to the Ephesians there is an allusion to the seal as a pledge of purchase. This would be very understandable to the Ephesians, for Ephesus was a maritime city, and an extensive trade in timber was carried on there by shipmasters of the neighboring ports. This was the method of purchase: the merchant, after selecting the timber, would stamp it with his own signet, which was accepted as a sign of ownership. Often it was inconvenient for him to carry off his purchase at that time, so it would be left in the harbor with floats of other timber. In due time, the merchant sent a trusty agent with the signet, who finding the timber with the corresponding impress, claimed it and brought it away for the master's use. Thus it is that the Holy Spirit impresses on the soul the image of Jesus Christ, and this is the sure pledge of our everlasting inheritance.

The secret of the life of a lovely young girl, who was always beautiful in a home where the other members of the family did not know Christ, was discovered when she died. Around her neck she had always worn a locket which she said contained her lover's picture. Friends had often wished they might see what was in it. When they opened it, there was no picture there but the words, "Whom having not seen, ye love."

Who are this band before this throne of light? They are those who have died with the mark of the Christ upon them; they are the ones that bore the seal of their Purchaser; they are the ones He has then claimed as His own. You can belong to this band who have come out of great tribulation if your life is marked for the Lord.

PRAYER: *Our hearts are warm with gratitude, Lord, for the gift of Your love, and the assurance that through it we are marked for everlasting life. What a prospect is ours! Give us an urgency to share this with others. In Jesus' name. Amen.*

Behold a Host, Arrayed in White

Their voices they in worship raise

Revelation 7:15, 16

"Therefore are they before the throne of God,
and serve him day and night within his temple;
and he who sits upon the throne will shelter them with his presence."

THE THINGS that we are told about heaven are to us somewhat of a paradox. What a joy it has been to me, when I have been very weary with the multitudinous tasks that engage a mother in any given day, to contemplate heaven as a place of rest. Yet here we are told that the saints will be serving God day and night. Our trouble in trying to get a picture of heaven, is that we can only think in finite terms, and with finite limitations. Knowing the Lord, and the way He keeps His promises, I am very sure that this service will be the most delightful experience that can be. In fact, even in this life there is a foretaste of it, for when one is on the errands of the Lord, one knows the greatest possible happiness.

A bright young girl was suddenly paralyzed on one side and became nearly blind. She heard her family doctor say to her parents standing by her bedside: "She has seen her best days, poor child!" "No doctor," she roused herself to say. "My best days are yet to come."

In the Letter to the Hebrews the writer suggests that, with the cloud of witnesses, we should put away every weight, and run the race that is set before us. There is the suggestion that our race here is very closely connected with winning the prize. If we run with the pioneer and perfector of our faith, here, and if we know the joy of serving Him in this life, it is not at all hard to anticipate the overwhelming joy in the fulfillment of His promise.

A minister preached one day about heaven, and his sermon was greatly enjoyed by the people. The next morning, a wealthy member of his church stopped him and said, 'That was a good sermon about heaven, but you did not tell us where it was!" "Oh," said the minister, "I can tell you that right now. You know those poor cottages on the other side of the track. In the one at the end of the block lives a member of our church. She is sick in one bed, and her two children are sick in another. She hasn't a bit of fuel in her home, nor a loaf of bread. If you will go down town and buy provisions and some coal, and send them to that home, and then go yourself to the house, and promise her to do all that you can to see that she is taken care of, then read to her the Twenty-third Psalm, and kneel and pray with her, you will know where heaven is."

PRAYER: *Today, Lord, make us sensitive and alert to the needs You would have us fill. We want to serve You here, too. Thank You for the joy there is in running Your errands. In Jesus' name. Amen.*

Behold a Host, Arrayed in White

Who from the great affliction came

2 Corinthians 4:16-18; 5:1

So we do not lose heart. Though our outer nature is wasting away, our inner nature is being renewed every day. For this slight momentary affliction is preparing for us an eternal weight of glory beyond all comparison, because we look not to the things that are seen, but to the things that are unseen; for the things that are seen are transient, but the things that are unseen are eternal.

For we know that if the earthly tent we live in is destroyed, we have a building from God, a house not made with hands, eternal in the heavens.

THE THINGS that are most worth while are not often the things that are most easily attained. When there has been a struggle, the prize seems of greater value. Those things that are come by easily are not the things that are appreciated the most. The winning of the crown of Life comes from being faithful unto death. The Apostle Paul speaks of counting it a joy to suffer on behalf of Christ. Of the Lord himself we are told that He, "for the joy that was set before him endured the cross." The great white host are those who have won through the trials and vicissitudes of life.

Sometimes, when I hear the complaints of church members about the things they are asked to do for the kingdom, I wonder what kind of Christian fortitude and love we have. Often in soliciting workers for the Church school or other avenues of service, one feels that there is such a resistance as almost to make the solicitor apologetic. Where is the sense of the prize for which we are striving? Where is the joy in forgetting your own comforts to share kindness with others?

In the matter of courage for our Christian witness, how often have we not remained silent or compromised ourselves, rather than in any way be bold in what Christ has done for us, or in what He wants us to be? Where is there such self-forgetfulness, today, that Christians are seeking new opportunities of service, new ways of making His love known?

It is good for us to think of the men and the women who through tribulation have won the crown. Was it easy for a Livingstone to seek the heart of Africa for Christ? Do you not think that Dr. Schweitzer is human enough so that he could enjoy the physical comforts that you and I hold so essential, and complain about so readily when we lack them? What of a Florence Nightingale, a Jane Addams, a Muriel Lester? How do you rate in comparison with these?

Perhaps the devil's deadliest weapon is the one named "at ease." When we are "at ease" in Zion, then let us beware. When you are satisfied with what you have done, search out the Pharisee within you. Those at the great white throne have through the fire of trials come.

PRAYER: *Stir us, Lord out of our ease. Help us to know that we are running a race, and there are obstacles. Keep the prize so ever before us, that we will not waver, but press on to the goal. In Jesus' name. Amen.*

Behold a Host, Arrayed in White

And praise the Lord, who with His Word
Sustained you on the way

John 5:24

"Truly, truly, I say to you, he who hears my word and believes him who sent me, has eternal life; he does not come into judgment, but has passed from death to life."

Revelation 2:10

"Do not fear what you are about to suffer. Behold, the devil is about to throw some of you into prison, that you may be tested, and for ten days you will have tribulation. Be faithful unto death, and I will give you the crown of life."

IF THERE is one quality that often seems to be diminishing in the rush and confusion of our modern living, that quality is faithfulness. We flit like butterflies from one thing to another. Loyalties are thin, and our interests so easily vary from day to day. How much more we need an inner loyalty and faith that we will take with us wherever we go. It is good for us to plumb our faith, to measure its depth. In the Letter to the Romans, the Apostle Paul relates the faithfulness of Abraham in his covenant with God. Of him Paul says, "No distrust made him waver . . . but he grew strong in faith. . . ." You will remember that Abraham was called a friend of God, and entrusted himself so completely into the hands of this Friend, that he was willing even to sacrifice his son.

How do we evidence whether or not we are faithful? For us, it may not be some dramatic choice like the one Abraham had to make. In his life, too, there were the daily choices. In our lives this is perhaps the testing: what we do with our every day. Do you remember the words of our Lord in the parable of the steward? "You have been faithful over a little. I will set you over much." The test of our faithfulness comes in our everyday experiences.

What do you do with your time? How do you spend your energies? What is the pattern of your thought? How do you use your money? What is the goal for which you are striving?

A boy hired himself out to a man who kept a hardware store. He was sent up into an attic where there was a great box full of nails and screws of all sizes, hinges, old tools, and bits of iron. The attic was gloomy and dusty, and the work seemed useless and tiresome. Nobody was watching him, and he was tempted to take a nap. But instead he set about his work with a determination to do it well. For three days he worked at it, and then reported to the head clerk when it was done. "All right," the latter said, "you will be given a place at my counter. That box is a test job which we give to see whether a boy will be worthy of a better place."

PRAYER: *There are so many winds of doctrine in the air today, Lord. Help us to be faithful to the gospel, to the hope of everlasting life that we know in Your sacrificial love. We ask this in Jesus' name. Amen.*

Behold a Host, Arrayed in White

Ye did the joys of earth disdain

Isaiah 52:11

Depart, depart, go out from thence, touch no unclean thing; go out from the midst of her, purify yourselves, you who bear the vessels of the Lord.

John 15:19

"If you were of the world, the world would love its own; but because you are not of the world, but I chose you out of the world, therefore the world hates you."

THE CHOICE that Christians had to make in the day in which this hymn was written, is exactly the same as the one they have to make today. It is to choose God or mammon; it is to choose the Christ or material possessions; it is to choose eternal life with the Lord, or a life built around self. Dr. D. L. Moody has well said, "Christians should live in the world, but not be filled with it. A ship lives in water; but if water gets into the ship, she goes to the bottom. So Christians may live in the world; but if the world gets into them, they sink."

Scientists tell us of an insect which, though you immerse it in water, yet never touches the water. The reason for this wonder in nature is that it carries with it its own atmosphere. Even though it is submerged in this other atmosphere, it is untouched by it, because it is enveloped in its own. If we walk close to the Lord, we shall have about us the atmosphere of His presence, and that will keep us from conforming to the pattern of sin around us. We will be "in the world," but not "of the world."

Do you not find that the world presses in on all sides? You give in a little here in principle, and give in a little there in your ideals, until there is neither white nor black in the realm of conduct, but everything is gray. We have become a generation of compromisers, and so are thrashing about unrooted or anchored, being tossed about by every wind that blows.

How fleeting are the pleasures of the world! How bitter are the results of worldly living! The poet Robert Burns in "Tam O' Shanter" expresses well the "here today, and gone tomorrow" pleasures. He says:

"But pleasures are like poppies spread,
You seize the flower, its bloom is shed;"

The psalmist has put the contrast in simple words: "Thou dost show me the path of life; in thy presence there is fullness of joy, in thy right hand are pleasure for evermore." The great white host consists of those who chose the Christ instead of the world.

PRAYER: *Lord, You know how the pressures are on all sides. Keep our relationship so intimate in prayer and through Your Word, that nothing will separate us from You. Today, help us to make the choices that will indicate for what country we are headed. We ask this in Jesus' name. Amen.*

SATURDAY

Behold a Host, Arrayed in White

Ye toiled and sowed in tears and pain

Psalm 126:5, 6

May those who sow in tears reap with shouts of joy!
He that goes forth weeping, bearing the seed for sowing,
shall come home with shouts of joy, bringing his sheaves with him.

THE MIRACLE of a seed is one that makes you aware of a Creator. A poet has said:

"Who plants a seed beneath the sod
Believes in God."

Yet an even greater miracle is the way the Seed, God's Word, takes root and grows and bears fruit. Here again in Scripture, we have the interchange of the Word with Christ, for "seed" is used in each instance to speak of both. A prophecy of Christ speaks of "the seed of a woman" and Christ in giving us the parable of the sower speaks of the seed's being the Word. Our song writer indicates that it may be necessary for some of the seed to be sown through tears.

The men that the Lord chose to serve Him through difficult times, even in the Old Testament, were not men who came out of the plush life. Joseph was sold into slavery, David began as a shepherd boy, Gideon's family was the poorest in Manasseh and Gideon was the least in his father's house. Daniel was carried away to a strange land as a young boy. When Jesus chose men to preach the Word about himself to the nations, He chose poor fishermen and farmers. This preaching and sharing was done through great vicissitudes and personal hardship.

The churches that are strong around the world today are the young churches that are having to stand persecution and difficulties, and to count the cost of discipleship.

In our own personal lives the same thing pertains. When the power of God has made you victorious in difficult situations, when you have been able to persevere in love through trying circumstances because of the undergirding of the "Everpresent One," then there is this feeling that the psalmist speaks about, this coming home "with shouts of joy." Maybe there is a tense situation in your home to which you can bring patience and love and forgiveness; maybe there are problems in your church that need your prayers, your energies, your best. The world needs desperately those who are willing to believe what the Word teaches, so that they are willing to sow the seed of love, regardless of the circumstances. Then shall we be one with that great company arrayed in white.

PRAYER: *We want things so easy, Lord, and we rebel at the least little inconvenience on behalf of the kingdom. Forgive us, and awaken in us such a sense of commission in the knowledge of salvation that is ours, that we shall be willing to sow even in tears. This day make our choices right. In Jesus' name. Amen.*

Just As I Am, without One Plea

Woodworth. L. M. WILLIAM BATCHELDER BRADBURY, 1849.

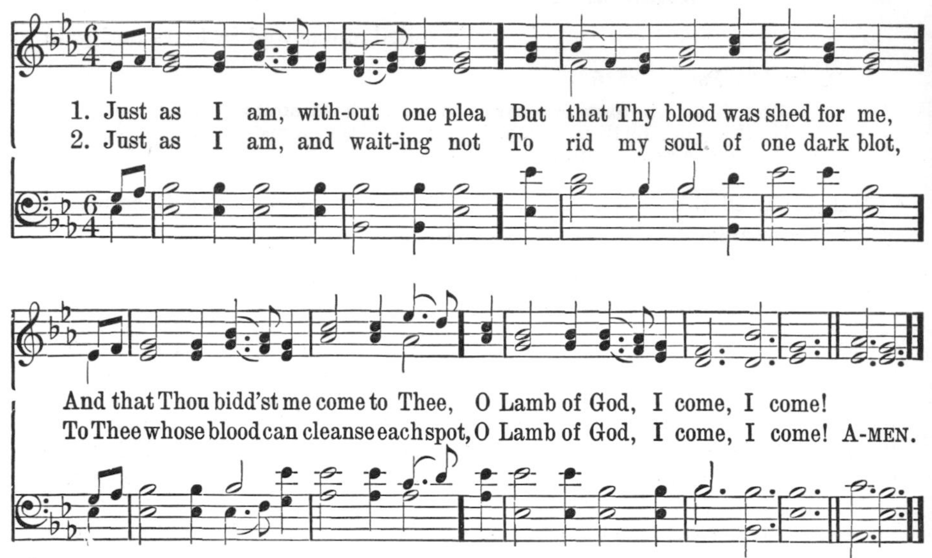

3 Just as I am, though tossed about
With many a conflict, many a doubt,
Fightings and fears within, without,
O Lamb of God, I come, I come!

4 Just as I am, poor, wretched, blind;
Sight, riches, healing of the mind,
Yea, all I need in Thee I find,
O Lamb of God, I come, I come!

5 Just as I am; Thou wilt receive,
Wilt welcome, pardon, cleanse, relieve,
Because Thy promise I believe;
O Lamb of God, I come, I come!

6 Just as I am; Thy love unknown
Hath broken every barrier down;
Now to be Thine, yea, Thine alone,
O Lamb of God, I come, I come!

Charlotte Elliott, 1836.

Just as I Am, without One Plea

But that Thy blood was shed for me

John 6:37-40

"All that the Father gives me will come to me; and him who comes to me I will not cast out. For I have come down from heaven, not to do my own will, but the will of him who sent me; and this is the will of him who sent me, that I should lose nothing of all that he has given me, but raise it up at the last day. For this is the will of my Father, that every one who sees the Son and believes in him should have eternal life; and I will raise him up at the last day."

AND him who comes to me I will not cast out." These are the words of Scripture that inspired the writing of this hymn. Its roots had been planted years before the hymn came to flower, but it was on the statement of Christ's reception to anyone who would turn to Him, that Charlotte Elliott based her hymn. This had been the key to her own spiritual experience. Although a daughter of the church, and brought up in a pious home, it seems that Miss Elliott had never found true peace with God. She had the conception that men must do something to win salvation, instead of their accepting what Christ has done. It was when Dr. Caesar Malan, a noted Swiss preacher from Geneva, came to visit in her home that he discovered her spiritual perplexity. He told her that she had nothing of merit to bring to God; that she must come as she was, a sinner.

This poem was written 14 years later. The story is told that, while she was living at Brighton, her clergyman brother was trying to establish a school where at a nominal cost the daughters of poor clergymen could come for an education. A bazaar was planned to help raise some money. During fifty years of Miss Elliott's life she was an invalid, and on the opening day of the bazaar she was ill, and unable to get up and help. She had such a feeling of uselessness, and taking inventory of her situation, she wrote this hymn. "She gathered up in her soul the great certainties, not of her emotions but of her salvation—her Lord, His power, His promise—and deliberately set down for her own comfort the formula for her faith; restated to herself the gospel of pardon, peace, and heaven." The sale of this hymn aided the cause more than any bazaar. On the title page was written: "Sold for the benefit of St. Margaret's Hall, Brighton."

In this hymn is found the evangelical message of the gospel. There are those who rebel against the philosophy of the "blood," and belittle a God who has such a method. I am grateful that eternal life is my heritage in the shed blood of Jesus Christ. This knowledge has transformed my whole life, and gives me new purpose in living. The struggle to achieve can be released into the channels of bearing the fruit of the presence of the Lord in your life.

PRAYER: *We thank You Lord, for using Your servant to tell the Gospel message so simply in song that anyone can understand. We thank You that the way of salvation is a way of faith. In Jesus' name. Amen.*

Just as I Am, without One Plea

And waiting not
To rid my soul of one dark blot

Jeremiah 3:13

"Only acknowledge your guilt, that you rebelled against the Lord your God and scattered your favors among strangers under every green tree, and that you have not obeyed my voice, says the Lord."

1 John 1:9

If we confess our sins, he is faithful and just, and will forgive us our sins and cleanse us from all unrighteousness.

IN THIS line of the hymn the writer calls attention to a mistaken idea that so many people have in regard to their coming to Christ. The pastor in calling, bidding people to come, will often get the response, "I'm not good enough." Or again, he will frequently have people say, "Why should I join the church? I'm as good as a lot of your members." Shamefully enough, we have to admit the latter, but all the while we are aware of the misconception of Christ's invitation. He himself said, "For I came not to call the righteous, but sinners." The very fact that you feel unworthy means that the invitation is extended to you. If you are going to wait until you yourself rid your soul of sin, you will wait until eternity, and then not arrive.

Have we too often given the impression that the church is for "respectable" people? We may not be prostitutes or drunkards or dope addicts, but we are guilty of pride, and selfishness, and of lack of faith; we are often guilty of judging our neighbors, and of a slanderous tongue. Believe me, every one of us is plenty guilty. Every time I go out to the district prison and stand before those girls to share the love of God in Christ, I feel that I am one with them in approaching the mercy seat of God. My opportunities in life hold me doubly accountable.

Bishop Thoburn, after spending twenty-five years in India as a missionary, was asked, when he returned to America what changes he had noted. He answered, "I no longer see the very poor or the wicked in our churches; they used to come to the church I knew best in my home town. It is my firm belief that wherever the Friend of sinners is lifted up, there sinners will come. Next to my church in Calcutta was a Magdalen home. I asked the matron if the inmates might come to church. They came, and some of them sat on the side seats where they could look out over the audience. One of them afterwards said to the matron: 'That was the queerest church I ever saw. All the bad people in Calcutta were there.' That was one of the best things ever said about my church. I knew that sinners would not come here if they did not know that the Savior of whom I spoke was the Friend of sinners."

PRAYER: *Thank You, Lord, that the requirement for coming is one that every single soul can meet: a broken and a contrite heart. Amen.*

Just as I Am, without One Plea

Though tossed about
With many a conflict, many a doubt

Mark 9:23, 24

And Jesus said to him, "If you can! All things are possible to him who believes." Immediately the father cried out and said, "I believe; help my unbelief!"

SOMETHING OF the "being tossed about" that is mentioned in this hymn was evidenced in Miss Elliott's titles to two poems that were printed in a collection: "Hours of Sorrow," "Cheered and Comforted." There are such titles as these in this book: "To One Deprived of Hearing in Church Through Deafness," "On a Restless Night in Illness," "To a Mother on the Death of a Child of Great Promise," "To One Whose Mind Was Disordered by Grief," and "A Vision, Composed During a Thunderstorm." It is understandable that a woman who was natural and gay in her earlier years, who wrote humorous poems within the "propriety" for females of that age, and who later was so beset with sickness that she was a cripple for fifty years of her life, might have moments of doubt. Which one of us does not? There are many things in the Bible that I cannot understand, and if I dwelt on these, I could get myself into a dither. But there is so much that I can understand! There is One whom I trust completely, and I leave all my doubts with Him. It, however, is not once and for all. That is why the apostle tells us to "fight the good fight of the faith." That fight will go on until the Lord takes us home.

In the gospel story, the man who came to the Lord had his troubles. There must have been a measure of faith in the beginning, because he had come to the disciples for help. They had been ineffective. One then understands better his saying to the Lord, "If you can do anything, have pity on us." When Jesus chides him because of his "if," you will notice his response. We are told: "Immediately the father of the child cried out and said, 'I believe; help thou my unbelief.'" And such a cry the Lord always honors. The whole point of the song writer and the point of the gospel is that we come to Jesus—as we are—and let Him work His wonders in our lives. No one who has ever come has gone away empty, if he was willing to take what the Lord had to offer.

There was a father and son combination where each professed to be infidels. The father became ill, and as he lay on his deathbed, his confidence in his unbelieving principles broken down. His son, desiring that his father should die as he had lived, went to fortify him and said, "Father, be a man and stick to it." "Ah," he replied, "but there's nothing to stick to."

PRAYER: *Lord, we are so grateful that even in our doubtings we may come to You. We are so grateful for Your understanding heart. Help our faith to grow that it may be a beacon for others. In Jesus' name. Amen.*

Just as I Am, without One Plea

Poor, wretched, blind

Psalm 40:17

As for me, I am poor and needy; but the Lord takes thought for me.
Thou art my help and my deliverer; do not tarry, O my God!

Isaiah 56:10

His watchmen are blind, they are all without knowledge;
they are all dumb dogs, they cannot bark;
dreaming, lying down, loving to slumber.

IN ONE hymn line for today we are reminded of the words of the psalmist: "Out of the pit have I cried to thee, O Lord!" From the depth of despair and misery a soul may yet seek God. In this hymn there is almost an antiphonal effect in the listing of man's wretchedness and then God's effectiveness. Here are the limitations and failures of which the soul is conscious: conflicts, doubts, fears, poverty of accomplishment, wretchedness, spiritual blindness. Then we have listed the opposites that are found in Christ: sight, riches, healing of the mind, welcome, pardon, cleansing, relief. Here is the compulsion of the Christian to share. He who has known the first state, and now is experiencing the second, will of necessity want to witness to this to all whom he meets.

In every heart there is a yearning for salvation. What devious paths men have taken to satisfy this yearning! I shall never forget standing by the *Scala Sancta* in Rome. These are the "holy steps" that were brought over from Palestine to be a shrine for seeking pilgrims. The pattern is that you make your way up these steps on your knees, saying prayers at given intervals, and this act of devotion will bring you such merit as to erase years from your stay in purgatory. Luther was brought to Rome when he was seeking peace and started up these steps. Halfway up, he rebelled, saying within himself, "No, this can't be God's way. There is no peace in this!"

As we stood watching the pilgrims, we saw a cripple painfully pull one knee up after the other; we saw young folks go through the ritual and then skip away feeling that a job had been well done. My heart was heavy at the blind way these pilgrims were going, when the Lord has provided an open door. It was the succession of these man-made devices for salvation against which Luther protested. In the Letter to the Romans, as well as throughout all Scripture, he discovered the wonderful truth that salvation is a free gift of God.

The apostle gives a glorious answer to the question, "Who will deliver me?" "Thanks be to God through Jesus Christ our Lord! . . . There is therefore now no condemnation for those who are in Christ Jesus."

PRAYER: *Thank You, Lord, that whatever my condition, You will receive me, if I come seeking. Thank You that the burden does not need to be carried on my back. Thank You for forgiveness of sins in Christ Jesus, my Lord. Amen.*

Just as I Am, without One Plea

And that Thou bidd'st me come to Thee

Revelation 22:17
The Spirit and the Bride say, "Come." And let him who hears say, "Come." And let him who is thirsty come, let him who desires take the water of life without price.

AGAIN WE have extended to us the Great Invitation! In the social life of Washington there often is a great deal of "to do" about who will be included in a guest list when a V.I.P. is to be entertained. There are those who would give their right eye to be included in some of these invitations. Yet the invitation extended by the King of kings is ignored! The invitation that promises a feast that will last forever is given a deaf ear. As you read this today, if you have not already accepted it, the invitation comes anew, through God's Word which you have just read. No one can say that he was not included.

This is one of those hymns in our family life that has special meaning. It was my mother's favorite hymn, and was a part of every prayer that she prayed. The way of salvation was clear to her, and she wanted to make sure that each of her children knew about God's wonderful plan and invitation. Rest assured, we can never forget.

In this month is the birthday of our second son. There is something rather special in this hymn of Mother's being used at this time, for I believe that here is evidence of the blessings that come to the third and fourth generation of those that love God. Dave's life has been spared miraculously so many times. It almost seems as if his whole life has been a series of escapes from physical danger. Last year we were reminded of it again, when coming up from underneath the diving tower, he hit an aluminum ladder rung with his head, and had to have several stitches taken. No one knew that he was under the board, and he could easily have been drowned without anyone's being aware of it. As a little boy he fell down a whole flight of steps resulting in a concussion of the brain. In his very coming into the world, there was a divine Hand that protected the little one. This sense of destiny, of sharing God's great invitation, has now become the purpose of his life, because he knows what enrichment of life there is for those who come; knowing this, there is the overwhelming compulsion to share it with others. How I pray that my prayers may bless his life as my mother's have blessed ours!

Absolute surrender—that is the requirement for anyone who would know the joy of accepting Christ's invitation; surrender of your heart and your life to follow His will.

PRAYER: *Again, Lord, we would thank You for the inclusiveness of Your invitation. We thank You for the banquet that You spread in Your Word. We thank You for the "overnight hospitality" that is included in Your invitation. Bless young folks everywhere, and let Your Holy Spirit so work in their hearts that they may accept what You have to offer. In Jesus' name. Amen.*

Just as I Am, without One Plea

**Thou wilt receive;
Wilt welcome, pardon, cleanse, relieve**

Luke 15:1, 2

Now tax collectors and sinners were all drawing near to him. And the Pharisees and the scribes murmured, saying, "This man receives sinners and eats with them."

Isaiah 55:6, 7

"Seek the Lord while he may be found, call upon him while he is near;
let the wicked forsake his way, and the unrighteous man his thoughts;
let him return unto the Lord, that he may have mercy upon him, and
to our God, for he will abundantly pardon."

IT IS A beautiful experience to go through the Gospels and take note of the folks who came to Jesus, and the way that He received them.

There was the woman in the crowd who had had an issue of blood for many years. She thought, "If I only can touch the hem of his garment!" Can you imagine how she would have to push her way through the crowd to get to Him? It happened! She was well! She was about to slip back, when He turned to ask who touched Him? As she tremblingly and fearfully fell down before Him, He said to her, "Take heart, daughter; your faith has made you well."

How many times did not He say, "Your sins are forgiven you!" How many times give new life to a withered hand, new spring to a faltering limb, new sight to eyes, and a new lift to weary souls? If we beggar the language, there yet are not words enough to describe the gratitude this sinner feels for such a Savior.

Charles Wesley was speaking to a Moravian friend about the sense of pardon which had come to him. "I suppose that I had better keep silent about it," he said. "Oh no, my brother," was the reply, "if you had a thousand tongues, go and use them all for Jesus." And Wesley went home and wrote the hymn: "Oh, for a thousand tongues to sing my great Redeemer's praise."

In the Letter to the Romans we read: "Welcome one another, therefore, as Christ has welcomed you." Can there be the danger of our taking for granted the gift of pardon and love that is ours in Christ, and not be concerned that the whole world should know about it? Would our mission budgets go begging unless this were true? It is as simple as one redeemed soul telling another, and inviting him to share, too. How quickly we give recipes, and are flattered when a friend asks for one of ours. If you know the recipe for abundant living, you will lose it, unless you share it.

PRAYER: *Give us, Lord, tongues ready to witness of Your love. As You have received us, help us, in turn, to seek out the lonely and downtrodden, and love them in Your name. Amen.*

Just as I Am, without One Plea

Thy love unknown
Has broken every barrier down

1 John 3:16

By this we know love, that he laid down his life for us; and we ought to lay down our lives for the brethren.

WILL YOU recount the victorious phrases that ring through our Christian faith? "And of his kingdom there shall be no end." "Whom shall I fear?" "We are more than conquerors through him who loved us." "Every knee shall bow." "I can do all things in him who strengthens me." "With God all things are possible." You add to the list. As the conclusion to this hymn there is the great swell of all of these. God's love is the most powerful force in the world; God's love has broken down every barrier; God's love is eternal; God's love is for everybody. Here, then, is the note of victory that the song of every heart should have. Here, then, is our commission: to make that love known.

In a hospital in a large city there was a woman who had been very, very ill. She looked with somber eyes around her, for it was visitors' hour, and everybody else except her had a visitor. She almost wished that she had died, she was so lonely. What did anyone care? Suddenly a gentle hand touched her shoulder, and a kind voice spoke: "I have brought you some flowers. They are from a friend of yours." The woman's eyes opened wide in surprise. "I have no friend that would send me flowers," she said. "Nevertheless your friend has sent you these," said the stranger with a smile. "He thought that you would like for-get-me-nots best. You are tired now, so I will not stay, but I shall see you again. This card will tell you who sent the flowers," and with another smile the stranger was gone. Eagerly the woman read the card. "A great poet has said that flowers are messengers from us to God. He is wanting to say to you 'I have not forgotten you, and will rescue you even now. I will draw you to me and make you my own.'" The woman looked at the flowers. Forget-me-nots! Had she indeed forgotten the wonderful Friend that she once knew? Tears came to her eyes, and she remembered the lines of Browning:

All I could never be,
All men ignored in me,
This I was worth to God.

There is no barrier which the Lord cannot surmount. Yes, "we are more than conquerors through him who loved us!"

PRAYER: *Conquering Son of God, loving Savior, in adoration and praise we lift our hearts to worship You. Empower us to be the conveyors of Your love to others. Give us a faith in the power of love, so that nothing will daunt us. In Your name. Amen.*

A Mighty Fortress Is Our God

Ein feste Burg ist unser Gott. 8 7, 8 7, 6 6, 6 6 7. MARTIN LUTHER, 1529.

3 Though devils all the world should fill,
All watching to devour us,
We tremble not, we fear no ill,
They cannot overpower us.
For this world's prince may still
Scowl fiercely as he will,
We need not be alarmed,
For he is now disarmed;
One little word o'erthrows him.

4 The Word they still shall let remain,
Nor any thanks have for it;
He's by our side upon the plain,
With His good gifts and Spirit,
Take they, then, what they will,
Life, goods, yea, all; and still,
E'en when their worst is done,
They yet have nothing won,
The kingdom ours remaineth,

Martin Luther, 1529.

A Mighty Fortress Is Our God

A trusty Shield and Weapon

1 Samuel 17:45

Then David said to the Philistine, "You come to me with a sword and with a spear and with a javelin; but I come to you in the name of the Lord of hosts, the God of the armies of Israel, whom you have defied."

Romans 13:12

The night is far gone, the day is at hand. Let us then cast off the works of darkness and put on the armor of light.

THE BIBLE is full of passages that give us this picture of the way God has equipped us for the battle against evil in life. All the weapons are those related to love. Actually, this kind of warfare no nation has ever really tried. No nation has been Christian enough, apparently, to have such faith in God that it would believe that returning good for evil would bring victory; that feeding the enemy was God's offensive; that praying for them was a source of limitless reserve. I have been grateful for the measure in which our country has wanted to share with the starving around the world, but too often there has been consideration of the strategy of it, rather than a daring and fearless sharing because of love for others. If enough of us will believe in the power of love over hate; will have the faith of a David to know that all the weapons and strength of a giant are insignificant when pitted against the power of God, then we shall live to see the day of a new battle, the battle for the human heart.

It is not to be wondered at that Martin Luther chose the figurative language of the Bible to write his great Reformation hymn. It was the Bible that had unlocked the prison that was enslaving his soul. It was the Bible that provided the key to everlasting life through faith. Before that he had been locked in the bondage of fear and damnation because he had been taught that his salvation had to be earned by good works. It was the Bible that was his defense when he was pressed by foes on all sides; it was the Christ that came alive to him in that Book, and that made him defy pope and emperor to defend the truth as his conscience dictated.

Do you know what it means to be within the fortress of God? Do you know the strength of His weapons in your everyday living? With Him as a shield, and with the sword of the Spirit in your hand, there is no foe that you need ever fear. In God there is the answer to every one of these needs; in Him there is sufficiency to meet anything that comes.

PRAYER: *Lord of the Universe, God, our fortress, we thank You for the strong protection we know in Your love. We thank You that Yours is a victorious cause, and that Your weapons are never outdated. We thank You that you are sufficient for anything that may happen to us this day. In Jesus' name. Amen.*

A Mighty Fortress Is Our God

The old malignant foe
E'er means us deadly woe

Ephesians 6:10-13

Finally, be strong in the Lord and in the power of his might. Put on the whole armor of God, that you may be able to stand against the wiles of the devil. For we are not contending against flesh and blood, but against the principalities, against the powers, against the world rulers of this present darkness, against spiritual hosts of wickedness in the heavenly places. Therefore take the whole armor of God that you may be able to withstand in the evil day, and having done all, to stand.

ALTHOUGH THE Bible tells us that the devil goes around seeking whom he may devour, it also suggests that he sometimes disguises himself, for it speaks of "wolves in sheep's clothing" and of the "prince of darkness." Too many times we think of the power of evil with a couple of horns and a tail, and all the while such an enemy might be lingering in our own hearts. It is this that the Apostle Paul speaks about when he warns us about the kind of enemy we face. "Spiritual hosts of wickedness in the heavenly places" could well mean that the devil comes to church, too.

The fact that evil may disguise itself is well portrayed in Greek mythology. Jupiter was impressed with the beauty of Europa. He took the form of a snow-white bull, and mingled with the herd that grazed in the meadow where the young princess was gathering flowers. Attracted by his beauty and gentleness, she caressed him, crowned him with flowers, and fearlessly mounted on his back. He immediately plunged into the sea and carried her to an unknown shore, which later was called Europe after her. This is a tale of fancy, but the way the devil disguises himself to lead us his way is anything but fanciful. The power of the devil, Dr. Luther felt so strongly, even when he was in his study in holy preparation, that he flung an ink well at him. This is not to say that he actually saw him, but Satan's power in that room with him was that real.

We can never meet an enemy unless we acknowledge him. We can never overcome unhappy traits in our characters unless we are willing to face up to them. How Satan uses the weapon of alibi! Adam became a victim of it when he said, "The woman thou gavest me . . ." We build up our defenses and side-step responsibility; we assume a sanctimonious air when we criticize others. All of this is Satanic strategy to divert us from following the One who said that if we are to be master, we must first of all be servant; that in order to bring forth fruit, we must be a seed willing to die to self and be buried.

Do not minimize the foe; but maximize the Fortress!

PRAYER: *Within us, Lord, there is this constant battle between good and evil. Gird us with Your weapons, and help us this day to "fight the good fight of the faith." Thank You that Your reserves are at our command and that they can never be exhausted. In Jesus' name. Amen.*

A Mighty Fortress Is Our God

**With might of ours can naught be done . . .
But for us fights the Valiant One**

Psalm 44:4-7

Thou art my King and my God, who ordainest victories for Jacob. Through thee we push down our foes; through thy name we tread down our assailants. For not in my bow do I trust, nor can my sword save me. But thou hast saved us from our foes, and hast put to confusion those who hate us.

1 John 5:4, 5

For whatever is born of God overcomes the world; and this is the victory that overcomes the world, our faith. Who is it that overcomes the world but he who believes that Jesus is the Son of God?

HAVE YOU had the experience with little children of their thinking they are stronger than they really are, and wanting to do something that is far too difficult for them? Maybe it is a pail of water they want to be "big" about, and carry "all alone." But when the burden becomes heavy, and the little arms begin to ache, how happy they are to have Father's hand reach down and give them a lift. People will say, "I can fight my own battle; I don't need any help." But to every individual there comes a time when his own resources are utterly inadequate, and when he needs someone who will help.

There is Someone whom to have is to know victory. When you choose Him, you are sure to win. Why do you act as if you were defeated, fretting and worrying about the outcome, if you have chosen to be on His side? Perhaps it is because you do not call out His reserves often enough.

A man dreamed that he was traveling, and came to a little church with a steeple. On the cupola of the church, there was a devil, fast asleep. The man went along farther, and came to a log cabin. He found that it was surrounded by devils. He asked one of them what this meant. The reply was: "I will tell you. The fact is that the whole church is fast asleep, and one devil can take care of all the people; but here are a man and a woman who pray and they have power that we are concerned about."

"Who is it that overcomes the world but he who believes that Jesus is the Son of God?" Is this faith so strong in you that you rely upon Him in prayer? Do you sense the strong shoulders of the Son of God at your side, and flanking you against all foes?

How the church today needs to look to its resources; how it needs to inventory the strength that it has in Christ! There has been too much dress parade and too little battling for souls; there has been too much dissipation of energies on conferences discussing strategy, and too little calling upon the One who has the plan.

PRAYER: *Lord, forgive us our prayerlessness as a church and as individuals. We grovel around in our own strength and lose heart. Make us aware constantly that there is One who fights for us, and with Him there is no defeat. Amen.*

A Mighty Fortress Is Our God

Though devils all the world should fill,
All watching to devour us

Matthew 13:18, 19

"Hear then the parable of the sower. When any one hears the word of the kingdom and does not understand it, the evil one comes and snatches away what is sown in the heart; this is what was sown along the path."

1 Peter 5:8, 9

Be sober, be watchful. Your adversary the devil prowls around like a roaring lion, seeking some one to devour. Resist him, firm in your faith, knowing that the same experience of suffering is required of your brotherhood throughout the world.

DR. MARTIN LUTHER, the author and composer of our hymn for the week, is known as the father of evangelical hymnody. The lost art of congregational singing was restored through his efforts. It is said that the march of the Reformation gained speed and power because of the gospel message that was being sung from the throats of thousands of people.

There is something about singing a hymn that puts to rout the devil. Try it. Let the mood of depression be yours, and by the power of the Holy Spirit start singing a hymn and see what happens! Suppose you are afraid of some physical circumstance, like the darkness or a storm. Strike up a hymn, think on the words, and observe the result. Evil thoughts lurk in your mind; thoughts of suspicion and ill will. Sing a hymn of the love and mercy of God, and put the enemy to shame. This battle for the human soul is not something that we withdraw from; that was not the way of our Lord. It is something we pitch into with all the resources of heaven at our command.

There are those who think that they can retreat into seclusion, and so be protected. In Westmeal, near Antwerp, there is a convent of Trappist monks who try to do this. Thirty-six monks live there under the vow of separation from the world and perpetual silence. They dress in rough sackcloth with ropes about their waists, heads shaven and long beards. They live on bread and sour milk and vegetables, and sleep on hard boards. They spend their days in solemn silence. Each day they walk in a garden and look into an open grave, ready for the member of the group who will die first. This is supposed to be the high ideal of Christian living.

This, however, is not the kind of followers our Lord prayed for. He was right down in the busiest byways of His day, at the center of the trade traffic of that part of the world. He walked among men, and knew the buffeting of evil on all sides. In His day, too, there were plenty of devils to make the battle hot. But He enjoins us to get into the thick of it; He wants us to be on offensive. He is not satisfied just to hold the territory He has; He wants us to be part of His conquering army.

PRAYER: *Lord, help us to conquer in the opportunities immediately about us; give us faith to know there is victory in Your love. In Jesus' name. Amen.*

A Mighty Fortress Is Our God

One little word o'erthrows him

Revelation 19:13, 14

He is clad in a robe dipped in blood, and the name by which he is called is The Word of God. And the armies of heaven, arrayed in fine linen, white and pure, followed him on white horses.

Mark 3:11

And whenever the unclean spirits beheld him, they fell down before him and cried out, "You are the Son of God."

WORDS CAN take on such different meanings, depending upon the way they are used. Many of our strong words have lost their efficacy because they have been used carelessly. Superlatives no longer are effective, because modern advertising has super duped everything. Unfortunately this is also true about the "name which is above every name." Often one hears it used in a curse or carelessly.

But in the full force of what God meant it to be, what a name it is: "Jesus, the Son of God"! In the power of this Name, devils are defeated; in the power of this Name, the lame are made to walk; in the power of this Name, people are cured of all manner of diseases; and in the power of this Name, the world is redeemed. Try breathing this Name in prayer when you are sore pressed. Try making it your first call in the morning. Know the peace of its echo on your lips as you fall into slumber. In a single Name, you have a power that can overcome the world.

I am reminded of a story that Dickens relates in his *Child's History of England.* He there tells of a worthy merchant of London, Gilbert Becket, who made a pilgrimage to the Holy Land, and was taken prisoner by a Saracen lord, who treated him kindly and not as a slave. The lord's daughter fell in love with the merchant, and told him she wanted to be a Christian and was willing to marry him and go to a Christian country. The merchant returned the love until he found opportunity to escape to his country. The lady was more loving than the merchant, and leaving her father's house in disguise, she attempted to follow her lover. He had taught her two words: London, and Gilbert. Coming to the seashore, she went about among the ships saying "London, London." The sailors directed her to ships going there, and with some of her jewels she purchased passage. Then when she came to London, she went up and down the streets saying, "Gilbert, Gilbert." One day the merchant's servant noticed her and recognized her. Remembering the tenderness she had shown him in his captivity, the merchant ran to meet her, and with a cry of joy, she fainted in his arms.

There is a Name, that needs to be spoken on the streets of the world. It has in it the power to dispel darkness, to dissipate sadness, and forever to conquer defeat. And the name by which He is called is, "the Son of God."

PRAYER: *Holy Son of God, we thank You that in Your Name there is power to make victory out of any defeat. Amen.*

A Mighty Fortress Is Our God

The Word they still shall let remain

Psalm 119:89-93

For ever, O Lord, thy word is firmly fixed on the heavens.
Thy faithfulness endures to all generations;
thou hast established the earth and it stands fast.
By thy appointment they stand this day; for all things are thy servants.
If thy law had not been my delight, I should have perished in my affliction.
I will never forget thy precepts; for by them thou hast given me life.

THE STORY of the cataclysmic effect of the Word of God in Martin Luther's life has been repeated again and again in other lives when the Word has been released. More and more I am convinced that if we can get people studying their Bibles, the Holy Spirit of God will do the rest. We have the promise that His Word will not return void, but will accomplish that for which it was sent. One of the great things that Luther did was to get the Bible into the hands of the people, and into a language they could understand. Dr. Laubach and his workers are doing a tremendous work today, teaching people to read, and then seeing that the Bible is translated into their dialects and languages. If families together, neighbors together, church groups together, would gather around this Word, study it, and apply it to their lives, revolutionary things would happen.

A Christian teacher in India returned from an inland field. She was asked how things were coming. Unwittingly she gave a vivid description: "We are having a 'rebible' time," she said.

The Christian Church will be strong and virile and effective, if it is alive and sensitive to the leading of God. This is possible as His Word lives in us.

Volumes could be written relating the fascinating experiences of people around the world having their lives completely changed by a couple of pages of this book. Just the other day I read about an English diamond merchant who was packing gems which he was sending to a trader in India. Each was wrapped with special care. As he came to the last and costliest, he used as an outer wrapping the soft India paper torn from an old Bible—the first three chapters of the Gospel of John. A Hindu to whom this precious stone was sent, while unwrapping it had his attention drawn to the wrapping. He soon discovered that it was a message from the Book of Life. At the words, "God so loved the world . . ." he tarried, and then he began to ask what these words meant. By simple faith he accepted these words, and became a Christian. When a European missionary later reached the town, he found a large group of Indian Christians gathered about this man.

God's Word has power for your life. It can break the bondage of any sin; it can overcome any evil. More than that, it can give you a vision and purpose that will make life abundant.

PRAYER: *Use us as instruments to make Your Word come alive today, Lord. Help us to study it and live. Help us today to live some portion of it into somebody else's life. In Jesus' name. Amen.*

SATURDAY

A Mighty Fortress Is Our God

The kingdom ours remaineth

Isaiah 9:7

Of the increase of his government and of peace there will be no end, upon the throne of David and over his kingdom, to establish it, and to uphold it with justice and with righteousness from this time forth and for evermore. The zeal of the Lord of hosts will do this.

WHAT GREAT words are these, and what a surge of victory is ours to be a part of such a kingdom! These words are repeated in the Gospel of Luke, as the coming of the King is imminent. Is there this awareness of the everlastingness and sureness of our cause in the Christian Church today? We need a new sense of commission, both as a church and as individuals. We need a new injection of the fearlessness of the Reformation; we need men of the calibre who are willing to stand for truth and right, regardless of the consequences, knowing that God is their stay. We need a rebirth of God's dream for His world, when men will live together as brothers and bear one another's burdens. We need a new faith in the power of the Holy Spirit to accomplish this, if we will permit ourselves to be His vessels. How can this be?

Do you remember His words when Christ talked to His disciples about the time when He will come to reign over His kingdom?

He said, "For I was hungry and you gave me food, I was thirsty and you gave me drink, I was a stranger and you welcomed me. I was naked and you clothed me, I was sick and you visited me, I was in prison and you came to me." You know the rest of this passage: "as you did it to one of the least of these . . . ." It is no paradox, then, that the Reformer, who staked his life to proclaim the gospel of salvation by grace as he found that clearly expounded in Scripture, also made the statement that we have used before: "By this shall men know whether the birth of Christ is effective in you, whether or not you take upon yourself the need of your neighbor." There is the thermometer that indicates the temperature of your soul. What does yours read?

How quickly we are weary in well-doing; how ready we are to list what we have done. Yet the virility of the kingdom within us is witnessed by the way we take upon ourselves the need of our neighbor. How concerned are you about the bigotry of some of the stipulations of our immigration act? What does it mean to you that thousands are starving behind the bamboo curtain? What concern do you give to the "apartheid" policy of South Africa that often in the name of Christians belies the Fatherhood of God and the brotherhood that we know in Jesus Christ? Or closer home, what are you doing to live the principle of the kingdom in your own community?

PRAYER: *What a cause is ours and Yours, Lord! As we read these great words of Scripture, we know a holy thrill and are given a new purpose in living. Make us bold to be a part of Your kingdom work. In Jesus' name. Amen.*

The Church's One Foundation

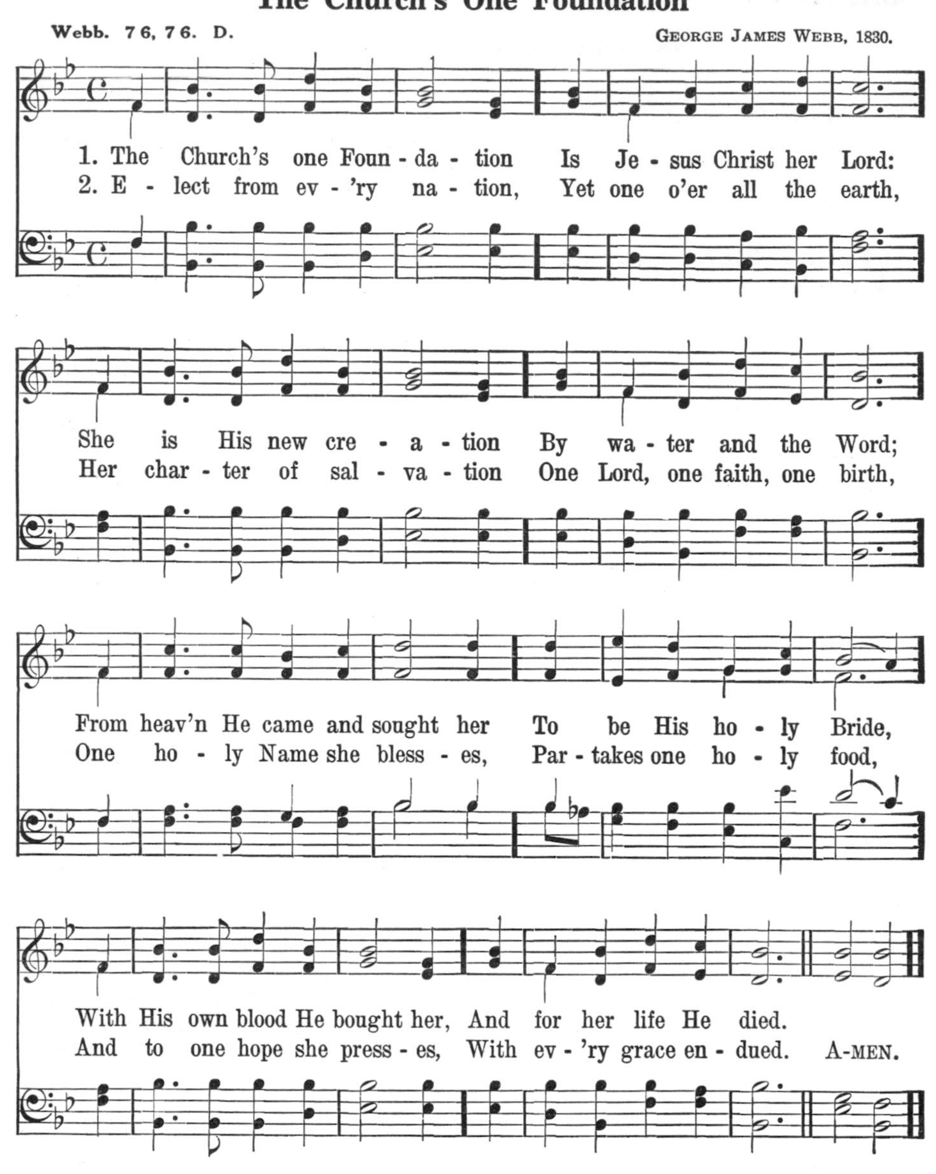

3 Though with a scornful wonder
Men see her sore opprest,
By conflicts rent asunder,
By heresies distrest,
Yet saints their watch are keeping,
Their cry goes up, "How long?"
And soon the night of weeping
Shall be the morn of song.

4 'Mid toil, and tribulation,
And tumult of her war,
She waits for consummation
Of peace forevermore;
Till with the vision glorious
Her longing eyes are blest,
And the great Church victorious
Shall be the Church at rest.

Samuel John Stone, 1866.

SUNDAY

The Church's One Foundation

Is Jesus Christ her Lord

1 Corinthians 3:11

For no other foundation can anyone lay than that which is laid, which is Jesus Christ.

OUR HYMN for the next seven days is built on a series of Bible verses. It was born out of rather a turbulent controversy in the church, but has come to be a unifying force as it challenges us to look to our Source. Samuel John Stone, the author, was a man of virility and sympathy. He found a little girl being beaten by a bully. He beat the bully black and blue with his fists, like an avenging angel. In sober thought later, he realized that there might have been other ways. He captained his college crew on the Thames. Though he might have been a soldier, he could not resist the call to the ministry. Most of his parishes were in very poor districts, and he devoted himself to his people with sensitivity, having a particular interest in young people and the working class. He was a real pastor, a shepherd.

In spite of his rigidity along certain lines, he was quite adaptable in others. He was sent to the parish of All Hallows, London Wall. This was a small city church in an area that had 10,000 by day, and 150 by night, consisting of caretakers and charwomen for the surrounding office buildings. He was equal to this opportunity. Largely at his own expense he renovated the church building and opened it at 6:30 a.m. to accommodate the crowds of office workers who arrived early on the commuters' train and had no place to go until their offices opened. He shared the church as a place for meditation and prayer during this waiting period. Our modern churches might well learn something from the adaptability of this man to his surroundings.

The hymn was written to help interpret the Apostles' Creed to some of his cottagers, who did not seem to know what the Creed meant and yet repeated it as one of their prayers. It was also an answer to his part of the conflict in the thought realm of the church of his day.

Think of what would happen if the Christian Church in the world today would look to its Foundation. Here is a real basis for unity. When we share what it means to know forgiveness in Jesus Christ; when we share what it means to have experienced answered prayer; when we share our concern for the whole world—we are one in the family of God. Our household of faith is built on the foundation of Jesus Christ. Surely this is the oneness that the Father desires in His children. Surely this is the end for which He would have us strive.

PRAYER: *There is no other foundation on which we would build, Lord, than on You and Your redemptive love. We thank You that this foundation holds through all the storms of life. Send a new Pentecostal experience upon Your church today, that with one voice we may witness to Your love around the world. In Your name. Amen.*

The Church's One Foundation

**She is His new creation
By water and the Word**

John 3:4, 5

Nicodemus said to him, "How can a man be born when he is old? Can he enter a second time into his mother's womb and be born?" Jesus answered, "Truly, truly I say to you, unless one is born of water and of the Spirit, he cannot enter the kingdom of God."

HOW THE Apostle Paul takes us to task for our divisions! In the letter to the Corinthians he raises the question: "Is Christ divided? Was Paul crucified for you? Or were you baptized in the name of Paul?" Around the subject of baptism there has grown much controversy, and I would not want to presume to enter into a discussion of the divisive elements here. Surely we can be together on the things that Scripture makes clear, and on the others we will each believe according to the enlightenment of our conscience. I think we are all agreed that when baptism simply becomes a "name-giving" ceremony, it is not what the Lord meant it to be. The Bible often combines baptism and teaching as in our Lord's great command, "Go into all the world . . . baptizing . . . teaching . . . ."

It is interesting to note the place of baptism in the Book of Acts. In the first chapter of Acts, we are reminded that John baptized with water, but that there would be the baptism of the Holy Spirit. In Acts 2, Peter, after reminding the people of the death and resurrection of Christ, enjoins them to repent and be baptized. Philip's experience with the Ethiopian eunuch ended in that man's asking, "What is to prevent my being baptized?" Chapter 10 records the story of Peter's baptizing the Gentiles, after they had received the Holy Spirit. Later in Acts the wonderful story tells us that the jailer and his whole family were baptized.

It is sufficient for me to know that to baptize is to follow the command of our Lord, and that what happens is the miracle of His word and our faith. I leave the rest to Him. I know that in Him I am a new creature; that my name through faith is written in the Book of Life, and that I am His child.

The hymn writer suggests also that the church is created on the Word. Sometimes I think that we forget that the church is a fellowship of believers. Being such, it is also a fellowship of the concerned; for if you love God, says Scripture, you must also love your neighbor. As Christians, in both the horizontal and the vertical channels, we should be one.

Let us never forget in our attitudes and in our devotion that Christ established the church; that it is His body here on earth; that if we love Him, we will love His Church, and give our best energies to His work.

PRAYER: *Where the church is in error, O Lord, correct it. Where it is divided unite it. Help us each to make our relationship with You personal and real. Give us joy in our fellowship one with another. In Jesus' name. Amen.*

The Church's One Foundation

From heav'n He came and sought her
To be His holy bride

Ephesians 5:25-27

Husbands, love your wives, as Christ loved the church and gave himself up for her, that he might sanctify her, having cleansed her by the washing of water with the word, that the church might be presented before him in splendor, without spot or wrinkle or any such thing, that she might be holy and without blemish.

2 Corinthians 11:2

I feel a divine jealousy for you, for I betrothed you to Christ to present you as a pure bride to her one husband.

THE FIGURE that the Bible uses to clarify the relationship of Christ and the church is one that we can all understand. The church, we are told, is the bride of Christ, and He will come to claim it for His own. That is why Paul in his Letter to the Corinthians speaks of having a "divine jealousy" for the young church; he wants her to be a pure bride for her one husband. Could it be that today's church has become polygamous? Is it that our oneness of purpose has been lost?

Dr. Phillips, in his Introduction to his translation of the Book of Acts has some very significant things to say in this regard. He says: "The new-born Church, as vulnerable as any human child, having neither money, influence nor power in the ordinary sense, is setting forth joyfully and courageously to win the pagan world for God through Christ." He goes on to describe them as "a body of ordinary men and women joined in an unconquerable fellowship never before seen on this earth." Here is the bride preparing for the advent of the One who will come to claim her! This young church is vigorous and flexible "for these are the days before it ever became fat and short of breath through prosperity, or muscle-bound by over-organization." (Can you see this kind of bride?)

We find it very easy to criticize "the church." It is a favorite indoor sport of many people. But perhaps we had better ask ourselves the question: Who comprise the church? When we discover that we are talking about ourselves, and that everything we say about the church is really an indictment of our own spirituality, maybe we will say less, pray more, and dedicate ourselves to making the "bride" of Christ ready for His coming. Is our faith manufactured? Have we encased our relationship to Christ in so many outward ceremonials that He is lost for the trimmings? Is the involvement of our modern life such as to submerge the One whom to know is life eternal? We need to pray, as individuals and as churches, that we might be channels for the Holy Spirit, so that the bride will expectantly await the day of His appearing.

PRAYER: *Stir us, Lord, so that we may bring to the church a sense of mission. Arouse Your Church, O God. In Jesus' name. Amen.*

The Church's One Foundation

Elect from ev'ry nation
Yet one o'er all the earth

John 11:51, 52

He prophesied that Jesus should die for the nation, and not for the nation only, but to gather into one the children of God who are scattered abroad.

Ephesians 4:4, 5

There is one body and one Spirit, just as you were called to the one hope that belongs to your call, one Lord, one faith, one baptism, one God and Father of us all, who is above all and through all and in all.

THIS LAST description of Christian unity welds us pretty closely together. How do we get so far apart? Sometimes I think that we cling to things of the past, not even knowing the reason for them; and these separate us. In our American churches many of the early divisions were due to language, necessitated by the waves of immigration from various countries. This reason for division is now a thing of the past; yet what a difficult time we are having to effect unity. Dr. E. Stanley Jones tells the story of the order of monks who, when they went to prayer, always tied a cat to one certain leg of the chair by which they were kneeling. When asked why the cat, no one could answer. Finally someone became curious enough to investigate, and discovered that centuries earlier one of the monks of the order was bothered by mice when he knelt to pray. So he brought in the cat to keep the mice away. No longer did this situation pertain, but each night a cat was tied to the certain leg of each monk's chair, because that was the way that it always had been done. (Where have I heard those words before?)

Christ is for the world, and the church is one in Him. Should people have to by-pass one church and go to another farther away, because their skin is of a different color, even though their faith is the same? Did it have to take a Supreme Court decision to awaken Christians to the fact that the soul has no color, and the elect of God will come from the ends of the earth, and gather together around the throne? Where is our vision and our daring? Our Scripture tells us that Jesus died to gather into one the children of God scattered over the earth. Could it be that we are crucifying Him afresh?

We are told that the Roman censors refused to let the debauched son of Africanus wear a ring on which was his father's likeness because "he who was so unlike the father's person was unworthy to wear the father's picture." If we are so destitute of the likeness of Christ on earth, it will not be granted us to enjoy His likeness in heaven.

PRAYER: *Search out our hearts, Lord, for bigotry and prejudice. Help us so to dwell together here, that it will be a foretaste of our oneness in the life to come. In Jesus' name. Amen.*

The Church's One Foundation

Though with a scornful wonder
Men see her sore opprest

2 Peter 2:1

But false prophets also arose among the people, just as there will be false teachers among you, who will secretly bring in destructive heresies, even denying the Master who bought them, bringing upon themselves swift destruction.

Matthew 24:4, 5

And Jesus answered them, "Take heed that no one leads you astray. For many will come in my name, saying 'I am the Christ,' and they will lead many astray."

THE APOSTLE PAUL needed to write constantly to the young churches to true them up in regard to their beliefs. Teachers would come along and get them all confused on issues that often were not even vital. There was a great controversy over whether circumcision was necessary for the Gentiles. Paul had a very definite word from the Lord in respect to this. He was able to teach, through the enlightenment of the Holy Spirit, that when we are born in Christ, the old things have passed away, and we are now new creatures in Him.

Peter, too, warned about the false prophets and teachers who "would secretly bring in destructive heresies." And Christ himself prophesied that many would come in His name, pretending to be His. What a dilemma this puts us in! What shall we believe, and how are we to know the truth?

In our day there are myriads of movements, claiming to have the truth, and having only a part of it. Often the part they emphasize is something that the church may have neglected, and many, many good people are captivated by an ethic or a philosophy that is not Christian, even though at times it is called such by its proponents. What is the test by which we can know if faith is real?

Use the measuring stick of Scripture. Does it square up with what Christ taught about himself? How can some of these folks reject Scripture and yet teach that Christ was a great teacher? How can they accept certain things of the Bible and discard others? The final criterion is, How does the teaching stand the test of time and the test of living? Men may hurl derisive names at the Church of Jesus Christ, but nobody can argue away love living on your street. They may impugn the intelligence of your faith, but they cannot deny its efficacy, if it gives you grace to bear any vicissitudes with patience and triumph. There is no argument that can hold a candle to the witness of Christ in you.

It is the pseudo Christians that do the cause so much harm. It is the Pharisee in each of us that skeptics can point to; it is the lip service, but not the life service that is such a strange paradox.

PRAYER: *Alert us, Lord, to the Truth. Help us to be living witnesses of it. In Jesus' name. Amen.*

FRIDAY

The Church's One Foundation

Yet saints their watch are keeping

Joshua 1:5

"No man shall be able to stand before you all the days of your life; as I was with Moses, so will I be with you; I will not fail you or forsake you. Be strong and of good courage; for you shall cause this people to inherit the land which I swore to their fathers to give them."

2 Timothy 2:19

But God's firm foundation stands, bearing this seal: "The Lord knows those who are his," and, "Let every one who names the name of the Lord depart from iniquity."

WITH BOLD honesty we have tried to speak of our failures as a church to bring the witness of Christ's concern in many of the areas of contemporary life. We would be remiss if we did not acknowledge those in every church who are keeping the fire burning brightly; who in self-forgetfulness are giving themselves to the underprivileged, the forgotten, and the lonely. They are the salt of the earth; they are the saints who are keeping the watch.

I think of a woman whose first two children were born spastic; and who lost a normal little boy at the age of four. She "had a nose" for the lonely and the needy, serving these people in love, and alerting others to serve them. She did not have a halo, but believe me, she had a shine. I think of a beauty operator that a great Scotch evangelist told us about. She was from his church, and was a woman who was shy with words. She had come to a new sense of her love for the Lord, and after her work on Mondays she went to the slums and conducted a class for girls, in which she showed them the beauty of Jesus, as she began by delousing them and washing them up. All through Saturday night she worked in the hospitals, because they were so short of help, and scrubbed floors and did other menial tasks. Little did her fashionable clients realize how she spent her "leisure" time! She had just come to the pastor with the proceeds of her Saturday night's work to be used in some cause for Christ.

I know a government worker who gives a night a week to children in the settlement house, and her Saturdays to those in the T.B. ward of the General Hospital; who teaches a Church school class and loves the members so much that, if any are absent Sunday morning, she visits them on Sunday afternoon. (She has no car.) This saint who is keeping her watch gives a large part of her income to the kingdom work.

What would the pattern of your everyday life look like to the Lord? Stand back a bit and take a look at it, against the backdrop of the cross. Is your striving for the things of the kingdom or for the things that perish?

PRAYER: *Lord, we would be of that company who keep watch and build the ramparts of Zion. Give us such a compulsion of love that we will be Your hands and feet in our community today. Live in us. In Jesus' name. Amen.*

SATURDAY

The Church's One Foundation

**And the great Church victorious
Shall be the Church at rest**

Exodus 15:1, 2, 18

"I will sing to the Lord, for he has triumphed gloriously; the horse and his rider he has thrown into the sea. The Lord is my strength and my song, and he has become my salvation; this is my God, and I will praise him, my father's God, and I will exalt him." "The Lord will reign for ever and ever."

IT IS a rewarding study to go through the Bible and read the songs of victory. Some of them have been sung under times of greatest duress. It was with a song that our Lord went up to Jerusalem; it was in prison that Paul sang. The song, of which here we have recorded a section, is the one that Moses and the Children of Israel sang. The wilderness was the setting; an unknown land their destination; but the Lord was with them. We remember how they faltered in faith again and again, and we are reminded of ourselves. But we recall that when they trusted in the Lord, He never failed them.

To champion His cause, the Lord had to use a woman in the person of Deborah. A handful of people led by a woman triumphed over chariots and man-made weapons. The song of Deborah and her people is an interesting study.

The song in Revelation 15 is the triumphant song of the victorious church, as Christ comes to claim His bride. The Church Militant is a part of the Church Triumphant. Ours is a victorious cause.

It is interesting to study in the Bible, too, the people of whom it can be said, "But the Lord was with him." Those words are the difference between victory and defeat. They change despair to hope; they change depression to joy. They still work!

No man or woman is ever used of God to build up His kingdom who has lost hope. When you know the presence and undergirding of the Lord, hope is eternal. We are told that "underneath are the everlasting arms." Has anyone who has tried the Lord found himself lower than underneath?

In a granite quarry in North Carolina the manager was showing a visitor about. He said: "We supplied the granite for the Municipal Building in New York City. We can lift an acre of solid granite, ten feet thick, to almost any height that we desire for the purpose of moving it. We do it by compressed air. It can be done as easily as I can lift that piece of paper and move it through the air." Man-made devices are wonderful, but the Holy Spirit of God has power beyond our wildest conceptions. He can change hearts; He can bring victory out of defeat. He can break a stubborn will.

The Church of Jesus Christ is a victorious church. In our walk as Christians there should be the song of victory.

PRAYER: *We thank You, Lord, for Your power that turns defeat into victory. We thank You for the knowledge that You have overcome the world. Help us to walk victoriously as Christians, and guide and direct the destiny of the Church. In Your name. Amen.*

Now Thank We All Our God

Nun danket alle Gott. 6 7, 6 7, 6 6, 6 6.

JOHANN CRÜGER, 1648.

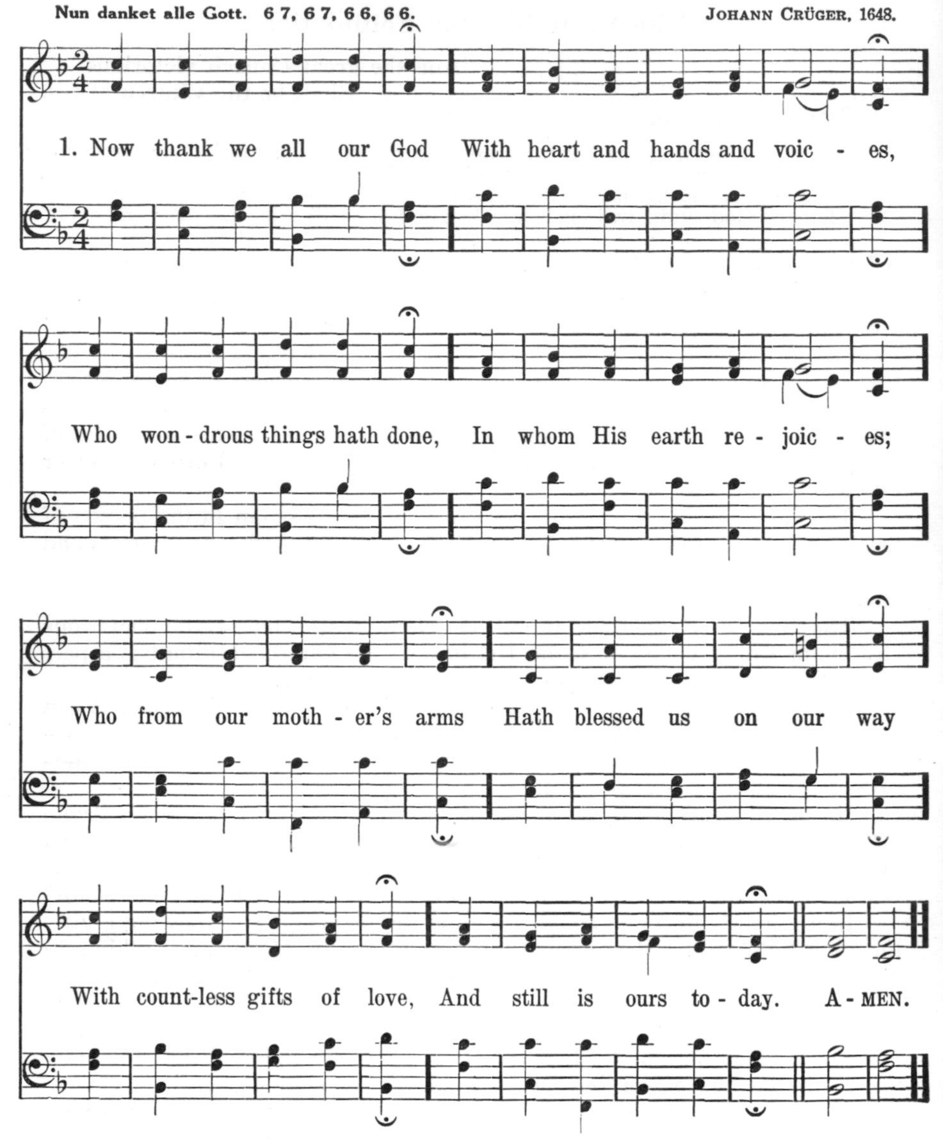

2 O may this bounteous God
Through all our life be near us,
With ever joyful hearts
And blessèd peace to cheer us;
And keep us in His grace,
And guide us when perplexed,
And free us from all ills
In this world and the next.

3 All praise and thanks to God
The Father now be given,
The Son, and Him who reigns
With them in highest heaven:
The One eternal God,
Whom earth and heaven adore;
For thus it was, is now,
And shall be evermore.

Martin Rinkart, 1630.

Now Thank We All Our God

With heart and hands and voices

Colossians 3:17

And whatever you do, in word or deed, do everything in the name of the Lord Jesus, giving thanks to God the Father through him.

WOULD YOU ever guess that this hymn was born out of a background of distress and death? Dr. Rinkart, the author, lived in the town of Eilenberg during the Thirty Years' War. Because this was a walled city, it became a refuge for fugitives from far and near. Unable to cope with the hundreds that crowded its streets and lived wherever they could, the city became a breeding place for disease and death because of lack of sanitation and of famine. The other two pastors died, and Pastor Rinkart was left to bury the dead and minister as best he could to the living. He read the burial service for from forty to fifty people a day, totaling about 4,480. At last the burials were in trenches without services. Rinkart's wife was one of those he had to bury.

But this was not enough. There followed three sackings, one by the Austrians and two by the Swedes. An indication of the man's faith is given in the incident connected with the Swedes. A levy of 30,000 thaler had been made on the town to aid in the Protestant cause. Knowing the impoverishment of his townsmen, Rinkart went out to the Swedish camp to plead their case. The General was adamant. The pastor turned to those who accompanied him and said, "Come, my children, we can find no mercy with men, let us take refuge in God." He then fell on his knees in the presence of those from whom he had sought relief, and uttered a fervent prayer, after which they sang the hymn: "When in the hour of utmost need." The Swedish commander was so impressed with the scene, that he relented and reduced the levy to 1,350 thaler.

The inspiration for the first part of the song was taken from the apocryphal book of Ecclesiasticus; the last verse is the author's paraphrase of the Gloria Patri, written in Greek some hundreds of years earlier. It was originally written as a table prayer, possibly for his own family. In Germany, it has become the national Te Deum and is sung at all festive occasions. The composer was a musician and a writer, having also authored plays that were produced. The bloody war, and its concomitant misery took its toll on Rinkart's health and he died a year after its end.

Somehow the song comes to mean a great deal more to me from out of this background. To be able to sing praise to God when circumstances were this difficult certainly is to witness to faith. Then to follow through with the work of one's hands in alleviating suffering, and to use the voice to encourage and help—this is thanks indeed!

PRAYER: *Forgive us, Lord, for our ready complaint, and our slowness to say "thank you." Let our living have the lilt of gratitude and our hands have the eagerness of praise. In Jesus' name. Amen.*

Now Thank We All Our God

Who wondrous things hath done

Psalm 105:1-5

O give thanks to the Lord, call on his name, make known his deeds among the peoples! Sing to him, sing praises to him, tell of all his wonderful works! Glory in his holy name; let the hearts of those who seek the Lord rejoice! Seek the Lord and his strength, seek his presence continually! Remember the wonderful works that he has done, his miracles and the judgments he uttered.

THIS MATTER of thanksgiving is a wonderful therapy for the soul. As you are remembering in a special way this week to thank God, why don't you help yourself to a wonderful experience, and each day thank some person for what he has meant in your life? One year I wrote a letter each day of November to thank someone who had blessed my life in the years past. It was a great experience. I remembered the Sunday school teacher who had loved her little girls so that in her they saw something of the Christ about whom she taught them.

I remembered a doctor who carried with him the presence of the Great Physician, and so blessed every bedside that he attended, including my children's. I remembered the kind lady who used to come in and clean, and be a real lift to a mother whose days had long hours in caring for her children and trying to help in the parish. Thanksgiving is good for the soul.

Psalm 105 is a recounting of the wonderful things that the Lord had done for the Children of Israel. The psalmist begins by reminding the Children of Israel from what roots they have sprung. Then he recounted God's covenant with Abraham, His promise to Isaac, confirmed to Jacob. He takes them back to the hard days when they wandered from nation to nation. He recalls how God directed the destiny of Joseph's life so that he could succor his people in time of want. Then he reminds them how God preserved and provided Moses to be their leader during very difficult times. He lists the plagues that the Lord sent to Pharaoh in order that he would let the people go. Then he concludes with:

So he led forth his people with joy,
his chosen ones with singing. . . .
Praise the Lord!

For each one of us during this Thanksgiving month it would be a wonderful thing to write down the guidance of the Lord in our lives. Is there in your living this note of thanksgiving? Is there in your home this melody to God? Is your first waking thought one of gratitude? Is your last remembrance at night one of trustful thanksgiving? What might you be fretting about right now as you read this? Stop—and say "thank you" to God for His gift of prayer, and then show your gratitude by using it.

PRAYER: *It is good for us, Lord, to think about the wonderful things You have done. Today we want the song of gratitude to be heard in our living. Amen.*

Now Thank We All Our God

In whom His earth rejoices

Deuteronomy 8:7-10

"For the Lord your God is bringing you into a good land, a land of brooks of water, of fountains and springs, flowing forth in valleys and hills, a land of wheat and of barley, of vines and fig trees and pomengranates, a land of olive trees and honey, a land in which you will eat bread without scarcity, in which you will lack nothing, a land whose stones are iron, and out of whose hills you can dig copper. And you shall eat and be full, and you shall bless the Lord your God for the good land he has given you."

Psalm 65:11-13

Thou crownest the year with thy bounty; the tracks of thy chariot drip with fatness. The pastures of the wilderness drip, the hills gird themselves with joy, the meadows clothe themselves with flocks, the valleys deck themselves with grain, they shout and sing together for joy.

THIS DESCRIPTION in the Book of Deuteronomy sounds as if it might have been written about America. How the Lord has blessed us! It is frightening, because with this thought comes the realization that "to whom much is given, of him will much be required." As surely as this applies to the individual, it applies to the nation as well. What a debt is ours to God!

Autumn is the fulfillment of the promise of spring. There is a sense of rejoicing in the harvest. "Thou crownest the year with thy bounty." Every time you go to the grocery store, there should be gratitude in your heart for the provisions of the Lord! Has not your heart rejoiced over the beauty of bins of fruits and vegetables? They witness to the providence of God. Do you stop to listen to the singing of the birds? They are joining their voices with the chorus of the earth. Here are more variations and harmonies than in any choir you ever heard; for all of nature has its own way of witnessing to its Creator. The incessant lapping of the wave on shore speaks of the everlastingness of God's love; the chirp of the cricket at your door is a reminder of God's awareness of the minutest of His creatures; the soughing of the winds in the pine trees is a reminder of prayer, which one cannot see but knows is there.

It is said that Beethoven had his piano placed in the middle of a field, and then, "under the smiling sky, with the birds singing around him, flowers shining and grain glistening in the sun, the master musician composed some of his great oratorios." You and I will bring to our day a more inspiring melody, if the undertones as well as the theme are the rejoicing of gratitude. All nature has set us the example. The crown of God's creation, man, should lift the most beautiful paean of praise, for we have seen all beauty culminated in a Savior.

PRAYER:

For the creation of the earth, we thank You, Lord;
For the miracle of seedtime and harvest, we give You thanks.
For the beauty around us that witnesses to Your love,
We praise You. *In Jesus' name. Amen.*

Now Thank We All Our God

**Who from our mother's arms
Hath blessed us on our way**

Acts 2:39

"For the promise is to you and to your children and to all that are far off, every one whom the Lord our God calls to him."

2 Timothy 3:14

But as for you, continue in what you have learned and have firmly believed, knowing from whom you learned it and how from childhood you have been acquainted with the sacred writings which are able to instruct you for salvation through faith in Christ Jesus.

AS WE think of things for which we should thank God, it would be well for us to take a backward look today. Do you remember the child you used to be? Has your life been blessed with "sweet home" memories? It is interesting in a group to share with each other our earliest remembrance. One might have an amateur study of psychology in determining what, in each instance, made the person remember that particular incident. Surely there are very few of us who will not bless the Lord in the remembrance of how, through our parents, God has blessed us on our way.

Perhaps a mistake that parents make without realizing it is in over-indulging a child. In one of my visits to the women's prison of the District of Columbia, I had a talk with a girl who was "in" ten years for using and peddling dope. She claims that she was framed in the peddling, and I am inclined to believe her. However, the pathos of her story was in another direction. At her request, I had visited her mother in Baltimore, and had a fine experience with a Christian mother, who would do anything for her daughter, and who was showing real love of Christ in helping to rebuild the wrecked life. As I talked to the daughter about my visit, she said, "Oh, I'm so glad that you love my mother. She would do anything for me. I'm sure that you will understand when I say this, Mrs. Nelson, because the last thing in the world that I would want to do, is to criticize my mother, but her being willing to do everything for me is part of my trouble. She didn't make me take any responsibility, and always gave me everything I wanted. I had my own way too much, and that way was no good."

How can parents, then, bless children on their way? It must be first to teach them the fear of the Lord, and their responsibility to Him. Then it must be to teach them the resources they have in prayer, and the directions for life that they have in God's Word. Then it must be to show them the joy of walking God's way, and serving their fellow men. Those of us with this kind of remembrance want to say "thank you" to God.

PRAYER: *For children everywhere, we would pray, Lord. Give us to share the love we know in You in our homes and with others. Thank You for parents who have shown the way. In Jesus' name. Amen.*

Now Thank We All Our God

With countless gifts of love,
And still is ours today

Proverbs 13:22

A good man leaves an inheritance to his children's children, but the sinner's wealth is laid up for the righteous.

Proverbs 22:6

Train up a child in the way he should go, and when he is old he will not depart from it.

THE OLD gospel hymn, "Count your blessings, name them one by one," has some very simple but happy suggestions for each one of us. I recommend taking a pencil and paper and writing them down. If some of them concern the people near you, I would suggest that you let them know your gratitude. We do not thank God enough; nor do we thank those about us as often as we should. It is so easy for us to take for granted the things that are done for us each day. If things are not just right, we are quick enough to point that out. But when things are right, how often do we mention it? A child learns an attitude of gratitude from his home, or he learns the opposite. This learning will "dog" him all the days of his life.

A little girl really evidenced her discernment, when in a group one night the question of food came up. This little lass told cleverly what each member of the family liked best. Finally, it came to the father's turn to be described. "And what do I like, Nancy?" he asked laughing. "You," said the little girl slowly, "well, you like most anything that we haven't got."

Someone has suggested that, since we have one Thanksgiving Day in which a lot of us think that we take care of saying "thank you" to God for the whole year, we should have a Grumbling Day, when all of our grumbles would be packed into one day and we would forget them the rest of the time. Not a bad idea.

Take a look at the blessings in your life today. Think of the number of people involved in making possible your physical comforts. Think of being able to read and write, and how many have given themselves that this might be possible. How many people we have to be grateful to—plumbers, electricians, builders, grocers, farmers, policemen, firemen, teachers, musicians, preachers, doctors, lawyers, businessmen, manufacturers. . . . You finish the list.

But most of all, "Thanks be to God for his inexpressible gift." This still is ours today; it blesses our lives, as it did the lives of our parents and our grandparents; Christ is the Gift of gifts. Let us not forget to thank Him.

PRAYER: *Lord what a list of blessings is ours! "Countless" is the word we need. For all, but most of all for You, we give our thanks! Amen.*

Now Thank We All Our God

O may this bounteous God
Through all our life be near us

Psalm 143: 5, 6

I remember the days of old, I meditate on all that thou hast done;
I muse on what thy hands have wrought.
I stretch out my hands to thee;
my soul thirsts for thee like a parched land.

Psalm 145:4, 5

One generation shall laud thy works to another,
and shall declare thy mighty acts.
Of the glorious splendor of thy majesty, and of thy wondrous
works, I will meditate.

THE PSALMS repeatedly acknowledge the bounty of God and invoke His blessings. In Psalm 145, there is one expression after the other of praise to God. First the writer speaks of blessing the Lord's name forever. Then in the next verse he says: "Every day I will bless thee." The next measure of time that he uses is the term "generation." So the spirit of the hymn writer, "Through all our life be near us," is well illustrated in this Psalm. There is the long look of "forever," and the close look of "every day." It is interesting to note, too, the recurrence of the word "all" with its various references. "The Lord is good to all." "All thy works shall give thanks to thee." "Thy dominion endures throughout all generations." "The Lord is faithful in all his deeds." ". . . and raises up all who are bowed down." "The eyes of all look to thee." And still there are more! On the one hand, it is used in reference to us, is inclusive; and on the other hand, it is descriptive of God; in His totality He blesses us. "The Lord is just in all his ways, and kind in all his doings." It is this bounteous God who is all in all and in all, that we pray will be with us all our life.

How does this "allness" of Christ find its response in our hearts? Do we permit Him to share in all that we do? Is He a part of all of our thinking? I like the modern translation of one of Paul's letters which speaks of our "bringing into captivity every thought into the orbit of Christ." Christ is all for us in all ages. Are we all for Him in all our life? There is a beautiful little prayer of George Herbert's, written in the 17th century, that speaks for my heart:

Our Prayer

Thou hast given so much to me,
Give one thing more, a grateful heart;
Not thankful when it pleaseth me,
As if thy blessings had spare days;
But such a heart, whose pulse may be
Thy praise.

PRAYER: *For all Your goodness for all of life, we thank You, Lord. Help us to withhold nothing from You. In Jesus' name. Amen.*

Now Thank We All Our God

And free us from all ills

Isaiah 25:8, 9

He will swallow up death for ever, and the Lord God will wipe away tears from all faces, and the reproach of his people he will take away from all the earth; for the Lord has spoken. . . . It will be said on that day, "Lo, this is our God; we have waited for him, that he might save us. This is the Lord; we have waited for him; let us be glad and rejoice in his salvation."

2 Corinthians 6:10

As sorrowful, yet always rejoicing; as poor, yet making many rich; as having nothing, and yet possessing everything.

THE FREEING from all ills, does not mean we shall be spared trouble. That is not the history of the men and the women who have followed the Christ. That will be only in the world to come. But it means that God will be sufficient for whatever comes. Therefore we can sing; therefore we can praise Him. Our witness through singing and praising, even during the ill times, is an unforgettable one to those who do not know the Lord. Too many folks rejoice only when the going is good.

There is a bird from whom we could learn much. It is the thistlebird, which always sings persistently when in any trouble of any sort. In a little town in Nebraska, a man heard this singing under his window for several days. Finally he called the song to the attention of a naturalist who was a friend of his. Upon investigating they found that the thistlebird was a captive in its nest. A ladder was brought and the bird and nest were taken down for examination. One of the bird's legs had become entangled in the wool which formed the nest's lining, and it took twenty minutes of careful maneuvering to release the little fellow. When this was done, the bird flew away, a little unsteadily, but apparently uninjured. The bird had been kept alive by worms offered by its feathered friends during its captivity. If the thistlebird had not sung in its time of affliction, it never would have been released.

So it is with us humans. There is a release in singing and in giving praise that is a therapy all in itself. Try it and see. If you are carrying a burden, if things are going hard with you, discipline yourself to sing of God's providence and goodness; of His sufficiency and love, and you will find that the burden is eased, and you have been freed from the ill. This is what it does for you. What does your witness do for others? It makes them take stock of themselves; it makes them want the source of strength that is yours.

We are in the period of time marking the close of the church year. What has God done for you? Has there been any time when He has failed?

PRAYER: *Thank You, Lord, for the release to our spirits that you give. Thank You that there is no binding that is too hard for You. Thank You for the promise that You will always be with us if we follow You. In Jesus' name. Amen.*

O Come, O Come, Immanuel

St. Petersburg. 8 8, 8 8, 8 8. DIMITRI BORTNIANSKY, (1752–1828).

2 O come, Thou Rod of Jesse, free
Thine own from Satan's tyranny;
From depths of hell Thy people save,
And give them victory o'er the grave.

3 O come, Thou Dayspring, come and cheer
Our spirits by Thine advent here:
And drive away the shades of night,
And pierce the clouds and bring us light.

4 O come, Thou Key of David, come,
And open wide our heavenly home;
Make safe the way that leads on high,
And close the path to misery.

Latin Antiphons, XI Century.
Tr. John Mason Neale, 1861.

O Come, O Come, Immanuel

And ransom captive Israel

Isaiah 7:14

"Therefore the Lord himself shall give you a sign. Behold, a young woman shall conceive and bear a son, and shall call his name Immanuel."

Isaiah 52:1-3

Awake, awake, put on your strength, O Zion; put on your beautiful garments, O Jerusalem, the holy city; for there shall no more come into you the uncircumcised and the unclean. Shake yourself from the dust, arise; O captive Jerusalem; loose the bonds from your neck, O captive daughter of Zion. For thus says the Lord: "You were sold for nothing, and you shall be redeemed without money."

THE EXPECTANCY of the Advent season is a thrilling one. From now until Christmas in a very special way, there should be the recurring thought in every Christian's heart. "The King is coming! The King is coming! He will come to me!" And from Christmas through the rest of the year we should live in the awareness that the King has come into our lives. This is the beginning of the Church Year. These four Sundays in Advent are preparatory to Christmas. Many of our churches use the symbol of the four candles during these Sundays to make people more aware of the anticipation. Each Sunday an additional candle is lighted.

In the Scandinavian countries, and in Germany also, this is often done in the homes, too. We have loved the practice in our home of lighting the Advent candles every night before family devotions around the table. A special candle holder called a "Lode" has been prepared for this purpose. In a certain section of Germany red apples are used as candle holders. Four of them are chosen, and the bottoms cut off to make them stand level. Then holes are made in the top of them for the candles. They are set in a background of pine branches on the center of the table and really add a very pretty decorative touch.

So often I have heard people say this time of the year: "My, Christmas is upon you before you really know it! I never get the things done that I planned!" And their mind is a confusion of cooky baking, entertaining, hectic shopping, and related things! My prayer is that with this Advent preparation there may be a new sense in your heart of what Christmas really can mean.

What enslavement imprisons you? Is it concern about "things"? Is it a nasty temper? Is it a tongue that you cannot bridle? Is it melancholy and depression? Is it fear of the future? Of ill-health? Of losing face? The message of the Advent season is: "Rejoice! There is coming One who will set you free. He has ransomed you from this slavery!"

PRAYER: *For Your wonderful plan, Lord, and for Your great love and its eternal provisions for our souls, we thank You. Make these Advent days significant ones in our lives as we prepare anew for the King's coming. In His name. Amen.*

O Come, O Come, Immanuel

That mourns in lonely exile here
Until the Son of God appear

Isaiah 51:11

And the ransomed of the Lord shall return, and come with singing to Zion; everlasting joy shall be upon their heads; they shall obtain joy and gladness, and sorrow and sighing shall flee away.

Isaiah 52:10

The Lord has bared his holy arm before the eyes of all nations;
and all the ends of the earth shall see the salvation of our God.

TO BE exiled from God is hell. It is hopelessness, and despair, and defeat, thrown all together. But if in this state there is the promise of release, and of reunion, then the exile is bearable. It was so in the case of the Children of Israel; it is so in the life of an individual soul. Our song is an invitation for the coming of the Lord. In the invitation is the faith of a positive answer. "Rejoice, rejoice! Immanuel shall come to thee, O Israel!" is the chorus.

The story of this hymn is both interesting and varied. It is sung to a medieval plain song that has such a haunting melody that once you begin singing it, you will find it with you throughout the day. Its origin was in the ninth century when it was used as a series of seven Antiphons. These are short verses sung at the beginning or close of the Psalm or the Magnificat during Advent vespers. Antiphon suggests that the lines were sung alternately between two choirs sitting opposite each other in the chancel. Four or five centuries later someone took these seven separate sentences and discarded two of them, changing the order of the remaining five, weaving them into a hymn and adding a refrain. This is the hymn that has become such an Advent favorite in the Christian world today.

The key words of the remaining antiphons have their derivation from Scripture passages. These key words are Immanuel, Branch of Jesse, Dayspring, Key of David, Adonai. The latter word is a substitute for the name Jahweh, from which is derived our Jehovah, but which was considered too sacred to pronounce so Adonai was substituted.

The lines we have from our hymn for this day, are a reminder of the Babylonian Captivity, when Israel was separated from God's temple in Jerusalem. The church now separated from heaven is compared to this exile. It is from this sad state that Immanuel is to come to set free the captives.

The metaphors may be mixed, and the setting of the hymn medieval, but its basic pattern is as modern and everlasting as God is. We have broken the law, and therefore are in exile from God. Only as there will come One who will ransom us, can we ever have our freedom again and know the joy of anticipating going home. As Christians we sing the song of released captives because there was that first Christmas.

PRAYER: *We thank You, Lord, for the release from the exile which sin places us. Constrain us to share this freedom with all the world. Amen.*

O Come, O Come, Immanuel

O come, Thou Rod of Jesse, free
Thine own from Satan's tyranny

Isaiah 11:1-4

There shall come forth a shoot from the stump of Jesse, and a branch shall grow out of his roots. And the Spirit of the Lord shall rest upon him, the spirit of wisdom and understanding, the spirit of counsel and might, the spirit of knowledge and the fear of the Lord. And his delight shall be in the fear of the Lord. He shall not judge by what his eyes see, or decide by what his ears hear; but with righteousness he shall judge the poor, and decide with equity for the meek of the earth; and he shall smite the earth with the rod of his mouth, and with the breath of his lips he shall slay the wicked.

IT WOULD be an enriching experience for each of us, if during these weeks of Advent we would read the Book of Isaiah. It is so full of Messianic prophecies, and so vividly gives the anticipatory feeling one should have for Christmas, that it is indeed good preparation. Where is there a more remarkable picture of what Christ is like than in these lines of the eleventh chapter? For each one of the phrases there comes a picture from out of the life of Christ, as it is recorded in the Gospels.

"And the Spirit of the Lord shall rest upon him" called to mind the baptismal scene at the River Jordan when a voice from heaven said, "This is my beloved Son, with whom I am well pleased."

"The spirit of counsel and might, of wisdom and understanding," brings me to the scene on the mountain side when Jesus gave the Sermon on the Mount. Where since then has there been wisdom and understanding like that?

"And his delight shall be in the fear of the Lord" calls to mind the Gethsemane scene and Christ's immortal prayer, "Thy will be done." Or the portion of the Gospel of John where He speaks of himself and the Father as one, and of His coming to do the will of One who sent Him.

"He shall not judge by what his eyes see, or decide by what his ears hear" makes me think of his appraisal of the Pharisees. "Whitewashed tombs," He called them, as He pointed to their inconsistencies with their babbling about their religion, while they did not practice the love of God in their daily lives.

"With righteousness shall he judge the earth" calls to mind His remarkable handling of the situation when they brought to Him the woman taken in adultery. The accusers slunk away in the knowledge of their own sin, and the woman was left to His mercy.

And as for His teachings, the world has never been the same since He expounded His way of life, as God's interpreter to us. This is the One about whom Isaiah prophecies; this is the One whose birthday celebration we are now anticipating; this is the One who would daily reign in our hearts.

PRAYER: *From the tyranny of myself and my sin, free me, O Holy Son of God. There is no other who has power to do it. Make this Advent season a special blessing in my life. Amen.*

O Come, O Come, Immanuel

**From depths of hell Thy people save,
And give them victory o'er the grave**

Isaiah 53:6, 11

All we like sheep have gone astray; we have turned every one to his own way; and the Lord has laid on him the iniquity of us all . . . he shall see the fruit of the travail of his soul and be satisfied . . .

PEOPLE MAKE hell for themselves. They are the ones to choose between God and the voice of the evil one. While the latter conquers, there is nothing but death to anticipate, for the inevitable result of sin is death. But the coming of Immanuel—God with us—is life and victory over the grave. In South Africa a Christian illustrated well what the difference ought to be. He said: "When a heathen is dying the witch doctors put into his hand a dead bone as a passport into the world beyond. But we do not grasp a dead bone as we pass through the veil. We grasp the hand of the living Lord."

Sometimes we forget how closely related Christmas and Easter are.

December Twenty-fourth
Tomorrow you are born again
Who died so many times.
Do You like the candle-light,
Do You like the chimes?
Do You stop to wonder
Why men never see
How very closely Bethlehem
Approaches Calvary?
ELEANOR SLATER

It was on the First Sunday in Advent that my father went home, some twenty-two years ago. It was a spiritual experience to hear him pray, "Come Lord Jesus, come quickly," and to know how sure the faith was with which he was meeting his God. It was a real "Advent" for him, because the Rod of Jesse had broken the back of sin and death, and this obstacle was no longer an unconquerable one to the pilgrim that held the hand of the Victor.

Do the thoughts of anticipating Christmas and death seem incongruous to you? If the One whose birthday we shall be celebrating has been born in your heart, this will not be. An old slave, who was a fine Christian, gives the witness of which we speak. He had evidenced his faith in the way he did his work, always the best that he could do. When it came time for him to die, the doctor leaned over him and gently said, "Corporal, it is only right to tell you that you must die." He replied, "Bless you, doctor; don't let that bother you; that's what I have been living for."

PRAYER: *Thank You, Lord, for the victory that we can know because You were born and were willing to die to release us from sin and hell. Thank You for the life that You bring to our living and the difference that Your presence makes. Amen.*

O Come, O Come, Immanuel

O come, Thou Dayspring, come and cheer
Our spirits by Thine advent here

Luke 1:78, 79

"Through the tender mercy of our God,
when the day shall dawn upon us from on high
to give light to those who sit in darkness and
in the shadow of death,
to guide our feet into the way of peace."

ZECHARIAH'S BEAUTIFUL song at the birth of his son, John the Baptist, has in it all the joy for which the hymn lines plead. It is from this song that the name for Christ, "Dayspring" comes. The Revised standard version uses the term, "When the day shall dawn upon us from on high," and that is exactly what Dayspring would mean, is it not? What does "the dawn of a new day" signify to you? We are living in an age when the science of psychology, the science of the mind, is an expanding study. Its sister, psychiatry, has such practical implications, that everyone is aware of it. One of the basic principles that it teaches is that there is a chance to begin again; you can forget the past. This is essential in rebuilding mental health where the individual is sick because of "ghosts" that loom up to haunt him.

But this is not new. We Christians have had it in our Christ all along. It was promised back there in the days of Isaiah in the prophecies of Christ's coming; it was fulfilled when He walked on this earth, and offered a new beginning and healing to every one who came to Him; it continues today in our lives, as we accept the gift of the forgiveness of our past failures, and let each new day dawn with the knowledge that the Dayspring from on high has visited us.

Why, then, should we go heavy-hearted or be downcast? It can only be that we do not invite Him in. That is the implication in the line of our Advent song: "Come and cheer our spirits by Thine advent here."

You have heard about that experience in Martin Luther's life when his wife taught him a lesson. Luther had been pretty low in spirits, and it was bothering Kate to the point of doing something about it. So she dressed herself in mourning apparel, and greeted him with a sad, long face. "Why, Katie," he cried, "who is dead?" Somberly she replied, "God." "For shame on you," was his retort. "You know that isn't so!" And her womanly and wise answer was: "Well, that is the way you have been acting!"

Light an Advent candle in your heart today, and there will be cheer both for yourself and for others.

PRAYER: *For the joy of Your presence, we thank You, Lord. For the difference to all the world that Your coming made, we give You praise. Help us to reflect that joy in our living. In Your name. Amen.*

O Come, O Come, Immanuel

And drive away the shades of night
And pierce the clouds and bring us light

Isaiah 40:31

> But they who wait for the Lord shall renew their strength,
> they shall mount up with wings like eagles,
> they shall run and not be weary, they shall walk and not faint.

IT IS from the third chapter of Revelation that this name which the hymn writer uses in the last verse, comes. "The Key of David" is our Lord who unlocks the door to everlasting light. In Psalm 77 we have recorded what the Lord did with clouds to clear the way for the Children of Israel that they might pass through the Red Sea. There is no cloud but that it is "afraid" of God. There is no trouble in your life but that He can dispel it. There is no overhanging gloom that His presence will not disperse. You have but to try Him.

And so these lines of such a witness from the Book of Isaiah. The question that introduces them is pertinent: "Have you not known? Have you not heard? The Lord is the everlasting God, the Creator of the ends of the earth. . . . He gives power to the faint, and to him that has no might he increases strength." How can one "drive away the shades of night, and pierce the clouds"? It is to call upon the One who is the Light.

In a certain town there was a torchlight procession to honor a returned hero. As the parade started, one torch after the other blazed into radiance, as if by electricity, and one wondered what the source of their light was. A small child was discovered, crouching under some timbers to keep away from the wind, with a lighted candle in his hand. Every torch bearer came to him for light. This little fellow was lighting up the world of darkness.

There was a Child who was born in a manger in a dark corner of the world. He crouched under "wood," one day, too, to provide a Light for all the world. Every one who comes to Him gets his torch lighted for His is a light that never goes out, and it lights up everything that it touches. It is the "Key" to unlock everlasting light.

And do not forget that the person who carries such a light reflects it in the lives of all whom he meets. That is the way that the light spreads and grows. That is the way that the clouds of the world—the war clouds, the hate clouds, the clouds of selfishness, the better-than-thou clouds, are dispersed. Do you daily bring your torch to have it lighted that you, too, may be a dispeller of clouds?

PRAYER: *There is no shadow, Lord, if we place ourselves directly in the sunshine of Your presence. There is no cloud, when we are on the side of the sun. By the grace of Your Holy Spirit, may we keep Your light glowing steadily in our hearts. In Jesus' name. Amen.*

O Come, O Come, Immanuel

Make safe the way that leads on high

Isaiah 62:10-12

Go through, go through the gates, prepare the way for the people; build up, build up the highway, clear it of stones, lift up an ensign over the peoples. . . . Behold, the Lord has proclaimed to the end of the earth: Say to the daughter of Zion, "Behold your salvation comes; behold his reward is with him, and his recompense is before him."

"MAKE SAFE the way that leads on high"— this is what the coming of Immanuel did for the world! This proclaims the Magna Charta of the human soul. Is it any wonder that there is an inner compulsion that caused every verse of our hymn to have as its exclamation point: "Rejoice, Rejoice! Immanuel shall come to thee, O Israel."

Yes, Christmas should be a happy time, and our preparations for it should be happy. All the while there must be within us a sense of responsibility. If you were traveling on a highway and had been given information about the road ahead that was very vital, would you be satisfied just to make use of it yourself, and forget the fellow whose car had pulled up alongside of you? Suppose the information said that if you went one road, you would go to your own destruction, because there were evils that lurked all the way to the precipice at the end. This you would not be able to see because it was so skillfully hidden from view. The other road, according to the information (which, by the way, had been sent back by travelers who had gone the way) was not very smooth, but all along there were stations of help, and this guide would suffice to carry you over it. Its destination was the most beautiful view in the world, and a free resting place. Suppose this happened on your next trip. Would you tell the fellow next to you, or would you go your own way blithely and let him head for destruction? Before you told him, would you make sure that he is the same brand and breed that you are, had the same color hair, and the same income?

Friend, on the highways of life today are these millions of travelers, your neighbors and mine. Christmas brought to the world the only map that can safely lead a wayfarer home. You have in your possession that map in your knowledge of Christ and what He has done for the world. Can you complacently follow its sure directions and ignore the peril of your neighbor? Can you smugly light your Christmas candles, and not be concerned that the rest of the world is stumbling along in darkness?

Make this Advent something special in your life, by daily making it a point to share with someone your knowledge of the road that leads home.

PRAYER: *Awaken us to our responsibility, Lord, to share our knowledge of You with others. Help us to do it winsomely, Lord, that others will want to follow the path that we take. In Jesus' name. Amen.*

Winds Through the Olive Trees

Traditional
Arr. by R. Ekstrom

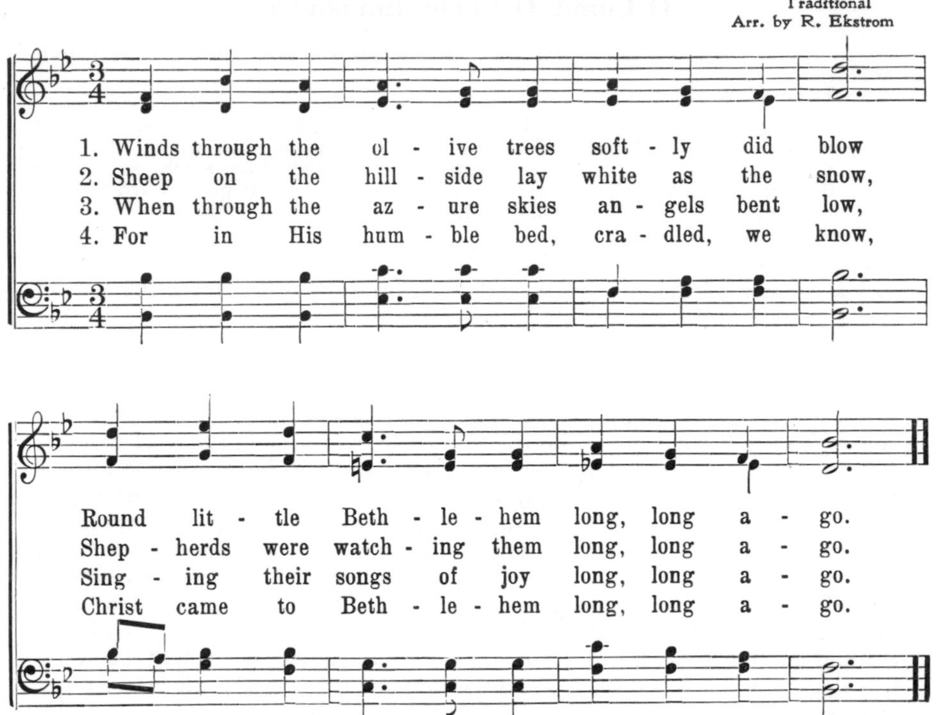

Winds Through the Olive Trees

Softly did blow

Psalms 128:3

Your wife will be like a fruitful vine within your house; your children will be like olive shoots around your table.

John 3:8

"The wind blows where it wills, and you hear the sound of it, but you do not know whence it comes or whither it goes; so it is with every one who is born of the Spirit."

Psalm 147:18

He sends forth his word, and melts them; he makes his wind blow, and the waters flow.

THE TIME for the singing of carols has come. They are such good preparation for the coming of the King. The simple carol for this week is unknown to many people. Its author is unknown, as well as its age. It has a haunting simplicity that particularly fits the Bethlehem story. Once learned, it will be within you and crop out at the most unexpected times.

I must confess that it has in it something special for me, for it is associated with crisp December evenings in Duluth, when the ground was beautiful with its white covering of snow. Then we would join our young people in caroling for the shut-ins. There would be a violin to give us a lift, and as we would pile out of the cars at each stop, somebody would pick up the tune, "Winds Through the Olive Trees." Another voice would join, and another, until we all would be marching down the path to the house, in sweet and simple harmony with the story of that first Christmas coming in song from our lips. We would be able to see our breath in the cold, but there were warm hearts underneath the mackinaws as we saw candles lighted in other hearts in response to the message of the Light of the World. Unforgettable memories!

The olive is one of the most sacred Bible trees. It is closely associated with the prayer hours of Jesus. It never thrives far from the sea, because it is dependent upon mists for its growth. It is known to be almost ageless, for from the old tree a new shoot is sent up before the former crashes to the earth.

Our song writer is giving us the setting for the story that is to be told. It was an ordinary day; soft winds blowing through the olive trees, just as they had in the days of Noah. (Remember, it was an olive branch that the dove found?) People were sitting in their homes eating their meals. It was a day just like today is in your life. On such a day, the Lord was born.

PRAYER: *Mighty Creator from whose hand have come all things, and in whose power is the wind and the seasons, help us to prepare our hearts for this season that celebrates Your coming to earth in the form of man. Help us to be aware that You will come anew into our hearts each day. Amen.*

MONDAY

Winds Through the Olive Trees

'Round little Bethlehem
Long, long ago

Micah 5:2

But you, O Bethlehem Ephrathah, who are little to be among the clans of Judah, from you shall come forth for me one who is to be ruler in Israel, whose origin is from of old, from ancient days.

BETHLEHEM WAS a favorite spot for me in the Holy Land. Possibly it was because it fulfilled my imaginings so well. As we drove down the hillside to make our way from Jerusalem to this city of Jesus' birth, we saw flocks of sheep, with their shepherds in their characteristic garb. Here was exactly the same kind of dress I had struggled to devise many Christmases at home for our "actor" shepherds in the Church school. Bending around a corner in the road, where olive trees lined the way, was this little city of some two thousand homes, set like an amphitheatre in the hollow of the hills. Today the streets are lined with little shops selling mementoes, but there must also have been shops there, when our Lord was born, for Palestine was a trade center, a crossroads, for the then known world. One bends low to enter the Church of the Nativity, for the door was cut down to size in the days of the Crusades so that horsemen would not ride their steeds into the place that was so sacred to many.

We made our way down to the grotto which has been designated as the place of the famous manger scene. If we had not been prepared, we would have been a little disturbed by all the ornate trimmings that surrounded the place. We had to close our eyes and remember the simplicity of that first setting, and the humility of the One who changed the course of history.

The streets of Bethlehem were filled with ordinary people, stopping to visit, or going on their devious errands. It was an ordinary Palestinian town. Yet Scripture makes us to know how extraordinary it was. Rachel was buried right outside of this place; here it was that Ruth and Naomi came, to effect the union that was connected with its later importance; from here King David had come, then only an ordinary shepherd boy, with his kingly days ahead. It was an ordinary place, but God chose it for the most extraordinary event of all time, the birth of our Lord.

Where do you live? Do you look to other places and think of how exciting it would be to live there? The Lord often chose the simple and unimportant places and people to do His greatest work. Christmas should make you remember that. He will come to your town, to your heart—and transform them!

PRAYER: *Give us such a reflection of Your values, Lord, that no place will ever be insignificant. Give us such a sense of expectancy in our daily living as to be constantly asking, "What if the Lord should come to me today?" Come, Lord Jesus! Amen.*

Winds Through the Olive Trees

Sheep on the hillside lay
White as the snow

Psalm 65:13
The meadows clothe themselves with flocks.

Psalm 79:13
Then we thy people, the flock of thy pasture, will give thanks to thee for ever.

Psalm 95:7
For he is our God, and we are the people of his pasture, and the sheep of his hand.

IT WAS such a natural for sheep to be a part of the Christmas story. They had represented the God—man relationship all through the Old Testament. They were as much a part of everybody's life as anything could be. They provided food and clothing, and companionship, too. In Bible times, every family in Palestine hoped to buy two lambs at the time of the Passover. One was killed and eaten to commemorate their protection by the hand of God when they were in Egypt, and to celebrate their Exodus from there and their safe deliverance from the hand of Pharaoh. The other was kept as a playmate for the children, whose job it then was to take care of it. It furnished wool for their looms and at last ended up in the larder. This was, of course, a sad day for the children, but there was always the prospect of another lamb coming up. The sheep slept with the children and ate from their hands. The pet sheep drank from the children's cup, as told in the story of the prophet Nathan to David, the story of the poor man who had but one ewe lamb.

Shepherds and sheep were a real part of Palestinian landscape—and still are. Shepherding was the most ordinary occupation a man could follow. Yet it was to shepherds that the angels announced the birth of the King of kings! It was to ordinary shepherds, whose names have never been recorded in mortal books, doing an ordinary job, on an ordinary night, in an ordinary place, that the greatest message of all time was given!

Our human values are so superficial. We look upon some work as being more important than other work. We are so quick to classify people and their jobs. It is not so with the Lord. Many people look out the windows of life to other people's fields and think, "Oh, if I only could be working at that job!" Yet all the while, in their own place there is an opportunity to hear the message of the angels: "For to you is born this day in the city of David, a Savior. . . ." There is born to *you*. . . .

Whatever your occupation, whether it be at a typewriter, or in kitchen; whether it be in office or in field; whether it be in the rural areas or the urban, the message is to you—and it can completely change a life.

PRAYER: *Help us to bring to the tasks of our every day, Lord, Your love and Your sense of the dignity of every man. Today give us grace to do well, whatever is at hand. In Jesus' name. Amen.*

Winds Through the Olive Trees

When through the cloven skies
Angels bend low

Psalm 103:20

Bless the Lord, O you his angels, you mighty ones who do his word, hearkening to the voice of his word!

Psalm 91:11, 12

For he will give his angels charge of you to guard you in all your ways. On their hands they will bear you up, lest you dash your foot against a stone.

ANGELS BEND low! It was an angel that the Lord placed at the entrance to the Garden of Eden to bar the way for those who had sinned. It was an angel who announced to Mary that she was to be the mother of the Savior. It was an angel who prepared Joseph for his part in this great event. It was an angel who announced at the tomb to Mary Magdalene that the entrance had been opened again for all who were willing to go the way of the cross. Scripture is full of instances of angels as messengers, and angels as guides. We are told there are guardian angels. In speaking of children, the Lord says, "I tell you that in heaven their angels always behold the face of my Father who is in heaven."

We often labor under the error that when we die we will become angels. This is not Scriptural. Angels are another order of beings who minister for the Lord. We were created, "a little lower than the angels," and yet, as Peter says in his Letter, the message which we have heard about the love of God in Christ is such that the very angels long to look into it.

Is it not a wonderful thing to know that the Lord has His angels watching over us to guide us? I have a friend who blesses my life by reminding me that she prays for the guardian angels to watch over our children.

So the Lord used His angels to tell to the shepherds this greatest of all messages; this word that meant a new hope for every creature, for all the world.

Are you sensitive to the message that the angels would bring you? We are told that if we show hospitality to strangers, it may be that we will be entertaining angels unawares. Have you known this joy, and been blessed three times over, when you have shared without expecting to receive in turn?

Try inviting someone who does not expect it. Seek out a lonely person, a destitute person, and share with him your heart, your hearth, and your board. There are strangers from around the world in your community who need to know Christian love as it is lived in an American home. Invite them in—and who knows! You may be entertaining—angels unaware!

PRAYER: *This Christmas time, Your birthday, Lord, help us to follow the pattern of remembering others, forgotten others, whose remembrance will be our birthday gift to You. In Your name. Amen.*

THURSDAY

Winds Through the Olive Trees

Singing their songs of joy

Isaiah 9:2, 6

The people that walked in darkness have seen a great light; those who dwelt in a land of deep darkness, on them has light shined. . . . For to us a child is born, to us a son is given; and the government will be upon his shoulders, and his name will be called "Wonderful Counselor, Mighty God, Everlasting Father, Prince of Peace."

"LUCIA DAY" in Sweden is a very special day, ushering in the Christmas season. It also is called "The Feast of Lights." Early on this morning in a Swedish home, a young girl of the household will arise and, dressed in white with a crown of candles on her head, will serve the family "lussekattor" *(rolls made to resemble cat faces)*, and "peppar kakor" *(ginger snaps)* with a cup of coffee. The story had its origin in Italy where Lucia was a beautiful girl engaged to be wed. Then she became a Christian, and in giving her heart to Christ, wanted also to give all her means. This infuriated her fiancé so that he burned her eyes out, and finally burned her at the stake. Her story as a Christian martyr traveled northward where it became interwoven with a pagan festival. Now according to legend, she wanders around in her bare feet, eyeless, but carrying a candle, and succouring the poor and helping the needy. She is the "Queen of Lights" for she brings with her into dark places the Light of men. The "Lucia fest" has now become a civic festival in many places and is a means for raising money for charity.

"Singing their songs of joy"—is this what the beginning of the Christmas festivities will mean to you? Or will it mean hurried last minute shopping for a gift that you had not expected to give, but because you received one you feel that you must give one in return? Will it mean a checking of your card list to be sure that you remembered every one who remembered you last year? Will there be so much baking and cooking that the Christ child will knock at your door and find no room?

Whom are you remembering for whom it will be as if it were unto Him? Where will your church, His Church, come in on your giving, or will it be that you have stretched your budget so far that there will be nothing left? Will you spend hours wrapping beautiful packages, and be too busy to visit the ill and the aged, to share with them the joys of Christmas? Will there be time, quiet time, to be apart with Him, so that you may hear the personal message He has for you?

Christmas is not here yet. There still is time. This Child that was born that first Christmas, whose birthday you are about to celebrate, would like to be included in your plans. Make it His birthday party!

PRAYER: *Light of the World, wherever You have come You have scattered darkness. Let Your light be the center of our Christmas activities. Let what You would want us to do be the guidance for our plans. Help us Lord, to put You back into Christmas. Amen.*

Winds Through the Olive Trees

For in a manger bed
Cradled we know

Luke 1:30, 31

And the angel said to her, "Do not be afraid, Mary, for you have found favor with God. And behold, you will conceive in your womb and bear a son, and you shall call his name Jesus."

Luke 2:7

And she gave birth to her first-born son and wrapped him in swaddling cloths, and laid him in a manger, because there was no place for them in the inn.

THE AVERAGE cubicle house in Palestine has one large space divided into two apartments. In the space nearest the door live the domestic animals, the ox and cattle and donkey. Mangers for the animals are placed on the lower level of the homes. Contrary to the pictures which artists have created of the manger, they are not made out of wood but rather hollowed out of stone, and set flat on the floor without any legs. Sometimes these have been excavated from caves.

Members of families in Palestine sleep side by side on mats, fully dressed. Do you remember the parable our Lord told about the man who would not heed the importunate knocking at his door by a neighbor's asking for bread? "Do not bother me; the door is now shut, and my children are with me in bed."

Mary must have longed for a regular cradle for her baby that Christmas night. The baby's cradle of those times was a woolen cradle swung from roof beams. These were slung on mother's back when she walked into the fields to reap. One wonders if Mary had such a cradle with her when the Holy Family fled into Egypt.

Though the cradle was a manger of stone with a bed of straw; though the attendants were the lowly animals whose home the Christ child shared, yet there was a mother's love to care. And the heart of Mary is laid bare in the Magnificat. Here was a woman who had faith; here was a woman who trusted when she could not understand the pattern at all. Here was one who was willing to be the "handmaid of the Lord."

I have wondered often what Mary must have thought as she felt the first stirrings of life within her. Surely there must have been those who raised their eyebrows at this unwed woman who was with child. Yet there was a serenity about her, as evidenced in her visit to Elizabeth, in her response to the angel, and in her hymn of praise. I am sure Mary called to mind the things that she had learned from Holy Writ, the things that concerned God's care and protection.

PRAYER: *We have paid so much attention, Lord, to the outward accoutrements of life, that often we have not had time for love. Forgive us, and give us a sense of values that will measure up to eternity. We ask it in Jesus' name. Amen.*

SATURDAY

Winds Through the Olive Trees

Christ came to Bethlehem
Long, long ago

Isaiah 25:1

O Lord, thou art my God; I will exalt thee, I will praise thy name; for thou hast done wonderful things, plans formed of old, faithful and sure.

WHO WOULD ever think that the coming of a little baby into the world could make such a difference? How little we know the ways of God!

The amazing effect that an ordinary child can have on a difficult situation is evidenced by an incident from the First World War. A day dawned on a battlefield in northern France with a fog so thick that no one could see more than a few yards from the trenches. In the night, the Germans had drawn back their lines a bit, and the French had gone forward, but between the two positions, a lonely farmhouse was still standing. As the sun rose, big guns began to boom. But suddenly on both sides the shooting stopped, and there was a deep silence. Midway between the trenches near the shattered farmhouse there was a situation that seemed impossible in such a setting. But there it was! Crawling on its hands and knees, a little baby! It appeared perfectly happy and contented, and the men in either trench heard its laughter as it plucked a dandelion. Not a shot was fired. There was hardly a breath. This spot which had been an inferno of explosion and hell was now a friendly little oasis in a desert. Suddenly a soldier jumped out and ran to where the child was. He tenderly took it up in his arms, and brought it back to shelter. No shots came from the trenches, but along each side rang out a mighty cheer. A little babe had been able to do what guns and generals could not do.

A little Babe born in Bethlehem changed the direction of a whole world from "an eye for an eye" philosophy, to one that bids you turn the other cheek.

And in despair I bowed my head:
"There is no peace on earth," I said,
"For hate is strong, and mocks the song
Of peace on earth, good will to men."

Then pealed the bells more loud and deep:
"God is not dead, nor doth He sleep;
The wrong shall fail, the right prevail,
With peace on earth, good will to men."

Till, ringing, singing on its way,
The world revolved from night to day,
A voice, a chime, a chant sublime,
Of peace on earth, good will to men!

H. W. Longfellow

PRAYER: *In the stillness of the pause before a Child in the manger, Lord, let the world hear again Your invitation to peace. Amen.*

Good News from Heaven the Angels Bring

Vom Himmel hoch da komm ich her. L. M.

VALENTIN SCHUMANN'S
Geistliche Lieder, Leipzig, 1539.

3 All hail, Thou noble Guest, this morn,
Whose love did not the sinner scorn:
In my distress Thou com'st to me,
What thanks shall I return to Thee?

4 Were earth a thousand times as fair,
Beset with gold and jewels rare,
She yet were far too poor to be
A narrow cradle, Lord, for Thee.

5 Ah, dearest Jesus, holy Child,
Make Thee a bed, soft, undefiled,
Within my heart, that it may be
A quiet chamber kept for Thee.

6 Praise God upon His heavenly throne,
Who gave to us His only Son;
For this His hosts, on joyful wing,
A blest New Year of mercy sing.

Martin Luther, 1535.

SUNDAY

Good News from Heaven the Angels Bring

Glad tidings to the earth they sing

Isaiah 61:1

The Spirit of the Lord God is upon me, because the Lord has anointed me to bring good tidings to the afflicted; he has sent me to bind up the brokenhearted, to proclaim liberty to the captives, and the opening of the prison to those who are bound.

SOMEWHERE I read of an incident connected with the writing of this song. The story seems highly probable. Dr. Martin Luther, the author, was a generous and hospitable man, but an abominable financier. His wife Katie had to take over that part of the household, and he acknowledged with gratitude what a wonderful manager she was. But she had to work hard and use all her ingenuity to make both ends meet.

Luther had the proclivity to invite to his home any and all students who had no place to go. Their table often held eighteen or twenty guests of this kind. You may have read some of the interesting Table Talk that ensued. This was fine, but it was costly to keep feeding such a mob, and sometimes Kate voiced her objections.

It was the night before Christmas, and Luther was in his study preparing to preach at the Christmas service on the morrow. Then he remembered that he had forgotten to tell Kate about the students that he had invited to dinner. There was quite a group of them. He left his study to find her in the kitchen, busy with the preparations. When he broke the news, she "broke," too! "How am I going to manage?" she said. "Where is the money coming from?" "There, there, Katie," was his response, "the good Lord will provide, you know that. He always does." She knew that it was useless to press this point more, so she said to him, "Well, you'll have to take care of the baby. I can't possibly rock him and get the food ready, too." So, the story goes, Luther took the little one's cradle into his study, and began rocking with his foot, as he turned to his books. Something about the peace of the little one in the cradle arrested his attention and he began musing: "It must have been a starlight night like this, the night that the Savior was born. What an experience to have the heavens open and hear an angels' chorus! And what a message they brought! Good news! The best that the world could ever hear! Good news from heaven!" And before he knew it, poet that he was, he was writing the song. In the original, there were eighteen verses, so one wonders if the baby were a long time getting to sleep.

What news in the Christmas message! Isaiah beautifully lists the details of what this message means: "good tidings to the afflicted, to bind up the brokenhearted, to proclaim liberty to the captives, and the opening of prison to those who are bound."

PRAYER: *Thank You, Lord, for the witness of all these song writers. Thank You for the reiteration of the Christmas message. Prepare my heart to receive it with joy. In Jesus' name. Amen.*

MONDAY

Good News from Heaven the Angels Bring

To us this day a Child is given

Isaiah 2:4

He shall judge between the nations, and shall decide for many peoples; and they shall beat their swords into plowshares, and their spears into pruning hooks; nation shall not lift up sword against nation, neither shall they learn war any more.

HOW THE world needs to stop and hear the angels' song today. A song of joy, yes, because there was born a Savior; and a song of peace: "Glory to God in the highest, and on earth peace among men with whom he is pleased!" What a change in the world the news of this Child's birth made! When we look about us and see all the turbulence and suspicion and armament; when we list the areas of tension around the world today, we begin to wonder if there are any men "with whom he is pleased!" We go again to the Book of Isaiah and read with nostalgia the promise that "nation shall not lift up sword against nation"; and again in Isaiah, "The wolf shall dwell with the lamb, . . . the lion shall eat straw like the ox." What can we do to help bring peace?

We must begin in our own household and in our own neighborhood. What is the primary cause of quarrels in a home? Determine that, and then multiply it by many people, and you have a major war. Basically I think we are all agreed that our selfishness is at the bottom. Each one wants to protect his own rights; each one wants to be the "big fish." The One about whom the angels sang their Christmas message set quite another example: He who was king of glory, "humbled himself and became obedient unto death, even death on a cross." What an example to follow! Are you able to remain silent when everything within you cries out to defend yourself, and show the other person to be wrong? Are you able to pray for those who oppose you?

A little girl came home to her mother one night and said, "I was a peacemaker today." "How was that?" asked the mother. "I knew something that I didn't tell," was the unexpected reply. We could learn from this little lass.

Martin Luther told the story of two goats that met upon a bridge over deep water. They could not go back; they durst not fight. After a short parley, one of them lay down and let the other go over him, and so no harm was done. The moral is that you are to be content if your person is trod upon for the sake of peace.

PRAYER: *Lord, we know that man-made schemes cannot bring peace, and yet You must work through us mortals. O bring peace to the world, Lord. Bless the United Nations, that it may be an instrument of peace. Help the Christian members to give a witness of Your presence in their lives. Still the noise of the warmongers, that we may hear the message of the Christmas angels. Amen.*

Good News from Heaven the Angels Bring

This is the Christ, our God and Lord,
Who in all need shall aid afford

John 1:1-5

In the beginning was the Word, and the Word was with God, and the Word was God. He was in the beginning with God; all things were made through him, and without him was not anything made that was made. In him was life, and the life was the light of men. The light shines in the darkness, and the darkness has not overcome it.

WHO IS this Babe that was born in Bethlehem? We would do well in our Christmas preparation to take a look at who He is! It might make a difference! The Gospel of John gives about as complete a picture of Him as we can get. He first tells us that He is the Word, one with God, and from the beginning of time. Next He is presented as Son of man when He is a guest at the marriage feast in Cana. To Nicodemus, He is the Divine Teacher. Bending over the pool where the sufferers are, He is the Great Physician. To the Samaritan woman, He is the Soul Winner. Listen to the other portraits of Him that John gives us: Bread of Life, Water of Life, Light of the World, Defender of the Weak, Good Shepherd, The Resurrection and Life, The King, A Servant, The Consoler, The Great Intercessor, The Model Sufferer, The True Vine, The Giver of the Spirit, The Uplifted Savior, The Victor over Death, and the Restorer of the Penitent.

Best of all to me is the fact that He is Redeemer and Friend. Dr. Elson, the pastor of President Eisenhower, tells of an unforgettable memory that he has. When in health, the President attended church regularly, so that the pastor hardly noticed that he was there. On this Sunday, at the end of the service, the congregation joined in the closing hymn, "What a Friend We Have in Jesus" which happens to be one of the President's favorites. As they were singing the last stanza, the pastor's eyes were drawn to the place where the President sat. There he was, with his glasses down a bit on his nose like any other grandpa, singing with all the vigor that he had:

"Are we weak and heavy laden,
Cumbered with a load of care?
Precious Saviour, still our Refuge,—
Take it to the Lord in prayer."

At a time when the balance of the peace of the world was on the shoulders of this man, he found his refuge in the Prince of Peace, the same source that you and I have. He believes with the song writer: "Who in all need shall aid afford." This is the One who was born in Bethlehem. This is the One who wants to be Your Savior. This is the One who will walk with you through every day of the year.

PRAYER: *Today, Lord, the world is dark. Help us to bring Your light to every corner of our living, and to every corner of the world. In Jesus' name. Amen.*

Good News from Heaven the Angels Bring

**He will himself our Saviour be,
And from our sins will set us free**

Galatians 4:4, 5

But when the time had fully come, God sent forth his Son, born of woman, born under the law, to redeem those who were under the law, so that we might receive adoption as sons.

IN THE first Book of the Bible, Genesis, we are told of God's plan of love to redeem mankind. To follow the pattern of the Messianic prophecies in the Old Testament, and to see their fulfillment in the New, is to have a rich experience in faith. That He was the promised seed of Abraham, of the lineage of David born of a virgin in the city of Bethlehem, these have all been fulfilled. That kings should come to His rising, that His name should be Immanuel, God with us, that there should be the massacre of the infants, that His family should have to flee into Egypt, these are all a part of the Christmas story.

Were we to follow His life into its maturity we should find the same amazing pattern. His rejection by the Jews, some of His characteristics, His triumphal entry, His being betrayed by a friend and sold for thirty pieces of silver, as well as His crucifixion, resurrection, and ascension, these all indicate a master plan and fulfillment by God for us.

This He did to set us free from sin. No wonder that poets and hymn writers through the ages have found their language beggared when trying to describe their gratitude. There come to mind the lines from a Lenten hymn:

What language shall I borrow
To thank Thee, dearest Friend!

There is a language! He himself told us about it. He made it very clear that, if we want to do something for Him, we should seek the hungry and the lonely and the naked and the stranger and the prisoner. He promised us that in serving them and helping them, we would be doing it for Him. In fact, He assures us that is how men will know that we love Him.

Christmas, His birthday, is a wonderful time. What do your preparations evidence about your gratitude and your love for Him? I am reminded of one of our boys when he was small. We had tried to teach them that the joy of Christmas was in doing for others. There was none of this: "What do you want Santa to bring?" I weakened, though, and took them to the train department of a toy shop. They loved watching those trains. That night this boy prayed, "And please, God, if I get two trains for Christmas, help me to give one to the poor."

PRAYER: *Search our hearts, O Lord, and make us honest about our plans. Give us the courage and the grace to put You at the heart of all of them. In Jesus' name. Amen.*

THURSDAY

Good News from Heaven the Angels Bring

In my distress Thou com'st to me

Genesis 35:3

"Then let us arise and go up to Bethel, that I may make there an altar to the God who answered me in the day of my distress and has been with me wherever I have gone."

2 Samuel 22:7

"In my distress I called upon the Lord; to my God I called. From his temple he heard my voice and my cry came to his ears."

THE HISTORY of the Christian Church is a witness to the way the Lord has helped men in their distress. Not always is it obvious at the time, but in the backward look one sees the marvelous guiding of Providence. This was evidenced again and again in the Old Testament; it has greater corroboration in the New Testament; the Lord of glory came to earth as a little child, to be a man like us that He might know the feeling of our infirmities. How many times people will say, "O you can't understand. You have never had it happen to you!" And you know how true it is, that when you have had a similar experience, your sympathy is much more real and discerning.

There have been human beings who have had such a heart of love that they have gone through various tortures better to understand and help. In recent experiments in mental health, people have subjected themselves to certain processes to make them mentally ill, in order that they might relate the reactions and feelings when one is under that stress. There have, for instance, been those who have gone with bound eyes in order that they might better serve those for whom the light is shut out, and understand the difficulties encountered because of it.

What God did for us in Christ is all of this and much more. He who was the King of glory, and had all power, left His kingly home to come to earth, to be born in a manger, to be born of a woman, to have to flee for safety, to work as a carpenter, to be misunderstood, even to be hated, and then to die on a cross.

Sometimes we get distressed because we do not see relief immediately! The King of Christmas asks us to take one step at a time, and trust Him for the rest. A tourist was taking a bicycle trip in Scotland. Sometimes it was difficult to follow the roads. Often he needed to ask for guidance. There were many times when the directions had so many details that they were puzzling, and he would forget them before he had hardly begun. But once a man told him how to proceed for two or three miles and then said, "I shan't burden you with any more. That is as much as you can remember. When you reach the point to which I have directed you, ask at the blacksmith shop for further directions."

PRAYER: *Thank You, Lord, for Your love for us. Thank You for coming to earth to be our Savior. Remind us again this Christmas and through our whole life of the miracle of Your love. Amen.*

Good News from Heaven the Angels Bring

Were earth a thousand times as fair

Psalm 27:4

> One thing have I asked of the Lord, that I will seek after; that I may dwell in the house of the Lord all the days of my life, to behold the beauty of the Lord, and to inquire in his temple.

WHAT IS the most beautiful thing you can think of, other than our beautiful Savior? Is it a rose, with all its lovely fragrance, just emerging from bud to flower? I love roses for Christmas, red roses symbolizing the One who is called the Rose of Sharon. Is it a baby, a happy, gurgling little one, fresh from its bath? Is it some older person, with all the marks of having walked with the Lord on her face? Is it a young girl, on the verge of full bloom? Or is it a starlit night on a placid lake, with a border of pines and birches? Maybe it is a snow-capped mountain in its mighty majesty against an azure sky, over which billowy clouds move in procession?

What is the most beautiful thing you can think of? Let the picture come before you now, and then know that more fair than this, more fair than all these, is the Savior who was born in Bethlehem that first Christmas.

With His awareness we can see beauty in the most unexpected places. A famous father taught his son this lesson. Edwin Markham wanted his lad to have discerning eyes. When the boy was about five years old, the father took him on a walk, and told him that there was poetry in everything—a tree, a board, a stone, a cliff; in food and drink and night and dark and everything. While the little boy was looking around, a bird's nest fell into the line of his vision. Rather defiantly, he pointed it out to his father and said, "There's a bird's nest, Father. Let's see you write a poem about that!" And the father wrote:

> There are three green eggs in a small brown pocket,
> And the breeze will swing and the gale will rock it,
> Till three little birds on the thin edge teeter,
> And our God will be glad and the world be sweeter!

Yes, the earth is beautiful, and there is beauty in everything, if you will look for it. But the most beautiful of all is the Savior who came to redeem mankind. When you watch a sunset, something of its glow will be reflected in your face.

A favorite chorus of the girls out at the prison is the popular one: "Let the beauty of Jesus be seen in me." They go back to their confinement, singing that chorus. And I have seen faces that come in, set and disgruntled, leave relaxed and beautiful, because of the power of God's Word, and the presence of the beautiful Savior in it.

PRAYER: *Give us discerning eyes, Lord, to recognize soul beauty. Help us to see, through all the tinsel and wrappings, the beauty of Your love that came to earth in a new revelation at Christmas. Amen.*

SATURDAY

Good News from Heaven the Angels Bring

Ah, dearest Jesus, holy Child,
Make Thee a bed, soft, undefiled,
Within my heart, that it may be
A quiet chamber kept for Thee

Jeremiah 24:7

"I will give them a heart to know that I am the Lord; and they shall be my people and I will be their God, for they shall return to me with their whole heart."

IN THIS stanza of the hymn is a Christmas prayer that pleases the heart of God; here is an open door for the One who comes knocking; here is room for the Christ child to dwell.

Here is what Christ looks for: a heart, open and yielded to the One who came to earth to dwell with men. Will that be happening to you this Christmas?

The Lord can do this for you, if this is your earnest prayer. In the Book of Jeremiah He says: "I will give them a heart to know that I am the Lord." As you read the Christmas stories these days, as you sing the Christmas carols, are you willing to pray, "Come into my heart, Lord Jesus"? What a Christmas this will be for each of us, if this is our prayer! What happens when the Lord comes in is the miracle of His grace. Enmity goes out, pride slinks away, old grudges are erased, self is sent scampering.

Bishop Taylor relates that he was once having a communion service for a group of natives. During the preparatory meditation, which dealt with the forgiveness of sins, the bishop saw a peculiar thing happen. One man, a former cannibal, turned and looked intently at the man sitting next to him. Then he abruptly arose and fled out of the church. A few minutes later he returned and quietly took his place at the communion rail beside the man from whose presence he had fled. After the service, the bishop asked the man about his sudden departure. Then he explained that he had recognized the man beside him as the man who had slain his father in a battle. After this man had helped to devour his father at a cannibal feast, the son had sworn revenge. Years had passed, during which he had found Christ. But as he identified the man at the communion rail, the old hatred awoke. He ran into the forest and prayed for power to forgive, and put this hatred out of his heart. On his knees he caught a vision of how Jesus had died to make his forgiveness possible. God gave him the victory, and he went back to take communion with the one he had vowed to destroy.

Be willing to kneel together with all people around the manger of the Christ, and know we are of one family. Accept from Him forgiveness and love, and in this glow go back to your everyday experiences.

PRAYER: *We would open the doors of our hearts now, Lord, so that You may come in and dwell with us. Help us to do a thorough house cleaning of every room of our hearts in preparation. In Jesus' name. Amen.*

O Little Town of Bethlehem

St. Louis. 8 6, 8 6, 7 6, 8 6. LEWIS HENRY REDNER, 1868.

3 How silently, how silently,
 The wondrous Gift is given!
So God imparts to human hearts
 The blessings of His heaven.
No ear may hear His coming,
 But in this world of sin,
Where meek souls will receive Him still,
 The dear Christ enters in.

4 O holy Child of Bethlehem!
 Descend to us, we pray;
Cast out our sin, and enter in,
 Be born in us to-day.
We hear the Christmas angels
 The great glad tidings tell:
O come to us, abide with us,
 Our Lord Immanuel!

Phillips Brooks, 1868.

O Little Town of Bethlehem

How still we see thee lie

Luke 2:1-5

In those days a decree went out from Caesar Augustus that all the world should be enrolled. This was the first enrollment, when Quirinius was governor of Syria. And all went to be enrolled, each to his own city. And Joseph also went up from Galilee, from the city of Nazareth, to Judea, to the city of David, which is called Bethlehem, because he was of the house and lineage of David, to be enrolled with Mary, his betrothed, who was with child.

THE GREAT wealth of Christmas carols has come from around the world. One of America's finest contributions to the carol collection is this much loved hymn, "O Little Town of Bethlehem," by Phillips Brooks. He took a trip to the Holy lands in 1865. It is said that his Sunday school children had gathered the money to make this trip possible for their pastor. Three years after his return, he was asked to write a song for the Children's Christmas service. In remembering his trip, he tried to think of what had impressed him most. On the night of Christmas Eve those three years before, he had gone out to the field where the shepherds must have been, and the sweet beauty of the starlit night stayed with him. Later he attended the service which lasted from 10 p.m. to 3 a.m. The day before Christmas he had ridden on horseback from Jerusalem to Bethlehem. But of all of his experiences, it was the remembrance of the quiet town in the stillness of the star-studded sky that stood out the most.

He gave this poem to his organist, and asked him to write some music for it. The man was always waiting for the right inspiration to come, and on Christmas Eve was much disturbed about his procrastination. In the middle of the night he dreamed that he heard the angels singing. He awoke with the melody still sounding in his ears. He quickly seized a piece of paper and recorded it, and the next morning filled out the harmony. He never wanted to take credit for it; he always insisted that it was a gift from heaven.

There was a beautiful affinity between Phillips Brooks and children, although he was a bachelor. He loved children, and they in turn responded to him. The story is told by Dr. McCutchan that when a mother told her little girl that Phillips Brooks had gone to heaven, the little lass said, "O mama, how happy the angels will be!"

The first stanza is an apostrophe to the little town. There were no street lights, no automobile headlights, and no home lights. People worked from dawn to sunset, and then were ready to retire. It was into this quiet little village that Jesus Christ was born.

PRAYER: *We marvel, Lord, at the wonder of Your plan. An emperor's order, a little village, a mother and a manger, and the King of glory is born. Thank You that there is nothing too insignificant to escape You. Thank You that we are in Your plan. Amen.*

O Little Town of Bethlehem

**Yet in thy darkness shineth
The everlasting Light**

Luke 2:7

And she gave birth to her first-born son and wrapped him in swaddling cloths, and laid him in a manger, because there was no place for them in the inn.

Isaiah 9:2

The people who walked in darkness have seen a great light; those who dwelt in a land of deep darkness, on them has the light shined.

Ephesians 5:14

Therefore it is said, "Awake, O sleeper, and arise from the dead, and Christ shall give you light."

INTO WHATEVER situation the Christ comes, there is light. Let it be a quarrel let it be a problem, let it be a burden, or whatever the darkness of the soul, He is the only Light that can dispel it. Bethlehem lay unsuspecting her destiny that winter's night; and to one of her streets came the Light of life. To all the world since then, Bethlehem has been a symbol of rest to weary travelers; and to those who have been walking in darkness has her light shined, because Jesus was born there.

One of the most striking stories I have ever read illustrates the miracle of The Light in a dark place. The great Christian, Dr. Kagawa, shares it. A man was brought into a hospital with a terrible Oriental skin disease. Science had yet found no cure for it. All that they could do was to submerge the man in a tub with a chemical solution that would relieve the suffering. Actually, then, he was condemned to a living death night and day, with even his arms submerged.

But into the darkness of that hellish prison the Light came. Somehow he came in contact with the gospel story. His spirit took on new life; his soul had been released. At his request, a New Testament was fastened on a long string, and tied to the ceiling. The Book hung on a level with his eyes. Day after day, and month after month, he drank in the life-giving words. His useless body was almost forgotten in the abiding peace that he found with the advent of Christ. As his physical strength failed, his soul gained new insights, until the prison bath tub became an altar. People from everywhere came to hear this story, and to see the Book that had wrought this miracle of a man's soul being vibrantly alive while his body was wasting in agony. As Dr. Kagawa said, "It is hard to have faith in a bath tub." Yet, who can say how far-reaching was the witness of this man during those seven years he spent in such a home, before his soul was released.

PRAYER: *Thank You, God, that You are a light that is everlasting. Your light is never variable, or its resources exhausted. Help us to walk daily in this light. In Jesus' name. Amen.*

TUESDAY

O Little Town of Bethlehem

The hopes and fears of all the years
Are met in thee tonight

Luke 2:14

"Glory to God in the highest,
and on earth peace among men
with whom he is pleased."

HOW QUICK man is to despair, and how slow is hope to grow in the human breast! Our attitude about the world situation today is a case in point. Who is there that really believes that Christ could change the heart of the Communists? We look at that situation as if it were hopeless, and continue to pile up our atom and hydrogen bombs and our instruments of war that are outdated before they are even manufactured. Christians will say as pagan a thing as can be said: "Well, that is human nature, and you can't change human nature," or "I can't do anything about it. You will just have to take me as I am." These are the devil's lies, and you might just as well, or better, be the iconoclast that the late H. L. Mencken was when he said: "Man is a sick fly on a dizzy wheel." At least he did not parade under the banner of another name!

Christmas says to all the world that there is hope. Christmas says that human nature can be changed. Christmas says that a King came to earth so that in every human breast there might be hope, and that fears might be dispelled.

Sometimes I think that we have heard the story so many times that we have become immune to it. But when the love of the Christ child is in your heart, the wonder of Christmas is ever new. Suppose you had been one of those shepherds on that night. From all appearances, it was exactly the same as all the nights that had preceded it, the monotony broken only by an occasional wolf, who would try to steal a sheep. But that was over in a hurry and you settled back either to blankness or to a reverie on the sameness of life. *Then It Happened!* All at once there was this amazing light, and the sound of music—the most beautiful that you had ever heard, come to think of it. You were frightened. All the while you were bored with the ordinary, you were also fearful of the unusual. Was it the end of the world? Then it was that you learned that it was really the beginning. For the angels, who came into focus through the light, spoke of "good tidings," "great joy," "to all people," "a Savior." Here was a speedy reversal. Instead of fear, there was now hope; instead of darkness, there was light; instead of monotony, there was something to do, Someone to see, something to tell, somewhere to go.

PRAYER: *Lord, help me to be willing to experience the cataclysmic change that Your presence can make in my life. Help me to believe that You can change anything. This Christmas season, O Lord, come with Your love and change the world. Begin with me. In Jesus' name. Amen.*

O Little Town of Bethlehem

While mortals sleep, the angels keep
Their watch of wond'ring love

Luke 2:15, 16

When the angels went away from them into heaven, the shepherds said to one another, "Let us go over to Bethlehem and see this thing that has happened, which the Lord has made known to us." And they went with haste, and found Mary and Joseph, and the babe lying in a manger.

IT MUST have been a great day in heaven too, as it was on earth, that first Christmas night. Phillips Brooks has given vent to his imagination, as he thought of the wonder of the angels whom the Lord used to help announce and herald His great plan. Can you not imagine the expectancy those heavenly messengers had, and the joy that was theirs, as they broke through the sky with their message? They had been used to prepare the people involved in this great drama, too. An angel had appeared to Mary and to Joseph. And what a difference it made to get the heavenly perspective on the events that were to come! Think of what a difference this viewpoint meant to Mary! And imagine the change in attitude that there was in Joseph! Zechariah, too, had a heavenly visitor to make him aware of how the Lord was going to use the son of his old age to prepare the way for the promised Messiah. The jubilance in this father's heart is beautifully recorded in the song he sang at the birth of his son. Read those opening words again: "Blessed be the Lord God of Israel, for he has visited and redeemed his people . . ." When mortals were filled with so much joy, there must have been great rejoicing in heaven, too. Jesus told us that there is rejoicing over one sinner who repents, so we are sure there was jubilation on the night when God's plan of salvation was announced.

Homer, in his great masterpiece of Greek mythology, describes the warrior Hector parting from his family. He is standing outside the city walls, ready to depart on what proved to be his last campaign. His wife and child, accompanied by a nurse, had come to say farewell. The father put out his arms to take the little boy to kiss him, but when the child sees the shining helmet flashing in the sun, and the wild plume waving in the wind he cries out with fear. The warrior then takes off his helmet and lays it aside, and again puts out his hand to the child. At once the little one recognizes his loving father, and happily springs into his arms.

Without the revelation of Christmas, God might have remained the austere judge that is pictured so often in the Old Testament. His loving Father heart is revealed there too, in His having mercy again and again on His wayward people. But the revelation in Christ of the heart of love that is our God is irresistible; or, so it seems, it ought to be!

PRAYER: *For the revelation of Your wondrous love in Christ, we thank You, God our Father. For the message of Christmas and its hope for the world, we give You praise. Amen.*

O Little Town of Bethlehem

So God imparts to human hearts
The blessings of His heaven

Luke 2:29-35

"Lord, now lettest thou thy servant depart in peace, according to thy word; for mine eyes have seen thy salvation which thou hast prepared in the presence of all peoples, a light for revelation to the Gentiles, and for glory to thy people Israel." And his father and his mother marveled at what was said about him: and Simeon blessed them and said to Mary his mother, "Behold, this child is set for the fall and rising of many in Israel, and for a sign that is spoken against (and a sword will pierce through your own soul also) that thoughts out of many hearts may be revealed."

"HOW SILENTLY, how silently, the wondrous Gift is given!" So, says our hymn writer, God imparts His blessings to human hearts. Sometimes you do not know there has been a blessing until much later. There is no fanfare, no flourish, in the giving. It is like daily bread, and like day and night; it is like sun and rain and winter and summer.

We had a most enriching experience in an early parish. The pastor had been called to the city hospital to visit a lonely little old man who had no friends. After he left the hospital, he started to come to our church. It was just before Christmas, and this was to be the first Christmas with our first-born. We had looked forward to a sacred family hour. But I was haunted by the thought of this little old fellow alone at Christmas, and so I asked my husband to invite him to spend the holiday with us. What an experience that was! When the pastor mentioned his errand the fellow said, "Oh, did you already get my letter? How could you get it so fast?" The pastor told him that we had received no letter, but just wanted him as our guest. Then he told how he had written to ask if he might join our church. His comment was, "Will your people have me? I know Jesus Christ will!" He had added, "I do not know what will happen to me at Christmas, but I know God will take care of me." While Emil's letter was on its way, God was working in our hearts to answer his prayer. Well, he became "Uncle Emil" in our home, and ate every Sunday dinner with us. Our church had been in a basement eleven years. These were depression times, and our people were skilled laborers. One Sunday, Emil came to my husband after dinner and said, "Do you know what I am going to do? When I get my relief money on Tuesday, I'm bringing ten dollars of it (the total was twenty dollars for the month) to start that building going." The details of the rest of the story are fascinating, but we have not the space to tell them. Suffice it to say that Emil was the inspiration for the upper structure, and it stands today as a monument to the faith of a man who did not have a cent of his own in the world. We thought we had been helping Emil. God was using him to build the kingdom.

PRAYER: *We praise You, Lord, for the wonderful way You work in our lives. We thank You for hidden blessings that we do not even know. Amen.*

O Little Town of Bethlehem

Where meek souls will receive Him, still
The dear Christ enters in

Luke 2:36-38

And there was a prophetess, Anna, the daughter of Phanuel, of the tribe of Asher; she was of a great age, having lived with her husband seven years from her virginity, and as a widow till she was eighty-four. She did not depart from the temple, worshiping with fasting and prayer night and day. And coming up at that very hour she gave thanks to God, and spoke of him to all who were looking for the redemption of Jerusalem.

YESTERDAY OUR Bible passage was a portion of the beautiful song of Simeon, that righteous man who had been looking for the Messiah. We are told that the Holy Spirit had made it known to him that he should not see death until he had seen the Lord's Christ. In the Lord Jesus, Simeon recognized immediately that this was He. He burst into the beautiful paean of praise that we know as the Nunc Dimittis.

No one would have picked out Simeon or Anna as being anyone special, but the Lord has told us that it is not to the wise that He reveals the things of the kingdom.

The story that tells us why holly has red berries has something of this wisdom in it. One day the trees heard a rumor that, if the king should walk in their shade, the first tree that would recognize him would become more beautiful than the others. Outside the town of Nazareth there grew a big forest of pines, and firs, and oaks, and one little holly tree. A boy came out of town, one day, and walked through the forest. Each of the big trees thought, "He is looking at me." But the little holly tree became so engrossed in watching him that it forgot all about itself. Pretty soon, the other trees did not pay any more attention to him. The holly tree was intrigued by the boy, he was so fair, and said, "Surely, if a king were to come, he would not be as beautiful as this boy. He is always kind, and even the animals are not afraid of him. I wish he were my king. I should like to obey him."

After a little time, the boy no longer went to the forest. The holly tree really missed him, but thought about him and tried to be like him, following his example in being kind to the birds and the other animals. The little boy grew to be a man, and traveled about the country telling people about God and how to love one another. But one day, wicked men took him and nailed him to a cross, and over his head placed a sign which read, "The King." A wonderful change came over the little holly tree. Between its dark leaves little red berries began to grow, until it was the most beautiful tree of all.

"Not many wise, after the flesh, not many mighty, not many noble are called. . . ." (K.J.V.)

PRAYER: *Forgive our pride and haughtiness, O Lord, and give us a spirit of meekness. May we invite Your indwelling. Make us more like You. Amen.*

O Little Town of Bethlehem

O Holy Child of Bethlehem!
Descend to us, we pray;
Cast out our sin, and enter in,
Be born in us today

Matthew 2:8-11

And he [Herod] sent them to Bethlehem, saying, "Go and search diligently for the child, and when you have found him bring me word, that I too may come and worship him." When they had heard the king they went their way; and lo, the star which they had seen in the East went before them, till it came to rest over the place where the child was. When they saw the star, they rejoiced exceedingly with great joy; and going into the house they saw the child with Mary his mother, and they fell down and worshiped him.

CHRISTMAS HAS come and gone. I wonder how many of us really have understood at all what its significance is. We are living in a day when all kinds of conjectures are being made as to whether or not there is life on other planets. There are those who say there is pretty good evidence for believing that there is. Does that frighten you? Does that shake your faith? I am sure there is so much that we know so very little about that the next years will amaze us all, even as the last years have done.

I like the term that Dr. Phillips uses in his book, *New Testament Christianity*. In the beginning of his book, he tells the fanciful story of a senior angel showing a little angel about the universe. As they drew near to the star which we call our sun, the senior angel called attention to a small and rather insignificant sphere turning slowly on its axis. The little angel's comment was that it looked spretty small and dirty. But solemnly the senior angel informed its pupil that that was the *Visited Planet*. The rest of the story continues with the explanation of how the Prince of glory visited this planet in person, in order that He might redeem those who dwelt thereon.

The story is fanciful, but the fact of the *"Visited Planet"* is the truth of Christmas. No matter what they find anywhere else, it was to our little planet, the earth, that God came in the form of man, to redeem man and release him from the curse of the law, and to put into his hand the key to everlasting life in the glorious home from which He came and to which He has gone.

The very course of history was changed by this visit; the calendar that most men use had its turning point in relation to this event.

But how can one talk in generalities and argumentation, when one's heart has been the recipient of a personal visit from this same Prince of glory? What need for argument is there, when the visit has transformed a life, completely changed it? What answer is there to that?

PRAYER: *We need Your grace to cast out our sin, Lord, so that there may be room in our hearts for You. Thank You that You will dwell with anyone who will open the door. Come into my heart, Lord Jesus. Amen.*

Jesus Christ Is Passing By

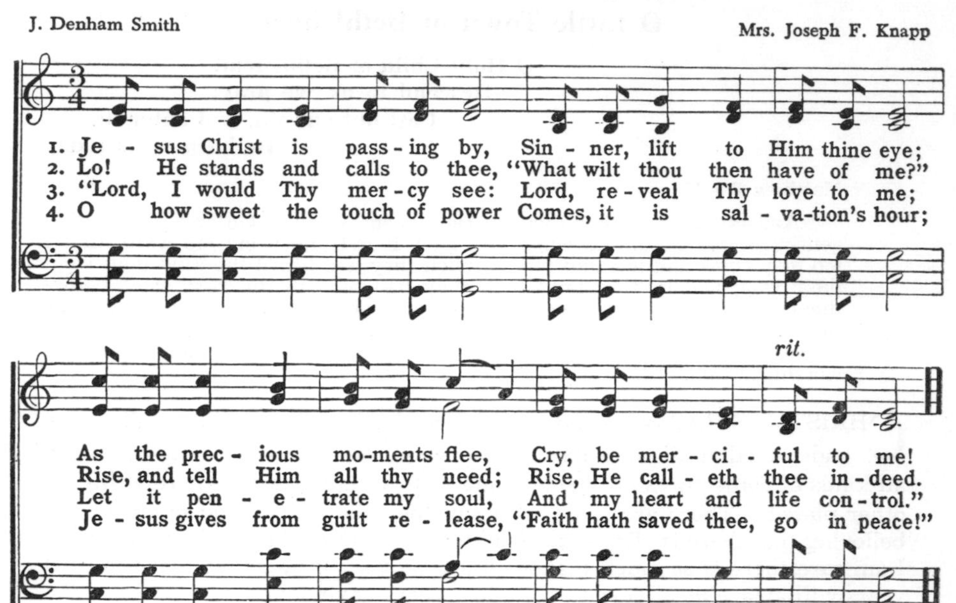

Jesus Christ Is Passing By

Sinner, lift to Him thine eye

Mark 8:17, 18

"Why do you discuss the fact that you have no bread? Do you not yet perceive or understand? Are your hearts hardened? Having eyes do you not see, and having ears do you not hear? And do you not remember?"

Mark 8:34, 35

"If any man would come after me, let him deny himself and take up his cross and follow me. For whoever would save his life will lose it; and whoever loses his life for my sake and the gospel's will save it."

WHAT A million attractions there are in the world! Some few years ago man's wants were comparatively few. Today they are so numerous as to make living very complicated. It is interesting when in a group of people to explore their interests. So often we are concerned so much with our own that we do not take time to listen to theirs. (I speak for myself!) In almost any ordinary group you will find as wide a variety as there are people.

But I wonder, if one were able to probe underneath the professional surface of the person that lies awake at night and thinks, to the one who wonders what life is all about, to the hidden fears of the man who has had pains around the heart, I wonder if underneath all these you would not find a common denominator—a hunger for God. It is no poetic figure of speech merely, when the psalmist says, "As a hart longs for flowing streams, so longs my soul for thee, O God."

Is there a hunger in your heart? Do you know the rejoicing of which the apostle speaks again and again, and through all manner of vicissitudes? Is there a hollow sound to your living, which in your quiet moments frightens you? The song writer expresses the invitation: "Sinner, lift to Him thine eye!"

In our Scripture the Lord is talking to His disciples. They were wondering about how they were going to be fed. Already they had forgotten how He had fed the multitude before. He has to remind them, fact by fact. He would do that with each one of us. It is what He wanted to do during the recent Christmas season.

A church bell was out of order, and gave a shrill sound. They sent to the firm which had made the bell—they must know what was wrong. And the firm sent a man to discover the secret. And he did. Just a few drops of oil had dropped down when someone had oiled the bearings above, and had settled upon the lower rim of the great bell! That was all; but it was enough to raise the tone of the bell several steps. The man wiped the oil away and the bell came back to its real tone.

PRAYER: *Lord, sin is so subtle, and we are so blind. Open our eyes to see You passing by. Abide with us, and transform us into vessels fit for Your use. Amen.*

Jesus Christ Is Passing By

Faith hath saved thee; Go in peace

1 Timothy 6:11, 12

But as for you, man of God, shun all this; aim at righteousness, godliness, faith, love, steadfastness, gentleness. Fight the good fight of the faith; take hold of the eternal life to which you were called when you made the good confession in the presence of many witnesses.

THE YEAR is at an end. How swiftly it has gone—never to come back. What things stand out as good, and what cause you regrets? I am very sure that those things connected with the Christ are the things that you now hold most precious.

How has the memory of your hymns been? If each day you have tried to make them a part of you, they will be yours now. But if you began to get careless, you are right where you were before. When will we learn that it is the daily practice that makes the tone of a life? It is the quality of the hours that determines the richness of the day.

Speaking of learning hymns, a part of the rich background of Phillips Brooks was due to his childhood training. Each Sunday in the Brooks' home the children were required to memorize a hymn. When the father conducted the family altar in the evening, the children recited the hymns. When Dr. Brooks entered college, he could repeat no less than two hundred hymns from memory.

It is a thrilling thing to remember that each one of these hymns is the witness of a soul that fought the good fight; and they are making their good confession before many witnesses. Down through all the ages they have come. Times have been different; circumstances have varied, but the experience of Jesus Christ in every age, and through every circumstance, has been the same. Each has given the witness: "He Leadeth Me," "Abide with Me," "A Mighty Fortress Is Our God," "What a Friend We Have in Jesus."

At the end of the year we take inventory. We evaluate our stock. Is salvation nearer than when you first believed? Are you fighting the good fight? Is the presence of Jesus with you more through each day than at the beginning of the year? And how about your fears? Have you given them to God? Do you greet each new day with joy and in His strength?

Jesus Christ is passing by. Have you asked Him to abide with you?

PRAYER: *As the bells of the old year toll, and the bells of the new year ring, give us, O Lord, the peace that comes from knowing that You are changeless, and that Your love is everlasting. All the sins of the past year we ask that You will forgive. And for tomorrow, Lord, we pray for a faith that will be victorious even unto everlasting life. In Jesus' name. Amen.*

Blessed is the man
who walks not in the counsel of the wicked,
nor stands in the way of sinners,
nor sits in the seat of scoffers;
but his delight is in the law of the Lord,
and on his law he meditates day and night.
He is like a tree
planted by streams of water,
that yields its fruit in its season,
and its leaf does not wither.
In all that he does, he prospers.

Psalm 1:1-3

Acknowledgments

GRATEFUL acknowledgment is made to authors and publishers who have permitted their copyrighted materials to be used in this book. If, in any instance, acknowledgment has been inadvertantly omitted, and information is furnished of such oversight, proper credit will be given in future editions.

To Charles Scribner's Sons for the use of the hymn, "This Is My Father's World."

To Leslie Savage Clark for the use of the poem, "A Baby's Hands."

To Harper and Brothers for permission to use material from "Life Together" by Dietrich Bonhoeffer. Also, for permission to use the poems, "Never Night Again" by Lillian Cox; "God's Plans" by Mary Riley Smith; "Lent" by Jane McKay Lanning; "Guilty" by Marguerite Wilkinson; "Out of the Vast" by Augustus W. Bamberger from *Masterpieces of Religious Verse,* Harper and Brothers, 1948.

To Lothrop, Lee Shepard Co., Inc., for the use of the poem, "When I Am Overmatched by Petty Cares" by Richard Burton.

To THE MACMILLAN COMPANY for the use of material from *Letters to Young Churches* by J. B. Phillips.

To Samuel M. Miller for the use of the words and the music of the hymn, "Jesus Only."

To Erica Oxenham for the use of the poem, "The Vision Splendid," by John Oxenham.

To E. E. Ryden for background material for some of the hymns from *The Story of Our Hymns.* Augustana, 1932.

To *The Christian Century* for permission to use the poems, "Revealment" and "His Hands" by John R. Moreland; "A Ballad of Wonder" and "December Twenty-fourth" by Eleanor Slater.

To The Faith Mission for the use of "Unafraid" from *Songs of Victory.*